PRAISE FOR
SPEAKING WHILE FEMALE

"Dana Rubin has put together a remarkable collection that amplifies the diverse voices of women in American history. Each woman is introduced and her historical context set. This is a valuable resource for teaching that both illuminates and instills pride in women, their thinking, and their courage."

BETTINA APTHEKER
Distinguished Professor Emerita, Feminist Studies Department, University of California, Santa Cruz

"Why hasn't anyone done something like this before? This splendid anthology brings together some voices that will be familiar and a great many more that are not — and should be. I hope it will encourage many more women and girls to make themselves heard at a time when some of the gains they've made in recent decades are under threat."

ADAM HOCHSCHILD
Author of *King Leopold's Ghost*, finalist for the National Book Critics Circle Award,
and *American Midnight: The Great War, a Violent Peace, and Democracy's Forgotten Crisis*

"The legacy of women's speech in America is strong, showing us the importance of celebrating our history with future generations."

BILLIE JEAN KING
Winner of thirty-nine Grand Slam tennis titles and gender activist

"It's hard to overstate the value of Dana Rubin's work as a critical counter to a culture that persistently erases what women think, believe, know, and say. It's more important than ever to recognize that we have always spoken publicly and made vital contributions to history, politics, and society. *Speaking While Female* is a tool for doing exactly this."

SORAYA CHEMALY
Cofounder of the Women's Media Center Speech Project
and author of *Rage Becomes Her: The Power of Women's Anger*

"This is a vital book. By identifying and elevating the voices of women across the ages, Dana Rubin has successfully led all of us to examine our assumptions and to listen with new ears and open minds. Carefully curated, deftly edited, and brilliantly brought together, this is a collection that will not be silenced, but heard."

JON MEACHAM
Political speechwriter and author of the Pulitzer Prize-winning
biography *American Lion: Andrew Jackson in the White House*

"*Speaking While Female* is a welcome addition, featuring some of the most eloquent speeches ever delivered in America. Each of these women moved her listeners to join her cause or contemplate the plight of her community at an important point in the country's history. They deserve to be read and remembered."

LINDA CHAVEZ
Reagan White House advisor and author of *An Unlikely Conservative*

"*Speaking While Female* highlights an unassailable truth: women have always used their voices and ideas to actively engage in the public square. With speeches culled from a cross-section of women from the 17th century to the present, this book centers and normalizes diversity in the telling of American history. Without question, it should be required reading in every classroom in the United States."

CHARITY C. ELDER
Author of *Power: The Rise of Black Women in America*

"*Speaking While Female* finally sets the record straight about who spoke out in America and who made America. This book will make the voices of women today and tomorrow more powerful."

SIVA VAIDHYANATHAN
Professor of Media Studies at the University of Virginia and author of
Antisocial Media: How Facebook Disconnects Us and Undermines Democracy

SPEAKING WHILE FEMALE

75 EXTRAORDINARY SPEECHES BY AMERICAN WOMEN

DANA RUBIN

RealClear
Publishing

Publishing

www.realclearpublishing.com

Speaking While Female: 75 Extraordinary Speeches by American Women

Cover image
Isamu Noguchi, Helen Gahagan Douglas, 1935. Collection of the National Portrait Gallery, Smithsonian Institution. Photo: F. S. Lincoln.
© 2022 The Isamu Noguchi Foundation and Garden Museum, New York / Artists Rights Society (ARS), New York. Used with permission from the Eberly Family Special Collections Library, Penn State University Libraries.

For more information, please contact:
Amplify Publishing, an imprint of Amplify Publishing Group
620 Herndon Parkway, Suite 320
Herndon, VA 20170
info@amplifypublishing.com

Library of Congress Control Number: 2022919973

CPSIA Code: PRV0123A

ISBN-13: 978-1-63755-030-4

Printed in the United States

For women speakers everywhere.
If you speak in public, this book is for you.
And if you don't yet speak in public, this book is especially for you.

CONTENTS

INTRODUCTION

In September 1861, a young Black woman stepped up to speak at a church in Manhattan and described her escape from slavery. At a time when the Fugitive Slave Law was still in effect, a newspaper account identified her only as "Miss Paulyon."

She talked about growing up in Alabama and how, at age sixteen, she traveled hundreds of miles on the Underground Railroad, and the hunger, thirst, and cold she experienced along the way. For an hour and a half she spoke, interrupted by clapping and shouts of approval. At times she moved her audience to tears. According to the *Weekly Anglo-African*, "We never heard anything to equal it."

No record exists of Miss Paulyon's words, only a brief description of the event.

Nor is there a record of the words of Eliza Harriot O'Connor, who delivered a series of paid lectures in Philadelphia at the same time the Continental Congress was convening there in 1787. Thanks to recent scholarship, we can read five private letters she wrote — four of them to President George Washington — but there's no trace of her spoken words.

Clarissa Danforth was a popular itinerant preacher in New England in the early 19th century. When she was called to God in the Free Will Baptist Church in 1815, she became the nation's first female ordained minister. The press called her a "sensation." Yet we have none of her actual words.

Thousands of American women like Miss Paulyon, Eliza Harriot O'Connor, and Clarissa Danforth have courageously spoken in public over the past four centuries. Their speeches helped shape the beliefs, culture, and ideals of America. But their voices have been omitted from American history, and our storehouse of common knowledge. The same cannot be said about the many lionized male orators who appear in our history books, media, and public discourse.

I know because when I give talks and teach classes in public speaking, I ask my audience: "Which famous speakers in American history can you name?" Many people can rattle off at least half a dozen American male speakers like Abraham Lincoln, Franklin D. Roosevelt, Martin Luther King, Jr., John F. Kennedy, Robert F. Kennedy, Billy Graham, and Ronald Reagan. But when I ask which *women speakers* they remember, there's a long pause. Someone might mention Hillary Clinton or Michelle Obama. Mostly the faces are blank.

Could it be true, I wondered, that the "great men" in history gave all the greatest speeches? Or could it be we just don't know about great women speakers?

To answer that question, I began searching for speeches by American women. I began by looking at speech collections, published as far back as 1797. Out of nearly 250 anthologies, I found very few speeches by women. About a third of the volumes had none at all.

A pioneer in the field of women's speech, Karlyn Kohrs Campbell was among the first to try and set the record straight. In 1989, she published a landmark two-volume study, *Man Cannot Speak for Her*, "to call into question what has become the canon of public address in the United States," she wrote, "a canon that excludes virtually all works by women."

Three decades later, I embarked on my own historical excavation, looking for transcripts and other accounts of women's spoken words.

I searched in institutional repositories, history books and biographies, journals, old newspapers and out-of-print books. With a growing sense of urgency, I began publishing those speeches online. This collection formed a new global archive of women's speeches called the Speaking While Female Speech Bank. Some of the speeches in the archive had not been published in more than a century.

My project is just one part of an ongoing recovery of women's overlooked contributions in scholarship, the media, and the arts that is challenging accepted narratives and opening up new ways to view the past. Women's experiences, concerns, and ideas were different from men's. And yet, despite the work of Campbell and many other determined historians and researchers, the influence of women speakers to the formation of America, this great national experiment, is still largely unknown.

For a long time, the accepted belief among scholars was that no women speakers existed in America before 1830. That's clearly not true. Indigenous women used their voices in public communication for centuries, long before the United States became a country. In the many tribes that gave women broad communal authority, women spoke in matters of governance, politics, and diplomacy.

Other early American women speakers were itinerant preachers like Danforth, who traveled the rutted roads in a largely rural landscape. They spoke in open-air groves, under tents, in barns, churches, meetinghouses, and even prisons, delivering the divine word of God to audiences of both sexes and mixed races. Their work was not for the faint of heart — travelling alone was dangerous for women.

With the late 18th century came a hardening of the separate gendered realms — women who stepped outside their allotted role to speak in public were often met with disdain. Many were either laughed at or laughed about. Yet still they spoke.

In 1806 the British evangelist and abolitionist Dorothy Ripley preached a sermon in the US Capitol, with President Thomas Jefferson attending. We don't have a record of her words. Twenty years later, Anne Laura Clarke was travelling up and down the East Coast, giving paid speeches on history and cultural topics. She even used colorful charts and a newfangled "magic lantern" with slides to illustrate her talks. None of her lectures were published.

In January 1827, famed preacher Harriet Livermore — "the most interesting woman of the day," according to one account — preached on Capitol Hill to a hall packed with senators, congressmen, even President John Quincy Adams. But evidently no one considered her words that day important enough to write down.

Consider this: If a woman was scheduled to speak but no stenographer was on hand to record it, and no journalist thought it worthwhile to attend, then it's likely no one wrote down what she said. Without those recorded words, no newspaper or journal could publish them, no editor could anthologize them, no history book could include them, and no one could quote them. The result is that roomful of blank faces when I ask my students about women speakers.

What explains this colossal indifference toward women's speech, this historical erasure? Why was it, as Mary Wollstonecraft wondered in the late 18th century, that throughout history, men have been accorded the mantle of authority, while women were "excluded, without having a voice?"

British classicist Mary Beard, author of *Woman & Power: A Manifesto*, tells the story of Penelope, wife of Odysseus, who in the opening chapter of Homer's epic, *The Odyssey*, descends from her private quarters into the great hall and attempts to speak to the people gathered there, at which point her son Telemachus exclaims, "Mother, go back up into your quarters . . . speech will be the business of men."

Beard calls this the earliest recorded example of a man telling a woman, "Oh do shut up, dear."

But women refused to shut up. Behind every instance of "silencing" was a woman who wanted to be considered a thinking, rational, authoritative human being, a woman with a mind and a voice — and very often she did speak out.

The cost of ignoring those voices has been high. As Australian scholar Dale Spender has noted, that absence has led every generation of women to ask the same question women before have asked: *"How come I didn't know about her?"*

Imagine what a difference it could have made if women had access to the continuity of thought and language of those who came before them. Labor activist Ai-jen Poo, who speaks powerfully today on the rights of domestic workers and caregivers, builds on a long tradition that includes Californian Dolores Huerta's rousing speech to grape growers in the 1960s, Nannie Helen Burrough's defense of Black domestic workers at a conference in 1902, and Louise Mitchell's ardent plea to tailoresses in Manhattan in 1832.

Without a documented history of women's speech, as Spender says, most women speakers have to reinvent the wheel.

This volume puts a spotlight on 75 American women speakers, from 1637 to the present, and explains how each contributed to the making of the nation. It allows each woman to speak for herself. It invites us to consider our country's history from the perspective of women's experience. And it asks the question: whose voices should define who we are?

Included are Indigenous women who, for much of their history, had no written language. Some of their words come to us through the pens of the US treaty negotiators who kept government records. Included are Black women who were enslaved and in most cases forbidden to read or write, but who nevertheless found a way to speak out and document their histories. Included are Hispanic and Asian-American women who fought for the right to preserve their language and culture and gain equal access to jobs and fair wages. Included are White women of every class, background, and belief who spoke for just about every cause under the sun.

Each woman who spoke changed the world we know through her public voice, some in ways that were direct and obvious, others more nuanced. It is a reflection of the incremental pace of change that many of them did not live to see their work come to fruition.

Neither Elizabeth Cady Stanton nor Susan B. Anthony lived to see the passage of the 19th Amendment in 1919. Deborah Sampson Gannett, who dressed like a man to fight in the Revolutionary War, did not live to see the Pentagon allow women to serve in combat roles in 2013. Clara Shortridge Foltz, who argued that the poor deserved legal representation, did not live to see the US Supreme Court hand down its 1963 decision, *Gideon v. Wainwright*, requiring states to provide legal counsel to indigent criminal defendants.

Just think how Frances Harper, who in 1866 bristled with fury at being sent to the smoking car of the train in Washington, DC, because of her skin color, would have greeted the triumph of the Montgomery bus boycott in 1956. Just think how Emma Willard, who in 1819 advanced the outlandish notion that women should receive the same education as men, might have reacted to knowing that 200 years later, women in the US would not only be as well educated as men, but would significantly outnumber them at schools of higher education.

Speech creates change in ways often impossible to measure. Sarah Parker Remond's words didn't weaken Northern England's ties to cotton, but they opened eyes to the links between slavery and British commercial profit. Not many people in America became anarchists because of the thundering rhetoric of Voltairine de Cleyre, Lucy Parsons, or Emma Goldman, yet their words left an imprint, making it possible for less radical speakers and thinkers to be accepted and influential. Clare Boothe Luce's clear-eyed warning about Russia helped sharpen our sense of that country's territorial ambitions and authoritarian nature. Without women's speech, the world we inhabit would not exist.

One of my hopes is that this book will encourage more students and scholars to join the quest for missing women's speeches. So many more remain to be uncovered, and without them, the historical record is not only incomplete — it's inaccurate. To know American history, we must hear these women speak.

In tandem with that, I want teachers, textbook writers, and the media to include these women and their robust voices in the narrative of the nation.

A recent study by the National Women's History Museum found that less than one quarter of all the historical figures studied from kindergarten through 12th grade in the US were women. Let's change that.

At the top of my list is the desire for more women and girls to use their voices and speak out, bolstered by the knowledge that we do have an accessible and inspirational past. It's because those women spoke out then that we are able to speak out today.

We have the freedom and the privilege — so let's use them.

ANNE HUTCHINSON

In 1634, Anne Marbury Hutchinson left her native England, crossed the Atlantic, and arrived at the Massachusetts Bay Colony with her husband and ten children.

The colony had been settled thirteen years earlier by Puritans escaping religious persecution and what they saw as a degenerate England. Hutchinson's father, Francis Marbury, was a Puritan minister jailed for criticizing the Church of England. He never made it to America, but he taught his daughter to read.

Hutchison became an herbalist and a midwife, and was intensely spiritual. She began offering interpretations of the clergy's weekly sermons at her home on the Shawmut Peninsula, today's downtown Boston, and her followers grew. By all accounts she was charismatic and persuasive. John Winthrop, the new colony's first governor, called her "a woman of ready wit and bold spirit."

But in the Massachusetts Bay Colony, essentially a theocracy ruled by men, women were not allowed to participate in town meetings. They didn't speak in church or comment on scripture, except in all-female prayer groups.

So when Hutchinson began advancing religious beliefs at odds with the clergy — and drawing both women and men to her talks, even within the confines of her own home, became a threat. The ministers were outraged.

In November 1637 she was put on trial for challenging the established order. She was cross examined and forced to defend herself, which she did with verbal dexterity — so skillfully that some observers thought she was close to an acquittal.

But things took a sudden turn when she claimed to have direct communication with God, "by the voice of his own spirit to my soul." That was a step too far, a heresy. For views that were antithetical to Puritan theology, Hutchinson was condemned and banished from the colony.

She and her supporters resettled down the coast, first to the new settlement of Portsmouth, New Hampshire, and then to a spot known as Split Rock, in territory the Dutch called *Vreedelandt*, or "land of freedom."

That's where in 1643, her entire family except one daughter was murdered by the local Native tribe. The Hutchinsons were dragged into their home, along with their cattle, and the house was burned to the ground. Hutchinson's ashes are most likely buried beneath what's now Pelham Bay Park, in the eastern Bronx, just north of New York City.

Despite the odds against her, Hutchinson spoke out to assert her rights in a male-dominated community. We can still hear her pious, proud, and insistent words in the lengthy trial transcript:

"If you do condemn me for speaking what in my conscience I know to be truth, I must commit myself unto the Lord."

"HERESY TRIAL"

November 8, 1637
General Court, Newtown, Massachusetts Bay Colony

Mrs. Hutchinson: If you please to give me leave I shall give you the ground of what I know to be true. Being much troubled to see the falseness of the constitution of the church of England, I had like to have turned separatist; whereupon I kept a day of solemn humiliation and pondering of the thing; this scripture was brought unto me — he that denies Jesus Christ to be come in the flesh is antichrist — This I considered of and in considering found that the papists did not deny him to be come in the flesh, nor we did not deny him — who then was antichrist? Was the Turk antichrist only? The Lord knows that I could not open scripture; he must by his prophetical office open it unto me. So after that being unsatisfied in the thing, the Lord was pleased to bring this scripture out of the Hebrews. He that denies the testament denies the testator, and in this did open unto me and give me to see that those which did not teach the new covenant had the spirit of antichrist and upon this he did discover the ministry unto me and ever since. I bless the Lord, he hath let me see which was the clear ministry and which the wrong. Since that time I confess I have been more choice and he hath let me to distinguish between the voice of my beloved and the voice of Moses, the voice of John Baptist and the voice of antichrist, for all those voices are spoken of in scripture. Now if you do condemn me for speaking what in my conscience I know to be truth, I must commit myself unto the Lord.

Mr. Increase Nowell: How do you know that was the spirit?

Mrs. Hutchinson: How did Abraham know that it was God that bid him offer his son, being a breach of the sixth commandment?

Dep. Gov: By an immediate voice.

Mrs. Hutchinson: So to me by an immediate revelation.

Dep. Gov: How! an immediate revelation.

Mrs. Hutchinson: By the voice of his own spirit to my soul.

MARGARET BRENT

Who makes history, and who decides what goes in the history books? That question hovers over every entry in this volume.

Margaret Brent is a case in point. In her own place and time — the English colonies along the Eastern seaboard in the mid-17th century — she stood out as a woman of exceptional, unprecedented accomplishment.

She sailed from England to America in 1638 with three siblings, settling in Maryland when the colony was just four years old. The Brents were related to the wealthy Leonard Calvert, Governor of Maryland Colony, a connection that proved highly useful. Within a few years of her arrival Brent was flourishing as a landowner and businesswoman. She owned livestock, agricultural fields, and a mill, and she borrowed and lent money to local traders and merchants. We know because the transactions appear in the official record books.

In 1647, on his deathbed, Calvert appointed her to be executor of his Maryland estate, an unusually prominent role for a woman in those times, and surely a reflection of his confidence in her business skills. In that new role, Brent's responsibilities also included overseeing the vast holdings of Calvert's brother, Lord Baltimore, who lived across the Atlantic Ocean in North Yorkshire, England. Now she was a person of considerable stature.

But what cemented Brent's place in America's long march toward equality took place on January 21, 1648. That day, she went before the Maryland Assembly in St. Mary's, the provincial capital on the western shore of the Chesapeake Bay. As the official record states: "Came Mrs. Margaret Brent and requested to have vote in the house for her selfe and voyce allso . . . as his [Lord Baltimore's] Attorney."

In other words, she requested a seat in the assembly and two votes — one for herself as a landowner, and one as a representative of Lord Baltimore.

That was extraordinary. It took self assurance and a sense of entitlement to make such a claim. Women had no legal right to vote in the English colonies. But that didn't stop her from asking for it, and fully believing she deserved it.

For reasons that don't appear in the Maryland Archive, the Provincial Court turned Brent down. All we know is that the assembly "denied that the said Mrs. Brent should have any vote in the house."

The record also notes that she didn't take it lightly: "Mrs. Brent protested against all proceedings in this present Assembly unless she may be present and have vote as aforesaid."

Two centuries later, a group of upstart women gathered in a chapel in New York to demand more or less the same thing. Even then, most people thought the idea was far too radical and should be dropped.

But Brent had led the way.

"VOTE AND VOYCE"

January 21, 1648
Provincial Court, Maryland Assembly,
St. Mary's City, Colony of Maryland

Came Mrs. Margaret Brent and requested to have vote in the house for her selfe and voyce allso . . .

NANYE'HI

Nanye'hi was born around 1738 in Cherokee country, in what today is eastern Tennessee. Her name means "one who is with the spirit people."

Like many Indigenous tribes, the Cherokees were matriarchal, and women held leadership positions and made important pronouncements. Women served as ambassadors, diplomats, and, when the occasion arose, negotiators with US treaty commissioners.

Nanye'hi had even higher status among her people as a warrior. At the Battle of Taliwa in 1755, her husband was killed, and Nanye'hi picked up his rifle and killed his attacker. Then she took charge of the attack on the Muscogee, leading the Cherokees to victory.

A few years later she married again, to the Irish trader Bryant Ward, and took a second name, Nancy Ward.

Like other Indigenous people in the late 18th century, the Cherokee came in constant conflict with the land-hungry Anglo settlers coming over the Appalachians into their territory, eager to conquer the continent and build a new nation. Steadily the Cherokee lost more and more of their ancestral lands.

During the Revolutionary War, most of the Cherokee chose to side with the British against the rebel colonists, and in the summer of 1776 American military forces swept through Cherokee lands exacting revenge, destroying Native villages and crops.

In the 1780s, Nanye'hi and other female Cherokee diplomats represented their people in negotiations with US government representatives. In July 1781 she spoke at a meeting over a land dispute, one of five Cherokee women present. A torn and yellowed fragment of a handwritten account, now in the archives of the Library of Congress, is all that remains of her speech.

"We are your Mothers, you are our sons. Our cry is all for peace. Let your women's sons be ours; and let our sons be yours," she told the men.

Her final words were: "Let your women hear our words."

Scholars say each side baffled the other. The Anglos found it strange the Cherokee had women serving as negotiators, and the Cherokee found it strange the Anglos had no women leaders.

Nanye'hi lived until around 1822, having negotiated other treaties and witnessed the dislocation of her people and disruption to their way of life.

In 1830, President Andrew Jackson signed the Indian Removal Act, authorizing the US government to move Indigenous people from their land east of the Mississippi River. In 1838, some 15,000 Cherokees were forced to walk more than a thousand miles to Oklahoma, a death march known as the Trail of Tears.

"A PEACE TREATY"

July 1781
Long Island, Holston River, Tennessee

W e did never concern in the [for]mer Treaty, which has been broken, but we do in this, and on our account, who are your Mothers, let it never be broken. You know Women are always looked upon as nothing; but we are your Mothers, you are our sons. Our cry [is] all for Peace; let it continue because we are Your Mothers[.] This Peace must last forever. Let your women's sons be ours; and let our sons be yours. Let your women hear our words.

PRISCILLA MASON

In the spring of 1793, a young woman delivered a commencement speech at the Young Ladies Academy of Philadelphia. Chafing against the limitations of her sex, an indignant Priscilla Mason shared "a few thoughts in vindication of female eloquence," arguing for an expanded public role for women in the new American republic.

Education was highly valued in colonial America. A solid foundation of learning was considered essential to the cultivation of good citizenship. Since the mid-18th century, the number of academies and schools for boys had mushroomed, mostly catering to the families of European settlers who could afford to pay for private education.

The Young Ladies Academy of Philadelphia was the nation's first for girls and young women. Academic expectations were high but only up to a point. Even for the young women who benefitted from such a rare opportunity, their roles in society were still largely confined to the household and domestic sphere.

But change was in the air.

Just a few years earlier, the pathbreaking Eliza Harriot O'Connor had delivered a series of lectures in Philadelphia on the radical notion of "female genius" and the idea that women should be allowed to participate equally in public affairs. We know President George Washington heard one of her talks in May 1787, when he and the other delegates to the Constitutional Convention were gathered in the nation's capital to decide how the new country would be governed. O'Connor's ideas were percolating in the atmosphere when Mason and her fellow students were preparing for their graduation.

The commencement was an elaborate affair, a procession of teachers, administrators, students and trustees marching through the streets of Philadelphia to the Methodist church. Awaiting them inside the sanctuary inside were parents, friends, and local townspeople.

When her time came, Mason began her speech with a show of deference to her all-male teachers and an apology for the audacity of speaking to a "promiscuous" mixed-gender audience. But her tone quickly shifted into defiance and anger. Who decided that women should not be allowed to speak in public, she asked. "Who will say that the female mind is incapable?"

She blasted the "arbitrary" illogic and injustice of restricting women's opportunities for education while blaming them for their ignorance.

Even if women were to become orators, she asked, where could they use their talents? Men have barred women from all the avenues.

"The Church, the Bar, and the Senate are shut against us. Who shut them? *Man*; despotic man."

"SALUTORY ORATION"

May 15, 1793
**Year-end Ceremony, Philadelphia Young Ladies' Academy,
Methodist Church, Fourth Street, Philadelphia, Pennsylvania**

Venerable Trustees of this Seminary, Patrons of the Improvement of the Female Mind; suffer us to present the first fruits of your labours as an offering to you, and cordially to salute you on this auspicious day. Worthy Principal, Tutor, Friend and Parent, all in one! when we recollect our obligations to you, we feel, and would speak, but delicacy forbids.

The stern republican and polish'd citizen, will certainly join e'er long, to banish the barbarous custom of offering open adulation in such a place as this.

We therefore content ourselves with simply saluting you; and wishing the events of the day may speak your praise, in language suitable to your feelings.

Respected and very respectable audience; while your presence inspires our tender bosoms with fear and anxiety, your countenances promise indulgence, and encourage us to proceed. In the name of myself and sisters, therefore, I cordially salute you, and hope you will pardon the defects of an attempt to please you, defects arising in some measure from due respect.

A female, young and inexperienced, addressing a promiscuous assembly, is a novelty which requires an apology, as some may suppose. I therefore, with submission, beg leave to offer a few thoughts in vindication of female eloquence.

I mean not at this early day, to become an advocate for that species of female eloquence, of which husbands so much, and so justly, stand in awe, — a species of which the famous Grecian orator, Xantippe, was an illustrious example. Although the free exercise of this natural talent, is a part of the rights of woman, and must be allowed by the courtesy of Europe and America too; yet it is rather to be *tolerated* than *established*; and should rest like the sword in the scabbard, to be used only when occasion requires. — Leaving my sex in full possession of this prerogative, I claim for them the further right of being heard on more public occasions — of addressing the reason as well as the fears of the other sex.

Our right to instruct and persuade cannot be disputed, if it shall appear, that we possess the talents of the orator — and have opportunities for the exercise of those talents. Is a power of speech, and volubility of expression, one of the talents of the orator? Our sex possess it in an eminent degree.

Do personal attractions give charms to eloquence, and force to the orator's arguments? There is some truth mixed with the flattery we receive on this head. Do tender passions enable the orator to speak in a moving and forcible manner? This talent of the orator is confessedly ours. In all these aspects the female orator stands on equal, — nay, on *superior* ground.

If therefore she should fail in the capacity for mathematical studies, or metaphysical profundities, she has, on the whole, equal pretensions to the palm of eloquence. Granted it is, that a perfect knowledge of the subject is essential to the accomplished Orator. But seldom does it happen, that the abstruse sciences, become the subject of eloquence. And, as to that knowledge which is popular and practical, — that knowledge which alone is useful to the orator; who will say that the female mind is incapable?

Our high and mighty Lords (thanks to their arbitrary constitutions) have denied us the means of knowledge, and then reproached us for the want of it. Being the stronger party, they early seized the sceptre and the sword; with these they gave laws to society; they denied women the advantage of a liberal education; forbid them to exercise their talents on those great occasions, which would serve to improve them. They doom'd the sex to servile or frivolous employments, on purpose to degrade their minds, that they themselves might hold unrivall'd, the power and pre-eminence they had usurped. Happily, a more liberal way of thinking begins to prevail. The sources of knowledge are gradually opening to our sex. Some have already availed themselves of the privilege so far, as to wipe off our reproach in some measure.

A M'Caulley, a Carter, a Moore, a Rowe, and other illustrious female characters, have shown of what the sex are capable, under the cultivating hand of science. But supposing now that we possess'd all the talents of the orator, in the highest perfection; where shall we find a theatre for the display of them? The Church, the Bar, and the Senate are shut against us. Who shut them? *Man*; despotic man, first made us incapable of the duty, and then forbid us the exercise. Let us by suitable education, qualify ourselves for those high departments — they will open before us. They *will*, did I say? They have done it already. Besides several Churches of less importance, a numerous and respectable Society, has display'd its impartiality. — I had almost said gallentry in this respect. With *others,* women forsooth, are complimented with the wall, the right hand, the head of the table, — with a kind of mock pre-eminence in small matters: but on great occasions the sycophant changes his tune, and says, "Sit down at my feet and learn." Not so the members of the enlightened and liberal Church. They regard not the anatomical formation of the body. They look to the soul, and allow all to teach who are capable of it, be they male or female.

But Paul forbids it! Contemptible little body! The girls laughed at the deformed creature. To be revenged, he declares war against the whole sex: advises men not to marry them; and has the indolence to order them to keep silence in the Church —: afraid, I suppose, that they would say something against celibacy, or ridicule the old bachelor.

With respect to the bar, citizens of either sex have an undoubted right to plead their own cause there. Instances could be given of females being admitted to plead the cause of a friend, a husband, a son; and they have done it with energy and effect. I am assured that there is nothing in our laws or constitution, to prohibit the licensure of female Attornies; and sure our judges have too much gallantry, to urge *prescription* in bar of their claim. In regard to the senate, pre-scription is clearly in our favour. We have one or two cases exactly in point.

Heliogabalus, the Roman Emperor, of blessed memory, made his grand-mother a Senator of Rome. He also established a senate of women; appointed his mother President; and committed to them the important business of reg-ulating dress and fashions. And truly methinks the dress of our own country, at this day, would admit of some regulation, for it is subject to no rules at all — It would be worthy the wisdom of Congress, to consider whether a similar institution, established at the seat of our Federal Government, would not be a public benefit. We cannot be independent, while we receive our fashions from other countries; nor act properly, while we imitate the manners of governments not congenial to our own. Such a Senate, composed of women most noted for wisdom, learning and taste, delegated from every part of the Union, would give dignity, and independence to our manners; uniformity, and even authority to our fashions.

It would fire the female breast with the most generous ambition, prompting to illustrious actions. It would furnish the most noble Theatre for the display, the exercise and improvement of every faculty. It would call forth all that is human — all that is *divine* in the soul of woman; and having proved them equally capable with the other sex, would lead to their equal participation of honor and office.

DEBORAH SAMPSON GANNETT

In the spring of 1782, with the Revolutionary War raging, Deborah Sampson needed a job. So she cut her hair, bound her chest, put on men's clothes, and enlisted in the Continental Army.

Her disguise undetected, she joined the Fourth Massachusetts Regiment under the name Robert Shurtleff. She and the other recruits marched from Worcester, Massachusetts, to West Point, New York, where Sampson became part of the Light Infantry Troops.

By all accounts she fought bravely in several skirmishes against Loyalists and was even wounded in combat — lacerated in the head, and shot twice in the thigh. One of the musket balls she managed to extract herself, the other was embedded in her leg the rest of her life.

Seventeen months after she enlisted, Sampson's gender was revealed when she fell ill with a high fever and was treated at a Philadelphia hospital. A doctor discovered her disguise, and Sampson was mustered out of the army. She was granted an honorable discharge.

The next chapter in her life was equally extraordinary. Sampson launched a new career as an author and public speaker. With the help of a Massachusetts publisher, she wrote a book about her military service, *The Female Review: or, Memoirs of an American Young Lady.* Then she set out on the lecture circuit.

Traveling the countryside by horse, wagon, and cart, she appeared before audiences in Massachusetts, Rhode Island and New York, selling her book and getting paid for her speeches. She travelled alone, and as her diary records, she was often sick.

In the spring of 1802, Sampson performed four times at Boston's Federal-Street Theatre. On stage, dressed as a woman, she began with an apology: "My achievements are a breach of the decorum of my sex, unquestionably." And yet, she regarded the opportunity for women to serve in the military as "a natural privilege," one that she now recalled "with anguish and amazement."

Then she stepped behind a curtain and reappeared, this time in a blue-and-white Continental Army uniform. With her musket, she ran through a 27-step drill, the soldier's "manual exercise of arms."

Her reviews were positive — one writer even praised her "manly elocution." She recorded in her diary that her audiences were "polite" and "very agreeable."

Sampson married and had four children. Not until 1805 did she win her long campaign for a pension from the US government. She died of yellow fever at age 66 and is buried in Sharon, Massachusetts — where she's celebrated as a hometown hero.

"LIFE AS A REVOLUTIONARY WAR SOLDIER"

March 1802
Federal Street Theatre, Boston, Massachusetts

● ● ● **W**ithout further preliminary apologies, yet with every due respect towards this brilliant and polite circle, I hasten to a review of the most conspicuous parts of that path, which led to achievements, which some have believed, but which many still doubt. Their accomplishment once seemed to me as impossible, as that I am author of them, is now incredible to the incredulous, or wounding to the ear of more refined delicacy and taste. They are a breach in the decorum of my sex, unquestionably; and, perhaps, too unfortunately ever irreconcilable with the rigid maxims of the moralist; and a sacrifice, which, while it may seem perfectly incompatible with the requirements of virtue — and which of course must ring discord in the ear, and disgust to the bosom of sensibility and refinement, I must be content to leave to time and the most scrutinizing enquiry to disclose.

UNLETTERED in any scholastic school of erudition, you will not expect, on this occasion, the entertainment of the soft and captivating sounds of eloquence; but rather a naration of facts in a mode as uncouth as they are unnatural. *Facts* — which, though I once experienced, and of which memory has ever been painfully retentive, I cannot now make you feel, or paint to the life.

KNOW then, that my juvenile mind early became inquisitive to understand — not merely whether the principles, or rather the seeds of *war* are analagous to the genuine nature of *man* — not merely to know why he should forego every trait of *humanity*, and to assume the character of a *brute*; or, in plainer language, why he should march out tranquilly, or in a paroxism of rage against his fellow-man, to butcher, or be butchered? — for these, alas! were too soon horribly verified by the massacres in our streets, in the very streets which encompass this edifice — in yonder adjacent villas, on yonder memorable eminence, where now stand living monuments of the atrocious, the heart-distracting, mementous scenes, that followed in rapid succession!

THIS I am ready to affirm, though it may be deemed unnatural in my sex, is not a demoralization of human nature. The sluices, both of the blood of *freemen* and of *slaves*, were first opened here. And those hills and vallies, once the favorite resort, both of the lover and philosopher, have been drunk with their blood! A new subject was then opened to the most pathetic imagination, and to the rouzing of every latent spark of humanity, one should think, in the bosoms of the *wolves*, as well as in those of the *sheep*, for whose blood they were so thirsty.

BUT most of all, my mind became agitated with the enquiry — why a nation, separated from us by an ocean more than three thousand miles in extent, should endeavor to enforce on us plans of subjugation, the most unnatural in themselves, unjust, inhuman, in their operations, and unpractised even by the uncivilized savages of the wilderness? Perhaps nothing but the critical juncture of the times could have excused such a philosophical disquisition of politics in woman, notwithstanding it was a theme of universal speculation and concern to man. We indeed originated from her, as from a parent, and had, perhaps, continued to this period in subjection to her mandates, had we not discovered, that this, her romantic, avaricious and cruel disposition extended to *murder*, after having bound the *slave*!

CONFIRMED by this time in the justness of a defensive war on the one side, from the most aggravated one on the other — my mind ripened with my strength; and while our beds and our roses were sprinkled with the blood of indiscriminate youth, beauty, innocence and decrepit old age, I only seemed to want the *license* to become one of the severest *avengers* of the wrong.

FOR several years I looked on these scenes of havoc, rapacity and devastation, as one looks on a drowning man, on the conflagration of a city — where are not only centered his coffers of gold, but with them his choicest hopes, friends, companions, his all — without being able to extend the rescuing hand to either.

WROUGHT upon at length, you may say, by an enthusiasm and phrenzy, that could brook no control — I burst the tyrant bands, which *held my sex in awe*, and clandestinely, or by stealth, grasped an opportunity, which custom and the world seemed to deny, as a natural privilege. And whilst poverty, hunger, nakedness, cold and disease had dwindled the *American Armies* to a handful — whilst universal terror and dismay ran through our camps, ran through our country — while even WASHINGTON himself, at their head, though like a god, stood, as it were, on a pinacle tottering over the abyss of destruction, the last prelude to our falling a wretched prey to the yawning jaws of the monster aiming to devour — not merely for the sake of gratifying a fecetious curiosity, like that of my reputed Predecessor, in her romantic excursions through the garden of bliss — did I throw off the soft habiliments of *my sex* and assume those of the *warrior*, already prepared for battle.

THUS I became an actor in that important drama, with an inflexible resolution to persevere through the last scene; when we might be permitted and acknowledged to enjoy what we had so nobly declared we would possess, or lose with our lives — FREEDOM and INDEPENDENCE! — When the philosopher might resume his researches unmolested — the statesman be disembarrassed by his distracting theme of national politics — the divine find less occasion to invoke the indignation of heaven on the usurpers and cannibals of the inherent rights and even existence of man — when the son should again be restored to the arms of his disconsolate parent, and the lover to the bosom of her, for whom indeed he is willing to jeopard his life, and for whom alone he wishes to live!

A NEW scene, and, as it were, a new world now opened to my view; the objects of which now seemed as important, as the transition before seemed unnatural. It would, however, here be a weakness in me to mention the tear of repentence, or of that of temerity, from which the stoutest of my sex are, or ought not to be, wholly exempt on extreme emergencies, which many times involuntarily stole into my eye, and fell unheeded to the ground: And that too before I had reached the embattled field, the ramparts, which protected its internal resources — which shielded youth, beauty, and the delicacy of that sex at home, which perhaps I had forfeited in turning volunteer in their defence. *Temeritis* — when reflections on my former situation, and this new kind of being, were daggers more frightful, than all the implements of war — when the rustling of every leaf was an omen of danger, the whisper of each wind, a tale of woe! If then the poignancy of thought stared me thus haggardly in the face, found its way to the inmost recesses of my heart, thus forcibly, in the commencement of my career — what must I not have anticipated before its close!

THE curtain is now up — a scene opens to your view; but the objects strike your attention less forcibly, and less interestingly, than they then did, not only my own eyes, but every energetic sensation of my soul. What shall I say further? Shall I not stop short, and leave to your imaginations to pourtray the tragic deeds of war? Is it not enough, that I here leave it even to unexperience to fancy the hardships, the anxieties, the dangers, even of the best life of a soldier? And were it not improper, were it not unsafe, were it not indelicate, and were I certain I should be intitled to a pardon, I would appeal to the soft bosom of my own sex to draw a parallel between the perils and sexual inconveniences of a girl in her teens, and not only in the armour, but in the capacity, at any rate, obliged to perform the duties in the field — and those who go to the camp without a masquerade, and consequently subject only to what toils and sacrifices they please: Or, will a conclusion be more natural from those who sometimes take occasion to complain by their own domestic fire-sides; but who, indeed, are at the same time in affluence, cherished in the arms of their companions, and sheltered from the storms of war by the rougher sex in arms?

MANY have seen, and many can contemplate, in the field of imagination, battles and victories amidst garments rolled in blood: but it is only one of my own sex, exposed to the storm, who can conceive of my situation . . .

I AM indeed willing to acknowledge what I have done, an error and presumption. I will call it an *error* and *presumption*, because I swerved from the accustomed flowry paths of *female delicacy*, to walk upon the heroic precipice of feminine perdition! — I indeed left my morning pillow of roses, to prepare a couch of brambles for the night; and yet I awoke from this refreshed, to gather nought but the thorns of anguish for the next night's repose — and in the precipitancy of passion, to prepare a moment for repentance at leisure!

Had all this been achieved by the rougher hand, more properly assigned to wield the sword in duty and danger in a defensive war, the most cruel in its measures, though important in its consequences; these thorns might have been converted into wreaths of immortal glory and fame. I therefore yield every claim of honor and distinction to the hero and patriot, who met the foe in his own name; though not with more heartfelt satisfaction, with the trophies, which were most to redound to the future grandeur and importance of the country in which he lives.

BUT *repentance* is a sweet solace to conscience, as well as the most complete atonement to the Supreme Judge of our offences: notwithstanding the tongue of malevolence and scurrility may be continually preparing its most poisonous ingredients for the punishment of a crime which has already received more than half a pardon.

YET if even this be deemed too much of an extenuation of a breach in the modesty of the *female world* — humilized and contented will I sit down inglorious, for having unfortunately performed an important part assigned for another — like a bewildered star traversing out of its accustomed orbit, whose twinkling beauty at most has become totally obscured in the presence of the sun.

BUT as the rays of the sun strike the eye with the greatest lustre when emerging from a thick fog, and as those actions which have for their objects the extended hand of charity to the indigent and wretched — to restore a bewildered traveller to light — and, to reform in ourselves any irregular and forlorn course of life; so, allowing myself to be one or the greatest of these, do I still hope for some claim on the indulgence and patronage of the public; as in such case I might be conscious of the approbation of my GOD.

I CANNOT, contentedly, quit this subject or this place, without expressing, more emphatically, my high respect and veneration for my own SEX. The indulgence of this respectable circle supercedes my merit, as well as my most sanguine expectations. You receive at least in return my warmest gratitude. And though you can neither have, or perhaps need, from me the instructions of the sage, or the advice of the counsellor; you surely will not be wholly indifferent to my most sincere declaration of friendship for that sex, for which this checkered flight of my life may have rendered me the least ornamental example; but which, neither in adversity or prosperity, could I ever learn to forget or degrade . . .

EMMA WILLARD

Emma Hart Willard believed women deserved a role beyond hearth and home and should not be consigned to second-class status.

Although raised by parents who valued education for both their daughters and sons, her own school for girls convened for just twelve weeks in the wintertime. For the most part, the daughters of families of means were trained in "the accomplishments" — meaning painting, drawing, dance, and music.

In 1814, impressed with the curriculum at the male-only Middlebury College in Vermont, she applied to study there and was furious when she was rejected because of her gender.

And so she began working on a grand plan. Five years later, she presented to the Governor and legislators of New York her radical vision of an academy for young women, equal to the higher education available to young men. She published it as a pamphlet, paying for it out of her own pocket.

Appealing to the legislators' patriotism, she argued that educated women would participate in creating an enlightened future citizenry. Women versed in "republican manners and virtues" would strengthen the "body politic" and make the new American republic more resistant to tyrants.

She laid out a detailed blueprint for how her academy would be structured, what the coursework would include, and how students would be taught. As a public good, she argued, the academy should be financed through the state budget.

Some historians believe Willard read her plan aloud to a group of legislators, in which case it can be considered a speech. Regardless, her proposal reverberated through the state capital. Her educational roadmap has been called "the Magna Carta of higher education for women in America."

Although state legislators turned her down, Willard found the money she needed when the city council in Troy appropriated $4,000 to buy a three-story building, and local citizens raised the funds for renovation.

In the autumn of 1821, she opened the doors of the Troy Female Seminary — the world's first higher educational institute for women, and the first to teach women science, philosophy, history, geography, and other subjects previously reserved for men. She envisioned it as the first of many female seminaries across the country.

In later years, Willard traveled across the US to lecture about equal education, train teachers, and help communities set up public schools. She campaigned and advocated for women's higher education in Greece. In 1854 she spoke at a conference for educators in London.

Willard died in 1870, leaving a powerful educational legacy for generations of female students.

"IMPROVING FEMALE EDUCATION"

Spring 1819
**Read before influential members of the New
York State Legislature, Albany, New York**

The object of this Address, is to convince the public, that a reform, with respect to female education, is necessary; that it cannot be effected by individual exertion, but that it requires the aid of the legislature; and further, by shewing the justice, the policy, and the magnanimity of such an undertaking, to persuade that body to endow a seminary for females, as the commencement of such reformation.

The idea of a college for males will naturally be associated with that of a seminary, instituted and endowed by the public; and that absurdity of sending ladies to college, may, at first thought, strike every one to whom this subject shall be proposed. I therefore hasten to observe, that the seminary here recommended, will be as different from those appropriated to the other sex, as the female character and duties are from the male. The business of the husbandman is not to waste his endeavours, in seeking to make his orchard attain the strength and majesty of his forest, but to rear each, to the perfection of its nature.

That the improvement of female education will be considered by our enlightened citizens as a subject of importance, the liberality with which they part with their property to educate their daughters, is a sufficient evidence; and why should they not, when assembled in the legislature, act in concert to effect a noble object, which, though dear to them individually, cannot be accomplished by their unconnected exertions.

If the improvement of the American female character, and that alone, could be effected by public liberality, employed in giving better means of instruction; such improvement of one half of society, and that half, which barbarous and despotic nations have ever degraded, would of itself be an object, worthy of the most liberal government on earth; but if the female character be raised, it must inevitably raise that of the other sex: and thus does the plan proposed, offer, as the object of legislative bounty, to elevate the whole character of the community.

As evidence that this statement does not exaggerate the female influence in society, our sex need but be considered, in the single relation of mothers. In this character, we have the charge of the whole mass of individuals, who are to compose the succeeding generation; during that period of youth, when the pliant mind takes any direction, to which it is steadily guided by a forming hand. How important a power is given by this charge! yet, little do too many of my sex know how, either to appreciate or improve it. Unprovided with the means of acquiring that knowledge, which flows liberally to the other sex — having our time of education devoted to frivolous acquirements, how should we understand the nature of the mind, so as to be aware of the importance of those early impressions, which we make upon the minds of our children? — or how should we be able to form enlarged and correct views, either of the character, to which we ought to mould them, or of the means most proper to form them aright?

Considered in this point of view, were the interests of male education alone to be consulted, that of females becomes of sufficient importance to engage the public attention. Would we rear the human plant to its perfection, we must first fertilize the soil which produces it. If it acquire its first bent and texture upon a barren plain, it will avail comparatively little, should it be afterwards transplanted to a garden . . .

In inquiring, concerning the benefits of the plan proposed, I shall proceed upon the supposition that female seminaries will be patronized throughout our country.

Nor is this altogether a visionary supposition. If one seminary should be well organized, its advantages would be found so great, that others would soon be instituted; and, that sufficient patronage can be found to put one in operation, may be presumed from its reasonableness, and from the public opinion, with regard to the present mode of female education. It is from an intimate acquaintance, with those parts of our country, whose education is said to flourish most, that the writer has drawn her picture of the present state of female instruction; and she knows, that she is not alone, in perceiving or deploring its faults. Her sentiments are shared by many an enlightened parent of a daughter, who has received a boarding school education. Counting on the promise of her childhood, the father had anticipated her maturity, as combining what is excellent in mind, with what is elegant in manners. He spared no expense that education might realize to him, the image of his imagination. His daughter returned from her boarding school, improved in fashionable airs, and expert in manufacturing fashionable toys; but, in her conversation, he sought in vain, for that refined and fertile mind which he had fondly expected. Aware that his disappointment has its source in a defective education, he looks with anxiety on his other daughters, whose minds, like lovely buds, are beginning to open. Where shall he find a genial soil, in which he may place them to expand? Shall he provide them male instructors? — Then the graces of their persons and manners, and whatever forms the distinguishing charm of the feminine character, they cannot be expected to acquire. — Shall he give them a private tutoress? She will have been educated at the boarding school, and his daughters will have the faults of its instruction second-handed. Such is now the dilemma of many parents; and it is one, from which they cannot be extricated by their individual exertions. May not then the only plan, which promises to relieve them, expect their vigorous support.

Let us now proceed to inquire, what benefits would result from the establishment of female seminaries.

They would constitute a grade of public education, superior to any yet known in the history of our sex; and through them, the lower grades of female instruction might be controlled. The influence of public seminaries, over these, would operate in two ways; first by requiring certain qualifications for entrance; and secondly, by furnishing instructresses initiated in these modes of teaching, and imbued with their maxims.

Female seminaries might be expected to have important and happy effects, on common schools in general; and in the manner of operating on these, would probably place the business of teaching children, into hands now nearly useless to society; and take it from those, whose services the state wants in many other ways.

That nature designed for our sex the care of children, she has made manifest, by mental, as well as physical indications. She has given us, in a greater degree than men, the gentle arts of insinuation, to soften their minds, and fit them to receive impressions; a greater quickness of invention to vary modes of teaching to different dispositions; and more patience to make repeated efforts. There are many females of ability, to whom the business of instructing children is highly acceptable, and, who would devote all their faculties to their occupation. They would have no higher pecuniary object to engage their attention, and their reputation as instructors they would consider as important; whereas, whenever able and enterprizing men, engage in this business, they consider it, as a merely temporary employment, to further some other object, to the attainment of which, their best thoughts and calculations are directed. If then women were properly fitted by instruction, they would be likely to teach children better than the other sex; they could afford to do it cheaper; and those men who would otherwise be engaged in this employment, might be at liberty to add to the wealth of the nation, by any of those thousand occupations, from which women are necessarily debarred.

But the females, who taught children, would have been themselves instructed either immediately or indirectly by the seminaries. Hence through these, the government might exercise an intimate, and most beneficial control over common schools. Any one, who has turned his attention to this subject, must be aware, that there is great room for improvement in these, both as to the modes of teaching, and the things taught; and what method could be devised so likely to effect this improvement, as to prepare by instruction, a class of individuals, whose interest, leisure, and natural talents, would combine to make them pursue it with ardor. Such a class of individuals would be raised up, by female seminaries. And therefore they would be likely to have highly important and happy effects on common schools.

It is believed, that such institutions would tend to prolong, or perpetuate our excellent government.

An opinion too generally prevails, that our present form of government, though good, cannot be permanent. Other republics have failed, and the historian and philosopher have told us that nations are like individuals; that at their birth, they receive the seeds of their decline and dissolution. Here deceived by a false analagy, we receive an apt illustration of particular facts, for a general truth. The existence of nations, cannot, in strictness, be compared with the duration of animate life; for by the operation of physical causes, this, after a certain length of time, must cease: but the existence of nations, is prolonged by the succession of one generation to another, and there is no physical cause, to prevent this succession's going on, in a peaceable manner, under a good government, till the end of time. We must then look to other causes, than necessity, for the decline and fall of former republics. If we could discover these causes, and seasonably prevent their operation, then might our latest prosperity enjoy the same happy government, with which we are blessed; or of but in part, then might the triumphs of tyranny, be delayed, and a few more generations be free.

Permit me then to ask the enlightened politician of my country, whether amidst his researches for these causes, he cannot discover one, in the neglect, which free governments, in common with others, have shown, to whatever regarded the formation of the female character.

In those great republics, which have fallen of themselves, the loss of republican manners and virtues, has been the invariable precursor, of their loss of the republican form of government. But is it not in the power of our sex, to give society its tone, both as to manners and morals? And if such is the extent of female influence, is it wonderful, that republics have failed, when they calmly suffered that influence, to become enlisted in favour of luxuries and follies, wholly incompatible with the existence of freedom? . . .

The inquiry, to which these remarks have conducted us is this — What is offered by the plan of female education, here proposed, which may teach, or preserve, among females of wealthy families, that purity of manners, which is allowed, to be so essential to national prosperity, and so necessary, to the existence of a republican government.

1. Females, by having their understandings cultivated, their reasoning powers developed and strengthened, may be expected to act more from the dictates of reason, and less from those of fashion and caprice.
2. With minds thus strengthened they would be taught systems of morality, enforced by sanctions of religion; and they might be expected to acquire juster and more enlarged views of their duty, and stronger and higher motives to its performance.
3. This plan of education, offers all that can be done to preserve female youth from a contempt of useful labour. The pupils would become accustomed to it, in conjunction with the high objects of literature, and the elegant pursuits of the fine arts; and it is to be hoped that both from habit and association, they might in future life, regard it as respectable.

   To this may be added, that if housewifery could be raised to a regular art, and taught upon philosophical principles, it would become a higher and more interesting occupation; and ladies of fortune, like wealthy agriculturalists, might find, that to regulate their business, was an agreeable employment.
4. The pupils might be expected to acquire a taste for moral and intellectual pleasures, which would buoy them above a passion for show and parade, and which would make them seek to gratify the natural love of superiority, by endeavouring to excel others in intrinsic merit, rather than in the extrinsic frivolities of dress, furniture, and equipage.
5. By being enlightened in moral philosophy, and in that, which teaches the operations of the mind, females would be enabled to perceive the nature and extent, of that influence, which they possess over their children, and the obligation, which this lays them under, to watch the formation of their characters with unceasing vigilance, to become their instructors, to devise plans for their improvement, to weed out the vices from their minds, and to implant and foster the virtues. And surely, there is that in the maternal bosom, which, when its pleadings shall be aided by education, will overcome the seductions of wealth and fashion, and will lead the mother, to seek her happiness in communing with her children, and promoting their welfare, rather than in a heartless intercourse, with the votaries of pleasure: especially, when with an expanded mind, she extends her views to futurity, and sees her care to her offspring rewarded by peace of conscience, the blessings of her family, the prosperity of her county, and finally with everlasting happiness to herself and them.

Thus, laudable objects and employments, would be furnished for the great body of females, who are not kept by poverty from excesses. But among these, as among the other sex, will be found master spirits, who must have pre-eminence, at whatever price they acquire it. Domestic life cannot hold these, because they prefer to be infamous, rather than obscure. To leave such, without any virtuous road to eminence, is unsafe to community; for not unfrequently, are the secret springs of revolution, set in motion by their intrigues. Such aspiring minds, we will regulate, by education, we will remove obstructions to the course of literature, which has heretofore been their only honorable way to distinction; and we offer them a new object, worthy of their ambition; to govern, and improve the seminaries for their sex.

In calling on my patriotic countrymen, to effect so noble an object, the consideration of national glory, should not be overlooked. Ages have rolled away; — barbarians have trodden the weaker sex beneath their feet; — tyrants have robbed us of the present light of heaven, and fain would take its future. Nations, calling themselves polite, have made us the fancied idols of a ridiculous worship, and we have repaid them with ruin for their folly. But where is that wise and heroic country, which has considered that our rights are sacred, though we cannot defend them? that tho' a weaker, we are an essential part of the body politic, whose corruption or improvement must affect the whole? and which, having thus considered, has sought to give us by education, that rank in the scale of being, to which our importance entitles us? History shows not that country. It shows many, whose legislatures have sought to improve their various vegetable productions, and their breeds of useful brutes; but none, whose public councils have made it an object of their deliberations, to improve the character of their women. Yet though history lifts not her finger to such an one, anticipation does. She points to a nation, which, having thrown off the shackles of authority and precedent, shrinks not from schemes of improvement, because other nations have never attempted them; but which, in its pride of independence, would rather lead than follow, in the march of human improvement; a nation wise and magnanimous to plan, enterprising to undertake, and rich in resources to execute. Does not every American exult that this country is his own? And who knows how great and good a race of men, may yet arise from the forming hand of mothers, enlightened by the bounty of that beloved country, — to defend her liberties, — to plan her future improvement, — and to raise her unparalleled glory?

FRANCES WRIGHT

An orphan at three, she was raised by relatives in Scotland. Enthralled by the radical promise of the American Revolution, in 1818 she set sail for New York. Seven years later, Frances Wright, known as "Fanny," became a US citizen — and an ardent abolitionist.

Fired up by the ideals of the new nation, she earnestly believed she could change minds about slavery through rational thinking and planning. She came up with an experimental stratagem to purchase, educate, and emancipate a small group of enslaved people — by their labor, they would purchase their own freedom. Through hard work and cooperative farm labor, the settlement would undercut competitors and prosper.

With her own money, Wright bought a 640-acre tract in the wilderness of western Tennessee, purchased slaves, and set up a cooperative farming community. Members worked the fields during the day and studied in communal schools at night. She called it Nashoba, the Chickasaw word for "wolf."

It was a bold and seemingly practical scheme — and, like most utopian communities, a flop. After shutting Nashoba down, Wright chartered a ship to Haiti and freed the enslaved.

Then she set out on a lecture tour across the mid-Atlantic and Midwest. She advocated for free public education, equality between the sexes, birth control, liberalized divorce laws, and legal rights for married women, and she attacked slaveholders, legislators, and the clergy as ruling elites who exerted arbitrary power.

As her audiences grew, so did her notoriety — many came to her lectures just to see the spectacle of a female speaker. Ministers attacked her from the pulpit. Newspapers called her a "female monster," "the red harlot of infidelity," and "a disgusting exhibition of female impudence."

Undeterred, she bought an abandoned church in New York City and turned it into a "Hall of Science" in which many lectures were given, including her own — with room for 1,200, office space for her newspaper, the *Free Enquirer*, and a bookstore.

The vilification got worse. A barrel of turpentine was placed in a hall when she was speaking and set on fire. Another time, someone turned off the gas, leaving everyone in darkness. Wright's courage never faltered.

Her Fourth of July speech at New Harmony, Indiana, in 1828, blends patriotism with moral outrage. Wright identified "negro slavery and the degradation of our colored citizens" as the one area unreached by the US Constitution.

She called on her fellow citizens to "improve the victory" of the new nation so that "all mankind" could join in celebrating the America she so deeply admired.

"NEW-HARMONY HALL"

July 4, 1828
Celebration of 52nd Anniversary of American Independence,
New-Harmony Hall, New Harmony, Indiana

The custom which commemorates in rejoicing the Anniversary of the national independence of these States has its origin in a human feeling, amiable in its nature, and beneficial, under proper direction, in its indulgence.

From the era which dates the national existence of the American people, dates also a mighty step in the march of human knowledge. And it is consistent with that principle in our conformation which leads us to rejoice in the good which befalls our species, and to sorrow for the evil, that our hearts should expand on this day; — on this day, which calls to memory the conquest achieved by knowledge over ignorance, willing co-operation over blind obedience, opinion over prejudice, new ways over old ways, when, fifty-two years ago, America declared her national independence, and associated it with her republican federation. Reasonable is it to rejoice on this day, and useful to reflect thereon; so that we rejoice for the real, and not for any imaginary good, we reflect on the positive advantages obtained, and on those which it is ours farther to acquire.

Dating, as we justly may, a new era in the history of man from the Fourth of July, 1776, it would be well, that is, it would be useful, if on each anniversary we examined the progress made by our species in just knowledge and just practice. Each Fourth of July would then stand as a tide mark in the flood of time, by which to note the rise and fall of each successive error, the discovery of each important truth, the gradual melioration in our public institutions, social arrangements, and, above all, in our moral feelings and mental views. Let such a review as this engage annually our attention, and sacred, doubly sacred, shall be this day: and that not to one nation only, but to all nations capable of reflection!

The political dismemberment of these once British colonies from the parent island, though involving a valuable principle, and many possible results, would scarcely merit a yearly commemoration, even in this country, had it not been accompanied by other occurrences more novel, and far more important. I allude to the seal then set to the system of representative government, till then imperfectly known in Europe, and insecurely practised in America, and to the crown then placed on this system by the novel experiment of political federation. The frame of federative government that sprung out of the articles signed in '76, is one of the most beautiful inventions of the human intellect. It has been in government what the steam engine has been in mechanics, and the printing press in the dissemination of human knowledge.

But it needs not that we should now pause to analyse what all must have considered. It is to one particular feature in our political institutions that I would call attention, and this, because it is at once the most deserving of notice, and the least noticed. Are our institutions better than those of other countries? Upon fair examination most men will answer *yes*. But why will they so answer? It is because they are republican, instead of monarchical? Democratic, rather than aristocratic? In so far as the republican principle shall have been proved more conducive to the general good than the monarchical, and the democratic than the aristocratic — in so far will the reasons be good. But there is another and a better reason than these. There is, in the institutions of this country, one principle, which, had they no other excellence, would secure to them the preference over those of all other countries. I mean — and some devout patriots will start — I mean the principle of change.

I have used a word to which is attached an obnoxious meaning. Speak of "change" and the world is in alarm. And yet where do we not see change? What is there in the physical world *but* change? And what would there be in the moral world *without* change? The flower blossoms, the fruit ripens, the seed is received and germinates in the earth, and we behold the tree. The aliment we eat to satisfy our hunger incorporates with our frame, and the atoms composing our existence to day, are exhaled tomorrow. In like manner our feelings and opinions are moulded by circumstance, and matured by observation and experience. All is change. Within and about us no one thing is as it was, or will be as it is. Strange, then, that we should start at a word used to signify a thing so familiar? Stranger yet that we should fail to appreciate a principle which, inherent in all matter, is no less inherent in ourselves; and which as it has tracked our mental progress heretofore, so will it track our progress through time to come!

But, will it be said, *change* has a bad, as well as a good sense? It may be for the better, and it may be for the worse? In the physical world it can be neither the one nor the other. It can be simply such as it is. But in the moral world — that is, in the thoughts, and feelings, and inventions of men, change may certainly be either for the better or for the worse, or it may be for neither. Changes that are neither bad nor good can have regard only to trivial matters, and can be as little worthy of observation as of censure. Changes that are from better to worse can originate only in ignorance, and are ever amended so soon as experience has substantiated their mischief. Where men then are free to consult experience they will correct their practice, and make changes for the better. It follows, therefore, that the more free men are, the more changes they will make. In the beginning, possibly, for the worse; but most certainly in time for the better; until their knowledge enlarging by observation, and their judgment strengthening by exercise, they will find themselves in the straight, broad, fair road of improvement. Out of change, therefore, springs improvement; and the people who shall have imagined a peaceable mode of changing their institutions, hold a surety for their melioration. This surety is worth all other excellences. Better were the prospects of a people under the influence of the worst government who should hold the power of changing it, that those of a people under the best who should hold no such power. Here, then is the great beauty of American government. The simple machinery of representation carried through all its parts, gives facility for its being moulded at will to fit with the knowledge of the age. If imperfect in any or all of its parts, it bears within it a perfect principle — the principle of improvement. And, let us observe, that this principle is all that we can ever know of perfection. Knowledge, and all the blessings which spring out of knowledge, can never be more than progressive; and whatsoever *sets open the door* does all for us — does every thing.

The clearsighted provision as in the national constitution, by which the frame of government can be moulded at will by the public voice, and so made to keep pace in progress with the public mind, is the master-stroke in constitutional law. Were our institutions far less enlightened and well digested than they are — were every other regulation erroneous, every other ordinance defective — nay, even tyrannous — this single provision would counterbalance all. Let but the door be opened, and be fixed open, for improvement to hold on her unimpeded course, and vices, however flagrant are but the evils of an hour. Once launch the animal man in the road of iniquity, and he *shall* — he *must* — hold a forward career. He may be sometimes checked; he may seem occasionally to retrograde; but his retreat is only that of the receding wave in the inning tide. His master movement is always in advance. By *this* do we distinguish man from all other existences within the range of our observation. By *this* does he stand preeminent over all known animals. By *this* — by his capability of improvement; by his tendency to improve whenever scope is allowed for the development of his faculties. To hold him *still*, he must be chained. Snap the chain, and he springs forward.

But will it be said, that the chains which bind him are more than one? That political bonds are much, but not all; and that when broken, we may still be slaves? I know not, my friends. We tax our ingenuity to draw nice distinctions. We are told of political liberty — of religious liberty — of moral liberty. Yet, after all, is there more than one liberty; and these divisions, are they not the more and the less of the same thing? The provision we have referred to in our political institutions, as framed in accordance with the principle inherent in ourselves, insures to us all of free action that statues can insure. Supposing that our laws, constitutional, civil, or penal, should in any thing cripple us at the present, the power will be with us to amend or annul them so soon (and how might it be sooner?) as our enlarged knowledge shall enable us to see in what they err. All the liberty therefore that we yet lack will gradually spring up — *there*, where our bondage is — in our minds. To be free we have but to see our chains. Are we disappointed — are we sometimes angry, because the crowd or any part of the crowd around us bows submissively to mischievous usages or unjust laws? Let us remember, that they do so in ignorance of their mischief and injustice, and that when they see these, as in the course of man's progressive state they must see them, these and other evils will be corrected.

Inappreciable is this advantage that we hold (unfortunately) above other nations? The great national and political revolution of '76 set the seal to the liberties of North America. And but for one evil, and that of immense magnitude, which the constitutional provision we have been considering does not fairly reach — I allude to negro slavery and the degradation of our colored citizens — we could foresee for the whole of this magnificent country a certain future of uniform and peaceful improvement. While other nations have still to win reform at the sword's point, we have only to will it. While in Europe men have still to fight, we have only to learn. While there they have to cope with ignorance armed cap-a-pee, encircled with armies and powerful with gold, we have only peacefully to collect knowledge, and to frame our institutions and actions in accordance with it . . .

The very origin of the people is opposed to it. The institutions, in their principle, militate against it. The day we are celebrating protests against it. It is for Americans, more especially, to nourish a nobler sentiment; one more consistent with their origin, and more conducive to their future improvement.

It is for them more especially to know why they love their country, and to *feel* that they love it, not because it *is* their country, but because it is the palladium of human liberty — the favour'd scene of human improvement. It is for them more especially, to know, why they honour their institutions; and to *feel*, that they honour them because they are based on just principles. It is for them, more especially, to examine their institutions, because they have the means of improving them; to examine their laws, because at will they can alter them. It is for them to lay aside luxury, whose wealth is in industry; idle parade, whose strength is in knowledge; ambitious distinction, whose principle is equality. It is for them not to rest satisfied with words, who can seize upon things; and to remember, that Equality means, not the mere equality of political rights, however valuable, but equality of instruction, and equality in virtue; and that Liberty means, not the mere voting at elections, but the free and fearless exercise of the mental faculties, and that self-possession which springs out of well-reasoned opinions and consistent practice. It is for them to honour principles rather than men — to commemorate events rather than days; when they rejoice, to know for what they rejoice, and to rejoice only for what has brought, and what brings, peace and happiness to men. The event we commemorate this day has procured much of both, and shall procure, in the onward course of human improvement, more than we can now conceive of. For this — for the good obtained, and yet in store for our race — let us rejoice! But let us rejoice as men, not as children — as human beings, rather than as Americans, — as reasoning beings, not as ignorants. So shall we rejoice to good purpose and in good feeling; so shall we improve the victory once on this day achieved, until all mankind hold with us the Jubilee of Independence.

MARIA MILLER STEWART

"What if I am a woman?" asked Maria Miller Stewart, throwing down a remarkable challenge to her audience.

In 1833 it was not common for a woman to speak in public, especially to both women and men. What's more, Stewart was a Black woman whose audience would have included some reform-minded Whites — therefore, also mixed race.

The African Meeting House — and surrounding Beacon Hill neighborhood — was not only a gathering spot for a close-knit community of educated free Blacks but also a number of White anti-slavery activists. One of the most prominent among them, and an early supporter of Stewart's work, was William Lloyd Garrison, who published her speeches in his abolitionist newspaper, *The Liberator*.

Born a free Black in Connecticut, orphaned at five, then an indentured servant, Stewart's life had been hard. But she believed in a higher purpose, and that she was called to do God's work.

She had been in Boston for less than a decade and had made a name for herself with provocative essays and speeches that generated admiration and also no small degree of controversy. This one, her fourth speech, would be her last in the city, a "farewell" to her friends before she left for New York City.

Many strands came together in this speech: religion and salvation, slavery and race prejudice, and, prominently, women's roles and rights — including women's right to express themselves in public. Many women throughout time "have had a voice in moral, religious, and political subjects," she said.

Stewart believed her own voice was divinely inspired. The Lord "hath unloosed my tongue," she told the audience, "and put his word into my mouth."

At a time when the Bible was routinely used to justify women's subjugation in both religious and secular life, she reproached the apostle Paul for writing in his letter to the Corinthians that women should keep silent in church. If Paul had known how women would be oppressed, she said, "he would make no objection to our pleading in public for our rights."

She also chided her audience for not doing more to support women who were striving to educate and improve themselves. "No longer ridicule their efforts," she said, for "it will be counted as sin."

Stewart's plea for gender equality is one that millions of women around the world are still demanding today.

A short time after this speech, she left Boston for good. Six months later she sent a copy to Garrison, who published a collection of her works in 1835, ensuring that Stewart's words would not perish like those of so many other outspoken women.

"FAREWELL ADDRESS TO HER FRIENDS IN THE CITY OF BOSTON"

September 21, 1833
African Meeting House, "Paul's Church," Boston, Massachusetts

❝ **I**s this vile world a friend to grace,
To help me on to God?"
Ah, no! for it is with great tribulation that any shall enter through the gates into the holy city.

My Respected Friends, You have heard me observe that the shortness of time, the certainty of death, and the instability of all things here, induced me to turn my thoughts from earth to heaven. Borne down with a heavy load of sin and shame, my conscience filled with remorse. Considering the throne of God forever guiltless, and my own eternal condemnation as just, I was at last brought to accept of salvation as a free gift, in and through the merits of a crucified Redeemer. Here I was brought to see —

> *"'Tis not by works of righteousness*
> *That our own hands have done;*
> *But we are saved by grace alone,*
> *Abounding through the Son."*

After these convictions, in imagination I found myself sitting at the feet of Jesus, clothed in my right mind. For I before had been like a ship tossed to and fro in a storm at sea. Then was I glad when I realized the dangers I had escaped; and then I consecrated my soul and body, and all the powers of my mind to his service, from that time henceforth; yea, even for evermore. Amen.

I found that religion was full of benevolence; I found there was joy and peace in believing, and I felt as though I was commanded to come out from the world and be separate; to go forward and be baptized. Methought I heard a spiritual interrogation: "Are you able to drink of that cup that I have drank of? and to be baptized with the baptism that I have been baptized with?" And my heart made this reply: Yea, Lord, I am able. Yet amid these bright hopes I was filled with apprehensive fears, lest they were false. I found that sin still lurked within; it was hard for me to renounce all for Christ, when I saw my earthly prospects blasted. O, how bitter was that cup. Yet I drank it to its very dregs. It was hard for me to say, Thy will be done; yet I was made to bend and kiss the rod. I was at last made willing to be anything or nothing for my Redeemer's sake. Like many I was anxious to retain the world in one hand and religion in the other. "Ye cannot serve God and mammon," sounded in my ear, and with giant strength I cut off my right hand, as it were, and plucked out my right eye, and cast them from me, thinking it better to enter life halt and maimed rather than have two hands or eyes to be cast into hell. Thus ended these mighty conflicts, and I received this heart-cheering promise: "That neither death, nor life, nor principalities, nor powers, nor things present, nor things to come should be able to separate me from the love of Christ Jesus our Lord."

And truly, I can say with St. Paul, that at my conversion I came to the people in the fullness of the gospel of grace. Having spent a few months in the city of _____ previously I saw the flourishing condition of their churches and the progress they were making in their Sabbath schools. I visited their Bible classes and heard of the union that existed in their female associations. On my arrival here, not finding scarce an individual who felt interested in these subjects, and but few of the whites, except Mr. Garrison and his friend, Mr. Knap; and hearing that those gentlemen had observed that female influence was powerful, my soul became fired with a holy zeal for your cause; every nerve and muscle in me was engaged in your behalf. I felt that I had a great work to perform, and was in haste to make a profession of my faith in Christ that I might be about my Father's business. Soon after I made this profession the Spirit of God came before me, and I spake before many. When going home, reflecting on what I had said, I felt ashamed, and knew not where I should hide myself. A something said within my breast, "press forward, I will be with thee." And my heart made this reply: "Lord, if thou wilt be with me, then will I speak for thee so long as I live." And thus far I have every reason to believe that it is the divine influence of the Holy Spirit operating upon my heart that could possibly induce me to make the feeble and unworthy efforts that I have.

But to begin my subject. "Ye have heard that it hath been said whoso is angry with his brother without cause, shall be in danger of the judgment; and whoso shall say to his brother Raca, shall be in danger of the council. But whosoever shall say thou fool, shall be in danger of hell fire." For several years my heart was in continual sorrow. And I believe the Almighty beheld from his holy habitation the affliction wherewith I was afflicted, and heard the false misrepresentations wherewith I was misrepresented; and there was none to help. Then I cried unto the Lord in my troubles. And thus for wise and holy purposes best known to himself, he has raised me in the midst of my enemies to vindicate my wrongs before this people, and to reprove them for sin as I have reasoned to them of righteousness and judgment to come. "For as the heavens are higher than the earth, so are his ways above our ways, and his thoughts above our thoughts." I believe, that for wise and holy purposes best known to himself, he hath unloosed my tongue and put his word into my mouth in order to confound and put all those to shame that have rose up against me. For he hath clothed my face with steel and lined my forehead with brass. He hath put his testimony within me and engraven his seal on my forehead. And with these weapons I have indeed set the fiends of earth and hell at defiance.

What if I am a woman; is not the God of ancient times the God of these modern days? Did he not raise up Deborah to be a mother and a judge in Israel? Did not Queen Esther save the lives of the Jews? And Mary Magdalene first declare the resurrection of Christ from the dead? Come, said the woman of Samaria, and see a man that hath told me all things that ever I did; is not this the Christ? St. Paul declared that it was a shame for a woman to speak in public, yet our great High Priest and Advocate did not condemn the woman for a more notorious offense than this; neither will he condemn this worthless worm. The bruised reed he will not break, and the smoking flax he will not quench till he send forth judgment unto victory. Did St. Paul but know of our wrongs and deprivations, I presume he would make no objection to our pleading in public for our rights.

Again: Holy women ministered unto Christ and the apostles; and women of refinement in all ages, more or less, have had a voice in moral, religious, and political subjects.

Again: Why the Almighty hath imparted unto me the power of speaking thus I cannot tell. "And Jesus lifted up his voice and said, I thank thee, O Father, Lord of heaven and earth, that thou hast hid these things from the wise and prudent and hast revealed them unto babes: even so, Father, for so it seemed good in thy sight."

But to convince you of the high opinion that was formed of the capacity and ability of woman by the ancients, I would refer you to "Sketches of the Fair Sex." Read to the fifty-first page, and you will find that several of the northern nations imagined that women could look into futurity, and that they had about them an inconceivable something approaching to divinity. Perhaps the idea was only the effect of the sagacity common to the sex, and the advantages which their natural address gave them over rough and simple warriors. Perhaps, also, those barbarians, surprised at the influence which beauty has over force, were led to ascribe to the supernatural attraction a charm which they could not comprehend. A belief, however, that the Deity more readily communicates himself to women, has at one time or other prevailed in every quarter of the earth; not only among the Germans and the Britons, put all the people of Scandinavia were possessed of it. Among the Greeks, women delivered the oracles. The respect the Romans paid to the Sybils is well known. The Jews had their prophetesses. The prediction of the Egyptian women obtained much credit at Rome, even unto the emperors. And in most barbarous nations all things that have the appearance of being supernatural, the mysteries of religion, the secrets of physic, and the rights of magic, were in the possession of women.

If such women as are here described have once existed, be no longer astonished, then, my brethren and friends, that God at this eventful period should raise up your own females to strive by their example, both in public and private, to assist those who are endeavoring to stop the strong current of prejudice that flows so profusely against us at present. No longer ridicule their efforts, it will be counted for sin. For God makes use of feeble means sometimes to bring about his most exalted purposes.

In the fifteenth century, the general spirit of this period is worthy of observation. We might then have seen women preaching and mixing themselves in controversies. Women occupying the chairs of Philosophy and Justice; women haranguing in Latin before the Pope; women writing in Greek and studying in Hebrew; nuns were poetesses and women of quality divines; and young girls who had studied eloquence would, with the sweetest countenances and the most plaintiff voices, pathetically exhort the Pope and the Christian princes to declare war against the Turks. Women in those days devoted their leisure hours to contemplation and study. The religious spirit which has animated women in all ages showed itself at this time. It has made them, by turns, martyrs, apostles, warriors, and concluded in making them divines and scholars.

Why cannot a religious spirit animate us now? Why cannot we become divines and scholars? Although learning is somewhat requisite, yet recollect that those great apostles, Peter and James, were ignorant and unlearned. They were taken from the fishing-boat, and made fishers of men.

In the thirteenth century, a young lady of Bologne devoted herself to the study of the Latin language and of the laws. At the age of twenty-three she pronounced a funeral oration in Latin in the great church of Bologne; and to be admitted as an orator, she had neither need of indulgence on account of her youth or of her sex. At the age of twenty-six she took the degree of doctor of laws, and began publicly to expound the Institutes of Justinian. At the age of thirty, her great reputation raised her to a chair, where she taught the law to a prodigious concourse of scholars from all nations. She joined the charms and accomplishments of a woman to all the knowledge of a man. And such was the power of her eloquence, that her beauty was only admired when her tongue was silent.

What if such women as are here described should rise among our sable race? And it is not impossible; for it is not the color of the skin that makes the man or the woman, but the principle formed in the soul. Brilliant wit will shine, come from whence it will; and genius and talent will not hide the brightness of its lustre.

But to return to my subject. The mighty work of formation has begun among this people. The dark clouds of ignorance are dispersing. The light of science is bursting forth. Knowledge is beginning to flow, nor will its moral influence be extinguished till its refulgent rays have spread over us from East to West and from North to South. Thus far is this mighty work begun, but not as yet accomplished. Christians must awake from their slumbers. Religion must flourish among them before the church will be built up in its purity or immorality be suppressed.

Yet, notwithstanding your prospects are thus fair and bright, I am about to leave you, perhaps never more to return; for I find it is no use for me, as an individual, to try to make myself useful among my color in this city. It was contempt for my moral and religious opinions in private that drove me thus before a public. Had experience more plainly shown me that it was the nature of man to crush his fellow, I should not have thought it so hard. Wherefore, my respected friends, let us no longer talk of prejudice till prejudice becomes extinct at home. Let us no longer talk of opposition till we cease to oppose our own. For while these evils exist, to talk is like giving breath to the air and labor to the wind, Though wealth is far more highly prized than humble merit, yet none of these things move me. Having God for my friend and portion, what have I to fear? Promotion cometh neither from the East or West; and as long as it is the will of God, I rejoice that I am as I am; for man in his best estate is altogether vanity. Men of eminence have mostly risen from obscurity; nor will I, although a female of a darker hue, and far more obscure than they, bend my head or hang my harp upon willows; for though poor, I will virtuous prove. And if it is the will of my Heavenly Father to reduce me to penury and want, I am ready to say: Amen; even so be it. "The foxes have holes, and the birds of the air have nests, but the Son of man hath not where to lay his head."

During the short period of my Christian warfare, I have indeed had to contend against the fiery darts of the devil. And was it not that the righteous are kept by the mighty power of God through faith unto salvation, long before this I should have proved to be like the seed by the wayside; for it has actually appeared to me, at different periods, as though the powers of earth and hell had combined against me, to prove my overthrow. Yet amidst their dire attempts, I found the Almighty to be "a friend that sticketh closer than a brother." He never will forsake the soul that leans on him; though he chastens and corrects, it is for the soul's best interest. "And as a father pitieth his children, so the Lord pitieth them that fear him."

But some of you said: "Do not talk so much about religion; the people do not wish to hear you. We know these things; tell us something we do not know." If you know these things, my dear friends, and have performed them, far happier and more prosperous would you now have been. "'He that knoweth his Lord's will, and obeyeth it not, shall be beaten with many stripes." Sensible of this, I have, regardless of the frowns and scoffs of a guilty world, plead up religion and the pure principles of morality among you. Religion is the most glorious theme that mortals can converse upon. The older it grows the more new beauties it displays. Earth, with its brilliant attractions, appears mean and sordid when compared to it. It is that fountain that has no end, and those that drink thereof shall never thirst; for it is, indeed, a well of water springing up in the soul unto everlasting life.

Again: Those ideas of greatness which are held forth to us are vain delusions — are airy visions which we shall never realize. All that man can say or do can never elevate us; it is a work that must be effected between God and ourselves. And how? By dropping all political discussions in our behalf; for these, in my opinion, sow the seed of discord and strengthen the cord of prejudice. A spirit of animosity is already risen, and unless it is quenched, a fire will burst forth and devour us, and our young will be slain by the sword. It is the sovereign will of God that our condition should be thus and so. "For he hath formed one vessel for honor, and another for dishonor." And shall the clay say to him that formed it: Why hast Thou formed me thus? It is high time for us to drop political discussions; and when our day of deliverance comes, God will provide a way for us to escape, and fight his own battles.

Finally, my brethren, let us follow after godliness, and the things which make for peace. Cultivate your own minds and morals; real merit will elevate you. Pure religion will burst your fetters. Turn your attention to industry. Strive to please your employers. Lay up what you earn. And remember that in the grave distinction withers and the high and low are alike renowned.

But I draw to a conclusion. Long will the kind sympathy of some much-loved friend be written on the tablet of my memory, especially those kind individuals who have stood by me like pitying angels and befriended me when in the midst of difficulty, many blessings rest on them. Gratitude is all the tribute I can offer. A rich reward awaits them.

To my unconverted friends, one and all, I would say, shortly this frail tenement of mine will be dissolved and lie mouldering in ruins. O, solemn thought! Yet why should I revolt, for it is the glorious hope of a blessed immortality beyond the grave that has supported me thus far through this vale of tears. Who among you will strive to meet me at the right hand of Christ? For the great day of retribution is fast approaching, and who shall be able to abide his coming? You are forming characters for eternity. As you live, so you will die; as death leaves you, so judgment will find you. Then shall we receive the glorious welcome: " Come, ye blessed of my Father, inherit the kingdom prepared for you from before the foundation of the world." Or hear the heart-rending sentence: "Depart, ye cursed, into everlasting fire prepared for the devil and his angels." When thrice ten thousand years have rolled away, eternity will be but just begun. Your ideas will but just begin to expand. O, eternity, who can unfathom thine end or comprehend thy beginning?

Dearly beloved, I have made myself contemptible in the eyes of many, that I might win some. But it has been like labor in vain. "Paul may plant and Apollos water, but God alone giveth the increase."

To my brethren and sisters in the church I would say, be ye clothed with the breast-plate of righteousness, having your loins girt about you with truth, prepared to meet the bridegroom at his coming; for blessed are those servants that are found watching.

Farewell! In a few short years from now we shall meet in those upper regions where parting will be no more. There we shall sing and shout, and shout and sing, and make Heaven's high arches ring. There we shall range in rich pastures and partake of those living streams that never dry. O, blissful thought! Hatred and contention shall cease, and we shall join with redeemed millions in ascribing glory and honor and riches and power and blessing to the Lamb that was slain and to Him that sitteth upon the throne. Nor eye hath seen nor ear heard, neither hath it entered into the heart of man to conceive of the joys that are prepared for them that love God. Thus far has my life been almost a life of complete disappointment. God has tried me as by fire. Well was I aware that if I contended boldly for his cause I must suffer. Yet I chose rather to suffer affliction with his people than to enjoy the pleasures of sin for a season. And I believe that the glorious declaration was about to be made applicable to me that was made to God's ancient covenant people by the prophet: "Comfort ye, comfort ye, my people; say unto her that her warfare is accomplished, and that her inquities are pardoned. I believe that a rich reward awaits me, if not in this world, in the world to come. O, blessed reflection. The bitterness of my soul has departed from those who endeavored to discourage and hinder me in my Christian progress: and I can now forgive my enemies, bless those who have hated me, and cheerfully pray for those who have despitefully used and persecuted me.

Fare you well! farewell!

ANGELINA GRIMKÉ

Sarah and Angelina Grimké were raised in elite, prosperous Charleston. Their father, a colonel in the Revolutionary Army, was a South Carolina Supreme Court judge, and a slaveholder.

But as eyewitnesses to the horrors of slavery, they rebelled. They fled North, became Quaker pacifists, and dedicated their lives to abolition and women's rights — writing essays, gathering anti-slavery petitions, and delivering fiery speeches in defiance of politicians and religious leaders who said slavery was inevitable and justified.

Attacked for leaving the drawing room and taking up the podium — repudiating their "proper sphere" — the Grimké sisters were unstoppable, buoyed by a network of female anti-slavery societies that arranged and financed their speaking tours. Futilely, they urged Southern women to join them in condemning slavery.

In 1837 they traveled from one Massachusetts town to another, calling for slavery's immediate end. They became nationally known, both praised and reviled. "If the Misses Grimké could find some sort of *employment adapted to the sphere of their sex,*" wrote one newspaper, "they would be more worthy of public respect."

In early 1938, Angelina spoke to Massachusetts legislators and told them she had been "exiled from the land of my birth by the sound of the lash, and the piteous cry of the slave."

That May she married Theodore Weld, a prominent and passionate abolitionist in his own right. Two days later, she spoke at Pennsylvania Hall in Philadelphia, just built by abolitionists because they were barred from other spaces. A stately neo-Classical building, it was designed as a "Temple of Free Discussion." In an arc over the podium were the words "Virtue, Liberty, and Independence."

On the ground floor were a bookstore, a reading room, and the offices of an abolitionist newspaper. Although Pennsylvania was a free state, it was bordered by the slave states of Maryland and Virginia, and full of Southerners and businessmen with financial ties to the South.

As the program got underway, an angry crowd gathered outside. Grimké was the third speaker. As she stepped up to the podium, the crowd became more aggressive. She could hear shouting from the streets.

"As a Southerner, I feel that it is my duty to stand up here to-night and bear testimony," she cried out. As she spoke, bricks and stones came crashing through the windows, shattering glass. Grimké kept speaking: "Every man and every woman present may do something by showing that we fear not a mob."

The next night, the crowd returned and set Pennsylvania Hall ablaze. The firemen stood by and watched it burn. Its gutted shell stood for several years, a pilgrimage spot for abolitionists.

"AT PENNSYLVANIA HALL"

Men, brethren and fathers — mothers, daughters and sisters, what came ye out for to see? A reed shaken with the wind? Is it curiosity merely, or a deep sympathy with the perishing slave, that has brought this large audience together? [A yell from the mob without the building.] Those voices without ought to awaken and call out our warmest sympathies. Deluded beings! "they know not what they do." They know not that they are undermining their own rights and their own happiness, temporal and eternal. Do you ask, "what has the North to do with slavery?" Hear it — hear it. Those voices without tell us that the spirit of slavery is *here*, and has been roused to wrath by our abolition speeches and conventions: for surely liberty would not foam and tear herself with rage, because her friends are multiplied daily, and meetings are held in quick succession to set forth her virtues and extend her peaceful kingdom. This opposition shows that slavery has done its deadliest work in the hearts of our citizens. Do you ask, then, "what has the North to do?" I answer, cast out first the spirit of slavery from your own hearts, and then lend your aid to convert the South. Each one present has a work to do, be his or her situation what it may, however limited their means, or insignificant their supposed influence. The great men of this country will not do this work; the church will never do it. A desire to please the world, to keep the favor of all parties and of all conditions, makes them dumb on this and every other unpopular subject. They have become worldly-wise, and therefore God, in his wisdom, employs them not to carry on his plans of reformation and salvation. He hath chosen the foolish things of the world to confound the wise, and the weak to overcome the mighty.

As a Southerner I feel that it is my duty to stand up here to-night and bear testimony against slavery. I have seen it — I have seen it. I know it has horrors that can never be described. I was brought up under its wing: I witnessed for many years its demoralizing influences, and its destructiveness to human happiness. It is admitted by some that the slave is not happy under the *worst* forms of slavery. But I have *never* seen a happy slave. I have seen him dance in his chains, it is true; but he was not happy. There is a wide difference between happiness and mirth. Man cannot enjoy the former while his manhood is destroyed, and that part of the being which is necessary to the making, and to the enjoyment of happiness, is completely blotted out. The slaves, however, may be, and sometimes are, mirthful. When hope is extinguished, they say, "let us eat and drink, for tomorrow we die." [Just then stones were thrown at the windows, — a great noise without, and commotion within.] "What is a mob? What would the breaking of every window be? What would the levelling of this Hall be? Any evidence that we are wrong, or that slavery is a good and wholesome institution? What if the mob should now burst in upon us, break up our meeting and commit violence upon our persons — would this be any thing compared with what the slaves endure? No, no: and we do not remember them "as bound with them," if we shrink in the time of peril, or feel unwilling to sacrifice ourselves, if need be, for their sake. [Great noise.] I thank the Lord that there is yet life left enough to feel the truth, even though it rages at it — that conscience is not so completely seared as to be unmoved by the truth of the living God.

Many persons go to the South for a season, and are hospitably entertained in the parlor and at the table of the slave-holder. They never enter the huts of the slaves; they know nothing of the dark side of the picture, and they return home with praises on their lips of the generous character of those with whom they had tarried. Or if they have witnessed the cruelties of slavery, by remaining silent spectators they have naturally become callous — an insensibility has ensued which prepares them to apologize even for barbarity. Nothing but the corrupting influence of slavery on the hearts of the Northern people can induce them to apologize for it; and much will have been done for the destruction of Southern slavery when we have so reformed the North that no one here will be willing to risk his reputation by advocating or even excusing the holding of men as property. The South know it, and acknowledge that as fast as our principles prevail, the hold of the master must be relaxed. [Another outbreak of mobocratic spirit, and some confusion in the house.]

How wonderfully constituted is the human mind! How it resists, as long as it can, all efforts made to reclaim from error! I feel that all this disturbance is but an evidence that our efforts are the best that could have been adopted, or else the friends of slavery would not care for what we say and do. The South know what we do. I am thankful that they are reached by our efforts. Many times have I wept in the land of my birth, over the system of slavery. I knew of none who sympathized in my feelings — I was unaware that any efforts were made to deliver the oppressed — no voice in the wilderness was heard calling on the people to repent and do works meet for repentance — and my heart sickened within me. Oh, how should I have rejoiced to know that such efforts as these were being made. I only wonder that I had such feelings. I wonder when I reflect under what influence I was brought up that my heart is not harder than the nether millstone. But in the midst of temptation I was preserved, and my sympathy grew warmer, and my hatred of slavery more inveterate, until at last I have exiled myself from my native land because I could no longer endure to hear the wailing of the slave. I fled to the land of Penn; for here, thought I, sympathy for the slave will surely be found. But I found it not. The people were kind and hospitable, but the slave had no place in their thoughts. Whenever questions were put to me as to his condition, I felt that they were dictated by an idle curiosity, rather than by that deep feeling which would lead to effort for his rescue. I therefore shut up my grief in my own heart. I remembered that I was a Carolinian, from a state which framed this iniquity by law. I knew that throughout her territory was continual suffering, on the one part, and continual brutality and sin on the other. Every Southern breeze wafted to me the discordant tones of weeping and wailing, shrieks and groans, mingled with prayers and blasphemous curses. I thought there was no hope; that the wicked would go on in his wickedness, until he had destroyed both himself and his country. My heart sunk within me at the abominations in the midst of which I had been born and educated. What will it avail, cried I in bitterness of spirit, to expose to the gaze of strangers the horrors and pollutions of slavery, when there is no ear to hear nor heart to feel and pray for the slave. The language of my soul was, "Oh tell it not in Gath, publish it not in the streets of Askelon." But how different do I feel now! Animated with hope, nay, with an assurance of the triumph of liberty and good will to man, I will lift up my voice like a trumpet, and show this people their transgression, their sins of omission towards the slave, and what they can do towards affecting Southern mind, and overthrowing Southern oppression.

We may talk of occupying neutral ground, but on this subject, in its present attitude, there is no such thing as neutral ground. He that is not for us is against us, and he that gathereth not with us, scattereth abroad. If you are on what you suppose to be neutral ground, the South looks upon you as on the side of the oppressor. And is there one who loves his country willing to give his influence, even indirectly, in favor of slavery — that curse of nations? God swept Egypt with the besom of destruction, and punished Judea also with a sore punishment, because of slavery. And have we any reason to believe that he is less just now? — or that he will be more favorable to us than to his own "peculiar people?" [Shoutings, stones thrown against the windows, &c.]

There is nothing to be feared from those who would stop our mouths, but they themselves should fear and tremble. The current is even now setting fast against them. If the arm of the North had not caused the Bastile of slavery to totter to its foundation, you would not hear those cries. A few years ago, and the South felt secure, and with a contemptuous sneer asked, "Who are the abolitionists? The abolitionists are nothing?" — Ay, in one sense they were nothing, and they are nothing still. But in this we rejoice, that "God has chosen things that are not to bring to nought things that are." [Mob again disturbed the meeting.]

We often hear the question asked, "What shall we do?" Here is an opportunity for doing something now. Every man and every woman present may do something by showing that we fear not a mob, and, in the midst of threatenings and revilings, by opening our mouths for the dumb and pleading the cause of those who are ready to perish.

To work as we should in this cause, we must know what Slavery is. Let me urge you then to buy the books which have been written on this subject and read them, and then lend them to your neighbors. Give your money no longer for things which pander to pride and lust, but aid in scattering "the living coals of truth" upon the naked heart of this nation, — in circulating appeals to the sympathies of Christians in behalf of the outraged and suffering slave. But, it is said by some, our "books and papers do not speak the truth." Why, then, do they not contradict what we say? They cannot. Moreover the South has entreated, nay commanded us to be silent; and what greater evidence of the truth of our publications could be desired?

Women of Philadelphia! allow me as a Southern woman, with much attachment to the land of my birth, to entreat you to come up to this work. Especially let me urge you to petition. *Men* may settle this and other questions at the ballot-box, but you have no such right; it is only through petitions that you can reach the Legislature. It is therefore peculiarly *your* duty to petition. Do you say, "It does no good?" The South already turns pale at the number sent. They have read the reports of the proceedings of Congress, and there have seen that among other petitions were very many from the women of the North on the subject of slavery. This fact has called the attention of the South to the subject. How could we expect to have done more as yet? Men who hold the rod over slaves, rule in the councils of the nation: and they deny our right to petition and to remonstrate against abuses of our sex and of our kind. We have these rights, however, from our God. Only let us exercise them: and though often turned away unanswered, let us remember the influence of importunity upon the unjust judge, and act accordingly. The fact that the South look with jealousy upon our measures shows that they are effectual. There is, therefore, no cause for doubting or despair, but rather for rejoicing.

It was remarked in England that women did much to abolish Slavery in her colonies. Nor are they now idle. Numerous petitions from them have recently been presented to the Queen, to abolish the apprenticeship with its cruelties nearly equal to those of the system whose place it supplies. One petition two miles and a quarter long has been presented. And do you think these labors will be in vain? Let the history of the past answer. When the women of these States send up to Congress such a petition, our legislators will arise as did those of England, and say, "When all the maids and matrons of the land are knocking at our doors we must legislate." Let the zeal and love, the faith and works of our English sisters quicken ours — that while the slaves continue to suffer, and when they shout deliverance, we may feel the satisfaction of *having done what we could.*

LUCRETIA MOTT

In 1849, the eminent politician and orator Richard Henry Dana gave a talk in Philadelphia on what he considered woman's proper place. The author of *Two Years Before the Mast*, Dana championed the rights of the downtrodden — from seaman to fugitive slaves — but his empathy did not extend to women. In Philadelphia, he upheld male superiority and declared the women's rights movement a "threat" to society.

In the audience was Lucretia Coffin Mott, a Quaker minister and outspoken reformer. Afterwards she went up to Dana and told him she disagreed. He scowled and turned away.

Mott took it as a challenge. Two months later at the city's Assembly Building she delivered a rebuttal, her most forceful, sweeping argument for the liberation and elevation of women. Part theological, part legal, part historical, her speech was a carefully-constructed argument rooted in Enlightenment values of egalitarianism, individualism, reason, and tolerance.

"The question is often asked," she declared, "'What does woman want, more than she enjoys? What is she seeking to obtain? Of what rights is she deprived? What privileges are withheld from her?' I answer: She asks nothing as favor, but as right, she wants to be acknowledged a moral, responsible being."

In her sixty-year career as an activist, Mott was in the vanguard of American social thought. Women's rights were essential to her, but only part of a broader agenda that included Native American rights, anti-slavery, anti-militarism, anti-clericism — in fact, "anti" every form of what she saw as an overweening abuse of authority.

She refused to separate out the various reform causes, a stance that led to tensions with her fellow suffragists. At times she didn't see eye to eye with her close friend Elizabeth Cady Stanton, who was more single-mindedly focused on women. At the historic 1848 Seneca Falls Women's Rights convention, Mott spoke more than any other person, yet quietly expressed reservations about an agenda that prioritized the rights of women over other causes.

She almost always spoke extemporaneously, but diligent historians have uncovered transcripts of some 190 of her lectures and sermons in archives, newspapers, minutes of meetings, and other sources.

She preached to working class and society women, prisoners, fugitives from slavery, and audiences of mixed races, genders, and faiths. If she met a slaveholder on the train, she would buttonhole him and not let go until she had spoken her mind.

She summed up her philosophy at an 1852 women's rights convention when she declared her firm belief in "the wisdom of not keeping still."

"DISCOURSE ON WOMAN"

December 17, 1849
Assembly Building, Philadelphia, Pennsylvania

There is nothing of greater importance to the well-being of society at large — of man as well as woman — than the true and proper position of woman. Much has been said, from time to time, upon this subject. It has been a theme for ridicule, for satire and sarcasm. We might look for this from the ignorant and vulgar; but from the intelligent and refined we have a right to expect that such weapons shall not be resorted to, — that gross comparisons and vulgar epithets shall not be applied, so as to place woman, in a point of view, ridiculous to say the least.

This subject has claimed my earnest interest for many years. I have long wished to see woman occupying a more elevated position than that which custom for ages has allotted to her. It was with great regret, therefore, that I listened a few days ago to a lecture upon this subject, which, though replete with intellectual beauty, and containing much that was true and excellent, was yet fraught with sentiments calculated to retard the progress of woman to the high elevation destined by her Creator. I regretted the more that these sentiments should be presented with such intellectual vigor and beauty, because they would be likely to ensnare the young.

The minds of young people generally, are open to the reception of more exalted views upon this subject. The kind of homage that has been paid to woman, the flattering appeals which have too long satisfied her — appeals to her mere fancy and imagination, are giving place to a more extended recognition of her rights, her important duties and responsibilities in life. Woman is claiming for herself stronger and more profitable food. Various are the indications leading to this conclusion. The increasing attention to female education, the improvement in the literature of the age, especially in what is called the "Ladies' Department," in the periodicals of the day, are among the proofs of a higher estimate of woman in society at large. Therefore we may hope that the intellectual and intelligent are being prepared for the discussion of this question, in a manner which shall tend to ennoble woman and dignify man.

Free discussion upon this, as upon all other subjects, is never to be feared; nor will be, except by such as prefer darkness to light. "Those only who are in the wrong dread discussion. The light alarms those only who feel the need of darkness." It was sound philosophy, uttered by Jesus, "He that doeth truth cometh to the light, that his deeds may be made manifest, that they are wrought in God."

I have not come here with a view of answering any particular parts of the lecture alluded to, in order to point out the fallacy of its reasoning. The speaker, however, did not profess to offer anything like argument on that occasion, but rather a sentiment. I have no prepared address to deliver to you, being unaccustomed to speak in that way; but I felt a wish to offer some views for your consideration, though in a desultory manner, which may lead to such reflection and discussion as will present the subject in a true light.

In the beginning, man and woman were created equal. "Male and female created he them, and blessed them, and called their name Adam." . . . [Paul's] epistle to the Corinthian church, where the supposed apostolic prohibition of women's preaching is found, contains express directions how woman shall appear, when she prayeth or prophesyeth. Judge then whether this admonition, relative to speaking and asking questions, in the excited state of that church, should be regarded as a standing injunction on woman's preaching, when that word was not used by the apostle. Where is the Scripture authority for the advice given to the early church, under peculiar circumstances, being binding on the church of the present day? Ecclesiastical history informs us, that for two or three hundred years, female ministers suffered martyrdom, in company with their brethren.

These things are too much lost sight of. They should be known, in order that we may be prepared to meet the assertion, so often made, that woman is stepping out of her appropriate sphere, when she shall attempt to instruct public assemblies. The present time particularly demands such investigation. It requires also, that "of yourselves ye should judge what is right," that you should know the ground whereon you stand. This age is notable for its works of mercy and benevolence — for the efforts that are made to reform the inebriate and the degraded, to relieve the oppressed and the suffering. Women as well as men are interested in these works of justice and mercy. They are efficient co-workers, their talents are called into profitable exercise, their labors are effective in each department of reform. The blessing to the merciful, to the peacemaker is equal to man and to woman. It is greatly to be deplored, now that she is increasingly qualified for usefulness, that any view should be presented, calculated to retard her labors of love.

Why should not woman seek to be a reformer? If she is to shrink from being such an iconoclast as shall "break the image of man's lower worship," as so long held up to view; if she is to fear to exercise her reason, and her noblest powers, lest she should be thought to "attempt to act the man," and not "acknowledge his supremacy;" if she is to be satisfied with the narrow sphere assigned her by man, nor aspire to a higher, lest she should transcend the bounds of female delicacy; truly it is a mournful prospect for woman. We would admit all the difference, that our great and beneficent Creator has made, in the relation of man and woman, nor would we seek to disturb this relation; but we deny that the present position of woman, is her true sphere of usefulness: nor will she attain to this sphere, until the disabilities and disadvantages, religious, civil, and social, which impede her progress, are removed out of her way. These restrictions have enervated her mind and paralysed her powers. While man assumes, that the present is the original state designed for woman, that the *existing* "differences are not arbitrary nor the result of accident," but grounded in nature; she will not make the necessary effort to obtain her just rights, lest it should subject her to the kind of scorn and contemptuous manner in which she has been spoken of.

So far from her "ambition leading her to attempt to act the man," she needs all the encouragement she can receive, by the removal of obstacles from her path, in order that she may become a "true woman." As it is desirable that man should act a manly and generous part, not "mannish," so let woman be urged to exercise a dignified and womanly bearing, not womanish. Let her culti-vate all the graces and proper accomplishments of her sex, but let not these degenerate into a kind of effeminacy, in which she is satisfied to be the mere plaything or toy of society, content with her outward adornings, and with the tone of flattery and fulsome adulation too often addressed to her. True, nature has made a difference in her configuration, her physical strength, her voice, &c. — and we ask no change, we are satisfied with nature. But how has neglect and mismanagement increased this difference! It is our duty to develop these natural powers, by suitable exercise, so that they may be strengthened "by reason of use." In the ruder state of society, woman is made to bear heavy burdens, while her "lord and master" walks idly by her side. In the civilization to which we have attained, if cultivated and refined woman would bring all her powers into use, she might engage in pursuits which she now shrinks from as beneath her proper vocation. The energies of men need not then be wholly devoted to the counting house and common business of life, in order that women in fashionable society, may be supported in their daily promenades and nightly visits to the theatre and ball room . . .

The time is coming when educated females will not be satisfied with the present objects of their low ambition. When a woman now leaves the immediate business of her own education, how often, how generally do we find her, sinking down into almost useless inactivity. To enjoy the social circle, to accomplish a little sewing, a *little* reading, a little domestic duty, to while away her hours in self-indulgence, or to enjoy the pleasures of domestic life, — these are the highest objects at which many a woman of elevated mind, and accomplished education aims. And what does she find of sufficient interest to call forth her cultivated energies, and warm affections? But when the cultivation and development of the immortal mind shall be presented to woman, as her especial and delightful duty, and that too whatever be her relations in life; when by example and experience she shall have learned her power over the intellect and the affections, . . . then we shall not find woman, returning from the precincts of learning and wisdom, to pass lightly away the bright hours of her maturing youth. We shall not so often see her, seeking the light device to embroider on muslin and lace, (and I would add, the fashionable crochet work of the present day;) "but we shall see her, with the delighted glow of benevolence, seeking for immortal minds, whereon she may fasten durable and holy impressions, that shall never be effaced or wear away."

A new generation of women is now upon the stage, improving the increased opportunities furnished for the acquirement of knowledge. Public education is coming to be regarded the right of the children of a republic. The hill of science is not so difficult of ascent as formerly represented by poets and painters; but by fact and demonstration smoothed down, so as to be accessible to the assumed weak capacity of woman. She is rising in the scale of being through this, as well as other means, and finding heightened pleasure and profit on the right hand and on the left. The study of Physiology, now introduced into our common schools, is engaging her attention, impressing the necessity of the observance of the laws of health. The intellectual Lyceum and instructive lecture room are becoming, to many, more attractive than the theatre and the ball room. The sickly and sentimental novel and pernicious romance are giving place to works, calculated to call forth the benevolent affections and higher nature. It is only by comparison that I would speak commendatory of these works of imagination. The frequent issue of them from the press is to be regretted. Their exciting contents, like stimulating drinks, when long indulged in, enervate the mind, unfitting it for the sober duties of life.

These duties are not to be limited by man. Nor will woman fulfill less her domestic relations, as the faithful companion of her chosen husband, and the fitting mother of her children, because she has a right estimate of her position and her responsibilities. Her self-respect will be increased; preserving the dignity of her being, she will not suffer herself to be degraded into a mere dependent. Nor will her feminine character be impaired. Instances are not few, of woman throwing off the encumbrances which bind her, and going forth in a manner worthy of herself, her creation, and her dignified calling . . .

The lecturer regarded the announcement of woman's achievements, and the offering of appropriate praise through the press, as a gross innovation upon the obscurity of female life — he complained that the exhibition of the attainments of girls, in schools' was now equal to that of boys, and the newspapers announce that "Miss Brown received the first prize for English grammar," &c.. If he objected to so much excitement of emulation in schools, it would be well; for the most enlightened teachers discountenance these appeals to love of approbation and self-esteem. But, while prizes continue to be awarded, can any good reason be given, why the name of the girl should not be published as well as that of the boy? He spoke with scorn, that "we hear of Mrs. President so and so; and committees and secretaries of the same sex." But if women can conduct their own business, by means of Presidents and Secretaries of their own sex, can he tell us why they should not? They will never make much progress in any moral movement, while they depend upon men to act for them. Do we shrink from reading the announcement that Mrs. [Mary] Somerville is made an honorary member of a scientific association? That Miss [Caroline] Herschel has made some discoveries, and is prepared to take her equal part in science? Or that Miss [Maria] MITCHELL of Nantucket has lately discovered a planet, long looked for? I cannot conceive why "honor to whom honor is due" should not be rendered to woman as well as man; nor will it necessarily exalt her, or foster feminine pride. This propensity is found alike in male and female, and it should not be ministered to improperly, in either sex.

In treating upon the affections, the lecturer held out the idea, that as manifested in the sexes, they were opposite, if not somewhat antagonistic; and required a union, as in chemistry, to form a perfect whole. The simile appeared to me far from a correct illustration of the true union. Minds that can assimilate, spirits that are congenial, attach themselves to each other. It is the union of similar, not opposite affections, which are necessary for the perfection of the marriage bond. There seemed a want of proper delicacy in his representing man as being bold in the demonstration of the pure affection of love. In persons of refinement, true love seeks concealment in man, as well as in woman. I will not enlarge upon the subject, although it formed so great a part of his lecture. The contrast drawn seemed a fallacy, as has much, very much that has been presented, in the sickly sentimental strains of the poet, from age to age.

The question is often asked, "What does woman want, more than she enjoys? What is she seeking to obtain? Of what rights is she deprived? What privileges are withheld from her?" I answer, she asks nothing as favor, but as right, she wants to be acknowledged a moral, responsible being. She is seeking not to be governed by laws, in the making of which she has no voice. She is deprived of almost every right in civil society, and is a cypher in the nation, except in the right of presenting a petition. In religious society her disabilities, as already pointed out, have greatly retarded her progress. Her exclusion from the pulpit or ministry — her duties marked out for her by her equal brother man, subject to creeds, rules, and disciplines made for her by him — this is unworthy her true dignity. In marriage, there is assumed superiority, on the part of the husband, and admitted inferiority, with a promise of obedience, on the part of the wife. This subject calls loudly for examination, in order that the wrong may be redressed. Customs suited to darker ages in Eastern countries, are not binding upon enlightened society. The solemn covenant of marriage may be entered into without these lordly assumptions, and humiliating concessions and promises.

There are large Christian denominations who do not recognise such degrading relations of husband and wife. They ask no magisterial or ministerial aid to legalize or to sanctify this union. But acknowledging themselves in the presence of the Highest, and invoking his assistance, they come under reciprocal obligations of fidelity and affection, before suitable witnesses. Experience and observation go to prove, that there may be as much harmony, to say the least, in such a union, and as great purity and permanency of affection, as can exist where the more common custom or form is observed. The distinctive relations of husband and wife, of father and mother of a family are sacredly preserved, without the assumption of authority on the one part, or the promise of obedience on the other. There is nothing in such a marriage degrading to woman. She does not compromise her dignity or self-respect; but enters married life upon equal ground, by the side of her husband. By proper education, she understands her duties, physical, intellectual and moral; and fulfilling these, she is a help meet, in the true sense of the word . . .

It is with reluctance that I make the demand for the political rights of woman, because this claim is so distasteful to the age. Woman shrinks, in the present state of society, from taking any interest in politics. The events of the French Revolution, and the claim for woman's rights are held up to her as a warning. But let us not look at the excesses of women alone, at that period; but remember that the age was marked with extravagances and wickedness in men as well as women. Indeed, political life abounds with these excesses, and with shameful outrage. Who knows, but that if woman acted her part in governmental affairs, there might be an entire change in the turmoil of political life. It becomes man to speak modestly of his ability to act without her. If woman's judgment were exercised, why might she not aid in making the laws by which she is governed? Lord [Henry] Brougham remarked that the works of Harriet Martineau upon Political Economy were not excelled by those of any political writer of the present time. The first few chapters of her *Society in America*, her views of a Republic, and of Government generally, furnish evidence of woman's capacity to embrace subjects of universal interest.

Far be it from me to encourage woman to vote, or to take an active part in politics, in the present state of our government. Her right to the elective franchise however, is the same, and should be yielded to her, whether she exercise that right or not. Would that man too, would have no participation in a government based upon the life-taking principle — upon retaliation and the sword. It is unworthy a Christian nation. But when, in the diffusion of light and intelligence, a convention shall be called to make regulations for self-government on Christian, non-resistant principles, I can see no good reason, why woman should not participate in such an assemblage, taking part equally with man . . .

May these statements lead you to reflect upon this subject, that you may know what woman's condition is in society — what her restrictions are, and seek to remove them. In how many cases in our country, the husband and wife begin life together, and by equal industry and united effort accumulate to themselves a comfortable home. In the event of the death of the wife, the household remains undisturbed, his farm or his workshop is not broken up, or in any way molested. But when the husband dies, he either gives his wife a *portion* of their joint accumulation, or the law apportions to her a *share;* the homestead is broken up, and she is dispossessed of that which she earned equally with him; for what she lacked in physical strength, she made up in constancy of labor and toil, day and evening. The sons then coming into possession of the property, as has been the custom until of latter time, speak of having to keep their mother, when she in reality is aiding to keep them. Where is the justice of this state of things? The change in the law of this State and of New York, in relation to the property of the wife, go to a limited extent, toward the redress of these wrongs; but they are far more extensive, and involve much more, than I have time this evening to point out.

On no good ground can the legal existence of the wife be suspended during marriage, and her property surrendered to her husband. In the intelligent ranks of society, the wife may not in point of fact, be so degraded as the law would degrade her; because public sentiment is above the law. Still, while the law stands, she is liable to the disabilities which it imposes. Among the ignorant classes of society, woman is made to bear heavy burdens, and is degraded almost to the level of the slave.

There are many instances now in our city, where the wife suffers much from the power of the husband to claim all that she can earn with her own hands. In my intercourse with the poorer class of people, I have known cases of extreme cruelty, from the hard earnings of the wife being thus robbed by the husband, and no redress at law.

An article in one of the daily papers lately, presented the condition of needle women in England. There might be a presentation of this class in our own country, which would make the heart bleed. Public attention should be turned to this subject, in order that avenues of more profitable employment may be opened to women. There are many kinds of business which women, equally with men, may follow with respectability and success. Their talents and energies should be called forth, and their powers brought into the highest exercise. The efforts of women in France are sometimes pointed to in ridicule and sarcasm, but depend upon it, the opening of profitable employment to women in that country, is doing much for the enfranchisement of the sex. In England also, it is not an uncommon thing for a wife to take up the business of her deceased husband and carry it on with success.

Our respected British Consul stated to me a circumstance which occurred some years ago, of an editor of a political paper having died in England; it was proposed to his wife, an able writer, to take the editorial chair. She accepted. The patronage of the paper was greatly increased, and she a short time since retired from her labors with a handsome fortune. In that country however, the opportunities are by no means general for Woman's elevation.

In visiting the public school in London, a few years since, I noticed that the boys were employed in linear drawing, and instructed upon the black board, in the higher branches of arithmetic and mathematics; while the girls, after a short exercise in the mere elements of arithmetic, were seated, during the bright hours of the morning, *stitching wristbands*. I asked, Why there should be this difference made; why they too should not have the black board? The answer was, that they would not probably fill any station in society requiring such knowledge.

But the demand for a more extended education will not cease, until girls and boys have equal instruction, in all the departments of useful knowledge. We have as yet no high school for girls in this state. The normal school may be a preparation for such an establishment. In the late convention for general education, it was cheering to hear the testimony borne to woman's capabilities for head teachers of the public schools. A resolution there offered for equal salaries to male and female teachers, when equally qualified, as practised in Louisiana, I regret to say was checked in its passage, by Bishop Potter; by him who has done so much for the encouragement of education, and who gave his countenance and influence to that convention. Still the fact of such a resolution being offered, augurs a time coming for woman, which she may well hail. At the last examination of the public schools in this city, one of the alumni delivered an address on Woman, not as is too common, in eulogistic strains, but directing the attention to the injustice done to woman in her position in society, in a variety of ways. The unequal wages she receives for her constant toil, &c., presenting facts calculated to arouse attention to the subject.

Women's property has been taxed, equally with that of men's, to sustain colleges endowed by the states; but they have not been permitted to enter those high seminaries of learning. Within a few years, however, some colleges have been instituted, where young women are admitted, nearly upon equal terms with young men; and numbers are availing themselves of their long denied rights. This is among the signs of the times, indicative of an advance for women. The book of knowledge is not opened to her in vain. Already is she aiming to occupy important posts of honor and profit in our country. We have three female editors in our state — some in other states of the Union. Numbers are entering the medical profession — one received a diploma last year; others are preparing for a like result.

Let woman then go on — not asking as favor, but claiming as right, the removal of all the hindrances to her elevation in the scale of being — let her receive encouragement for the proper cultivation of all her powers, so that she may enter profitably into the active business of life; employing her own hands, in ministering to her necessities, strengthening her physical being by proper exercise, and observance of the laws of health. Let her not be ambitious to display a fair hand, and to promenade the fashionable streets of our city, but rather, coveting earnestly the best gifts, let her strive to occupy such walks in society, as will befit her true dignity in all the relations of life. No fear that she will then transcend the proper limits of female delicacy. True modesty will be as fully preserved, in acting out those important vocations to which she may be called, as in the nursery or at the fireside, ministering to man's self-indulgence.

Then in the marriage union, the independence of the husband and wife will be equal, their dependence mutual, and their obligations reciprocal . . .

SOJOURNER TRUTH

Although she could neither read nor write, no one who heard her speak could ever forget the weight of Sojourner Truth's words, or her wit and intelligence — and at six-feet tall, her towering presence.

In the spring of 1851, at the Universalist's Old Stone Church in Akron, Ohio, she delivered what has become the most famous American speech on women's rights, "Ain't I a Woman?"

Except there was one glaring mistake that went unchallenged for years.

It took an astute scholar to point out what should have been obvious all along: Those words were never spoken by Sojourner Truth.

She was born around 1797, an enslaved woman in upstate New York. That's where she gave birth to five children and escaped to freedom. After hearing the Holy Spirit call her to preach, she launched her itinerant ministry. Her native language was "low Dutch," and historians say her English was lightly accented.

She certainly did not have a Southern accent, as the long-accepted version of the speech would have us believe — the one performed at countless oratory competitions and school recitals through the years.

Sojourner Truth never sounded like "an old Negro plantation mammy." Her famous rhetorical question — "Ain't I a Woman?" — wasn't hers at all. She didn't say "dat man over dar." That's a fiction promoted by abolitionist Frances Dana Barker Gage, who published the speech in 1863.

The question is: Why would Gage transform Sojourner Truth into a stereotypical Southern slave? Was it a way to generate more sympathy? Satisfy audience expectations? Or was she unconsciously falling back on a caricature?

As historian Nell Irvin Painter made clear in a 1994 essay, the more authentic and dignified version was there all along, published just a few weeks after the Ohio convention in *The Anti-Slavery Bugle*.

"I can't read, but I can hear," said Sojourner Truth, in this version. "I have heard the Bible and have learned that Eve caused man to sin. Well, if woman upset the world, do give her a chance to set it right side up again."

Sojourner Truth traveled and spoke before dozens of audiences, sometimes singing too, in her low contralto voice. She sold copies of her autobiography and photographs of herself to fund her travel.

Let's celebrate this majestic, iconic speech, and Sojourner Truth, for her ability to convey with moral clarity, irony and sly humor, themes of women's rights and Black rights — twelve years before the Emancipation Proclamation.

In this volume you'll find both versions, because both are part of American history. Reading them side by side is a reminder to listen harder, look closer, and never stop questioning.

"AIN'T I A WOMAN?"

May 29, 1851
Woman's Rights Convention, Old Stone Church, Akron, Ohio

Well, chillen, whar dar's so much racket dar must be som'ting out o'kilter.

I tink dat, 'twixt de niggers of de South and de women at de Norf, all a-talking 'bout rights, de white men will be in a fix pretty soon.

But what's all this here talking 'bout?

Dat man ober dar say dat women needs to be helped into carriages, and lifted over ditches, and to have de best place eberywhar.

Nobody eber helps me into carriages or ober mud-puddles, or gives me any best place.

And ain't I a woman?

Look at me.

Look at my arm.

I have plowed and planted and gathered into barns, and no man could head me.

And ain't I a woman?

I could work as much as eat as much as a man, when I could get it, and bear de lash as well

Ain't I a woman?

I have borne thirteen chillen, and seen 'em mos' all sold off into slavery, and when I cried out with a mother's grief, none but Jesus heard

And ain't I a woman?

Den dey talks 'bout dis ting in de head.

What dis dey call it?

Dat's it, honey.

What's dat got to do with women's rights or niggers' rights?

If my cup won't hold but a pint and yourn holds a quart, wouldn't ye be mean not to let me have a little half-measure full?

Den dat little man in black dar, he say women can't have as much rights as man 'cause Christ wa'n't a woman.

Whar did your Christ come from?

Whar did your Christ come from?

From God and a woman.

Man had nothing to do with him.

If de fust woman God ever made was strong enough to turn de world upside down all her one lone, all dese togeder ought to be able to turn it back and git it right side up again, and now dey is asking to, de men better let 'em.

Bleeged to ye for hearin' on me, and now ole Sojourner ha'n't got nothin' more to say.

"I AM A WOMAN'S RIGHTS"

May I say a few words? I want to say a few words about this matter.

I am a woman's rights.

I have as much muscle as any man, and can do as much work as any man.

I have plowed and reaped and husked and chopped and mowed, and can any man do more than that?

I have heard much about the sexes being equal; I can carry as much as any man, and can eat as much too, if I can get it.

I am as strong as any man that is now.

As for intellect, all I can say is, if women have a pint and man a quart — why can't she have her little pint full?

You need not be afraid to give us our rights for fear we will take too much, for we cant take more than our pint'll hold.

The poor men seem to be all in confusion, and dont know what to do.

Why children, if you have woman's rights, give it to her and you will feel better.

You will have your own rights, and they wont be so much trouble.

I cant read, but I can hear.

I have heard the bible and have learned that Eve caused man to sin.

Well if woman upset the world, do give her a chance to set it right side up again.

The Lady has spoken about Jesus, how he never spurned woman from him, and she was right.

When Lazarus died, Mary and Martha came to him with faith and love and besought him to raise their brother.

And Jesus wept — and Lazarus came forth.

And how came Jesus into the world?

Through God who created him and woman who bore him.

Man, where is your part?

But the women are coming up blessed be God and a few of the men are coming up with them.

But man is in a tight place, the poor slave is on him, woman is coming on him, and he is surely between-a hawk and a buzzard.

LUCY STONE

One person called her a "silver bell," another a "loaded cannon." From her impassioned speeches, it's easy to see why both descriptions applied to Lucy Stone.

At a time of few educational opportunities for women, Stone was thrilled to be accepted at Oberlin, the nation's first college to admit women and Blacks. In 1843, at age twenty-five, she traveled from Massachusetts by train, steamship, and stagecoach to get there. But when she arrived on campus, she was furious to discover that women were taught they should not speak in public.

After taking part in a demonstration over the issue, Stone and her fellow student and future sister-in-law Antoinette Brown organized a female debating club. But that opened a dispute that went up the ranks to the college administration, with the tireless and rebellious Stone never letting up.

She even refused to take part in her own graduation ceremony in 1847 to protest the administration's position that speeches by female graduates must be read by their male professors.

The hurdles and harassment that women speakers faced in antebellum America — including hissing, spitting, shouting, hooting, whistling, name calling, foot stomping, and all manner of projectiles such as fresh and rotten eggs and spitballs — never deterred Stone.

Once while she was speaking in the wintertime, a pane of glass was removed from a window behind her, the nozzle of a hose inserted, and she was deluged with cold water. "She put on a shawl and went on with her lecture," wrote her daughter, Alice Stone Blackwell.

"I thank God with never-ending gratitude that young women of today do not and can never know at what price their right to speak in public at all has been earned," Stone said later.

She spoke most often about the two causes near to her heart: freedom for American slaves and the liberation of the female sex. And she delivered this impromptu speech, "Disappointment is the Lot of Women," in 1855 at a women's rights gathering in Cincinnati.

In response to a heckler who disparaged the female speakers as "a few disappointed women." Stone angrily shot back that she was indeed disappointed — legitimately so.

She described the many limitations of "woman's sphere" that created frustration and disappointment for women: in education, professional life, religion, marriage, and motherhood.

More than a lament, it's an inspiring call to action: "The widening of women's sphere is to improve her lot," as she put it. "Let us do it, and if the world scoff, let it scoff — if it sneer, let it sneer."

"DISAPPOINTMENT IS THE LOT OF WOMAN"

October 17, 1855
Seventh Women's Rights Convention, Smith
& Nixon's Hall, Cincinnati, Ohio

The last speaker alluded to this movement as being that of a few disappointed women. From the first years to which my memory stretches, I have been a disappointed woman. When, with my brothers, I reached forth after the sources of knowledge, I was reproved with, "It isn't fit for you; it doesn't belong to women." Then there was but one college in the world where women were admitted, and that was in Brazil. I would have found my way there, but by the time I was prepared to go, one was opened in the young state of Ohio — the first in the United States — where women and negroes could enjoy opportunities with white men. I was disappointed when I came to seek a profession worthy an immortal being — every employment was closed to me, except those of the teacher, the seamstress, and the housekeeper. In education, in marriage, in religion, in everything, disappointment is the lot of woman. It shall be the business of my life to deepen this disappointment in every woman's heart until she bows down to it no longer. I wish that women, instead of being walking show-cases, instead of begging of their fathers and brothers the latest and gayest new bonnet, would ask of them their rights.

The question of Woman's Rights is a practical one. The notion has prevailed that it was only an ephemeral idea; that it was but women claiming the right to smoke cigars in the streets, and to frequent barrooms. Others have supposed it a question of comparative intellect; others still, of sphere. Too much has already been said and written about woman's sphere. Trace all the doctrines to their source and they will be found to have no basis except in the usages and prejudices of the age. This is seen in the fact that what is tolerated in woman in one country is not tolerated in another. In this country women may hold prayer-meetings, etc., but in Mohammedan countries it is written upon their mosques, "Women and dogs, and other impure animals, are not permitted to enter."

Wendell Phillips says, "The best and greatest thing one is capable of doing, that is his sphere." I have confidence in the Father to believe that when He gives us the capacity to do anything He does not make a blunder. Leave women, then, to find their sphere. And do not tell us before we are born even, that our province is to cook dinners, darn stockings, and sew on buttons. We are told woman has all the rights she wants; and even women, I am ashamed to say, tell us so. They mistake the politeness of men for rights — seats while men stand in this hall to-night, and their adulations; but these are mere courtesies. We want rights. The flour-merchant, the house-builder, and the postman charge us no less on account of our sex; but when we endeavor to earn money to pay all these, then, indeed, we find the difference. Man, if he have energy, may hew out for himself a path where no mortal has ever trod, held back by nothing but what is in himself; the world is all before him, where to choose; and we are glad for you, brothers, men, that it is so. But the same society that drives forth the young man, keeps woman at home — a dependent — working little cats on worsted, and little dogs on punctured paper; but if she goes heartily and bravely to give herself to some worthy purpose, she is out of her sphere and she loses caste. Women working in tailor-shops are paid one-third as much as men. Some one in Philadelphia has stated that women make fine shirts for twelve and a half cents apiece; that no woman can make more that [sp] nine a week, and the sum thus earned, after deducting rent, fuel, etc., leaves her just three and a half cents a day for bread. Is it a wonder that women are driven to prostitution? Female teachers in New York are paid fifty dollars a year, and for every such situation there are five hundred applicants. I know not what you believe of God, but I believe He gave yearnings and longings to be filled, and that He did not mean all our time should be devoted to feeding and clothing the body. The present condition of woman causes a horrible perversion of the marriage relation. It is asked of a lady, "Has she married well?" "Oh, yes, her husband is rich." Woman must marry for a home, and you men are the sufferers by this; for a woman who loathes you may marry you because you have the means to get money which she can not have. But when woman can enter the lists with you and make money for herself, she will marry you only for deep and earnest affection.

I am detaining you too long, many of you standing, that I ought to apologize, but women have been wronged so long that I may wrong you a little. A woman undertook in Lowell to sell shoes to ladies. Men laughed at her, but in six years she has run them out, and has a monopoly of the trade. Sarah Tyndale, whose husband was an importer of china, and died bankrupt, continued his business, paid off his debts, and has made a fortune and built the largest china warehouse in the world. [Mrs. Mott here corrected Lucy. Mrs. Tyndale has not the largest china warehouse, but the largest assortment of china in the world]. Mrs. Tyndale, herself, drew the plan of her warehouse, and it is the best plan ever drawn. A laborer to whom the architect showed it, said: "Don't she know e'en as much as some men?" I have seen woman at manual labor turning out chair-legs in a cabinet-shop with a dress short enough not to drag in the shavings. I wish other women would imitate her in this. It made her hands harder and broader, it is true, but I think a hand with a dollar and a quarter a day in it, better than one with crossed ninepence. The men in the shop didn't use tobacco, nor swear — they can't do those things where there are women, and we owe it to our brothers to go wherever they work to keep them decent. The widening of women's sphere is to improve her lot. Let us do it, and if the world scoff, let it scoff — if it sneer, let it sneer — but we will go emulating the example of the sisters Grimké and Abby Kelley. When they first lectured against slavery they were not listened to as respectfully as you listen to us. So the first female physician meets many difficulties, but to the next the path will be made easy.

Lucretia Mott has been a preacher for years; her right to do so is not questioned among Friends. But when Antoinette Brown felt that she was commanded to preach, and to arrest the progress of thousands that were on the road to hell; why, when she applied for ordination they acted as though they had rather the whole world should go to hell, than that Antoinette should be allowed to tell them how to keep out of it.

She is now ordained over a parish in the state of New York, but when she meets on the Temperance platform the Rev. John Chambers, or your own Gen. Carey, they greet her with hisses. Theodore Parker said; "The acorn that the school-boy carries in his pocket and the squirrel stows in his cheek, has in it the possibility of an oak, able to withstand, for ages, the cold winter and the driving blast." I have seen the acorn men and women, but never the perfect oak; all are but abortions. The young mother, when first the newborn babe nestles in her bosom, and a heretofore unknown love springs up in her heart, finds herself unprepared for this new relation in life, and she sends forth the child scarred and dwarfed by her own weakness and imbecility, as no stream can rise higher than its fountain.

JANE JOHNSON

"I had rather die than go back." With those words, an enslaved woman declared in an open courtroom what freedom meant to her.

Jane Johnson and her two children had come to Philadelphia in July 1855 with their owner, John Hill Wheeler. He was on his way to Nicaragua, where he'd been appointed to a government position. Wheeler locked them in a room at Bloodgood's Hotel, a block from the harbor, with instructions not to speak to a soul. His plan was to take them by ferry that night to New York City, then on to Nicaragua.

Johnson had a different idea. At the hotel, she let a porter know she wanted to escape. The porter contacted William Still, himself a former enslaved man, a member of the Pennsylvania Anti-Slavery Society, and head of its Vigilance Committee.

Meanwhile, Wheeler had stealthily taken Johnson and her children down to the docks and onto a ferry. Just as it was about to depart, Still arrived with a colleague. They boarded the ship and informed Johnson that according to the "free state" laws of Pennsylvania, she and her sons were free to go.

Unsurprisingly, Wheeler strenuously objected. A skirmish broke out, with five Black dockworkers holding Wheeler down while Johnson and her sons took off.

Over in a few minutes, those events would make history as one of the first challenges to the notorious Fugitive Slave Law of 1850, requiring that even in "free states," slaves must be returned to their owners.

The events captured the attention of the national press. Still and his colleague landed in jail, as did the dockworkers. Ensconced the safety of New York, Johnson had no intention of staying silent, and she spoke at several public meetings and declared her intention to remain free.

Up for debate was the question: Did the Fugitive Slave Law apply in this case? Technically Johnson was not a runaway. She had travelled with Wheeler of her own free will. And Pennsylvania law held that only "fugitives" on the run should be sent back.

At the trial, the defendants faced charges of riot, assault and battery. Johnson appeared as a surprise witness, entering the courtroom surrounded by a protective phalanx of local anti-slavery activists, including Lucretia Mott.

Johnson's testimony was brief but breathtaking. "Nobody forced me away; nobody pulled me, and nobody led me," she told the magistrate. "I went away of my own free will . . . I don't want to go back."

She never did.

Granted her freedom by the court, she settled in Boston and raised her sons as free men.

"RATHER DIE THAN GO BACK"

August 29, 1855
Civil Court, Philadelphia, Pennsylvania

My name is Jane — Jane Johnson; I was the slave of Mr. Wheeler of Washington; he bought me and my two children, about two years ago, of Mr. Cornelius Crew, of Richmond, Va.; my youngest child is between six and seven years old, the other between ten and eleven; I have one other child only, and he is in Richmond; I have not seen him for about two years; never expect to see him again; Mr. Wheeler brought me and my two children to Philadelphia, on the way to Nicaragua, to wait on his wife; I didn't want to go without my two children, and he consented to take them; we came to Philadelphia by the cars; stopped at Mr. Sully's, Mr. Wheeler's father-in-law, a few moments; then went to the steamboat for New York at 2 o'clock, but were too late; we went into Bloodgood's Hotel; Mr. Wheeler went to dinner; Mr. Wheeler had told me in Washington to have nothing to say to colored persons, and if any of them spoke to me, to say I was a free woman traveling with a minister; we staid at Bloodgood's till 5 o'clock; Mr. Wheeler kept his eye on me all the time except when he was at dinner; he left his dinner to come and see if I was safe, and then went back again; while he was at dinner, I saw a colored woman and told her I was a slave woman, that my master had told me not to speak to colored people, and that if any of them spoke to me to say that I was free; but I am not free; but I want to be free; she said: 'poor thing, I pity you;" after that I saw a colored man and said the same thing to him, he said he would telegraph to New York, and two men would meet me at 9 o'clock and take me with them; after that we went on board the boat, Mr. Wheeler sat beside me on the deck; I saw a colored gentleman come on board, he beckoned to me; I nodded my head, and could not go; Mr. Wheeler was beside me and I was afraid; a white gentleman then came and said to Mr. Wheeler, "I want to speak to your servant, and tell her of her rights;" Mr. Wheeler rose and said, "If you have anything to say, say it to me — she knows her rights;" the white gentleman asked me if I wanted to be free; I said "I do, but I belong to this gentleman and I can't have it;" he replied, "Yes, you can, come with us, you are as free as your master, if you want your freedom come now; if you go back to Washington you may never get it;" I rose to go, Mr. Wheeler spoke, and said, "I will give you your freedom," but he had never promised it before, and I knew he would never give it to me; the white gentleman held out his hand and I went toward him; I was ready for the word before it was given me; I took the children by the hands, who both cried, for they were frightened, but both stopped when they got on shore; a colored man carried the little one, I led the other by the hand. We walked down the street till we got to a hack; nobody forced me away; nobody pulled me, and nobody led me; I went away of my own free will; I always wished to be free and meant to be free when I came North; I hardly expected it in Philadelphia, but I thought I should get free in New York; I have been comfortable and happy since I left Mr. Wheeler, and so are the children; I don't want to go back; I could have gone in Philadelphia if I had wanted to; I could go now; but I had rather die than go back. I wish to make this statement before a magistrate, because I understand that Mr. Williamson is in prison on my account, and I hope the truth may be of benefit to him.

JANE [her X mark.] JOHNSON.

JULIA BRANCH

"The depths of indecency." That's how one newspaper described the words of a young woman from New York City, not yet thirty years old, who shattered moral conventions with a speech in 1858.

Unfortunately we don't much about Julia Branch. But she deserves a spotlight for her bravery and outspokenness, and the way she anticipated contemporary views on sex, marriage, and motherhood.

The occasion was the Vermont Free Convention, a tent gathering one summer weekend in the town of Rutland. More than 3,000 men and women — "white, black, partially black, badly sun-burned and fair in face," according to one account — came together to debate ideas on the fringes of American thought: abolitionism, spiritualism, free-love, Shakerism, free-trade, and, said one newspaper, "all other queer things."

Branch was a published poet and a spirit-medium, an intermediary between the living and the dead. Many of the earliest female speakers in America were women who, like her, found in the spiritualism movement a rare opportunity to use their voices in public.

In her speech that day, she unleashed a fierce attack on the institution of marriage and what she saw as its limitations on women. When a woman signed a marriage contract, she was "selling herself," she said. "It is the binding marriage ceremony that keeps woman degraded in mental and moral slavery."

That line of argument went beyond the pale for most 19th century reformers, especially women's rights advocates who struggled for legitimacy at a time when the majority of Americans valued wifely submission, female purity, and maternal devotion.

Branch believed that by focusing on suffrage, the women's movement over-looked the ways that marriage robbed women of independent status. That autonomy, she said, included a woman's control over her own body, her right to choose her own sexual partners, and "her right to bear children when she will, and by whom she will."

That control should be exercised by woman alone — not, she said sarcastically, by "wise men, who know very much better than you do when you want a child, and when you ought to become a mother."

The convention was roundly disparaged in the media. "Pestilent," "licentious," and "blasphemous," said *The New York Times,* which published her entire speech on its front page. A waste of time said the *Rutland Herald.* But was it? More than a century before "no-fault" divorce became law in most of the country, Branch was laying down a marker and setting a precedent.

What could a woman speak about in public? Anything. Everything.

"WOMAN'S RIGHTS IN A NEW ASPECT"

June 26, 1858
Under a Tent, Rutland Free Convention, Rutland, Vermont

To my mind this resolution (referring to the one reported by the committee) means nothing, or it is entirely incomprehensive, and I am aware that I have chosen almost a forbidden subject; forbidden from the fact that any one that can and dare look the marriage question in the face and openly denounce the marriage institution as the sole cause of woman's degradation and misery, is an object of scorn, of suspicion and opprobrious epithets.

I ask of that now as I did formerly of the Church, Is it so sacred that it cannot be questioned? Is it so absolute that it defies argument? . . .

The marriage ceremony is necessary to keep woman virtuous and respectable, and all intercourse with man out of its holy rites, renders her an outcast and a thing to be despised. Is it because she is naturally vicious and wicked that bonds are placed upon her? Has she no nature that may not be proscribed and estimated by man law-makers? Has she no inborn right that belongs to herself? As she stands here before the world, she has none. She has not even that kind compliment that is paid to man in the Constitution of the United States, "that man is endowed with certain inalienable rights." And to the marriage ceremony, I say she is indebted for her wrongs, for her aching heart, her chains, her slavery.

Woman must strike the blow if she would be free and become the equal of man.

You speak of her right to labor — her right to teach — her right to vote, and lastly though not least, her right to get married; but do you say anything about *her right to love when she will, where she will and how she will?*

Yes, here is a stipulation for her in this resolution.

"She is to have an isolated household with an exclusive conjugal love." This is very pretty in sentiment and [Thomas] MOORE beautifully expresses it in his "Fire Worshippers:"

Oft in my fancy's wanderings
I've wished that little isle had wings,
And we within its fairy bowers

Were wafted off to seas unknown,
Where not a pulse would beat but ours,
And we might *live, love, die* alone,
Where the bright eyes of Angels only
Should come around us to behold
A paradise so pure and lonely.

But this will not do for practical life where man and woman work from ten to eighteen hours out of the twenty four. The working class are by far the larger class, and the isolated household is the worst place in the world for them. The man comes home to his meals which are set on the table amid crying children and the sickly, despairing face of his wife — there is no social life. Even the exclusive conjugal love that bound them together in the marriage ceremony has long since settled into the mildest form of friendship. The enthusiasm and ardor, and poetry, and sacredness are forever destroyed by constant familiarity in the isolated household.

Just as woman is isolated and confined within the isolated and confined limits of a home, just so will her offspring be narrow-minded, bigoted and selfish; just as she is free in her thoughts, her affections, making her home wherever she chooses, just so will her children be broad and expansive in their ideas, noble, and great and honorable in virtuous deeds, benevolent in heart and tolerant in all things, however opposite to them, because they feel within that they have not only the perfections but the imperfections of humanity.

We have lived in the ideal life too long; we want something practical. We have planted rank weeds, and we are cultivating them with as much nicety as we would beautiful flowers. We have gone down into hidden lore and have lived in the eyes of the past as though the present was too weak to bear the weight of our thoughts. We crawl on our hands and knees in the childhood of knowledge, fearing to rise lest the weight of our *brains* should topple us over. We live in dead men's graves, waiting for some angel to roll away the stone and give us life and liberty and individuality. Let me draw a picture of the isolated home, and one that came under my own observation.

See the woman with a care-worn face; long lines of grief have made deep furrows — her thin hand and shriveled figure — her dejected, weary air — her desponding tones tell of something that lies heavy at her heart. Surely, never Christ, bearing the great heavy cross up to crucifixion, could feel the deep woe that presses against her soul.

"Ah me," comes with a sad sigh as we lay our hand upon her head; "tell us," we say, and she throws open the inmost recesses of her soul, and tells the story of her life. How she aspired to be great from childhood — how noble thoughts took possession of her; how she loved, and married the object of her love; how dear the first-born of her heart grew to her; how it died, and she clothed herself in the habiliments of woe, and shut out the light of day to her heart, and sat down alone at home without friends or hope or consolation; how other children came to her, but they did not fill the void; the black veil was drawn down from between her and happiness, and pinned to the soul by the arrow of affliction. There was no sympathy in the world, and she longed to lie down in the grave and rest.

We brush away the tears and bid her hope; hope has died out; we speak of husbands and children; they have no sympathy.

"Are you willing," we ventured to ask, "to look for one moment into your own soul?"

"I have always tried to do right, but circumstances were against me. My husband has long since ceased to love me, although he presses upon me the necessity of bearing children whenever he pleases. My children are perverse and wayward, and I don't know what to do with them. Some people go right through the world always light hearted and happy; I never saw an unhappy day till I was married."

"But of yourself, have you never thought of a plan whereby you might be relieved from these troubles?"

"Oh, yes, of many, but I have no right to think or speak my sentiments, for I am married; if I do, my husband says it is better for me to attend to the domestic affairs, and he will do the thinking. He deprives me of female friends because women love to gossip; of male friends, for the world might talk about it; besides, he says a mother ought always to be at home taking care of her house and children, and providing for her husband's wants; and I have nothing but death; when that comes I shall go where everything will be bright and happy, and my soul's longings will be satisfied."

Now, I ask, what is that woman's life? Is she what God intended she should be?

No! She was made fair and beautiful in childhood, given those noble aspirations to cultivate in the garden of her soul.

What did she do with them? *Sold them with herself* at sixteen, when she entered into the marriage contract, and thus bowed down her soul forever. In her isolated household, she threw away her life, and added to the too many already children thrust into the world half made up — children of chance, children of lust, abortions who feel that they have no right to existence — children of disease, *whose tainted flesh and running sores are a disgrace and an everlasting reproach to the morals and purity of any community.*

Byron cursed his mother for his deformed feet, and there are thousands and thousands of children cursing the sacred name of mother for their deformed bodies and moral conditions.

Mrs. [Matilda Joslyn] GAGE, Mrs. [Ernestine] ROSE, Mr. [Henry C.] WRIGHT, and others, go back to the mother's influence, and go a step further back, and say *it is the marriage institution that is at fault. It is the binding marriage ceremony that keeps woman degraded in mental and moral slavery.* She must demand her freedom — her right to receive the equal wages of man for her labor — *her right to bear children when she will, and by whom she will.*

Woman is not totally depraved. She will never abuse one right that is given to her, and she will never step aside from her own nature. If she desires to go to the ballot-box, it is because there is a wrong somewhere, and she takes that way to right it. If she desires to become a lawyer, it is because there are laws to be redressed and made better. If she desires to preach, it is because she feels the woes and afflictions of humanity. If she desires rights, it is because she needs them.

I believe in the absolute freedom of the affections, and it is woman's privilege, aye, her right, to accept or refuse any love that comes to her. *She should be the ruling power in all matters of love,* and when her love has died out for the man who has taken her to his heart, she is living a lie to herself, her own nature, and to him, if she continues to hold an intimate relation with him.

And so is man's relative position to woman. When his love has died out, and he continues to live with his wife, on any consideration, he strikes a blow at the morality of his nature, and lives a life of deception, not only to her and society, but he is responsible for all the crimes that his children, borne under those circumstances, are liable to commit.

A gentleman said to me, a little time ago, "My wife is a woman's rights woman. She talks about her rights, and I allow it, but she really has none. I am her husband; she is my property, and if I do not like a thing I say so; and I do not consider she has any right to dispute it. I do not hold any argument, for I consider my will law. And if I loved a woman, and was not bound to her by the marriage ceremony, I should not think of disputing her will or wishes, for fear she would show me the door, and I should have no alternative but to go out of it. Her will is absolute, for I have no claim upon her, and she is justified in all she does, so it is necessary to guard myself and movements in order to retain the love and respect of the woman I love." What a pleasing prospect is this for the wife, who is rearing her children in her isolated household, and imagining the husband immaculate in thought as well as action, and respecting her in the sacred office of wife and mother.

Why should woman tame herself into calm submission, and be the slave and toy and play-thing of man? What is marriage? Is it the linking together of two loving hearts in holy, sacred union? No! this is seldom the case when compared to the many thousands upon thousands of marriages of convenience. Women are bought and paid for, as the negro slave is. She is estimated as a thing of barter, for a man counts the cost of his intended wife as deliberately as if he thought of keeping a cow, a dog, or a pig.

Now, what are the rights and privileges of woman in the marriage institution?

It gives us the privilege to become *Mrs.* Brown instead of *Miss* Smith. That is an honor, no doubt, as it relieves woman from the stigma of *old maid*. It gives us the privilege of being supported and attending to domestic duties — the privilege to see that the dinner is served at proper hours for a hungry husband — the privilege, oftentimes, to sit up alone half the night to let the husband in from a delightful concert and oyster supper that he has enjoyed with Mr. Jones and his beautiful wife.

Then we have a right; and listen! women of the Nineteenth Century! The marriage institution gives you one right; one right that you have not, perhaps, hitherto valued — *it gives you the right to bear children.*

It is not a privilege; it is not an inheritance that your nature craves. But it is the law of wise men, who know very much better than you do when *you want a child, and when you ought to become a mother.*

Now, I say again, that resolution is incomprehensive. Love is not dependent on reason, or judgment, or education, or mental acquirements, or society, or control of any kind. It is an inspiration of the soul. It is a holy, sacred emanation from the most vital part of our natures, and to say when or where it shall be limited or restricted is a violation of our individual rights.

I may have taken an extreme side of the question, but only offer my views as *my own*, and wish that the resolution may be put in a more definite form, stating what conjugal love is, and to how few, or how many, an isolated household may be limited to. I will read a resolution that I think would bear more directly on the marriage question:

Resolved, That the slavery and degradation of woman proceeds from the institution of marriage; that by the marriage contract she loses the control of her name, her person, her property, her labor, her affections, her children and her freedom.

SARAH PARKER REMOND

Sarah Parker Remond delivered her first anti-slavery lecture at sixteen. Born into a large free Black family in Massachusetts, she and her brother Charles Lenox Remond were traveling lecturers who rallied support for the anti-slavery cause.

In September 1858, she set sail for Liverpool as an emissary of the Massachusetts Anti-Slavery Society. Her mission was to plead the ethical and economic case against "the monster evil" of American slavery and persuade the British to support the Northern cause.

From 1859 to 1862, she delivered 45 anti-slavery lectures to overflowing halls in cities and towns across northern England, Scotland, and Ireland. Newspapers on both sides of the Atlantic extensively covered her "eloquent style of address."

Most ordinary Britons supported the North, but not necessarily Remond's elite, upper-class audiences — especially in manufacturing and industrial cities such as Liverpool, Leeds, and Manchester that were heavily dependent on textiles.

Manchester was a booming financial and commercial center due to one crop: cotton. The city's nickname was "Cottonopolis."

More than a hundred textile mills operated in the city, plus weaving sheds, dyeing and finishing plants, warehouses, and entire docks dedicated to the cotton trade, a spectacular infrastructure that kept the Mancunians proud and prosperous. A huge colonnaded Cotton Exchange dominated the city center.

The only problem, as Remond told her audience, was that three-quarters of all cotton processed in Manchester and surrounding Lancashire came from thousands of miles across the Atlantic, from slaveholding American states in the South.

Remond delivered her speech in the autumn of 1959 at the city's Athenaeum. To her mostly White audience, it must have made for an awkward evening. She told them that their city was economically and morally intertwined with the cotton trade — and therefore they were complicit.

As she walked through the busy streets of Manchester, she saw "load after load of cotton." All she could hear were cries of "Cotton! Cotton!" But as she noted with fury: "Not one cent of all that money has ever reached the hands of the laborers."

When the Civil War broke out in 1861, Remond remained in Britain, where she continued to lecture and argue that the government should offer assistance to the North. Officially it remained neutral, which was a victory for the North in that the United Kingdom never officially recognized the Confederacy.

Remond went on to study medicine and become a doctor. She passed away in 1894 and is buried in Rome. A plaque near the cemetery entrance describes her as an "African American abolitionist and physician."

I would like to add the words "courageous public speaker."

"WHY SLAVERY IS STILL RAMPANT IN THE LAND"

September 14, 1859
The Manchester Athenaeum, Manchester, England

Although the anti-slavery enterprise was begun some thirty years ago, the evil is still rampant in the land. As there are some young people present — and I am glad to see them here for, it is important that they shall understand this subject — I shall briefly explain that there are thirty-two states, sixteen of which are free and sixteen slave-states. The free states are in the north. The political feeling in the north and the south are essentially different. So is the social life. In the north, democracy — not what the Americans call democracy but the true principal of equal rights, prevails — I speak of the white population, mind — wealth is abundant. The country, in every material sense, flourishes. In the south, aristocratic feelings prevail. Labor is dishonorable and five millions of poor whites live in the most degrading ignorance and destitution. I might dwell long on the miserable condition of these poor whites, the indirect victims of slavery. But I must go on to speak of the four millions of slaves.

The slaves are essentially *things*, with no rights, political, social, domestic or religious: the absolute victims of all but irresponsible power. For the slave there is no home, no love, no hope, no help; and what is life without hope? No writer can describe the slave's life; it cannot be told; the fullest description ever given to the world does but skim over the surface of this subject. You may infer something of the state of society in the southern States when I tell you that there are eight hundred thousand mulattoes, nine-tenths of whom are the children of white fathers, and these are constantly sold by their parents, for the slave follows the conditions of the mother. Hence we see every shade of complexion among the slaves, from the blackest African hue to that of women and men in whose cheeks the lily and the rose vie for predominance.

To describe to you the miserable poor whites of the south, I need only quote the words of Mr. [Hinton Rowan] Helper, a southerner, in his most important work on slavery, and the testimony also of a Virginian gentleman of my acquaintance. The five millions of poor whites are all most of them in as gross a state of ignorance as Mrs. [Harriet Beecher] Stowe's Topsy, in *Uncle Tom's Cabin*.

The free coloured people of the northern States are, for no crime but merely the fact of complexion, deprived of all political and social rights. Whatever wealth or eminence in intellect or refinement they may attain to, they are treated as outcasts; and white men and women who identify themselves with them are sure to be insulted in the grossest manner. I do not ask your political interference in any way. This is a moral question. Even in America the Abolitionists generally disclaim every other ground but the moral and religious one on which this matter is based. You send missionaries to the heathen. I tell you of professing Christians practicing what is worse than any heathenism on record. How is it that we have come to this state of things, you ask? I reply, the whole power of the country is in the hands of the slaveholders. For more than thirty years we have had a slaveholding President, and the slave power has been dominant. The consequence has been a series of encroachments, until now at last the slave trade is re-opened and all but legitimised in America. It was a sad backward step when England last year fell into the trap laid by America, and surrendered the right of search. Now slavers ply on the seas which were previously guarded by your ships. We have, besides, an international slave trade. We have states where, I am ashamed to say, men and women are reared like cattle, for the market. When I walk through the streets of Manchester, and meet load after load of cotton, I think of those eighty thousand cotton plantations on which was grown the one hundred and twenty-five millions of dollars' worth of cotton which supply your market, and I remember that not one cent of that money has ever reached the hands of the labourers. Here is an incident of slave life for you — an incident of common occurrence in the south. In March 1859, a slave auction took place in the city of Savannah. Three hundred and forty-three slaves, the property of Pierce Butler, the husband of your own Fanny Kemble, were sold, regardless of every tie of flesh and blood, old men and maidens, young men and babes of fifteen months. There was but one question about them, and that was decided at the auction block. Pierce Butler, the owner, resides in Philadelphia and is a highly respected citizen and a member of a church. He was reputed a kind master who rarely separated the families of his slaves. The financial crisis took place, and I have given you the result to his human property. But Mr. Butler has in no wise lost face among his friends. He still moves among the most respectable in society, and his influence at church is so great that with other members he has removed from the pulpit of the Reverend Dudley Tyne, who had uttered a testimony against slavery. And in that pulpit, the man who now preaches, Mr. Prentiss by name, is the owner of a hundred slaves.

Such is the state of public opinion in America, and you find the poison running through everything. With the exception of the Abolitionists, you will find people of all classes thus contaminated. The whole army and navy of the United States are pledged to pursue and shoot down the poor fugitives, who, panting for liberty, fly to Canada, to seek the security of the British flag. All dominations of professing Christians are guilty of sustaining or defending slavery. Even the Quakers must be included in this rule. Now I ask for your sympathy and your influence. And whoever asked English men and women in vain? Give us the power of your public opinion — it has great weight in America. Words spoken here and read there are as no words written in America are read. Lord [Henry] Brougham's testimony on the first of August resounded through America; your [Thomas] Clarkson and your [William] Wilberforce are names of strength to us. I ask you, raise the moral public opinion until its voice reaches the American shores. Aid us thus until the shackles of the American slave melt like dew before the morning sun. I ask especial help from the women of England. Women are the worst victims of the slave power. I am met on every hand by the cry, "Cotton! Cotton!" I cannot stop to speak of cotton while women and men are being brutalised. But there is an answer for the cotton cry too, and the argument is an unanswerable one.

Before concluding, I shall give you a few passages from the laws of the slave states. By some of these laws, free coloured people may be arrested in the discharge of their lawful business; and, if no papers attesting their freedom be found on them, they are committed to gaol; and if not claimed within a limited time, they may be sold to pay the gaol fees. By another law any person who speaks at the bar, bench, on the stage, or in private, to the slaves, so as to excite insurrection, or brings any paper or pamphlet of such nature into the state, shall be imprisoned for not less than three nor more than twenty-one years, or shall suffer death as the judge decides. I could read such laws for hours, but I shall only add that in Maryland there is at present a gentleman in prison, condemned for ten years, because a copy of *Uncle Tom's Cabin* was found in his possession. The laws are equally severe against teaching a slave to read — against teaching even the name of the good God.

ANNA DICKINSON

The daughter of Quaker abolitionists, Anna Dickinson took to the podium as a teenager, speaking about temperance, women's rights, and the evils of slavery. Her poise and self-possession won raves.

Then came the Civil War, which made harsh demands on many citizens — but for Dickinson's speaking career it opened doors. By 1863, with President Abraham Lincoln's party in danger of losing the pivotal elections the following year, Dickinson was enlisted to campaign across New England to whip up support for pro-Union Republican candidates. She was a smash hit, winning praise for keeping the Union together.

Suddenly she was one of America's most famous women and the toast of Northern society. But she was also despised by those who rejected her radicalism, or simply believed that women had no place on the podium. They accused her of being motivated by money, fame, or vanity.

"Her looks have inspired us," wrote one newspaperman, "but her voice! Can anything — beauty or dramatic effect — carry us over that voice!"

"You talk well, talk fast, talk long and loud," scoffed another. "In fact, there is no end to your talk."

That summer, six months after the Emancipation Proclamation, with Northern enlistments falling sharply and the nation facing an unpopular draft, Dickinson spoke alongside orator Frederick Douglass and encouraged Black soldiers to enlist — although, as she shamefully acknowledged, they would receive less pay than their White counterparts.

This was "not a war for territory," Dickinson roared, "not a war for martial power, for mere victory; it is a war of the races, of the ages."

Six months later, to honor her for keeping their party in power, Republican legislators invited her to speak before Congress. She was just twenty-one.

The hall was packed with legislators, civic leaders, and businessmen. Dickinson was introduced by Vice President Hannibal Hamlin, who compared her to Joan of Arc.

Characteristically, she pulled no punches. She criticized the prosecution of the war, the State and War departments, and Lincoln's leadership. A half hour after she began, the President and Mrs. Lincoln slipped in — just as she was attacking the President's Amnesty Proclamation: "The men of the South must be punished!" The Lincolns sat and listened, quietly.

As the *Independent Democrat* noted, the evening was "a triumph of Woman's rights! A lady admitted to the Halls of Congress, and earnestly listened to during a set speech of an hour and a half! Truly, this is an age of innovations!"

"WHY COLORED MEN SHOULD ENLIST"

July 6, 1863
**Mass meeting promoting black enlistment,
National Hall, Philadelphia, Pennsylvania**

The People of the United States have decreed justice; the Almighty has answered them with victory. Month after month we have struggled with rebellion in arms; month after month, through more than two years of war, have waited for decisive victory in the East. In vain. Why? We had wealth and strength, numbers and power, intellect and energy, in the North. No one questions the heroism of the men we have sent into the field; men represented by that one who, left dying on a battle-field of the West, was asked by a friend, "Do you regret?" answered, "No, I — we all, are willing that our bodies should form the bridges and ladders, that the coming thousands may cross and mount, to plant their victorious banners on the shattered citadel and conquered wall;" and so died. No one questions the heroism of these men, sent by the North to martyrdom. We were unselfish, too; those who stayed gave freely of treasure, as those who went of life. We had culture to put against their ignorance; schools against rum-shops; churches against race-courses; the brain of New England against the degradation of South Carolina. We have twenty millions against eight millions. We failed. The South gained battles, won victories, trampled our banners in the dust; demanded and received from the world the recognition of the courage and determination of her soldiers.

Yet to-night we are rejoicing over a victory which wipes off all old scores of the army of the Potomac. This South, triumphant through the hatred which is genius; which in its strength reminds one of the story of an old Scotch king, who, seeing a great robber, with his splendid surroundings and the equipments of his band, turned to a knight, saying, "What lacks that knave a king should have?" "Sire," was the answer, "right and legitimacy." So this South, chiefly victorious through all this terrible conflict, aided by all despotism, almost recognized by the governments of the earth — what has it needed that beseems a nation? It has needed the corner stone of justice and the foundation of liberty. To-night, with its walls rocking to and fro, its supporters are flying from Gettysburg, with its ruins falling on their heads. The North stands triumphant, because the people have clambered up to the stand-point of freedom, and from thence have hurled their missiles on the advancing hosts of despotism. The President's threatened proclamation of September 22d, 1862; — the actual proclamation of January 1st, 1863, has had the stamp and seal of everlasting endurance set to it, by the people, in the Mass. 54th and 55th, and the Pennsylvania 3d United States Colored Volunteers.

True, through the past we have advocated the use of the black man. For what end? To save ourselves. We wanted them as shields, as barriers, as walls of defence. We would not even say to them, fight beside us. We would put them in the front; their brains contracted, their souls dwarfed, their manhood stunted; mass them together; let them die! That will cover and protect us. Now we hear the voice of the people, solemn and sorrowful, saying, "We have wronged you enough; you have suffered enough; we ask no more at your hands; we stand aside, and let you fight for your own manhood, your future, your race." Anglo-Africans, we need you; yet it is not because of this need that I ask you to go into the ranks of the regiments forming, to fight in this war. My cheeks would crimson with shame, while my lips put the request that could be answered, "Your soldiers? why don't you give us the same bounty, and the same pay as the rest?" I have no reply to *that*.

But for yourselves; because, after ages of watching and agony, your day is breaking; because your hour is come; because you hold the hammer which, upheld or falling, decides your destiny for woe or weal; because you have reached the point from which you must sink, generation after generation, century after century, into deeper depths, into more absolute degradation; or mount to the heights of glory and of fame.

The cause needs you. This is not our war, not a war for territory; not a war for martial power, for mere victory; it is a war of the races, of the ages; the stars and stripes is the people's flag of the world; the world must be gathered under its folds, the black man beside the white.

Thirteen dollars a month and bounty are good; liberty is better. Ten dollars a month and no bounty are bad; slavery is worse. The two alternatives are put before you; you make your own future. The to be will, in a little while, do you justice. Soldiers will be proud to welcome as comrades, as brothers, the black men of Port Hudson and Milliken's Bend. Congress, next winter, will look out through the fog and mist of Washington, and will see how, when Pennsylvania was invaded and Philadelphia threatened, while white men haggled over bounty and double pay to defend their own city, their own homes, with the tread of armed rebels almost heard in their streets; black men, without bounty, without pay, without rights or the promise of any, rushed to the beleaguered capital, and were first in their offers of life or of death. Congress will say, "These men are soldiers; we will pay them as such; these men are marvels of loyalty, self-sacrifice, courage; we will give them a chance of promotion." History will write, "Behold the unselfish heroes; the *eager* martyrs of this war." You hesitate because you have not all. Your brothers and sisters of the South cry out, "Come to our help, we have nothing." Father! you hesitate to send your boy to death; the slave father turns his face of dumb entreaty to you, to save his boy from the death in life; the bondage that crushes soul and body together. Shall your son go to his aid? Mother! you look with pride at the young manly face and figure, growing and strengthening beside you! he is yours! your own. God gave him to you. From the lacerated hearts, the wrung souls of other mothers, comes the wail, "My child, my child, give me back my child!" The slave-master heeds not; the government is tardy; mother the prayer comes to *you*; will you falter?

Young man! rejoicing in the hope, the courage, the will, the thews and muscles of young manhood — the red glare of this war falls on the faces and figures of other young men, distorted with suffering, writhing in agony, wrenching their manacles and chains — shouting with despairing voices to you for help — shall it be withheld?

The slave will be freed — with or without you. The conscience and heart of the people have decreed that. Xerxes scourging the Hellespont; Canute commanding the waves to roll back, are but types of that folly which stands up and says to this majestic wave of public opinion, "Thus far." The black man will be a citizen, only by stamping his right to it in his blood. Now or never! You have not homes — gain them. You have not liberty — gain it. You have not a flag — gain it. You have not a country! — be written down in history as the race who made one for themselves, and saved one for another.

FRANCES THOMPSON

In the spring of 1866, one year after the end of the Civil War, a brawl broke out on the streets of Memphis, Tennessee. In a city bristling with racial tension, that was enough to spark three days of violence. By the time federal troops brought it to a halt, 46 members of the Black community were dead, hundreds wounded, and dozens of homes, schools and churches reduced to ash.

Among the crimes recorded were the rapes of five Black women.

The Memphis riots shocked the nation during the early days of Reconstruction — a stark reminder that the war may have ended, but the peace that replaced it was fragile and combustible.

The previous year, Colonel Samuel Thomas traveled the South and reported to Congress on the condition of freed Blacks. "Wherever I go — the street, the shop, the house, or the steamboat — I hear the people talk in such a way as to indicate that they are yet unable to conceive of the Negro as possessing any rights at all . . . To kill a Negro they do not deem murder; to debauch a Negro woman they do not think fornication."

Within weeks of the riots, a Congressional committee traveled to Memphis and interviewed 170 women and men.

On June 1, the committee heard from a young Black woman. Frances Thompson identified herself as a former slave who worked as a tailor and laundress. She described how on the first night of rioting, seven men, including two policemen, came to the house she shared with sixteen-year-old Lucy Smith. Drawing their pistols, the men forced Thompson to cook for them, then gang raped both women and robbed them.

Thompson made it clear she did not consent to the assaults: "I said we were not that sort of women, and they must go. They said, 'that didn't make a damned bit of difference.'"

Afterwards, she told the committee, she was bedridden for two weeks.

What went unsaid in her testimony was that Thompson was transgender, born male but living her life as a female. Her account not only bore witness to those terrible crimes, but also made her the first known transgender person to testify before Congress.

Ten years later, Thompson reappeared in the historical record when she was arrested, examined by doctors, and pronounced a man. She was imprisoned, forced to wear men's clothing, and sentenced to "work the streets" on a chain gang. A few months later, she died.

The coroner's report said Thompson was anatomically male. But really, was it anybody's business besides her own?

We are indebted to her for courageously speaking out, sharing her suffering, and demonstrating human dignity.

"MEMPHIS RIOTS
AND MASSACRES"

June 1, 1866
US Congressional Committee Select Committee on the Memphis
Riots and Massacre, Gayoso House, Memphis, Tennessee

Q: State your name and residence.
A: My name is Frances Thompson; I live in Gayoso Street, here in Memphis.

Q: What is your occupation?
A: I sew and take in washing and ironing.

Q: Have you been a slave?
A: Yes sir.

Q: Where were you raised?
A: I was raised in Maryland. All our people but mistress got killed in the rebel army.

Q: Have you been injured?
A: I am a cripple. [the witness used crutches] I have a cancer in my foot.

Q: Were you here during the late riots?
A: Yes, sir.

Q: State what you know or saw of the rioting.
A: Between one and two o'clock Tuesday night seven men, two of whom were policemen, came to my house. I know they were policemen by their stars. They were all Irishmen. They said they must have supper, and asked me what I had, and said they must have some eggs, and ham, and biscuit. I made them some biscuit and some strong coffee, and they all sat down and ate. A girl lives with me; her name is Lucy Smith; she is about 16 years old. When they had eaten supper, they said they wanted some woman to sleep with. I said we were not that sort of women, and they must go. They said, "that didn't

make a damned bit of difference." One of them then laid hold of me and hit me in the side of my face, and holding my throat, choked me. Lucy tried to get out of the window when one of them knocked her down and choked her. They drew their pistols and said they would shoot us and fire the house if we did not let them have their way with us. All seven of the men violated us two. Four of them had to do with me, the rest with Lucy.

Q: Were you injured?
A: I was sick for two weeks. I lay for three days with a hot, burning fever.

Q: Did anyone attend you?
A: I had a cold before, and Dr. Rambert attended me after this.

Q: Were you robbed?
A: After they got through with us, they just robbed the house. They took the clothes out of my trunk and took one hundred dollars that I had in green-backs belonging to me, and two hundred dollars that belonged to a colored woman, that was left with me to keep safe for her.

Q: Did they take anything else?
A: They took three silk dresses of mine and a right nice one of Lucy's. They put the things into two pillow slips and took them away.

Q: How long did these men stay?
A: They were there, perhaps, for nearly four hours: it was getting day when they left.

Q: Did they say anything?
A: They said they intended to "burn up the last God damned nigger."

Q: Do you know any of them?
A: They were all Irishmen; there was not an American among them.

Q: Did anything else take place?
A: There were some quilts about that we had been making. They asked us what they were made for. When we told them we made them for the soldiers, they swore at us, and said the soldiers would never have them on their beds, and they took them away with the rest of the things. They said they would drive all the Yankees out of the town, and then there would be only some rebel niggers and butternuts left. I thought all the time they would burn the house down, but they didn't.

CLARA BARTON

Clara Barton became a teacher at seventeen and worked as a clerk in the US Patent Office in her thirties, but she found her life's mission on the bloody battlefields of the Civil War.

With the outbreak of fighting, she recognized the Union Army's lack of preparedness and tried to fill the gap by helping soldiers in need. She learned to pack, store and distribute medical supplies, treat injuries, and provide emotional support to the wounded and dying.

In 1862 she was granted permission to work on the front lines, setting up field hospitals, dispensing supplies and aiding soldiers wounded in combat. Time and again she put herself in harm's way, because that's where she was needed. In one of her most famous, oft-told stories, on the battlefield at Antietam a bullet whizzed through the sleeve of her dress without hitting her, but killing the soldier she was attending. "There was no more to be done for him and I left him to his rest," she said. "I have never mended that hole in my sleeve."

Despite having survived life's most harrowing experiences, one thing that frightened her was public speaking. She spent hours writing out her lecture notes in longhand. Yet in 1865, after the war, she traveled the country giving dozens of speeches about her wartime experiences, earning $75 to $100 per lecture.

She also personally lobbied Capitol Hill in support of the first Geneva Convention and the Red Cross — both eventually gained congressional approval — and she became the founder and first head of the American Red Cross.

In late 1865 Congress created the Joint Committee on Reconstruction to determine whether to readmit the Southern states to the Union. Barton, the only woman to testify, spoke about Georgia's notoriously brutal prisoner of war camp, Andersonville. In her testimony she described the hideous conditions in the camp, where prisoners were left to scorch in the sun and starve to death. Many of the living looked like skeletons.

When she discovered that thousands of letters from distraught relatives to the War Department had gone unanswered, she and her assistants set about locating the men in question, many in unmarked graves. Altogether she helped find more than 22,000 missing soldiers.

In 1900, she led her final field operation as American Red Cross president, helping victims of the 1900 Galveston hurricane, the nation's worst natural disaster. She distributed supplies, established an orphanage for storm victims, and acquired lumber to rebuild houses.

Four years later, Barton was forced to resign as American Red Cross president because of her domineering leadership style. Wasting no time, she promptly founded the National First Aid Society. She was 83 and determined to never stop saving lives.

"TESTIMONY ON CIVIL WAR PRISON CONDITIONS"

February 21, 1866
Joint Committee on Reconstruction,
US House of Representatives, Washington, DC

Miss Clara Barton sworn and examined.
By Mr. Howard:

Question. Of what State are you a native?
Answer. I am a native of Massachusetts.

Question. Were you raised and educated there?
Answer. I was; in Worcester county, Massachusetts.

Question. What has been your employment during the last year?
Answer. I have been searching for the missing men of the Union army.

Question. Where have you been engaged in that business?
Answer. I have been engaged in it here in Washington.

Question. Where else?
Answer. Nowhere else in that business. That business has led to other matters which have called me away.

Question. State where else you have been, and in what you have been engaged.
Answer. I commenced to search in the spring of 1865. In the latter part of June, 1865, I formed the acquaintance of a young man who had been a prisoner at Andersonville, and who had brought away the death record of that prison. He requested an interview, and, on giving it, I learned from him how the dead were buried in Andersonville, and I became satisfied that it was possible to identify them. I carried the question before General Hoffman, who, with the assistance, I think, of the Assistant Secretary of War, laid before the Secretary, Mr. Stanton, who sent for me to come to him the next day. I did so, and stated

to him my impressions, requesting that parties be sent out to identify the graves at Andersonville, and mark to them. He declared his gratitude even at the suggestion, all having thought it impossible; stated that an expedition should be started immediately, and that he would select some officer for the purpose, and he invited me to accompany it. We were ready in a week, and on the 8th of July we left Washington. I requested that the young man should also go with the party to identify the graves. We reached Andersonville, Georgia, on the 25th of July, and very soon the colored people there commenced to gather around me.

Question. What did you discover in relation to the colored people?
Answer. I discovered that they were in a state of ignorance, generally, at that time of their own condition as freedmen. Some of them knew it. They all, of course, mistrusted it. They had all heard it from one another. A few knew it from their masters, and only a few ; and what they did hear they had very little confidence to believe. Hearing that a party of Yankees, and especially a Yankee lady, was there, and they commenced to gather around me for the facts, asking me their little questions in their own way, which was to the effect, if they were free, and if Abraham Lincoln was really dead. They had been told that he was dead; that he had been killed; but at the same time they had been informed that, now that he was dead, they were no longer free, but would be all slaves again; and with that had come the suspicion, on their part, that he was not dead, but that it was a hoax to hold them in slavery. They would travel twenty miles in the night, after their day's work was done, and I would find them standing in front of my tent in the morning to hear me say whether it was true that Abraham Lincoln was dead, and that they were free. I told them Abraham Lincoln was dead; that I saw him dead; that I was near him when he died; and that they were free as I was. The next question was, what they should do. There were questions between the negro and his master in regard to labor and in regard to pay. I saw or discovered that the masters were inclined to get their labor without pay. Of course I had no way of proving that, but I inferred it. They were at work. Most of them offered to work until Christmas time, and to take a part of the profits. General [Rufus] Saxton, I should think, made some regulation specifying just what portion of each crop the negroes should have. They were all very anxious to hear the rules read. The commandant of each post had issued certain rules and regulations. These they had never heard read, and they came to me to know what the paper said. The rules were published daily in the Macon papers. They said they had been told that General [James H.] Wilson's orders said that they should work six days in the week hard, and half a day on Sunday. They wanted to know if it was so. My course with them was to read General Wilson's paper, as they called it. I have read it through sometimes forty times a day. They stood

around my tent in great numbers on a Sunday ; more than a hundred, men, women, and children, and every day more or less. Perhaps there were very few hours that I was not engaged in advising them, and attempting to decide some causes for them.

Question. Did General Wilson's order contain such a thing as that?

Answer. Oh, no, sir; General Wilson's order was protective of them in its character. The order was good, and the best of it was that they could understand it. When it was read to them they never failed to comprehend the most important parts of it. It was well drawn. I found that, if it had been read to them properly by their owners or masters, they would have understood it; for, as I read along to them, I would ask if they understood that; "Oh, yes," they would say, "we understand that." Then I would read another passage, and ask them if they understood that; "Oh, yes." "What do you understand by it?" They would put it in their own terms, and I saw that they understood it.

Question. Did they pretend to you that their old masters had given that peculiar version of General Wilson's order — that they should work six days in the week hard and half a day a Sunday?

Answer. In many instances they gave me that impression. They told me that in so many words, and said that they had been told so by the men for whom they worked. Some of them were not with their old masters, but were hired out, as they called it, to other parties . . . Perhaps I ought to state how the negroes came into southwestern Georgia. It is a poor section of the country, and the people there have been poor. They have been emphatically "poor whites." They were not wealthy enough to own slaves. They did their own work. But when the border States found it politic to sell their slaves, they sold them at a lesser price to speculators, who found it to their interest to purchase them and to run them into southwestern Georgia, and put them at a price at which these poor people could buy them, so that every poor man bought one or two slaves, as he could afford it, just as he would buy an ox or a cow. They kept them in their families and worked them like cattle. The slaves had no respect for their masters. The slaves have no respect for a poor man who owns them. They all seemed to apologize when they were asked where they came from. They would say, "We were not raised here." They all dated back to better days. They had been all raised in wealthy families in Virginia or South Carolina. This man that I have been speaking of had been taken away from his wife and five children, taken to southwestern Georgia, and sold to one Nick Wylie. Nick Wylie had a large number of slaves. During the years of the war he had not been on his own plantation, but some two hundred miles away, perhaps in the service; I do not know. He had an overseer by the name of Jim Bird, who must have been the personification of cruelty. This negro told me that some two years before, he married, after their style of marrying, a young women about eighteen years old, who was a slave on the Wylie plantation. They had one child, who was then a little over one year old. This man was a blacksmith. While he was at work, a few days before, his wife had proved unable to do the task of spinning which was given her. She was again within two months of her confinement, and was unable to do her task. She complained that she could not do it, and failed by a knot or two, as their term was, of completing it. When he came home at night from his day's work he found her lying in her hut. She had been bucked and gagged.

Question. Describe the process.

Answer. The person is seated upon the ground, the knees drawn up, the hands put under the knees, and a stick run through over the arms and under the knees, the hands being tied in front; that makes them utterly immovable; then there is a gag put in the mouth and tied at the back of the head — this woman had been treated in that way — then the overseer had come behind her, kicked her on the back, and thrown her over. She had been stripped in the mean time, for they never whip the negro with the clothes on; she was thrown on her face, and lashed on her back, so that, when her husband found her, he said she was a gore of blood, and she must have been; she had been untied, and was lying there as she had been left. He did not tell me that he remonstrated very much; I suppose he dared not. Next day the woman was ordered again to her task; she was utterly unable to do it, and scarcely able to stand; she bought all the yarn she could to try and make up the eight knots that she had to turn in; she failed to get quite enough, failing by a knot, or half a knot. The overseer sent to her the next night, when her task was counted, and she had failed again, ordering her to come to him the next morning at seven o'clock, as he was going to whip her; that he had not whipped her yet, but should do so the next morning. Arnold then had no way but to gather up his wife, walking as well as she could; and, after night time, they started for Americus, twelve miles below Anderson-ville. They were some twenty miles in the country from Americus; they dared not take the direct road, for they knew the overseer would mistrust that had gone to Americus, and would overtake them; they, therefore, went around, travelling some thirty or forty miles. After two days they reached Americus by a circuitous route. The overseer had been there, and had warned the military authorities that he had two runaway slaves, a man and a woman, who were coming there, and he wanted them returned. I think he stated he had punished them. They went into Americus without going direct to the military authorities; but the people saw them, and saw that she was lame and hurt, and took her in somewhere. He went to work for people there at blacksmithing at a dollar a day. He heard of me at Andersonville, and he thought to reach me there; he heard there was a settlement of Yankees forming at Andersonville; he started with his wife, for, after being a week there, she had got a little better. He had been paid for his work in confederate money, and, when he found himself on the train, the conductor would not take that money, and put them both off. He left the wife at Americus, came to me at Andersonville, and told his story. I wrote immediately to the commandant at Americus, stating the case to him, and asking him to send a sergeant and wagon, or team of some kind, with that man back to Nick Wylie's to get whatever he had left — (he spoke of having left chickens, furniture, bed, and bedding, and the baby which he had been obliged to leave) — and send them to me. He took the note to the commandant at Americus, and it was done as I requested. Two days after, the whole assemblage drove up in front of my tent — Cater, his wife and the baby, the chickens, and the bed and bedding. I took his wife into my tent and examined her back; she was a young, bright-colored woman, a little darker than he, with a fair, patient face, with nothing sulky in her look; I found across her back twelve lashes or gashes, partly healed and partly not, some of them cut into the bone. She must have been whipped with a lash half as large as my little finger — it may have been larger; any of these gashes was from eight to ten inches in length; the flesh had been cut completely out most of the way. It had been a curling whip; it had curled around her arms, cut out inside the arm, over the back, and the same on the other side. There were twelve of those long lashes, partly healed and partly not; she could not bear her clothing on her at that time, except thrown loosely over her shoulders; she had got strong enough so as to be able to walk, but she was feeble, and must have been unable to work before that occurred; she was in no condition to work.

Question. She was in a state of pregnancy, then?
Answer. Yes, sir; that was the difficulty. She was one who, from her face, would never have rebelled against labor that she could have done; of that I am satisfied.

Question. Do you know what became of her?
Answer. I referred them to Colonel Griffin, then in charge at Andersonville. The colonel put Cater to work at his trade as a blacksmith, and gave them a house to live in. I would have taken them away with me if I could; but it was impossible, and I left them there working for Colonel Griffin, he at his trade and she as a waiting girl . . .

Question. Did you examine the prison ground at Andersonville?
Answer. I did very thoroughly, every inch of ground used.

Question. Of course you found it difficult to discover any trace of the barbarities practiced there?

Answer. Of course there were no prisoners there then: but the appearance of the whole ground was sufficient evidence, considering the number of prisoners who had been there. All spoke of inhumanity. It was impossible that that number of men could be kept within the enclosure without the most intense suffering.

Question. Was the enclosure standing when you were there?

Answer. Yes, sir. It is a stockade formed of pine trees twenty feet long, and from a foot to a foot and a half through, set five or six feet in the ground, close together, and pointed at the top.

Question. What was the area of the enclosure?

Answer. From twenty-five to twenty-seven acres, more or less. It had been much less at one time. It was originally only eleven acres. They had got some thirty thousand men within that eleven acres. But they found it impossible, as prisoners were constantly sent there, to keep them in that space, and the stockade was increased to the size that they called twenty-seven acres. I had it measured while I was there, and I made it some twenty-five or twenty-six acres.

Question. Do you know how many prisoners they had there at any one time during the war?

Answer. From thirty to thirty-four thousand . . .

Question. What contrivances had there been for the protection of the prisoners from the rain, the sun, and the storms?

Answer. There were a few sheds, with simply a covering over the tops, but no sides, on the top of either hill; but I have been told by prisoners that at first there were none of them, and that the last five sheds (five on one end and five on the other) were only erected a few weeks before the stockade was abandoned. I may almost say that there was no protection. Some of the men had blankets and some of them had the little shelter tent. They put these together as well as they could and gathered under them; there was no other protection . . .

Question. So far you have been able to collect information, and so far as you believe, what is the state of feeling on the part of secessionists in Georgia towards the government of the United States.

Answer. I think they have no respect for it.

Question. How do they feel towards the freed negroes?

Answer. I think far less kindly than when they owned them themselves.

Question. Would they, or would they not, if they had the power, reduce them again to slavery?

Answer. That I cannot say; but I should not want to take the chances of being a slave there, were it in their power.

Question. Is there any other fact that you wish to state?

Answer. I am not aware of any; I think not.

Question. How did you find the feeling of the blacks towards the government of the United States, and towards the loyal people?

Answer. The very best of feeling — friendly, full of confidence in the United States government, loving the northern people.

Question. Did you meet with any blacks during your journey who were friendly to the rebel cause?

Answer. I cannot say that I did meet one; I heard no black person express himself or herself in that way.

Question. How did the blacks tell you they had conducted themselves during the war?

Answer. They said they had been "mity fraid."

Question. Did they seem to understand what was the object of the war, or what was to be its final result as to them?

Answer. They began to comprehend it. I think they understood it. I think, so far as their intelligence will permit, they understand it as clearly to-day as we do; they now grasp it distinctly.

Question. Have you any reason to suppose that there were secret associations among the negroes during the war, or before the war, by which intelligence was communicated from one locality to another?

Answer. If I may believe what they say, it was so; I have been repeatedly told so. They have, in their crude way, attempted to describe to me their evening meetings, as they stole away from one plantation to another, previous to the war and during the war.

Question. You have had a good deal of intercourse with the blacks; what is your idea about their capacity to acquire knowledge? Do they possess a capacity equal to that of the whites, generally speaking?

Answer. In their present condition they can hardly be compared with the whites; still, to a certain extent they learn as easily, as readily. I do not think that their reasoning powers have been educated up to a standard that enables them to grasp subjects which whites can grasp, but their imitation leads them to acquire many things as readily as white people do.

Question. What can you say in regard to their general truthfulness? How, in that respect, do they compare with white people in a similar condition of life, if it were possible to suppose such a similarity?
Answer. They have been, in a great measure, taught to speak falsely and to act falsely.

Question. Taught by whom?
Answer. Their very condition has taught them that; the condition of slavery teaches false hood. But there is a principal of religious character in their nature which holds them above white people of as low a grade. They are more religious, but the nature of their condition has not made them more moral.

Question. Are they wanting in truthfulness in their communications with one another?
Answer. To a certain extent I think they are; but not more so, probably, than white people under similar circumstances — if it were possible to imagine them. But that I mean that I do not think they are untruthful because they were created negroes, but from the condition and station in which they have been placed. Naturally, I think the negro not less moral, not less religious, not less truthful than any other race, only as his condition has made him so.

FRANCES ELLEN WATKINS HARPER

One year after the end of the Civil War, a Black woman stepped up to speak at a church in New York City. She looked out at the audience of mostly White women and began with a half-apology. "I feel I am something of a novice upon this platform," she said, then went on to deliver one of the most stirring, scathing speeches in American history.

The event was the Eleventh National Woman's Rights Convention, and the speaker was Frances Ellen Watkins Harper, the well-known poet, abolitionist, suffragist, and lecturer. After teaching for a few years, she began writing abolitionist materials and helping enslaved people along the Underground Railroad to Canada.

Her 1866 speech lasted only ten minutes, but no one who heard it could forget the blunt force of her words.

As she told the audience, six years earlier her husband had died suddenly, in debt, leaving her with four small children to raise. That's when she discovered how women, "unequal before the law," have little to protect themselves from the tribulations of life.

And yet, having the vote would not solve all women's problems, she said — not until America extended equality to all its citizens.

"You white women speak here of rights. I speak of wrongs," she said, a direct indictment of her supposedly enlightened, liberal-minded fellow suffragists in the audience.

Black soldiers had fought and died for the Union, their bones "bleaching" in the soil, she said, yet — as she had recently discovered — a Black person could not ride alongside a White in a train from Washington, DC, to Baltimore. "They put me in the smoking car!" she cried, incredulous. "Have women nothing to do with this?"

White women were not "dew-drops just exhaled from the skies," she said. "I tell you that if there is any class of people who need to be lifted out of their airy nothings and selfishness, it is the white women of America."

Despite it all, Harper painted a transcendent vision of the potential greatness of America, united in universal equality, "one great privileged nation."

She speaks to each of us directly by arguing that the oppression of the meekest ultimately harms everyone. "We are all bound up together in one great bundle of humanity, and society cannot trample on the weakest and feeblest of its members without receiving the curse in its own soul."

As long as there is injustice and oppression in the world, she reminds us, we are all morally responsible.

"WE ARE ALL BOUND UP TOGETHER"

May 10, 1866
11th National Woman's Rights Convention,
Founding meeting of the American Equal Right Association,
Church of the Puritans, Union Square, New York City

I feel I am something of a novice upon this platform. Born of a race whose inheritance has been outrage and wrong, most of my life had been spent in battling against those wrongs. But I did not feel as keenly as others, that I had these rights, in common with other women, which are now demanded. About two years ago, I stood within the shadows of my home. A great sorrow had fallen upon my life. My husband had died suddenly, leaving me a widow, with four children, one my own, and the others stepchildren. I tried to keep my children together. But my husband died in debt; and before he had been in his grave three months, the administrator had swept the very milk-crocks and wash tubs from my hands. I was a farmer's wife and made butter for the Columbus market; but what could I do, when they had swept all away? They left me one thing — and that was a looking glass! Had I died instead of my husband, how different would have been the result! By this time he would have had another wife, it is likely; and no administrator would have gone into his house, broken up his home, and sold his bed, and taken away his means of support.

I took my children in my arms, and went out to seek my living. While I was gone, a neighbor to whom I had once lent five dollars, went before a magistrate and swore that he believed I was a non-resident, and laid an attachment on my very bed. And I went back to Ohio with my orphan children in my arms, without a single feather bed in this wide world, that was not in the custody of the law. I say, then, that justice is not fulfilled so long as woman is unequal before the law.

We are all bound up together in one great bundle of humanity, and society cannot trample on the weakest and feeblest of its members without receiving the curse in its own soul. You tried that in the case of the negro. You pressed him down for two centuries; and in so doing you crippled the moral strength and paralyzed the spiritual energies of the white men of the country.

When the hands of the black were fettered, white men were deprived of the liberty of speech and the freedom of the press. Society cannot afford to neglect the enlightenment of any class of its members. At the South, the legislation of the country was in behalf of the rich slaveholders, while the poor white man was neglected. What is the consequence today? From that very class of neglected poor white men, comes the man who stands to-day, with his hand upon the helm of the nation. He fails to catch the watchword of the hour, and throws himself, the incarnation of meanness, across the pathway of the nation. My objection to Andrew Johnson is not that he has been a poor white man; my objection is that he keeps "poor whites" all the way through. That is the trouble with him.

This grand and glorious revolution which has commenced, will fail to reach its climax of success, until throughout the length and brea[d]th of the American Republic, the nation shall be so color-blind, as to know no man by the color of his skin or the curl of his hair. It will then have no privileged class, trampling upon and outraging the unprivileged classes, but will be then one great privileged nation, whose privilege will be to produce the loftiest manhood and womanhood that humanity can attain.

I do not believe that giving the woman the ballot is immediately going to cure all the ills of life. I do not believe that white women are dew-drops just exhaled from the skies. I think that like men they may be divided into three classes, the good, the bad, and the indifferent. The good would vote according to their convictions and principles; the bad, as dictated by preju[d]ice or malice; and the indifferent will vote on the strongest side of the question, with the winning party.

You white women speak here of rights. I speak of wrongs. I, as a colored woman, have had in this country an education which has made me feel as if I were in the situation of Ishmael, my hand against every man, and every man's hand against me. Let me go to-morrow morning and take my seat in one of your street cars — I do not know that they will do it in New York, but they will in Philadelphia — and the conductor will put up his hand and stop the car rather than let me ride.

Going from Washington to Baltimore this Spring, they put me in the smoking car. Aye, in the capital of the nation, where the black man consecrated himself to the nation's defence, faithful when the white man was faithless, they put me in the smoking car! They did it once; but the next time they tried it, they failed; for I would not go in. I felt the fight in me; but I don't want to have to fight all the time. Today I am puzzled where to make my home. I would like to make it in Philadelphia, near my own friends and relations. But if I want to ride in the streets of Philadelphia, they send me to ride on the platform with the driver. Have women nothing to do with this? Not long since, a colored woman took her seat in an Eleventh Street car in Philadelphia, and the conductor stopped the car, and told the rest of the passengers to get out, and left the car with her in it alone, when they took it back to the station. One day I took my seat in a car, and the conductor came to me and told me to take another seat. I just screamed "murder." The man said if I was black I ought to behave myself. I knew that if he was white he was not behaving himself. Are there not wrongs to be righted?

In advocating the cause of the colored man, since the Dred Scott decision, I have sometimes said I thought the nation had touched bottom. But let me tell you there is a depth of infamy lower than that. It is when the nation, standing upon the threshold of a great peril, reached out its hands to a feebler race, and asked that race to help it, and when the peril was over, said, You are good enough for soldiers, but not good enough for citizens. When Judge Taney said that the men of my race had no rights which the white man was bound to respect, he had not seen the bones of the black man bleaching outside of Richmond. He had not seen the thinned ranks and the thickened graves of the Louisiana Second, a regiment which went into battle nine hundred strong, and came out with three hundred. He had not stood at Olustee and seen defeat and disaster crushing down the pride of our banner, until words was brought to E.N. Hallowell, "The day is lost; go in and save it;" and black men stood in the gap, beat back the enemy, and saved your army.

We have a woman in our country who has received the name of "Moses," not by lying about it, but by acting it out — a woman who has gone down into the Egypt of slavery and brought out hundreds of our people into liberty. The last time I saw that woman, her hands were swollen. That woman who had led one of Montgomery's most successful expeditions, who was brave enough and secretive enough to act as a scout for the American army, had her hands all swollen from a conflict with a brutal conductor, who undertook to eject her from her place. That woman, whose courage and bravery won a recognition from our army and from every black man in the land, is excluded from every thoroughfare of travel. Talk of giving women the ballot-box? Go on. It is a normal school, and the white women of this country need it. While there exists this brutal element in society which tramples upon the feeble and treads down the weak, I tell you that if there is any class of people who need to be lifted out of their airy nothings and selfishness, it is the white women of America.

SUSAN B. ANTHONY

On November 1, 1872, Susan B. Anthony entered a barbershop in her hometown of Rochester, New York. After reading the Fourteenth Amendment on the rights of citizens out loud to the registrars, she signed up to vote in the upcoming presidential election. Four days later, she and several others dropped their votes in the ballot box.

For that, Anthony alone was arrested and charged with a crime, making headlines around the world.

In the months leading up to her trial, she brought her case to the public, giving dozens of speeches across northern New York state, in meeting halls, churches, schoolhouses — and if nowhere else was available, the front parlors of private homes. One newspaper called her "a female steamboat."

More than one door slammed in her face. She got used to it.

The daughter of a Quaker cotton-mill owner who lost his business because he refused to use slave-grown cotton, she made countless impassioned speeches for temperance and abolition, both widely despised causes at the time.

But with the end of the Civil War and the 15th Amendment granting Black men the vote, she turned fulltime to "the woman's vote."

In 1872 her question was, "Is it a Crime for a US Citizen to Vote?"

Her answer was "no." The basis of her argument was that as a citizen, she was indeed entitled to vote, and therefore could not be guilty of criminal intent or action. Nevertheless, in June 1873, she was found guilty before a local US Circuit Court. She refused to pay the $100 fine.

Dogged, determined, both idealistic and ruthlessly strategic, Anthony devoted more than a half century to the suffrage cause. Together with Elizabeth Cady Stanton and hundreds of thousands of women of every race, ethnicity, and creed, she revolted against a system that would not grant half its citizens a say in how they were governed.

Anthony did not live to see US women get the vote. But by the end of her life, she was recognized as the foremother of the suffrage movement. Many found her ideas eccentric, extreme, even despicable.

At the same time, she was beloved by Black women for championing their rights. "Our friend for many years — our champion," said Black activist Hester Jeffrey at Anthony's funeral in 1906.

Working with Stanton, Anthony spent significant effort monopolizing and molding the public image of the women's rights movement, a predominantly White women's version. The six-volume *History of Woman's Suffrage* tells only selected parts of the story, leaving yawning gaps that historians have been seeking to fill ever since.

"IS IT A CRIME FOR A US CITIZEN TO VOTE?"

Winter and spring, 1872-1873
Monroe and Ontario Counties, New York

F*riends and Fellow-citizens*: I stand before you to-night, under indictment for the alleged crime of having voted at the last Presidential election, without having a lawful right to vote. It shall be my work this evening to prove to you that in thus voting, I not only committed no crime, but, instead, simply exercised my *citizen's right*, guaranteed to me and all United States citizens by the National Constitution, beyond the power of any State to deny.

Our democratic-republican government is based on the idea of the natural right of each individual member thereof to a voice and a vote in making and executing the laws. We assert the province of government to be to secure the people in the enjoyment of their unalienable rights. We throw to the winds the old dogma that governments can give rights. Before governments were organized no one denies that each individual possessed the right to protect his own life, liberty, and property. And when one hundred or one million people enter into a free government, they do not barter away their natural rights, they simply pledge themselves to protect each other in the enjoyment of them through prescribed judicial and legislative tribunals. They agree to abandon the methods of brute force in the adjustment of their differences and adopt those of civilization.

Nor can you find a word in any of the grand documents left us by the fathers that assumes for government the power to create or confer rights. The Declaration of Independence, the United States Constitution, the constitutions of the several states, and the organic laws of the territories, all alike, propose to protect the people in the exercise of their God-given rights; not one of them pretends to bestow rights.

All men are created equal and endowed by their creator with certain unalienable rights; among these are life, liberty, and the pursuit of happiness. That, to secure these, governments are instituted among men, deriving their just powers from the consent of the governed.

Here is no shadow of government authority over rights, no exclusion of any class of men from their full and equal enjoyment. Here is pronounced the right of all men, and, "consequently," as the Quaker preacher said, "of all women," to a voice in the government. And here, in this very first paragraph of the Declaration, is the assertion of the natural right of all to the ballot; for how can the "consent of the governed" be given if the right to vote be denied? Again:

That whenever any form of government becomes destructive of these ends, it is the right of the people to alter or abolish it, and to institute a new government, laying its foundations on such principles, and organizing its powers in such form, as to them shall seem most likely to effect their safety and happiness.

Surely the right of the whole people to vote is here clearly implied. However destructive to their happiness this government might become, a disfranchised class could neither alter nor abolish it, nor institute a new one, except by the old brute-force method of insurrection and rebellion. One-half of the people of this nation, to-day, are utterly powerless to blot from the statute-books an unjust law, or write there a new and just one. The women, dissatisfied as they are with this form of government that enforces "taxation without representation" — that compels them to obey laws to which they have never given their consent — that imprisons and hangs them without a trial by a jury of their peers — that robs them, in marriage, of the custody of their own persons, wages, and children, are — this half of the people — left wholly at the mercy of the other half, in direct violation of the spirit and letter of the declarations of the framers of this government, every one of which was based on the immutable principles of "equal rights to all." By them kings, priests, popes, aristocrats were, all alike, dethroned and placed on a common level, politically, with the lowliest-born subject or serf. By them, too, men were deprived of their authority and placed on a political level with women. By their practice all class and caste distinction must be abolished, and slave, serf, plebeian, wife, woman, all alike, bound from their subject position to the proud platform of equality.

The preamble of the Federal Constitution says:

We, the people of the United States, in order to form a more perfect union, establish justice, insure domestic tranquility, provide for the common defense, promote the general welfare, and secure the blessings of liberty to ourselves and our posterity, do ordain and establish this Constitution for the United States of America.

It was we, the people, not we, white male citizens, nor yet we, male citizens; but we the whole people, who formed this Union. And we formed it, not to give the blessings of liberty, but to secure them — not to the half of ourselves and the half of our posterity, but to the whole people, women as well as men. And it is downright mockery to talk to women of their enjoyment of the blessings of liberty while they are denied the use of the only means of securing them provided by this democratic-republican government — the ballot.

The early journals of Congress show that when the committee reported to that body the original articles of confederation, the very first article which became the subject of discussion was that respecting equality of suffrage. Article 4th said: "The better to secure and perpetuate mutual friendship and intercourse among the people of the different states of this Union, and free inhabitants of each of the states (paupers, vagabonds, and fugitives from justice excepted) shall be entitled to all the privileges and immunities of the free citizens of the several states."

Thus, as the very beginning, did the fathers see the necessity of the universal application of the great principle of equal rights to all — in order to produce the desired result — a harmonious Union and a homogeneous people . . .

And it is upon this conclusion of "the citizens' constitutional right to vote" that our National Woman Suffrage association has based its argument and action for the last four years. We no longer petition legislature nor congress to give us the right to vote. We appeal to the women everywhere to assume their too long neglected "citizen's right to vote." We appeal to the inspectors of elections everywhere to receive the votes of all United States citizens as it is their duty to do. We appeal to United States commissioners and marshals to arrest the inspectors who reject the names and votes of United States citizens, as it is their duty to do, and leave alone those who, like our eighth ward inspectors, perform their duties faithfully and well.

We ask the courts to render true and unprejudiced opinions of the law, and wherever there is room for a doubt to give its benefit on the side of liberty and equal rights to all citizens, remembering that "the true rule of interpretation under our national constitution, especially since its amendments, is that anything for human rights is constitutional, everything against human rights unconstitutional."

We ask the juries to fail to return a verdict of "guilty" against honest, law-abiding, tax paying United States citizens for offering their votes, at our elections. Or against intelligent, worthy young men, inspectors of elections, for receiving and counting such citizens' votes.

And it is on this line that we propose to fight our battle for the ballot — all peaceably, but nevertheless persistently through to complete triumph, when all United States citizens shall be recognized as equals before the law.

MARIA MITCHELL

Maria Mitchell grew up on the island of Nantucket, where after sundown she would climb to the roof to observe the heavens, helping her father with his astronomical instruments and measurements.

Fame came unexpectedly in October 1847 when, at twenty nine, she discovered a comet. Overnight she was thrust into the public eye, with articles about her published around the world, a showering of accolades, even a gold medal from the King of Denmark. The following year she became the first woman elected to the American Academy of Arts and Sciences.

Still, her life on Nantucket was quiet. As a librarian at the Atheneum, she organized public lectures. Naturally, the speakers were all male. There were few models of women in American life leading independent intellectual lives and making significant contributions aside from a handful of reformers like Margaret Fuller and Dorothea Dix, about whom Mitchell wrote admiringly in her diary.

Even as her own reputation grew, Nantucket remained her home.

In 1857, an editorial in *United States* magazine noted that even though "the barren island of Nantucket" seemed like the ideal place to "promote solitary star-gazing . . . We wish, for the sake of her sex, and from the love of promoting science therein, Maria Mitchell would be induced to exhibit her fine talents in a lecture room."

And that's exactly what she did when she returned from a liberating trip to Europe.

In Rome she applied to visit the Vatican observatory, which required permission from the Pope. After much lobbying, she finally was allowed in, but as dusk approached, she was escorted to the door. Her permit "did not extend beyond the daylight."

As one door slammed shut, another opened in her mind: The belief that she could advocate for women's access to knowledge and intellectual advancement.

In 1865 she accepted a position as professor of astronomy at Vassar College, even though she herself had never attended college. She remained at Vassar for the next twenty-three years, nurturing a generation of science and astronomy graduates who went on to distinction. She taught them the importance of close observation and analysis and encouraged them to present their research at conferences and in scientific journals.

In 1875 Mitchell helped found the Association for the Advancement of Women. At its annual gathering the next year, she rebutted the argument that women were incapable of original insight. All that's needed she said, was for women to be freed from the drudgery of housework, "the hurry and worry of daily toil," and given an open door.

"THE NEED OF WOMEN
IN SCIENCE"

c. October 4-6, 1876
**Fourth Congress of Women, Association for the Advancement
of Women, St. George's Hall, Philadelphia, Pennsylvania**

When we inquire in regard to the opportunities afforded to women for the study of science, we are not surprised to find them meagre and unsatisfactory. Nor, with one exception, are we surprised at the localities in which the little culture of science is found; they have the range of latitude and longitude which we expected. The light shading on the map of the world, which in the old school books used to divide the enlightened from the barbarian countries, might be used to-day to designate the scientific and the unscientific.

Taking our whole country into consideration, there is very little attention paid to science. The same influences which deter men in scientific research, operate only more forcibly upon women; the want of leisure, and the unremunerative character of intellectual pursuits. And yet the fact that a few women give themselves so determinedly to scientific studies, and that so many make a beginning, would seem to show that they have a decided fitness for its demand. Young girls almost all study the natural sciences in schools, and quite a moiety of them take up the abstract sciences. I do not believe it is because the science of the ordinary schools requires little brain work, although that is true, but because it is the work to which they instinctively incline. I should like to urge upon young women a course of solid scientific study in some one direction for two reasons: —

1st. The needs of science.

2nd. Their own needs.

The needs of science. For the very reason that a woman's methods are different from those of a man, are women needed in scientific work. All her nice perceptions of minute details, all her delicate observation of color, of form, of shape, of change, and her capability of patient routine would be of immense value in the collection of scientific facts.

When I see a woman put an exquisitely fine needle at exactly the same distance from the last stitch which that last stitch was from its predecessor, I think what a capacity she has for an astronomical observer; unknowingly, she is using a micrometer — unconsciously she is graduating circles. And the eye which has been trained in the matching of worsteds is specially fitted for the use of prism and spectroscope. Persons who are in charge of the scientific departments of colleges are always mourning over the scarcity of trained assistants. The directors of observatories and museums not infrequently do an enormous amount of routine work which they would gladly relinquish; their time and strength are wasted on labor which students could do equally well, if students could be found who would be ready to make science a life work.

Women are needed, too, as lecturers in schools; it needs only the supply, and the demand will come. Persons who are known to be in a line of scientific work, are continually besieged with applications to give lectures, to write short articles for periodicals, to translate foreign works. Such lectures and such articles would do little directly for the advance, but much in directly in forming taste and arousing interest.

I am far from the intention of encouraging young women to scientific study on account of its outward utility; at best its wages to-day are little above those of manual labor, and were they those of royal revenues, I should still raise the objection that it is an ignoble following of nature, which looks for gain. Better dig in the earth for gold, than study its rocks for pay.

But for themselves, for young women who have a love of nature and a longing to study her laws, how shall the taste be developed and how shall they be encouraged? We must have a different kind of teaching. It must not be text-book teaching. I doubt if science can be taught in school-rooms at all. Certainly it cannot be taught by hearing recitations. There is a touch of the absurd, in a teacher's asking any but a very young person a question, the answer to which he already knows. In the old-fashioned books the dialogue method is better used; the pupils [sic] *asks* and the teacher *answers*. Eudora asks how far the earth is from the sun, and Tutor answers. Eudora then asks how this was found out, and Tutor explains.

The method of teaching science by lectures is questionable; it is liable to the objection that the lecturer impresses himself and his views upon the listener, rather than nature and her ways. It is a feeble kind of science that can be put upon a black-board, placed in array upon a table, or arranged upon shelves — the facts of science may be taught by such means — the spirit of science, which is the love of investigation, they cannot arouse. If science can be developed at all in class rooms, it must be by debate; freethought, and free inquiry are the very first steps in the path of science. Only the "hardpan" of scientific truths should be accepted, and scarcely that. I should have more hope of a girl who questioned if three angles of a triangle equaled two right angles, than of one who learned the demonstration and accepted it in a few minutes.

It will be easier to reform the in-school work than to take young women over the next years, when they leave the class rooms and college; but it will be less difficult, if, in the class room, they have learned to think for themselves and to plan their own lives. What lies before the true lover of nature, if she be a woman, when she leaves college? Almost always entire renunciation of her own wishes. An account which comes to me from one of the large cities of New York must be too strongly expressed, and yet it is somewhat true of any town. The writer says:

"If an unfortunate female should happen to possess a lurking fondness for any special scientific or literary pursuit, she is careful (if of any social position) to hide it as she would some deformity."

The young woman who leaves college, belongs to one of two classes. She must either enter at once upon some business which shall enable her to be self-supporting, or she must accept parental support.

If there is any class of women for whom I have a deep compassion, it is the unmarried and unoccupied daughters of rich men; all the more do I pity them, if, as often happens, they are born with a good deal of brain power. I shudder as I recall the speech of the editor of a widely-read newspaper: "The first duty of a woman is to be ornamental in the parlor." That is, she is to be the marble Clyteor.

Psyche that stands on the bracket! For such young women there is only the slow change of the ages; the conversion of public sentiment, or a struggle to which almost no one is equal. In most cases, she

"Suffers, recoils, then, thirsty and despairing

Of what she would, descends and sips the nearest draught."

There is more hope for the poor young woman. For her, there is work. But in her poverty there are the elements of destruction. She is, perhaps, a lover of nature, and dreams of a life devoted to study — she is a born investigator and knows that she has special power as well as peculiar tastes. She stifles her longings and enters upon work — distasteful work — work which is fettering — because the home needs her and there are younger ones to be aided. I question if a young woman who knows she has peculiar gifts, who can say of nature, "Her Priest I am, her holy fillets wear," has any right to turn aside from this call of God. That self abnegation is not a virtue, which urges the nearest, and on the whole the easiest, rather than the highest duty. The woman who has a definite line marked out for her in her natural gifts, has a duty as imperative as that which family tie imposes.

For these cases of rarely gifted souls, we should care. Does any one *suppose* that any woman in all the ages has had a fair chance to show what she could do in science? Let me bring you two cases— one is Tycho Brahé of the sixteenth, and the other is Caroline Herschel of the eighteenth century.

Sixteenth century: Tycho Brahé. King Frederic of Denmark gave him a delightful island for his habitation, large enough for him not to feel imprisoned (the circumference being about five miles), yet little enough for him to feel as much at home as in a high walled park. He built a great house in the midst of the isle, a palace of art and science. Uniting the ease of a rich nobleman's existence with every aid to science, he lived far enough from Copenhagen to enjoy the most perfect tranquility, yet near enough to escape the consequences of too absolute isolation. Aided in all that he undertook by a staff of assistants that he himself had trained, supported in his labor by the encouragement of his sovereign, he led the ideal intellectual life.

Journal of Caroline Herschel; Eighteenth Century.

At fourteen years. With my constant attendance at church and school, and besides the time I was employed in doing the drudgery of the scullery, it was but seldom I could make one in the group when the family were assembled together.

At twenty years. For my brother I knit as many cotton stockings as would last two years.

At thirty-seven years. A salary of £50 a year was settled on me as assistant to my brother, and in October I received £12 10s., being the eighteenth quarterly payment, and the first money I ever in all my lifetime thought myself to be at liberty to spend to my own liking.

For a certain class of students there are the summer schools, like that of Peni-kese — and there is the "society to encourage home studies," at present almost entirely literary in its aims. For a smaller and a more decided type of women, we should become a Bureau of Advice, and also originators of ways and means. Young women should be encouraged to state their case, and our committee should be able to suggest methods — ways of increasing facilities — perhaps to find opportunities for work in science. But what a scientist most needs is leisure — time to think. We ought to be able to give aids, in the shape of a year's residence near large libraries, museums, laboratories, or observatories. How eagerly such opportunities would be sought, we all know.

The laws of Nature are not discovered by accident; theories do not come by chance, even to the greatest minds; they are not born of the hurry and worry of daily toil; they are diligently sought, they are patiently waited for, they are received with cautious reserve, they are accepted with reverence and awe. And until able women have given their lives to investigation, it is idle to discuss the question of their capacity for original work.

SUSETTE LA FLESCHE

Throughout the early to mid-19th century, as more Caucasian settlers moved westward across North America, they increasingly came into conflict with Indigenous peoples who had made the land their home for centuries.

In response, the US government launched the "removal" program, forcing tribes to resettle, often with calamitous results. In 1868, the US government gave land in Nebraska reserved for the Ponca to the Sioux, then drove the Ponca from their homeland to "Indian Territory," in modern-day Oklahoma.

It was a humanitarian disaster. Many hundreds died along the grueling 500-mile march. Even more passed away from malaria and starvation when they reached the reservation.

One powerful advocate for the Ponca was Susette La Flesche. She was from the Omaha tribe, close cousins to the Ponca. Her bilingual skills, speaking savvy, and incandescent anger at government policies made her among the most effective voices for her people.

In the fall of 1879, La Flesche joined Chief Standing Bear, her brother Francis La Flesche, and journalist Thomas Tibbles of the *Omaha Daily Herald* on a speaking tour of the East Coast. Standing Bear's landmark civil rights case against the US government had been decided the previous May, and they were drawing huge crowds to hear about Native American rights.

In city after city, she translated for Standing Bear while adding her own emotional appeals. Entranced reporters praised her eloquence and called her Inshata Theumba, or "Bright Eyes."

Before an audience of 800 in Boston's Faneuil Hall, she issued an urgent plea. "We are human beings; God made us as well as you."

In a speech the following year, she pointed out the hypocrisy of the government's position. "When the Indian . . . fights for his property, liberty and life, they call him a savage," but when the first settlers in America did the same, "they were called heroes."

La Flesche and Tibbles married and continued lecturing on Native American issues. In 1881, Congress passed a Ponca reparation bill to pay tribe members for their losses. The following year a law was passed preserving land for the Ponca in perpetuity.

Today, Ponca women are still using their voices. At Joe Biden's inauguration, tribe elder Casey Camp-Horinek sent a letter to the new president, reminding him that the pact between the Ponca and the government included the language, "as long as the waters flow and the grass grows."

"PLIGHT OF THE PONCA INDIANS"

November 25, 1879
Faneuil Hall, Boston, Massachusetts

I have lived all my life, with the exception of two years, which I spent at school in New Jersey, among my own tribe, the Omahas, and I have had an opportunity, such as is accorded to but few, of hearing both sides of the "Indian question." I have at times felt bitterly toward the white race, yet were it not for some who have shown all kindness, generosity and sympathy toward one who had no claims on them but that of common humanity, I shudder to think what I would now have been. As it is my faith in justice and God has sometimes almost failed me but, I thank God, only almost.

It crushed our hearts when we saw a little handful of poor, ignorant, helpless, but peaceful people, such as the Poncas were, oppressed by a mighty nation, a nation so powerful that it could well have afforded to show justice and humanity if it only would. It was so hard to feel how powerless we were to help those we loved so dearly when we saw our relatives forced from their homes and compelled to go to a strange country at the point of the bayonet. The whole Ponca tribe were rapidly advancing in civilization; cultivated their farms, and their school houses and churches were well filled, when suddenly they were informed that the government required their removal to Indian Territory. My uncle said it came so suddenly upon them that they could not realize it at first, and they felt stunned and helpless. He also said if they had had any idea of what was coming, they might have successfully resisted; but as it was, it was carried rigidly beyond their control. Every objection they made was met by the word "soldier" and "bayonet." The Poncas had always been a peaceful tribe, and were not armed, and even if they had been they would rather not have fought. It was such a cowardly thing for the government to do! They sold the land which belonged to the Poncas to the Sioux, without the knowledge of the owners, and, as the Poncas were perfectly helpless and the Sioux well armed, the government was not afraid to move the friendly tribe.

The tribe has been robbed of thousands of dollars' worth of property, and the government shows no disposition to return what belongs to them. That property was lawfully theirs; they had worked for it; the annuities which were to be paid to them belonged to them. It was money promised by the government for land they had sold to the government I desire to say that all annuities paid to Indian tribes by the government are in payment for land sold by them to the government, and are not charity. The government never gave any alms to the Indians, and we all know that through the "kindness" of the "Indian ring" they do not get the half of what the government actually owes them. It seems to us sometimes that the government treats us with less consideration than it does even the dogs.

For the past hundred years the Indians have had none to tell the story of their wrongs. If a white man did an injury to an Indian he had to suffer in silence, or being exasperated into revenge, the act of revenge has been spread abroad through the newspapers of the land as a causeless act, perpetrated on the whites just because the Indian delighted in being savage. It is because I know that a majority of the whites have not known of the cruelty practiced by the "Indian ring" on a handful of oppressed, helpless and conquered people, that I have the courage and confidence to appeal to the people of the United States. I have said "A conquered people." I do not know that I have the right to say that. We are helpless, it is true; but at heart we do not feel that we are a conquered people. We are human beings; God made us as well as you; and we are peculiarly his because of our ignorance and helplessness. I seem to understand why Christ came upon the earth and wandered over it, homeless and hated of all men. It brings him so much nearer to us to feel that he has suffered as we suffer, and can understand it all — suffered that we might feel that we belonged to him and were his own.

I will relate a single instance out of many, given me by my father, who knows the individuals concerned in it. I do not select it because it exceeds in horrors others told me by my Indian friends, but because it happens to be freshest in my memory. My father said there was in the Pawnee tribe a warrior holding prominent position and respected by all the Indians. A white man was given the position on the reservation of government farmer for the Pawnee tribe. The Pawnees expected, of course, that he would go around among them and teach them how to plough and plant. Instead of doing that, he had fenced in a large piece of land, and had that sown and planted with grain and produce of all kinds. The Indians planted it and thought they would receive a part, at least, of the harvest. They never got any of it.

The warrior mentioned above was one day in the field killing the blackbirds which had alighted in the field in large numbers. While engaged in doing this the powder gave out. He went to the government farmer's house to ask for more. He saw a jeweled flask hanging up in the outside of the door, and as the farmer came to the door he pointed his gun to show that it was empty, and motioned to the flask to make known that he wanted some more powder. The government farmer shook his head and refused. The Indian, thinking he had misunderstood, raised his arm to take the flask to show him what he wanted. The government farmer, I suppose, thinking he, the Indian, intended to take the flask without his permission, raised a broadax lying on the ground, swung it in the air, and at one blow chopped the man's arm and cut into his side. The farmer then fled.

The Pawnee Indians gathered around the dying warrior, and were making preparations for war on the white people in revenge for the dead, but the dying man made them promise him that they would do nothing in return. He said, "I am dying, and when I am dead you cannot bring me back to life by killing others. The government will not listen to you, but will listen to the farmer and send its soldiers and kill many of you, and you will all suffer for my sake. Let me die in peace and know you will not have to suffer for me." They promised him, and none but the Indian people ever knew anything about it.

It is wrongs such as these which, accumulating, exasperate the Indians beyond endurance and prompt them to deeds of vengeance, which, to those who know only one side of the story, seem savage barbarism, and the Indians are looked upon with horror as beings whose thirst for blood is ever unslaked. I tell you we are human beings, who love and hate as you do. Our affections are as strong, if not stronger, than yours; stronger in that we are powerless to help each other, and can only suffer with each other.

Before the tribal relations were voluntarily broken up by the Omahas, my father was a chief. He helped make some of the treaties with the government. He had been acquainted with the last eighteen agents who have transacted the business for one tribe on the part of the government, and out of those eighteen agents four only were good and honest men.

The following instance will show how these agents squandered the money of the tribe: About four years ago one of them, without counselling the tribe, had a large handsome house built at a cost of about five thousand dollars, at the expense of the Omaha tribe. The building was intended by the agent, he said, for an infirmary, but he could not get any Indian to go into it, and it has never been used for anything since. It is of no use to the tribe, but it was a good job for the contractors. The tribe is now endeavoring to have it altered, to use it as a boarding school for the Indian children.

I have been intimately acquainted with the affairs of the Poncas. The Poncas and Omahas speak the same language and have always been friends, and thus I have known all their sorrows and troubles. Being an Indian, I, of course, have a deep interest in them. So many seem to think that Indians fight because they delight in being savage and are bloodthirsty. Let me relate one or two instances which serve to show how powerless we are to help ourselves. Some years ago an Omaha man was missed from one of our tribes. No one could tell what had become of him. Some of our people went to look for him. They found him in a pigpen, where he had been thrown to the hogs after having been killed by the white men.

Another time a man of our tribe went to a settlement about ten miles distant from our reserve to sell potatoes. While he stood sorting them out two young men came along. They were white men, and one of them had just arrived from the East; he said to his companion, "I should like to shoot that Indian, just to say that I had shot one." His companion badgered him to do it. He raised his revolver and shot him. Four weeks ago, just as we were starting on this trip, a young Indian boy of sixteen was stabbed by a white boy of thirteen. The stabbing took place near my house. The white people in the settlements around wondered that the Indian allowed the white boy to stab him, when he was so much older and stronger. It was because the Indian knew, as young as he was, that if he struck a blow to defend himself, and injured the boy in defending himself, the whole tribe would be punished for his act; that troops might be sent for a war made on the tribe. I think there was heroism in that boy's act. For wrongs like these we have no redress whatever. We have no protection from the law. The Indians all know that they are powerless. Their chiefs and leading men had been to Washington, and have returned to tell their people of the mighty nation which fill[s] the land once theirs. They know if they fight that they will be beaten, and they only fight when they are driven to desperation or are at the last extremity; and when they do at last fight, they have none to tell their side of the story, and it is given as a reason that they fight because they are bloodthirsty.

I have come to you to appeal for your sympathy and help for my people. They are immortal beings, for whom Christ died. They asked me to appeal to the churches, because they had heard that they were composed of God's people, and to the judges because they righted all wrongs. The people who were once owners of this soil ask you for their liberty, and law is liberty.

SARAH WINNEMUCCA

Sarah Winnemucca got her first stage experience in the 1860s, performing with her family as a traveling entertainment troupe, the Paiute Royal Family. She was the "Indian Princess."

White audiences loved the romanticized depiction of her tribe, the Northern Paiutes. For centuries they had lived a mostly nomadic existence living off small game and roots, seeds, and berries in modern day California, Nevada and Oregon.

Beginning in the 1840s, the Northern Paiutes came into contact with European-descended settlers. Winnemucca's grandfather, Chief Truckee, had welcomed the arrival of his "white brothers" and worked with them as a guide. But eventually it became clear the newcomers were competing with the Indigenous for scarce land and resources.

Because of her knowledge of English, Winnemucca worked for the Bureau of Indian Affairs as an interpreter between the two peoples. As she came to realize that her tribe was facing an existential threat, she became a vocal advocate for their rights, speaking and writing letters to newspapers, US Army generals, and the Bureau of Indian Affairs.

Sponsored by Boston's wealthy Peabody sisters — Elizabeth Palmer Peabody and Mary Peabody Mann — Winnemucca delivered nearly 300 speeches across New England. In April 1884, she testified before a Congressional subcommittee in Washington, DC.

Winnemucca portrayed a people in profound distress. She explained how, five years earlier, they had been forcibly marched 300 miles north from their traditional land, through the mountains, to a reservation in remote Washington Territory.

The Paiutes "were poor and had no clothing and no blankets and no buffalo robes," she said, "and nothing to make them warm, because we did not belong to a buffalo country. We took up our march and marched over drifting snow, my people carrying their little children." The ground was frozen stiff, she said, and "it was impossible to dig a hole to bury the infants who had frozen to death in their mothers' arms."

Winnemucca asked that her people be permanently resettled on land along the Nevada-Oregon border. That never happened.

She later wrote *Life Among the Paiutes: Their Wrongs and Claims* — a personal memoir and chronicle of her people and their initial contact with Anglo settlers.

Winnemucca and her brother also built a school for Indian children in Nevada to teach English and preserve the Paiute language and culture.

When her husband died and the school closed, she wrote: "I lost everything that was dear to me. Now only my book shall live on to tell the story of the Paiute people."

"TESTIMONY ON INDIAN AFFAIRS"

April 22, 1884
Subcommittee on Indian Affairs, Indian Affairs Committee
Room, US House of Representatives, Washington, DC

Chairman Robert W. S. Stevens: Please state, Winnemucca Hopkins, how it came that your people were dispossessed of this reservation? . . .

Mrs. Hopkins: My father had nothing. We never had guns issued to us like other tribes. We never received anything and had nothing to fight people with, and my people had to flee away upon the outbreak of Bannocks. The Bannocks took my people as prisoners and held them as prisoners until they would say they would fight the white people. I enlisted the United States troops and they went into the Bannock camp and rescued my people away in the night under orders of General [Oliver] Howard, and took them to Camp McDermot [Fort McDermit]. The campaign of course lasted all summer and then of course the Bannocks surrendered. They were going to be sent away to the fort where they belonged, awaiting orders, when late in the fall, in the month of November, I was given an instruction, that if I gathered all my people in Nevada, they were to go from Camp Harney back to this reservation. I did as I bargained, and I went from place to place throughout Nevada and I got five hundred of my people that were not within two hundred miles of Bannock Camp.

Chairman Stevens: Who gave you that order?

Mrs. Hopkins: The President sent the order to Major Cochrane, United States Army Officer at Camp Harney.

Chairman Stevens: What was the name of that agent, who was the brother-in-law of a Judge in Oregon?

Mrs. Hopkins: I think you must all be acquainted with it, Mr. [William V.] Rinehart. So I gathered my people there and in December when I got them there at Camp Harney, under military care, I expected every day to have my people go back under the permission of a new agent, and go on making our homes the same as before. But here came an order from the President to take all the five hundred Paiutes under you care there and take them across the Blue Mountains, and across the Columbia River, to Yakima Reservation.

This order came in December. Imagine what a severe winter it is out there at that time. They could not disobey the order although everything was said that could be in our [defense?]. But we took up the march, and the soldiers had good buffalo shoes and buffalo robes and prepared for their comfort, and here were my people. They were poor and had no clothing and no blankets and no buffalo robes, and nothing to make them warm, because we did not belong to a buffalo country. We took up our march and marched over drifting snow, my people carrying their little children. Well it took us a good while. Some times after we camped here and there, something was coming come along making a great noise. Some white people would mimic and mock them. Women would be coming along crying, and it was not because they were cold, for they were used to the cold. It was not because they were sick, for they suffered a great deal. The woman was crying because she also was carrying her little frozen child in her arms, and of course the soldiers never could stop, and they would dig into the snow as deep as over your head, to dig a grave, and even if they wanted to dig a grave they could not, and the only way the mother could do was to stop off onto one side and dig out a little hole and stick her little frozen child under the snow.

This was the way my people marched three hundred miles, and the dear little children strung along side of the road frozen to death for nothing but to punish us for all those thirty that went off with the Bannocks. Sometimes a wagon would be left behind too late to get in on account of the snow storm and an old man would be left in the wagon and when we would go back next day to get the wagon he would be found frozen to death.

My people's dead bodies were strung all along the road across the Columbia River to this Yakima Reservation. When we got there we were turned over to another man, and then after we got there we died off like a lot of beasts, and of course then the following winter I came right here to Washington. I began to lecture about it in San Fransisco [sic], and they sent for me and my father, the President did. We came on here and I pleaded — at least my father did — and of course my father asked for that same reservation back again. Says he I did not do anything. He said my people did not do anything. He said that our people had saved the lives of white people, and were now scattered everywhere and why should my people be punished like that. He asked them to give it back to us, which they did, and I will show you how I got it.

I got the reservation. I got 100 acres for each head of a family to work on and to live on, and I got it all back and I went home with my father. We could not sleep at night, we were so happy. We were happy [illegible] . . . we had gained the whole world when we were taking back these beautiful things to make our people happy again. I got it and took it home and carried it from place to place.

It has never been fulfilled, it is there on that paper, and I was also appointed as interpreter for my people at the same time, for whom I strived, but never got a penny for it. This is the way we are trifled with. On account of that people I would not come back and plead, because I had lost confidence and I come pleading to you, to the people, trying to interest the people in this thing and have the people give me a home. That is why I am pleading and begging from place to place and have been for a year and three months. Now my people say it is useless for me to ask for that Reservation back, and they say they would like to take anything you will give them and they will take this Camp McDermot, although Camp McDermot is worthless.

[Illegible] . . . thing has been said in behalf of my people returning; even the army officers have interceded for my people and told their testimony that the people they were keeping as prisoners had done nothing, had not raised an arm against anybody and it was a shame that they should be treated so. yet, it was not listened to and they were held there long enough, three years or four years open the reservation called the Malheur; and today I should not wonder if any of you were to go on that reservation that you would find that Judge Curry and Mr. Rinehart had got a good portion of that reservation.

So you see they could not get back. How could any one get back to any place where they wanted to go and were not permitted to go while the lion was lying there with his mouth open ready to shut his teeth down upon them if they made the attempt. But they did not care after they had thrown their reservation open; they let them go back the best way they could last spring and now they are at camp McDermot. Judge Pennyfield writes to my friends in Boston Mrs. Horace Mann and Miss Peabody that my people were really in need of food and of clothing, and those two ladies have interested their friends so they have sent out there first 13 barrels of clothes, and this last week they sent out five more to relieve these poor people that are naked and in want.

So we have no reservation, no home and now I ask you for my people to restore us and put us I do not care where as long as it is in our own home, in the home where we were born, and that is all.

Mr. George: Where was your original home?

Mrs. Hopkins: All through that portion of the Dalles was our country long ago before we were disturbed.

Mr. George: Tell the committee how far Camp McDermot is from your original home?

Mrs. Hopkins: It is two hundred and odd miles from the one we lost and the Malheur or south of it and eighty miles from Winnemucca station in Nevada north.

Mr. George: Would all this land you are asking for be in the northern part of Nevada?

Mrs. Hopkins: Yes.

Chairman Stevens: You say that you do not care to go back to the Malheur reservation because that is already occupied by white people?

Mrs. Hopkins: My people say it is useless for them to apply for this reservation because they well know that no reservation that is worth anything has ever been restored to Indians anywhere. But send them to Camp McDermot or Humboldt or along Humboldt River or any such place . . .

ELIZABETH CADY STANTON

In 1892 Elizabeth Cady Stanton traveled to Washington, DC, to deliver her final suffrage speech. She was 76. Age and infirmity made travel — even standing up for any length of time at the podium — a challenge.

But her speech that day is widely acknowledged as her finest.

Stanton had enthusiastically taken up social reform as a young woman in upstate New York, and abolition was her first cause. She and her husband traveled on their honeymoon in 1840 to an anti-slavery convention in London, where she was offended by the treatment of Lucretia Mott and the other women delegates who were forced to sit in silence in the gallery.

It was that first encounter between Stanton and Mott, a meeting of minds, that led to the historic Seneca Falls convention eight years later.

Susan B. Anthony entered the story when she traveled to Seneca Falls in 1851 and was introduced to Stanton. Friends and allies in the fight for suffrage, Stanton and Anthony worked side by side for nearly half a century, crisscrossing the country, writing, strategizing, and giving hundreds of speeches. Often criticized for working with Southerners who were racist, Stanton and Anthony in reality had little choice if they were to win the cause.

America was a completely segregated society. Racism was woven into the fabric of the nation, and Southerners were dead set against changing their way of life. Resolutely racist White men, whose votes the suffragists needed, held all the power in key state legislatures, and in Congress.

Back in 1848, when Stanton originally wanted to include women's enfranchisement in the Declaration of Sentiments, many considered it to a step too far. Eventually suffrage became the focus of women's rights advocates. But to Stanton it was always just one piece of a larger, far more encompassing and radical vision.

That vision was what she returned to in "Solitude of Self." By then, she was no longer involved in day-to-day operations of the movement. With no vote for women in sight, she was bone weary and discouraged, and searching for a philosophical way to sum up her thoughts.

Her speech, delivered to a Congressional committee and to a suffrage gathering, was no rousing call to action. It offered no strategy or road map. Instead, Stanton argued for suffrage as part of the complete independence of women, including self development, self governance, and the ability to define themselves on their own uncompromising terms.

Ultimately, she said, each woman must have the means to take responsibility for herself "because of her birthright to self-sovereignty; because, as an individual, she must rely on herself."

"SOLITUDE OF SELF"

January 18, 1892
Judiciary Committee, US House of Representatives, Washington, DC

Mr. Chairman and gentlemen of the committee:

We have been speaking before Committees of the Judiciary for the last twenty years, and we have gone over all the arguments in favor of a sixteenth amendment which are familiar to all you gentlemen; therefore, it will not be necessary that I should repeat them again.

The point I wish plainly to bring before you on this occasion is the individuality of each human soul . . .

The isolation of every human soul and the necessity of self-dependence must give each individual the right, to choose his own surroundings.

The strongest reason for giving woman all the opportunities for higher education, for the full development of her faculties, forces of mind and body; for giving her the most enlarged freedom of thought and action; a complete emancipation from all forms of bondage, of custom, dependence, superstition; from all the crippling influences of fear, is the solitude and personal responsibility of her own individual life. The strongest reason why we ask for woman a voice in the government under which she lives; in the religion she is asked to believe; equality in social life, where she is the chief factor; a place in the trades and professions, where she may earn her bread, is because of her birthright to self-sovereignty; because, as an individual, she must rely on herself. No matter how much women prefer to lean, to be protected and supported, nor how much men desire to have them do so, they must make the voyage of life alone, and for safety in an emergency they must know something of the laws of navigation. To guide our own craft, we must be captain, pilot, engineer; with chart and compass to stand at the wheel; to match the wind and waves and know when to take in the sail, and to read the signs in the firmament over all. It matters not whether the solitary voyager is man or woman; nature having endowed them equally, leaves them to their own skill and judgment in the hour of danger, and, if not equal to the occasion, alike they perish.

To appreciate the importance of fitting every human soul for independent action, think for a moment of the immeasurable solitude of self. We come into the world alone, unlike all who have gone before us; we leave it alone under circumstances peculiar to ourselves. No mortal ever has been, no mortal ever will be like the soul just launched on the sea of life. There can never again be just such environments as make up the infancy, youth and manhood of this one. Nature never repeats herself, and the possibilities of one human soul will never be found in another. No one has ever found two blades of ribbon grass alike, and no one will ever find two human beings alike. Seeing, then, what must be the infinite diversity in human character, we can in a measure appreciate the loss to a nation when any large class of the people is uneducated and unrepresented in the government.

We ask for the complete development of every individual, first, for his own benefit and happiness. In fitting out an army we give each soldier his own knapsack, arms, powder, his blanket, cup, knife, fork and spoon. We provide alike for all their individual necessities, then each man bears his own burden . . .

In youth our most bitter disappointments, our brightest hopes and ambitions are known only to ourselves, even our friendship and love we never fully share with another; there is something of every passion in every situation we conceal. Even so in our triumphs and our defeats. The successful candidate for Presidency and his opponent each have a solitude peculiarly his own, and good form forbids either in speak of his pleasure or regret. The solitude of the king on his throne and the prisoner in his cell differs in character and degree, but it is solitude nevertheless.

We ask no sympathy from others in the anxiety and agony of a broken friendship or shattered love. When death sunders our nearest ties, alone we sit in the shadows of our affliction. Alike amid the greatest triumphs and darkest tragedies of life we walk alone. On the divine heights of human attainments, eulogized land worshiped as a hero or saint, we stand alone. In ignorance, poverty, and vice, as a pauper or criminal, alone we starve or steal; alone we suffer the sneers and rebuffs of our fellows; alone we are hunted and hounded thro dark courts and alleys, in by-ways and highways; alone we stand in the judgment seat; alone in the prison cell we lament our crimes and misfortunes; alone we expiate them on the gallows. In hours like these we realize the awful solitude of individual life, its pains, its penalties, its responsibilities; hours in which the youngest and most helpless are thrown on their own resources for guidance and consolation. Seeing then that life must ever be a march and a battle, that each soldier must be equipped for his own protection, it is the height of cruelty to rob the individual of a single natural right.

To throw obstacles in the way of a complete education is like putting out the eyes; to deny the rights of property, like cutting off the hands. To deny political equality is to rob the ostracized of all self-respect; of credit in the market place; of recompense in the world of work; of a voice among those who make and administer the law; a choice in the jury before whom they are tried, and in the judge who decides their punishment. Shakespeare's play of "Titus and Andronicus" contains a terrible satire on woman's position in the nineteenth century. Rude men (the play tells us) seized the king's daughter, cut out her tongue, cut off her hands, and then bade her go call for water and wash her hands." What a picture of woman's position. Robbed of her natural rights, handicapped by law and custom at every turn, yet compelled to fight her own battles, and in the emergencies of life to fall back on herself for protection.

The girl of sixteen, thrown on the world to support herself, to make her own place in society, to resist the temptations that surround her and maintain a spotless integrity, must do all this by native force or superior education. She does not acquire this power by being trained to trust others and distrust herself. If she wearies of the struggle, finding it hard work to swim upstream, and allow herself to drift with the current, she will find plenty of company, but not one to share her misery in the hour of her deepest humiliation. If she tries to retrieve her position, to conceal the past, her life is hedged about with fears lest willing hands should tear the veil from what she fain would hide. Young and friendless, *she* knows the bitter solitude of self.

How the little courtesies of life on the surface of society, deemed so important from man towards woman, fade into utter insignificance in view of the deeper tragedies in which she must play her part alone, where no human aid is possible?

The young wife and mother, at the head of some establishment with a kind husband to shield her from the adverse winds of life, with wealth, fortune and position, has a certain harbor of safety, secure against the ordinary ills of life. But to manage a household, have a desirable influence in society, keep her friends and the affections of her husband, train her children and servants well, she must have rare common sense, wisdom, diplomacy, and a knowledge of human nature. To do all this she needs the cardinal virtues and the strong points of character that the most successful stateman possesses. An uneducated woman, trained to dependence, with no resources in herself must make a failure of any position in life. But society says women do not need a knowledge of the world, the liberal training that experience in public life must give, all the advantages of collegiate education; but when for the lack of all this, the woman's happiness is wrecked, alone she bears her humiliation; and the attitude of the weak and the ignorant is indeed pitiful in the wild chase for the price of life they are ground to powder.

In age, when the pleasures of youth are passed, children grown up, married and gone, the hurry and hustle of life in a measure over, when the hands are weary of active service, when the old armchair and the fireside are the chosen resorts, then men and women alike must fall back on their own resources. If they cannot find companionship in books, if they have no interest in the vital questions of the hour, no interest in watching the consummation of reforms, with which they might have been identified, they soon pass into their dotage.

The more fully the faculties of the mind are developed and kept in use, the longer the period of vigor and active interest in all around us continues. If from a lifelong participation in public affairs a woman feels responsible for the laws regulating our system of education, the discipline of our jails and prisons, the sanitary conditions of our private homes, public buildings, and thoroughfares, an interest in commerce, finance, our foreign relations, in any or all of these questions, here solitude will at least be respectable, and she will not be driven to gossip or scandal for entertainment.

The chief reason for opening to every soul the doors to the whole round of human duties and pleasures is the individual development thus attained, the resources thus provided under all circumstances to mitigate the solitude that at times must come to everyone. I once asked Prince Krapotkin, the Russian nihilist, how he endured his long years in prison, deprived of books, pen, ink, and paper. "Ah," he said, "I thought out many questions in which I had a deep interest. In the pursuit of an idea I took no note of time. When tired of solving knotty problems I recited all the beautiful passages in prose or verse I have ever learned. I became acquainted with myself and my own resources. I had a world of my own, a vast empire, that no Russian jailor or Czar could invade." Such is the value of liberal thought and broad culture when shut off from all human companionship, bringing comfort and sunshine within even the four walls of a prison cell.

As women ofttimes share a similar fate, should they not have all the consolation that the most liberal education can give? Their suffering in the prisons of St. Petersburg; in the long, weary marches to Siberia, and in the mines, working side by side with men, surely call for all the self-support that the most exalted sentiments of heroism can give. When suddenly roused at midnight, with the startling cry of "fire! fire!" to find the house over their heads in flames, do women wait for men to point the way to safety? And are the men, equally bewildered and half suffocated with smoke, in a position to more than try to save themselves? At such times the most timid women have shown a courage and heroism in saving their husbands and children that has surprise everybody. Inasmuch, then, as woman shares equally the joys and sorrows of time and eternity, is it not the height of presumption in man to propose to represent her at the ballot box and the throne of grace, do her voting in the state, her praying in the church, and to assume the position of priest at the family altar?

Nothing strengthens the judgment and quickens the conscience like individual responsibility. Nothing adds such dignity to character as the recognition of one's self-sovereignty; the right to an equal place, everywhere conceded; a place earned by personal merit, not an artificial attainment, by inheritance, wealth, family, and position. Seeing, then that the responsibilities of life rests equally on man and woman, that their destiny is the same, they need the same preparation for time and eternity. The talk of sheltering woman from the fierce storms of life is the sheerest mockery, for they beat on her from every point of the compass, just as they do on man, and with more fatal results, for he has been trained to protect himself, to resist, to conquer. Such are the facts in human experience, the responsibilities of individual sovereignty. Rich and poor, intelligent and ignorant, wise and foolish, virtuous and vicious, man and woman, it is ever the same, each soul must depend wholly on itself.

Whatever the theories may be of woman's dependence on man, in the supreme moments of her life he cannot bear her burdens. Alone she goes to the gates of death to give life to every man that is born into the world; no one can share her fears, on one can mitigate her pangs; and if her sorrow is greater than she can bear, alone she passes beyond the gates into the vast unknown.

From the mountain-tops of Judea, long ago, a heavenly voice bade His disciples, "Bear ye one another's burdens," but humanity has not yet risen to that point of self-sacrifice, and if ever so willing, how few the burdens are that one soul can bear for another. In the highways of Palestine; in prayer and fasting on the solitary mountain top; in the Garden of Gethsemane; before the judgment seat of Pilate; betrayed by one of His trusted disciples at His last supper; in His agonies on the cross, even Jesus of Nazareth, in these last sad days on earth, felt the awful solitude of self. Deserted by man, in agony he cries, "My God! My God! why hast Thou forsaken me?" And so it ever must be in the conflicting scenes of life, on the long weary march, each one walks alone. We may have many friends, love, kindness, sympathy and charity to smooth our pathway in everyday life, but in the tragedies and triumphs of human experience, each mortal stands alone.

But when all artificial trammels are removed, and women are recognized as individuals, responsible for their own environments, thoroughly educated for all the positions in life they may be called to fill; with all the resources in themselves that liberal thought and broad culture can give; guided by their own conscience an judgment; trained to self-protection by a healthy development of the muscular system and skill in the use of weapons of defense, and stimulated to self-support by the knowledge of the business world and the pleasure that pecuniary independence must ever give; when women are trained in this way they will, in a measure, be fitted for those hours of solitude that come alike to all, whether prepared or otherwise. As in our extremity we must depend on ourselves, the dictates of wisdom point to complete individual development.

In talking of education how shallow the argument that each class must be educated for the special work it proposed to do, and all those faculties not needed in this special walk must lie dormant and utterly wither for want of use, when, perhaps, these will be the very faculties needed in life's greatest [emergencies]. Some say, Where is the use of drilling girls in the languages, the sciences, in law, medicine, theology? As wives, mothers, housekeepers, cooks, they need a different curriculum from boys who are to fill all positions. The chief cooks in our great hotels and ocean steamers are men. In large cities men run the bakeries; they make our bread, cake and pies. They manage the laundries; they are now considered our best milliners and dressmakers. Because some men fill these departments of usefulness, shall we regulate the curriculum in Harvard and Yale to their present necessities? If not why this talk in our best colleges of a curriculum for girls who are crowding into the trades and professions; teachers in all our public schools rapidly filling many lucrative and honorable positions in life?

They are showing too, their calmness and courage in the most trying hours of human experience. You have probably all read in the daily papers of the terrible storm in the Bay of Biscay when a tidal wave made such havoc on the shore, wrecking vessels, unroofing houses and carrying destruction everywhere. Among other buildings the woman's prison was demolished. Those who escaped saw men struggling to reach the shore. They promptly by clasping hands made a chain of themselves and pushed out into the sea, again and again, at the risk of their lives until they had brought six men to shore, carried them to a shelter, and did all in their power for their comfort and protection.

What special school training could have prepared these women for this sublime moment of their lives? In times like this, humanity rises above all college curriculums and recognizes Nature as the greatest of all teachers in the hour of danger and death. Women are already the equals of men in the whole of realm of thought, in art, science, literature, and government. With telescope vision they explore the starry firmament, and bring back the history of the planetary world. With chart and compass they pilot ships across the mighty deep, and with skillful finger send electric messages around the globe. In galleries of art the beauties of nature and the virtues of humanity are immortalized by them on their canvas and by their inspired touch dull blocks of marble are transformed into angels of light. In music they speak again the language of Mendelssohn, Beethoven, Chopin, Schumann, and are worthy interpreters of their great thoughts. The poetry and novels of the century are theirs, and they have touched the keynote of reform in religion, politics, and social life. They fill the editor's and professor's chair, and plead at the bar of justice, walk the wards of the hospital, and speak from the pulpit and the platform; such is the type of womanhood that an enlightened public sentiment welcomes today, and such the triumph of the facts of life over the false theories of the past.

Is it, then, consistent to hold the developed woman of this day within the same narrow political limits as the dame with the spinning wheel and knitting needle occupied in the past? No! no! Machinery has taken the labors of woman as well as man on its tireless shoulders; the loom and the spinning wheel are but dreams of the past; the pen, the brush, the easel, the chisel, have taken their places, while the hopes and ambitions of women are essentially changed.

We see reason sufficient in the outer conditions of human beings for individual liberty and development, but when we consider the self dependence of every human soul we see the need of courage, judgment, and the exercise of every faculty of mind and body, strengthened and developed by use, in woman as well as man.

Whatever may be said of man's protecting power in ordinary conditions, mid all the terrible disasters by land and sea, in the supreme moments of danger, alone, woman must ever meet the horrors of the situation; the Angel of Death even makes no royal pathway for her. Man's love and sympathy enter only into the sunshine of our lives. In that solemn solitude of self, that links us with the immeasurable and the eternal, each soul lives alone forever. A recent writer says:

> *I remember once, in crossing the Atlantic, to have gone upon the deck of the ship at midnight, when a dense black cloud enveloped the sky, and the great deep was roaring madly under the lashes of demoniac winds. My feelings was not of danger or fear (which is a base surrender of the immortal soul), but of utter desolation and loneliness; a little speck of life shut in by a tremendous darkness. Again I remember to have climbed the slopes of the Swiss Alps, up beyond the point where vegetation ceases, and the stunted conifers no longer struggle against the unfeeling blasts. Around me lay a huge confusion of rocks, out of which the gigantic ice peaks shot into the measureless blue of the heavens, and again my only feeling was the awful solitude!*

> *And yet, there is a solitude, which each and every one of us has always carried with him, more inaccessible than the ice-cold mountains, more profound than the midnight sea; the solitude of self. Our inner being, which we call ourself, no eye nor touch of man or angel has ever pierced. It is more hidden than the caves of the gnome; the sacred adytum of the oracle; the hidden chamber of Eleusinian mystery, for to it only omniscience is permitted to enter.*

Such is individual life. Who, I ask you, can take, dare take on himself the rights, the duties, the responsibilities of another human soul?

IDA B. WELLS

Born into slavery, journalist Ida B. Wells grew up in the South and intended to stay there, believing that with rising wealth and education, thrift, and economy — the doctrine of self help — Blacks would be accepted into the wider American culture.

But everything changed for her in March 1892, when a fight outside a store in a Memphis neighborhood known as "the Curve" led to the wounding of two White police officers.

Three Black men were arrested, including her close friend, Tom Moss. While in police custody, the men were tortured, and as Wells put it, "found in an old field horribly shot to pieces."

In a 1893 speech at Boston's Tremont Temple, Wells did not spare her audience the wrenching details. Moss, she said, had "begged for his life, for the sake of his wife, his little daughter and his unborn infant." His last word to his tormenters were: "If you will kill us, turn our faces to the West."

As Wells put it: "I have no power to describe the feeling of horror that possessed every member of the race in Memphis when the truth dawned upon us that the protection of the law which we had so long enjoyed was no longer ours; all had been destroyed in a night."

Death threats in the wake of those events drove Wells to Chicago, where she made her life's mission the campaign against lynching — essentially, mob-driven murder of individuals with no due process of law. She investigated dozens of abhorrent cases, conducted countless interviews, collected data, and used her own insubstantial funds to publish her findings.

She also wrote and spoke bluntly about "that old threadbare lie that Negro men rape White women" as a would-be justification for lynching.

An impassioned speaker, she made her case at large conferences, in meeting halls, and in modest churches, helping turn the tide against the atrocity of lynching with her words.

It was an uphill battle. She endured harassment and financial hardship. Most of her editorials and articles were published in the Black-owned press, and only occasionally picked up by mainstream publications.

In 1898, she went to the White House to plead with President William McKinley for federal response to a lynching in South Carolina, and for compensation for the victim's widow and children. She told him that in the previous twenty years, some ten thousand Black citizens had been lynched in America.

Wells passed away in 1931. At the National Museum of African American History and Culture in Washington, DC, one of her most enduring lines is emblazoned on the wall: "The way to right wrongs is to turn the light of truth on them."

"LYNCH LAW IN ALL ITS PHASES"

February 13, 1893
Tremont Temple, Boston, Massachusetts

I am before the American people today through no inclination of my own, but because of a deep seated conviction that the country at large does not know the extent to which lynch law prevails in parts of the Republic nor the conditions which force into exile those who speak the truth. I cannot believe that the apathy and indifference which so largely obtains regarding mob rule is other than the result of ignorance of the true situation. And yet, the observing and thoughtful must know that in one section, at least, of our common country, a government of the people, by the people, and for the people, means a government by the mob; where the land of the free and home of the brave means a land of lawlessness, murder and outrage; and where liberty of speech means the license of might to destroy the business and drive from home those who exercise this privilege contrary to the will of the mob. Repeated attacks on the life, liberty and happiness of any citizen or class of citizens are attacks on distinctive American institutions; such attacks imperiling as they do the foundation of government, law and order, merit the thoughtful consideration of far sighted Americans; not from a standpoint of sentiment, not even so much from a standpoint of justice to a weak race, as from a desire to preserve our institutions.

The race problem or negro question, as it has been called, has been omnipresent and all pervading since long before the Afro-American was raised from the degradation of the slave to the dignity of the citizen. It has never been settled because the right methods have not been employed in the solution. It is the Banquo's ghost of politics, religion, and sociology which will not down at the bidding of those who are tormented with its ubiquitous appearance on every occasion. Times without number, since invested with citizenship, the race has been indicted for ignorance, immorality and general worthlessness declared guilty and executed by its self constituted judges. The operations of law do not dispose of negroes fast enough, and lynching bees have become the favorite pastime of the South. As excuse for the same, a new cry, as false as it is foul, is raised in an effort to blast race character, a cry which has proclaimed to the world that virtue and innocence are violated by Afro-Americans who must be killed like wild beasts to protect womanhood and childhood.

Born and reared in the South, I had never expected to live elsewhere. Until this past year I was one among those who believed the condition of masses gave large excuse for the humiliations and proscriptions under which we labored; that when wealth, education and character became more general among us, the cause being removed the effect would cease, and justice being accorded to all alike. I shared the general belief that good newspapers entering regularly the homes of our people in every state could do more to bring about this result than any agency. Preaching the doctrine of self help, thrift and economy every week, they would be the teachers to those who had been deprived of school advantages, yet were making history every day and train to think for themselves our mental children of a larger growth. And so, three years ago last June, I became editor and part owner of the Memphis *Free Speech*. As editor, I had occasion to criticize the city School Board's employment of inefficient teachers and poor school buildings for Afro-American children. I was in the employ of that board at the time, and at the close of that school term one year ago, was not re elected to a position I had held in the city schools for seven years. Accepting the decision of the Board of Education, I set out to make a race newspaper pay a thing which older and wiser heads said could not be done. But there were enough of our people in Memphis and surrounding territory to support a paper, and I believed they would do so. With nine months hard work the circulation increased from 1,500 to 3,500; in twelve months it was on a good paying basis. Throughout the Mississippi Valley in Arkansas, Tennessee and Mississippi on plantations and in towns, the demand for and interest in the paper increased among the masses. The newsboys who would not sell it on the trains, voluntarily testified that they had never known colored people to demand a paper so eagerly.

To make the paper a paying business I became advertising agent, solicitor, as well as editor, and was continually on the go. Wherever I went among the people, I gave them in church, school, public gatherings, and home, the benefit of my honest conviction that maintenance of character, money getting and education would finally solve our problem and that it depended us to say how soon this would be brought about. This sentiment bore good fruit in Memphis. We had nice homes, representatives in almost every branch of business and profession, and refined society. We had learned helping each other helped all, and every well conducted business by Afro-Americans prospered. With all our proscription in theatres, hotels and railroads, we had never had a lynching and did not believe we could have one. There had been lynchings and brutal outrages of all sorts in our state and those adjoining us, but we had confidence and pride in our city and the majesty of its laws. So far in advance of other Southern cities was ours, we were content to endure the evils we had, to labor and to wait.

But there was a rude awakening. On the morning of March 9, the bodies of three of our best young men were found in an old field horribly shot to pieces. These young men had owned and operated the "People's Grocery," situated at what was known as the Curve, a suburb made up almost entirely of colored people about a mile from city limits. Thomas Moss, one of the oldest letter carriers in the city, was president of the company, Cal McDowell was manager and Will Stewart was a clerk. There were about ten other stockholders, all colored men. The young men were well known and popular and their business flourished, and that of Barrett, a white grocer who kept store there before the "People's Grocery" was established, went down. One day an officer came to the "People's Grocery" and inquired for a colored man who lived in the neighborhood, and for whom the officer had a warrant. Barrett was with him and when McDowell said he knew nothing as to the whereabouts of the man for whom they were searching, Barrett, not the officer, then accused McDowell of harboring the man, and McDowell gave the lie. Barrett drew his pistol and struck McDowell with it; thereupon McDowell who was a tall, fine looking six footer, took Barrett's pistol from him, knocked him down and gave him a good thrashing, while Will Stewart, the clerk, kept the special officer at bay. Barrett went to town, swore out a warrant for their arrest on a charge of assault and battery. McDowell went before the Criminal Court, immediately gave bond and returned to his store. Barrett then threatened (to use his own words) that he was going to clean out the whole store. Knowing how anxious he was to destroy their business, these young men consulted a lawyer who told them they were justified in defending themselves if attacked, as they were a mile beyond city limits and police protection. They accordingly armed several of their friends not to assail, but to resist the threatened Saturday night attack.

When they saw Barrett enter the front door and a half dozen men at the rear door at 11 o'clock that night, they supposed the attack was on and immediately fired into the crowd, wounding three men. These men, dressed in citizen's clothes, turned out to be deputies who claimed to be hunting for another man for whom they had a warrant, and whom any one of them could have arrested without trouble. When these men found they had fired upon officer of the law, they threw away their firearms and submitted to arrest, confident they should establish their innocence of intent to fire upon officers of the law. The daily papers in flaming headlines roused the evil passions of whites, denounced these poor boys in unmeasured terms, nor permitted a word in their own defense.

The neighborhood of the Curve was searched next day, and about thirty persons were thrown into jail, charged with conspiracy. No communication was to be had with friends any of the three days these men were in jail; bail was refused and Thomas Moss was not allowed to eat the food his wife prepared for him. The judge is reported to have said, "Any one can see them after three days." They were seen after three days, but they were no longer able to respond to the greetings of friends. On Tuesday following the shootings at the grocery, the papers which had made much of the sufferings of the wounded deputies, and promised it would go hard with those who did the shooting, if they died, announced that the officers were all out of danger, and would recover. The friends of the prisoners breathed more easily and relaxed their vigilance. They felt that as the officers would not die, there was no danger that in the heat of passion the prisoners would meet violent death at hands of the mob. Besides, we had such confidence in the law. But the law did not provide capital punishment for shooting which did not kill. So the mob did what the law could not be made to do, as a lesson to the Afro-American that he must not shoot a white man, no matter what the provocation. The same night after the announcement was made in the papers that thee officers would get well, the mob, in obedience to a plan known to every eminent white man in the city, went to the jail between two and three in the morning, dragged out these young men, hatless and shoeless, put them on the yard engine of the railroad which was in waiting just behind the jail, carried them a mile north of the city limits and horribly shot them to death while the locomotive at a given signal let off steam and blew the whistle to deaden the sound of the firing.

"It was done by unknown men," said the jury, yet the Appeal Avalanche which goes to press at 3 a.m., had a two column account of the lynching. The papers also told how McDowell got hold of the guns of the mob and as his grasp could not be loosened, his hand was shattered with a pistol ball and all the lower part of his face was torn away. There were four pools of blood found and only three bodies. It was whispered that he, McDowell killed one of the lynchers with his gun, and it is well known that a police man who was seen on the street a few days previous to the lynching, died very suddenly the next day after.

"It was done by unknown parties," said the jury, yet the papers told how Tom Moss begged for his life, for the sake of his wife, his little daughter and his unborn infant. They also told us that his last words were, "If you will kill us, turn our faces to the West."

All this we learn too late to save these men, even if the law had not be in the hands of their murderers. When the colored people realized that the flower of our young manhood had been stolen away at night and murdered there was a rush for firearms to avenge the wrong, but no house would sell a colored man a gun; the armory of the Tennessee Rifles, our only colored military company, and of which McDowell was a member, was broken into by order of the Criminal Court judge, and its guns taken. One hundred men and irresponsible boys from fifteen years and up were armed by order of authorities and rushed out to the Curve, where it was reported that the colored people were massing, and at point of the bayonet dispersed these men who could do nothing but talk. The cigars, wines, etc., of the grocery stock were freely used by the mob, who possessed the place on pretence of dispersing the conspiracy. The money drawer was broken into and contents taken. The trunk of Calvin McDowell, who had a room in the store, was broken open, and his clothing, which was not good enough to take away, was throw out and trampled on the floor.

These men were murdered, their stock was attached by creditors and sold for less than one eighth of its cost to that same man Barrett, who is to day running his grocery in the same place. He had indeed kept his word, and by aid of the authorities destroyed the People's Grocery Company root and branch. The relatives of Will Stewart and Calvin McDowell are bereft of their protectors. The baby daughter of Tom Moss, too young to express how she misses her father, toddles to the wardrobe, seizes the legs of the trousers of his letter carrier uniform, hugs and kisses them with evident delight and stretches up her little hands to be taken up into the arms which will nevermore clasp his daughter's form. His wife holds Thomas Moss, Jr., in her arms, upon whose unconscious baby face the tears fall thick and fast when she is thinking of the sad fate of the father he will never see, and of the two helpless children who cling to her for the support she cannot give. Although these men were peaceable, law abiding citizens of this country, we are told there can be no punishment for their murderers nor indemnity for relatives.

I have no power to describe the feeling of horror that possessed every member of the race in Memphis when the truth dawned upon us that the protection of the law which we had so long enjoyed was no longer ours; all had been destroyed in a night, and the barriers of the law had been down, and the guardians of the public peace and confidence scoffed into the shadows, and all authority given into the hands of the mob, and innocent men cut down as if they were brutes the first feeling was one dismay, then intense indignation. Vengeance was whispered from ear to ear, but sober reflection brought the conviction that it would be extreme folly to seek vengeance when such action meant certain death for the men, and horrible slaughter for the women and children, as one of the evening papers took care to remind us. The power of the State, country and city, and civil authorities and the strong arm of the military power were all on the side of the mob and of lawlessness. Few of our men possessed firearms, our only company's guns were confiscated, and the only white man who sell a colored man a gun, was himself jailed, and his store closed. We were helpless in our great strength. It was our first object lesson in the doctrine of white supremacy; an illustration of the South's cardinal principle no matter what the attainments, character or standing of an Afro-American, the laws of the South will not protect him against a white man.

There was only one thing we could do, and a great determination seized the people to follow the advice of the martyred Moss, and "turn our faces to the

West," whose laws protect all alike. The *Free Speech* supported ministers and leading business men advised the people to leave a community whose laws did not protect them. Hundreds left on foot to walk four hundred miles between Memphis and Oklahoma. A Baptist minister went to the territory, built a church, and took his entire congregation out in less than a month. Another minister sold his church and took his flock to California, and still another has settled in Kansas. In two months, six thousand persons had left the city and every branch of business began to feel this silent resentment of the outrage, and failure of the authorities to punish lynchers. There were a number of business failures and blocks of houses for rent. The superintendent and treasurer of the street railway company called at the office of the *Free Speech*, to have us urge the colored people again on the street cars. A real estate dealer said to a colored man who returned some property he had been buying on the installment plan: "I see what you 'niggers' are cutting up about. You got off light. We first intend to kill every one of those thirty one niggers' in jail, but concluded to let all go but the 'leaders.'" They did let all go to the penitentiary. These so-called rioters have since been tried in the Criminal Court for the conspiracy of defending their property, and are now serving terms of three, eight, and fifteen years each in the Tennessee State prison.

To restore the equilibrium and put a stop to the great financial loss, the next move was to get rid of the *Free Speech*, the disturbing element which kept the waters troubled; which would not let the people forget, and in obedience to whose advice nearly six thousand persons had left the city. In casting about for an excuse, the mob found it in the following editorial which appeared in the Memphis *Free Speech*, May 21, 1892: "Eight negroes lynched at Little Rock, Ark., where the citizens broke into the penitentiary and got their man; three near Anniston, Ala., and one in New Orleans, all on the same charge, the new alarm of assaulting white women and near Clarksville, Ga., for killing a white man. The same program of hanging then shooting bullets into the lifeless bodies was carried out to the letter. Nobody in this section of the country believes the old threadbare lie that negro men rape white women. If Southern white men are not careful they will overreach themselves, and public sentiment will have a reaction. A conclusion will then be reached which will be very damaging to the moral reputation of their women." Commenting on this, *The Daily Commercial* of Wednesday following said: "Those negroes who are attempting to make lynching of individuals of their race a means for arousing the worst passions of their kind, are playing with a dangerous sentiment. The negroes well understand that there is no mercy for the negro rapist, and little patience with his defenders. A negro organ printed in this city in a recent issue published the following atrocious paragraph: 'Nobody in this section believes the old threadbare lie that negro men rape white women. If Southern men are not careful they will overreach themselves and public will have a reaction. A conclusion will be reached which will be very damaging to the moral reputation of their women.' The fact that a black scoundrel is allowed to live and utter such loathsome and repulsive calumnies is a volume of evidence as to the wonderful patience of Southern whites. There are some things the Southern white man will not tolerate, and the intimidation of the foregoing has brought the writer to the very uttermost limit of public patience. We hope we have said enough."

The Evening *Scimitar* of the same day copied this leading editorial and added this comment: "Patience under such circumstances is not a virtue. If the negroes themselves do not apply the remedy without delay, it will be the duty of those he has attacked, to tie the wretch who utters these calumnies to a stake at the intersection of Main and Madison streets, brand him in the forehead with a hot iron and —"

Such open suggestions by the leading daily papers of the progressive city of Memphis were acted upon by the leading citizens and a meeting was held at the Cotton Exchange that evening. *The Commercial* two days later had the following account of it:

ATROCIOUS BLACKGUARDISM.
There will be no Lynching and no Repetition of the Offense.

In its issue of Wednesday *The Commercial* reproduced and commented upon an editorial which appeared a day or two before a negro organ known as the *Free Speech*. The article was so insufferably and indecently slanderous that the whole city awoke to a feeling of intense resentment which came within an ace of culminating in one of those occurrences whose details are so eagerly seized and so prominently published by Northern newspapers. Conservative counsels, however, prevailed, and no extreme measures were resorted to. On Wednesday afternoon a meeting of citizens was held. It was not an assemblage of hoodlums or irresponsible fire eaters, but solid, substantial business men who knew exactly what they were doing and who were far more indignant at the villainous insult to the women of the south than they would have been at any injury done themselves. This meeting appointed a committee to seek the author of the infamous editorial and warn him quietly that upon repetition of the offense, he would find some other part of the country a good deal safer and pleasanter place of residence than this. The committee called a negro named Nightingale, but he disclaimed responsibility and convinced the gentlemen that he had really sold out his paper to a woman named Wells. This woman is not in Memphis at present. It was finally learned that one Fleming, a negro who was driven out of Crittenden Co. during the trouble there a few years ago, wrote the paragraph. He had, however, heard of the meeting, and fled from a fate he feared was in store for him, and which he knew he deserved. His whereabouts could not be ascertained, and the committee so reported. Later on, a communication from Fleming to a prominent Republican politician, and that politician's reply were shown to one or two gentlemen. The former was an inquiry as to whether the writer might safely return to Memphis, the latter was an emphatic answer in negative, and Fleming is still in hiding. Nothing further will be done in the matter. There will be no lynching, and it is very certain there will be no repetition of the outrage. If there should be — Friday, May 25.

The only reason there was no lynching of Mr. Fleming who was business manager and half owner of the *Free Speech*, and who did not write the editorials himself because this same white Republican told him the committee was coming and warned him not to trust them, but get out of the way. The committee scoured the city hunting him, and had to be content with Mr. Nightingale who was dragged to the meeting, shamefully abused (although it was known he had sold out his interest in the paper six months before.) He was in the face and forced at the pistol's point to sign a letter which was written by them, in which he denied all knowledge of the editorial, denounced it and condemned it as slander on white women. I do not censure Mr. Nightingale for his action because, having never been at the pistol's point myself, I do not feel that I am competent to sit in judgment on him, or say What I would do under such circumstances.

I had written that editorial with other matter for the week's paper before leaving home the Friday previous for the General Conference of the A.M.E. Church in Philadelphia. The conference adjourned Tuesday, and Thursday, May 25, at 3 p.m., I landed in New York City for a few days' stay before returning home, and there learned from the papers that my business manager had been driven away and the paper suspended. Telegraphing for news, I received telegrams and letters in return informing me that the trains were being watched, that I was to be dumped into the river and beaten, if not killed; it had been learned that I wrote the editorial and I was to be hanged in front of the court house and my face bled if I returned, and I was implored by my friends to remain away. The creditors attached the office in the meantime and the outfit was sold without more ado, thus destroying effectually that which it had taken years to build. One prominent insurance agent publicly declares he will make it his business to shoot me down on sight if I return to Memphis in twenty years, while a leading white lady had remarked she was opposed to the lynching of those three men in March, but she wished there was some way by which I could be gotten back and lynched.

I have been censured for writing that editorial, but when I think of the five men who were lynched that week for assault on white women and that not a week passes but some poor soul is violently ushered into eternity on this trumped up charge, knowing the many things I do, and part of which tried to tell in the

New York Age of June 25, (and in the pamphlets I have with me) seeing that the whole race in the South was injured in the estimation of the world because of these false reports, I could no longer hold my peace, and I feel, yes, I am sure, that if it had to be done over again (provided no one else was the loser save myself) I would do and say the very same again.

The lawlessness here described is not confined to one locality. In the past ten years over a thousand colored men, women and children have been butchered, murdered and burnt in all parts of the South. The details of these terrible outrages seldom reach beyond the narrow world where they occur. Those who commit the murders write the reports, and hence these blots upon the honor of a nation cause but a faint ripple on the outside world. They arouse no great indignation and call forth no adequate demand for justice. The victims were black, and the reports are so written as to make it appear that the helpless creatures deserved the fate which overtook them . . .

I beg your patience while we look at another phase of the lynching mania. We have turned heretofore to the pages of ancient and medieval history, roman tyranny, the Jesuitical Inquisition of Spain for the spectacle of a human being burnt to death. In the past ten years three instances, at least, have been furnished where men have literally been roasted to death to appease the fury of Southern mobs. The Texarkana instance of last year and Paris, Texas, case of this month are the most recent as they are the most shocking and repulsive. Both were charged with crimes from which the laws provide adequate punishment. The Texarkana man, Ed Coy, was charged with assaulting a white woman. A mob pronounced him guilty, strapped him to a tree, chipped the flesh from his body, poured coal oil over him and the woman in the case set fire to him. The country looked on and in many cases applauded, because it was published that this man had violated the honor of the white woman, although he protested his innocence to the last. Judge Tourjee in the Chicago *Inter Ocean* of recent date says investigation has shown that Ed Coy had supported this woman, (who was known to be a bad character,) and her drunken husband for over a year previous to the burning.

The Paris, Texas, burning of Henry Smith, February 1st, has exceeded the others in its horrible details. The man was drawn through the streets on a float, as the Roman generals used to parade their trophies of war, while scaffold ten feet high, was being built, and irons were heated in the fire. He was bound on it, and red-hot irons began at his feet and slowly branded his body while the mob howled with delight at his shrieks. Red hot irons were run down his throat and cooked his tongue; his eyes were burned out, when he was at last unconscious, cotton seed hulls were placed under him, coal oil poured all over him, and a torch applied to the mass. When the flames burned away the ropes which bound Smith and scorched his flesh he was brought back to sensibility and burned and maimed and as he was, he rolled off the platform and away from the fire. His half-cooked body was seized and trampled and thrown back into the flames while a mob of twenty thousand persons who came from all over the country howled with delight, and gathered up some buttons and ashes after all was over to preserve for relics. The man was charged with outraging and murdering a four year old white child, covering her body with brush, sleeping beside the body through the night, then making his escape. If true, it was the deed of a mad-man, and should have been clearly proven so. The fact that no time for verification of the newspaper reports was given, is suspicious, especially when I remember that a negro was lynched in Indianola, Sharkey Co., Miss. last summer. The dispatches said it was because he had assaulted the sheriff's eight year old daughter. The girl was more than eighteen years old and was found by her father in this man's room, who was a servant on the place . . .

Do you ask the remedy? A public sentiment strong against lawlessness must be aroused. Every individual can contribute to this awakening. When a sentiment against lynch law as strong, deep and mighty as that roused by slavery prevails, I have no fear of the result. It should be already established as a fact and not as a theory, that every human being must have a fair trial for his life and liberty, no matter what the charge against him. When a demand goes up from fearless and persistent reformers from press and pulpit, from industrial and moral associations that this shall be so from Maine to Texas and from ocean to ocean, a way will be found to make it so . . .

Then no longer will our national hymn be sounding brass and a tinkling cymbal, but every member of this great composite nation will be a living, harmonious illustration of the words, and all can honestly and gladly join in singing:

My country! 'tis of thee
Sweet land of liberty
Of thee I sing.
Land where our fathers died
Land of the Pilgrim's pride
From every mountain side
Freedom does ring.

CLARA SHORTRIDGE FOLTZ

At fifteen, she left her parents' home in Indiana and eloped with a Union Army veteran. "I will be a perfect wife, as near as in me lies, and then all will be well," she told herself. Fourteen years and five children later, her husband abandoned the family.

Economic need drove Clara Shortridge Foltz to public lecturing. She spoke for the suffrage cause and passed the hat to pay the bills. "Mrs. Foltz appears perfectly at home on the rostrum," reported one paper.

Her dream was to go to law school, but there was a small problem: the California Code of Civil Procedure allowed only White men over the age of twenty-one "and of good moral character" to take the bar exam and practice law. So Foltz did the obvious thing for a natural-born fighter — she lobbied for a bill that would change "white male" to "person."

The Woman Lawyer's Bill was signed into law in 1873.

Then came the next hurdle: California law schools didn't accept women. So Foltz and her fellow suffragist Laura de Force Gordon sued the Hastings College of Law in a legal battle that went up to the California Supreme Court, where they prevailed — a fight Foltz considered her finest moment.

By then she didn't have time for school; she was too busy working as the first female lawyer on the West Coast. She practiced probate, corporate, family, and criminal law, and saw first-hand the bias against the poor in the criminal justice system. An indigent defendant was almost always bulldozed by the legal might and resources of the public prosecutor.

If the legal system truly upheld the principle of "innocent until proven guilty," she argued, then the court had a responsibility to protect vulnerable defendants.

Foltz came up with the idea of a publicly-financed legal defense system for the poor, grounded in "equal justice under law" as guaranteed in the 14th Amendment to the US Constitution.

She shared that idea in an August 1893 speech at the National Congress of Jurisprudence and Law Reform, held in conjunction with the Chicago World's Fair.

"Let the criminal courts be re-organized upon a basis of exact, equal and free justice," she said. "Let our country be broad and generous enough to make the law a shield as well as a sword."

Not until 1914 was the country's first public defender office established in Los Angeles County — and Foltz was alive to see it.

Thanks to a campaign led by grateful female students at the Hastings College of Law, in 1991 Foltz was awarded a posthumous degree of Doctor of Laws.

The Criminal Courts Building in downtown Los Angeles was renamed for her in 2002 and is now called the Clara Shortridge Foltz Criminal Justice Center.

"PUBLIC DEFENDER RIGHTS OF PERSONS ACCUSED OF CRIME"

August 8, 1893
General Committee of The World's Congress Auxiliary on
Jurisprudence and Law Reform, World's Columbian Exposition,
Hall of Columbus, Memorial Art Palace, Chicago, Illinois

I f we were to inquire of wisdom through her sages and statesmen; of morality through her poets and preachers, and of sympathy through her orators and actors, what were the duty of the State toward those accused of crime, they would unite with a common voice in declaring that the citizens of a State are far more vitally interested in saving an innocent man from unmerited punishment than in the conviction of a guilty one. The common conscience of men, the great heart of the people, the law itself in its presumption of innocence and requiring twelve men to convict, all join in the fundamental idea that the protection of the innocent is far more important to the State than the prosecution of the guilty. Not only is the defense of the innocent important to the State, but it is an act that appeals to the better feelings and nobler impulses of men. It is the act that makes heroes, whom patriots praise and of whom poets sing.

It would naturally seem that an act so important as the defense of the innocent, and at the same time so consonant with the noblest impulses of the heart, would find a prominent and exalted place in our law and practice.

The innocent are, and of right ought to be, the special care of the law, and let it be remembered that in the eyes of the law every man is innocent until proven guilty, and the presumption of innocence goes with him and follows him through every step of the trial till the verdict is rendered. Every man brought to trial in a criminal court being presumed to be innocent, is entitled to be treated as an innocent man, and becomes of necessity the special object of the court's care.

On the court rests a double duty in every criminal cause, to punish the guilty and protect the innocent. But up to the finding of the verdict the court is bound to regard the accused as innocent. And this is not only consistent with a legal maxim, but it is a legitimate inference from established facts; for in over one-half the criminal cases the accused is actually found not guilty.

With a deeper motive and a higher duty to protect than to convict. We would expect to find in the criminal court a machinery for defense quite equal to that of the prosecution.

But how is it in fact? Connected with the court is a public prosecutor, selected for his skill in securing convictions, strong of physique, alert of mind, learned in the law, experienced in practice and ready of speech. Around and behind him is an army of police officers and detectives ready to do his bidding, and before him sits a plastic judge with a large discretion often affected by newspapers and police officers to the injury of the prisoner.

Not only is machinery for prosecution provided, but it is most effectively operated. The prosecuting attorney is usually imbued with the idea that he must convict at all hazards, and this idea takes deeper root because, in many instances, the State pays him a money bonus for each conviction. He misrepresents the facts he expects to prove, attempts to get improper testimony before the jury, garbles and misstates what is allowed, slanders the prisoner and browbeats the witnesses, all from the mistaken notion that it is the duty of the State to convict whoever is arrested.

A police, impelled by vanity to justify its arrests, and inoculated with the error that it is the State's d sire and duty to convict in any event, aids in the prosecution by colored testimony and overawing presence.

To the manifest prejudice of the prisoner in some States he has been manacled in court, and a few years ago in California the officers constructed cages in court-rooms and confined the accused in them like wild beasts, till an outraged public sentiment demanded and secured their removal.

Frequently hired counsel are joined in the prosecution, counsel in no sense representing the majesty of a great State, but rather the malice of a great prosecuting witness whose pride and vanity urge him to pay for a conviction to which he may point as a justification of his charge, and over which he may gloat in the unholy pleasure of his revenge.

When this mesalliance of the justice of the State and the revenge of little minds is made, then no pack of bloodhounds ever pursued a fleeing fugitive with more relentless vigor than do these officers and allies prosecute their victims. Trials which should be calm and solemn, investigations unmarked by prejudice and untainted by rancor, degenerate into a legal battle in which the highest personal rights are subordinated and trampled under foot in the reckless desire to win.

For the conviction of the accused every weapon is provided and used, even those poisoned by wrong and injustice. But what machinery is provided for the defense of the innocent? None. Absolutely none. For its lesser duty of convicting the guilty it has equipped and maintains an array and gives access to the public funds; for the higher one of defense of the innocent there is neither counsel nor officer nor money.

It was not always so. A hundred and fifty years ago, when the death penalty for one hundred offenses disgraced the Penal Code, when the Circuit judge in his rigorous enforcement of a cruel law was the herald of a hundred hangings, even then the accused was not without a defender, at least in name, for the law made it the duty of the State's' attorney to produce all the facts both for and against him, and of the judge to see that his rights were preserved to the uttermost; so that the judge announced himself as the counsel for the prisoner.

But times have changed. The State's attorney, once equally interested in the State and the accused, has so become a prosecutor that his very name is changed in common legal parlance to that of public prosecutor. The judge declines in every instance to interfere on behalf of the prisoner unless specially requested and urged to do so. The old defensive machinery is gone. There has been none supplied to take its place and the accused is thrown back on his original, natural right — the great right of self defense.

In his hour of need and peril — an hour when before him stands all the menacing machinery of the criminal law, when he is deserted by friends and assailed by foes; when, if ever the State should lend him its protection, the law relegates him to his savage state, and tells him, as if conferring a mighty boon, that he may have the pitiful privilege of defending himself if he can.

In criminal trials as at present conducted, particularly under the vicious notions that prevail among the public officers with regard to the State's duty toward the accused, counsel for the defense is an absolute essential to the just examination of a case. A trial without it would be little less than a farce and would be regarded as an invitation to the jury to convict. So true is this, so clearly did justice demand counsel for the defense, that the right to it is secured by Federal and State constitutional guaranty. It being necessary to justice in the trial of a cause, we would naturally look for it as one of the essentials provided by and in a court of justice, but we do not find it.

The unfortunate prisoner is not denied counsel, however; he is merely told that he may supply this essential to justice if he will but pay for it. If he is able to hire counsel he must do so or go without, and thereby go without justice.

While he has means to procure counsel the law compels him to procure his own. No matter what financial hardship or disaster may follow he must pay for his defense. It may ruin his business, impoverish his family and make his wife and children objects of charity merely to escape the malice of an enemy in the form of a prosecuting witness. Every criminal lawyer knows of scores of instances and illustrations of this fact.

If he is not able to hire counsel, if he pleads his poverty and announces himself a pauper, then generally it becomes the duty of the court to appoint counsel for him. Do not imagine however that this counsel is free. It is not. The accused is under actual legal obligations to pay for it, and if he ever gets any property the lawyer can enforce the payment for his services. The most that can be said for this system of furnishing counsel is that it is a system of compulsory credit by which the legal profession is compelled to give credit to the pauper.

Without detracting from the able men who sometimes do offer their services in behalf of a poor prisoner, the rule is that court appointees are wholly unequal to the public officers with whom they are to cope. Those whose ability commands a law business are seldom chosen. The appointees come from failures in the profession, who hang about courts hoping a stray dollar or two from the unfortunate, or from the kindergartens of the profession just let loose from college and anxious to learn the practice. They have no money to spend in an investigation of the case, and come to trial wholly unequipped either in ability, skill or preparation to cope with the man hired by the State who marshals the evidence for the prosecution. The defense is at most a sort of perfunctory one. It is wholly inadequate to the requirements of the case. It is but a shadow of the substance sought for. The prisoner has asked for bread and has received a stone. He is usually relieved of paying bread prices however for stone, for he is generally convicted. and the statute of limitations has run against his lawyer's claim by the time he gets out of prison.

Let me say again that a large percentage of those arrested for crime are actually proven not guilty, and all are presumed to be during the trial, and are entitled to be treated as innocent men. The only justification for any other treatment is the doctrine of necessity. We may detain, using so much force as is necessary, but only where it is necessary to secure the presence of the accused. Out of the presumption of innocence grows the right to bail, and necessity is the only justification for even a bail bond. So that at the trial every person accused of crime is rightfully regarded as innocent. and rightfully entitled to treatment as such. This system of compelling innocent (for they are innocent) to pay for their own counsel works untold evil. It places in the hands of the malicious and designing a weapon by which they can work injury and ruin upon the victims of their spite. Every lawyer knows that hundreds of arrests are made for no other purpose than to worry, harass, annoy, disgrace socially and bring financial disaster upon the accused. Under this system trials cease to be judicial inquiries with a view to justice and become acrimonious contests of men striving for verdicts. The forum degenerates into an arena and loses its dignity and sanctity.

Where defense for the poor is made it places the burden of a public duty on a single profession often to the injury of the business of the attorney. It operates a miscarriage of justice, for, in the wrangle of attorneys, the brow-beating of witnesses and the intrusion of irrelevant matters juries are bewildered and often take sides with attorneys, the innocent are convicted and the vicious and criminal are turned loose upon a helpless public by virtue of a vicious judicial system. The power of the court to appoint counsel for the defense places in the hands of the judge the power to enforce from any of the officers of his court a compulsory credit in favor of whomsoever he chooses — a power of doubtful constitutionality and one that would only be tolerated by a profession either the most servile or the most generous.

It affords to the poor man an inadequate and imperfect defense, for his counsel usually lacks skill and experience in criminal law and is without the aid of either personal aid or money in the discovery of evidence.

It works irreparable injury to the State by the wrong inflicted upon the individual. The accused, even if acquitted. comes from the court-house a changed man. He remembers a malicious arrest, an unjust incarceration, an expense that has impoverished him, atrial in which every court officer seemed doing his utmost for his conviction, the abuse of his witnesses and the slander of himself and possibly of his family., He remembers all this, and then he thinks of the heavy taxes he has paid, the heavy burdens he has borne for the support of the State, and the dangers he dared in order to protect the flag of his country when it was assailed, he thinks of all this, and is it any wonder that his love of country turns to bitterness and his soul is filled with hatred at the thought that the men whom he lifted to position and the government he fought to defend had only persecution for him when he needed a defender.

Henceforth his hand is against government and against men. Disgrace has crushed his manhood and injustice has murdered his patriotism.

The remedy for many of the evils of the present criminal court practice lies in the election or appointment of a public defender. For every public prosecutor there should be a public defender chosen in the same way and paid out of the same fund. Police and sheriffs should be equally at his command and the public treasury should be equally open to meet the legitimate expenses of the defense and the prosecution. With public defenders the injuries we have mentioned would be avoided, malicious prosecution would cease, the accused would have an adequate defense, trials would be judicial inquiries, courts would be freed from the squabbles that now disgrace them, the profession would be relieved from the burden of compulsory services and the expense would fall on the State at large, where it legitimately belongs. higher ideals of courts and government would be created, a deeper patriotism would be engendered and a deeper feeling of security would pervade the community, by reason of the com forting knowledge that a court of justice was not so merely in name, and a chamber of torture in fact, but a court to which rich and poor might freely go and equally expect the justice to which the law entitled them. But above and over all, the inauguration of the office of public defender would enable the State to do its duty to its citizens . . .

The chief and highest function of government is to secure the lives and liberties of its people. For this purpose taxes are levied, imposts laid and internal revenues collected. To this end the police is organized, courts are established, armies mustered and navies manned. To support them each citizen surrenders his natural right to defend himself and pays his share for the support of the State, under the implied contract that for such surrender of right and such contribution, the government will defend his life and liberty from unlawful invasion.

When therefore the rights of a person are assailed it is the duty of the government under its implied contract to provide him defense. This is not merely a privilege or latent function of government. It is a duty inseparably connected with its very existence — a duty it could not shirk if it were sufficiently ignoble to attempt it; an obligation it could not evade if it were base enough to wish it. And that duty exists at all times and in all cases, whether the invasion be under the form of law or under the more savage form of personal revenge.

Let the criminal courts be re-organized upon a basis of exact, equal and free justice; let our country be broad and generous enough to make the law a shield as well as a sword; let the citizen understand that his flag is his protection in his own home as well as when his foot is on foreign soil, and there will come to the State, as a natural sequence, all those blessings which flow from constitutional obligations conscientiously kept and government duties sacredly performed.

KA'IULANI

On a chilly March afternoon in 1893, a young woman stepped off a steamship that had just docked in New York harbor. Waiting on the pier was an army of journalists and curiosity seekers.

Her name was Victoria Kawēkiu Ka'iulani Lunalilo Kalaninuiahilapalapa Cleghorn — Ka'iulani, for short. Her mother was descended from the royal rulers of Polynesia, and her father was a Scottish financier. Until recently she had been heir to the throne of the Sandwich Islands, the last hope of the Hawaiian Kingdom.

But six weeks earlier, a US-backed coup planned by powerful sugar planters, led by lawyer Sanford Dole, had overthrown her aunt, Queen Lili'uokalani, in a coup. With America pulling the strings, a new government was installed. Indicative of its sympathies, 300 US Marines were sent in, ostensibly to protect American lives. Hawaii was no longer a sovereign nation.

Standing on the pier in New York, Ka'iulani made a short statement to the press, and took her case to the American people.

The United States had no right to interfere with a legitimate Hawaiian government, she said. "Today, I, a poor, weak girl. . . have the strength to stand up for the rights of my people. Even now I can hear their wail in my heart, and it gives me strength."

During her American stay, Ka'iulani made public appearances and speeches to protest the coup, arguing that her people were not "savages" and were perfectly capable of ruling themselves.

She appealed directly to President Grover Cleveland and his wife Frances, even meeting them in the White House. Cleveland was an outspoken anti-imperialist and thought the US had acted shamefully in Hawaii. He wanted to restore Lili'uokalani to the throne, but he lacked Congressional and public support.

Fueled by passion and indignation, Ka'iulani kept making public appearances and speeches, arguing for Hawaiian independence. In 1899, after a horse ride in a storm, she fell ill and died. She was buried in a tomb at Mauna Ala on Oahu, the final resting place of Hawaiian royalty.

Two years later, after the Spanish-American War demonstrated the strategic value of the naval base at Pearl Harbor, Congress voted to annex Hawaii. In 1959, Hawaii entered the United States as the 50th state.

Ka'iulani's rhetoric could not change the course of history. But her argument is remembered as a proud, defiant stand against American economic drive, colonialism, and territorial ambition.

In 1993, a joint Congressional resolution apologized for the 1893 overthrow of the Kingdom of Hawaii and declared it had been illegal.

"THE RIGHTS OF MY PEOPLE"

March 1, 1893
After alighting from the *Teutonic*, on the pier,
New York City, New York

Good morning.

Unbidden I stand upon your shores today, where I had thought so soon to receive a Royal welcome. I come unattended except for the loving hearts that have come with me over the winter seas. I hear that Commissioners from my land have been for many days asking this great nation to take away my little vineyard. They speak no word to me, and leave me to find out as I can from the rumors of the air that they would leave me without a home or a name or a nation.

Seventy years ago, Christian America sent over Christian men and women to give religion and civilization to Hawaii. Today three of the sons of those missionaries are at your capitol, asking you to undo their fathers' work. Who sent them? Who gave them the authority to break the Constitution which they swore they would uphold?

Today, I, a poor, weak girl, with not one of my people near me and all of these statesmen against me, have the strength to stand up for the rights of my people. Even now I can hear their wail in my heart, and it gives me strength and I am strong. Strong in the faith of God. Strong in the knowledge that I am right, strong in the strength of seventy million people who in this free land will hear my cry and will refuse to let their flag cover dishonour to mine!

ANNA JULIA COOPER

The Chicago World's Fair of 1893 — rising optimistically from the cinders of a city that had almost burned to the ground two decades earlier — was an extravaganza of American art and industry, with thousands of displays, exhibits and lectures celebrating everything that made America great.

But who exactly had contributed to that greatness?

Controversy broke out in the planning stages about whether, and how much, the accomplishments of women and Black Americans would be included. In the end, a monumental Italianate Women's Building was designed to host exhibits and lectures on women's achievements.

But what about Black Americans? Thirty years after the Emancipation Proclamation, their progress would largely go unnoted at the fair — despite the outraged protests of journalist Ida B. Wells and others.

Only six Black women were allowed to speak during the entire six-month exposition, among them the respected educator Anna Julia Cooper.

When it was her turn to step up to the podium, in May 1893, she held her head high. "I speak for colored women of the South," she said, "because it is there that the millions of blacks in this country have watered the soil with blood and tears."

Cooper's herself was born into slavery in North Carolina, and although her mother never discussed it, her father was almost certainly her mother's slave owner. Cooper spoke of the horrors of enslavement and abuse, paying homage to all Black women who had suffered and struggled in silence, and their "despairing fight, as of an entrapped tigress, to keep hallowed their own persons."

One of the first Black women in America to graduate from college, Cooper fought for the right to study alongside men. She was fueled by a sense of urgency to help her people gain access to education, which she saw as key to their success.

And indeed, as she pointed out, Black women were excelling at every educational level, even obtaining degrees from the nation's most prestigious universities.

She also told of their considerable advances in economic life, industry, and the community.

But what elevates her speech into a spiritual and political manifesto is her vision of amplitude and generosity for all, regardless of gender, race or status.

Born of pain and oppression, her vision champions right over might, universal equality, and the interdependence of humankind. Her words still enthrall and challenge us to do better.

"The colored woman feels that woman's cause is one and universal," she declared, with the future of the human race depending on "the solidarity of all humanity."

"WOMAN'S CAUSE IS ONE AND UNIVERSAL"

May 18, 1893
World's Congress of Representative Women, Chicago, Illinois

The higher fruits of civilization can not be extemporized, neither can they be developed normally, in the brief space of thirty years. It requires the long and painful growth of generations. Yet all through the darkest period of the colored women's oppression in this country her yet unwritten history is full of heroic struggle, a struggle against fearful and overwhelming odds, that often ended in a horrible death, to maintain and protect that which woman holds dearer than life. The painful, patient, and silent toil of mothers to gain a free simple title to the bodies of their daughters, the despairing fight, as of an entrapped tigress, to keep hallowed their own persons, would furnish material for epics. That more went down under the flood than stemmed the current is not extraordinary. The majority of our women are not heroines — but I do not know that a majority of any race of women are heroines. It is enough for me to know that while in the eyes of the highest tribunal in America she was deemed no more than a chattel, an irresponsible thing, a dull block, to be drawn hither or thither at the volition of an owner, the Afro-American woman maintained ideals of womanhood unshamed by any ever conceived. Resting or fermenting in untutored minds, such ideals could not claim a hearing at the bar of the nation. The white woman could least plead for her own emancipation; the black woman, doubly enslaved, could but suffer and struggle and be silent. I speak for the colored women of the South, because it is there that the millions of blacks in this country have watered the soil with blood and tears, and it is there too that the colored woman of America has made her characteristic history, and there her destiny is evolving. Since emancipation the movement has been at times confused and stormy, so that we could not always tell whether we were going forward or groping in a circle. We hardly knew what we ought to emphasize, whether education or wealth, or civil freedom and recognition. We were utterly destitute. Possessing no homes nor the knowledge of how to make them, no money nor the habit of acquiring it, no education, no political status, no influence, what could we do? But as Frederick Douglass had said in darker days than those, "One with God is a majority," and our ignorance had hedged us in from the fine spun theories of agnostics. We had remaining at least a simple faith that a just God is on the throne of the universe, and that somehow — we could not see, nor did we bother our heads to try to tell how — he would in his own good time make all right that seemed most wrong.

Schools were established, not merely public day schools, but home training and industrial schools, at Hampton, at Fisk, Atlanta, Raleigh, and other stations, and later, through the energy of the colored people themselves, such schools as the Wilberforce, the Livingstone, the Allen, and the Paul Quinn were opened. These schools were almost without exception co-educational. Funds were too limited to be divided on sex lines, even had it been ideally desirable; but our girls as well as our boys flocked in and battled for an education. Not even then was that patient, untrumpeted heroine, the slave-mother, released from self sacrifice, and many an unbuttered crust was eaten in silent content that she might eke out enough from her poverty to send her young folks off to school. She "never had the chance," she would tell you, with tears on her withered cheek, so she wanted them to get all they could. The work in these schools, and in such as these, has been like the little leaven hid in the measure of meal, permeating life throughout the length and breadth of the Southland, lifting up ideals of home and of womanhood; diffusing a contagious longing for higher living and purer thinking, inspiring woman herself with a new sense of her dignity in the eternal purposes of nature. Today there are 25,530 colored schools in the United States, with 1,353,352 pupils of both sexes. This is not quite the thirtieth year since their emancipation, and the colored people hold in landed property for churches and schools $25 million dollars. Two and one half million colored children have learned to read and write, and 22,956 colored men and women (mostly women) are teaching in these schools. According to Doctor [Jeremiah] Rankin, President of Howard University, there are 247 colored students (a large percentage of whom are women) now preparing themselves in the universities of Europe. Of other colleges which give the B.A. course to women, and are broad enough not to erect barriers against colored applicants, Oberlin, the first to open its doors to both woman and the Negro, has given classical degrees to six colored women, one of whom, the first and most eminent, Fannie Jackson Coppin, we shall listen to tonight. Ann Arbor and Wellesley have each graduated three of our women; Cornell University one, who is now professor of sciences in a Washington high school. A former pupil of my own from the Washington High School who was snubbed by Vassar, has since carried off honors in a competitive examination in Chicago University. The medical and law colleges of country are likewise bombarded by colored women, and every year some sister of the darker race claims their professional award of "well done." Eminent in their profession are Doctor [Halle Tanner] Dillon and Doctor [Sophia] Jones, and there sailed to Africa last month a demure little brown woman who had just outstripped a whole class of men in a medical college in Tennessee.

In organized efforts for self help and benevolence also our women have been active. The Colored Women's League, of which I am at present corresponding secretary, has active, energetic branches in the South and West. The branch in Kansas City, with a membership of upward of one hundred and fifty, already has begun under their vigorous president, Mrs. [Josephine] Yates, the erection of a building for friendless girls. Mrs. Coppin will, I hope, herself tell you something of her own magnificent creation of an industrial society in Philadelphia. The women of the Washington branch of the league have subscribed to a fund of about five thousand dollars to erect a woman's building for educational and industrial work, which is also to serve as headquarters for gathering and disseminating general information relating to the efforts of our women. This is just a glimpse of what we are doing.

Now, I think if I could crystallize the sentiment of my constituency and deliver it as a message to this congress of women, it would be something like this: Let woman's claim be as broad in the concrete as in the abstract. We take our stand on the solidarity of humanity, the oneness of life, and the unnaturalness and injustice of all special favoritisms, whether of sex, race, country, or condition. If one link of the chain be broken, the chain is broken. A bridge is no stronger than its weakest part, and a cause is not worthier than its weakest element. Least of all can woman's cause afford to decry the weak. We want, then, as toilers for the universal triumph of justice and human rights, to go to our homes from this Congress, demanding an entrance not through a gateway for ourselves, our race, our sex, or our sect, but a grand highway for humanity. The colored woman feels that woman's cause is one and universal; and that not till the image of God, whether in parian or ebony, is sacred and inviolable; not till race, color, sex, and condition are seen as the accidents, and not the substance of life; not till the universal title of humanity to life, liberty, and the pursuit of happiness is conceded to be inalienable to all; not till then is woman's lesson taught and woman's cause won — not the white woman's, nor the black woman's, not the red woman's, but the cause of every man and of every woman who has writhed silently under a mighty wrong. Woman's wrongs are thus indissolubly linked with undefended woe, and the acquirement of her "rights" will mean the final triumph of all right over might, the supremacy of the moral forces of reason, and justice, and love in the government of the nations of earth.

LILLIAN WALD

Lillian Wald found her calling one morning in 1894 when, as a community nurse, she was teaching new immigrants how to make a bed.

As she described it in *The House on Henry Street*, a child came up and said her mother was sick. Wald followed the child through the squalid, densely packed neighborhood. In a rear tenement she found the mother lying in filth, incapacitated, having just given birth.

The tenements were notorious for their extreme overcrowding, piles of trash, and lack of natural light or fresh air. They were also rife with cholera and tuberculosis.

In that instant, everything changed for Wald.

"Deserted were the laboratory and the academic work of the college," she later wrote. "I never returned to them. . . it seemed certain that conditions such as these were allowed because people did not *know,* and for me there was a challenge to know and to tell."

In 1893, she had founded the Henry Street Settlement to serve New York City's growing immigrant community. In the 1890s alone, millions of Italians and Yiddish-speaking Jews from Eastern Europe arrived. After sailing past the Statue of Liberty, they entered the country at the Castle Garden landing depot near the tip of the island. Many went to live on the Lower East Side, where rents were low.

Wald, a child of privilege from upstate New York, saw first-hand the problems caused by immigration, industrialization, and urban crowding. She moved into the settlement house and spent the rest of her life teaching, raising money, and devoting herself to public health, women's rights, children's welfare, and humanitarian causes.

In an 1896 she gave a speech to the National Council of Jewish Women in New York. In the audience were mostly upper-class women; many had come to America from highly cultured and assimilated German Jewish families, who tended to look down on the poorer, less educated Eastern European Jews.

Wald delivered an unsparing account of the depth of hardship and human suffering in the tenements, and the underlying social and environmental causes.

Over and over, she used the word, "you" — insisting on the duty of her listeners to their fellow human beings, and appealing to their conscience and pocketbook. "Say to yourself, 'If there is a wrong in our midst, what can I do?'" she said. "'What is my responsibility?'"

Her speech was a large-hearted plea for the obligations attendant upon membership in the human race. "As it is a crowded district of our metropolis, it belongs to all the country," she told her listeners, "and therefore is yours."

"CROWDED DISTRICTS OF LARGE CITIES"

November 17, 1896
National Council of Jewish Women, Tuxedo Hall,
New York City, New York

I n bringing a report of the crowded districts of great cities to you to-day, I am aware that whatever I could say to impress you would be from the personal experiences and conclusions obtained by some years' residence in such a quarter of one city only, or the less valuable observations made as visitor and stranger to like districts in other cities. But before we enter into particular descriptions or the ethics of their existence anywhere, I would remind you of the real insight that may be obtained by all, not only of the congested regions of great cities, but of the causes and results of their existence.

Such important education is to be found in the clear reading of official reports, vital statistics, labor reports and annuals, tenement-house reports, police reports, police records, school reports, charity organization and institution year-books — such literature as may be had for the asking, yet is, in many ways, the important social, history-making literature of our times. Then, more interesting, perhaps, are the evidences that may be found in stories and magazine articles, by the residents of social settlements and missions, the thoughts of visiting philosophers, who, eager to know the crowds, have camped for a time in these back-yards of our great cities, and have given the fruit of their meditations to others. There are the deeper works of students of sociology, who have looked upon these crowded districts as human laboratories, coldly, or inspired by a higher than scientific interest, a human one, to know the people, the men and the women, the children and the conditions that make "masses" and "districts" and "East Sides," have known their experiences to scholarly consideration. Knowing that these things are, they must next see why, and perhaps have thus furnished what has been likened to the ophthalmoscope, the instrument that made it possible to see into the eye, and thus revealing the disease, gave the physician the opportunity of curing it. Furnished with such an ophthalmoscope, the physician of social wrongs may heal and take from modern civilization its most baneful growth.

Such reading as this suggests might be called "dry," mere skeletons of figures to be recognized only by people "interested in that sort of thing," literature not to be found in any but the specialist's library. But it is not dry; and even if so, it is a literature that concerns us all, more than any news compiled, and if awaiting readers now, will some day *force* the attention of the whole world. But read each figure a human being; read that every wretched unlighted tenement described is a *home* for people, men and women, old and young, with the strength and the weaknesses, the good and the bad, the appetites and wants common to all. Read, in descriptions of sweat-shops, factories, and long-hour work-days, the difficulty, the impossibility of well-ordered living under the conditions outlines. Understanding reading of these things must bring a sense of fairness outraged, the disquieting conviction that something is wrong somewhere, and turning to your own contrasting life you will feel a responsibility of the *how* and the *why* and the *wherefore*. Say to yourself, "If there is a wrong in our midst, what can *I* do? What is *my* responsibility? Who is to blame? Do *I* owe reparation?

All this is a plea for the intelligent reading of the things that pertain to the people of the crowded districts of *all* cities, that something more may be given to the subject than the few moments in a convention's program; that the suggestion may be made, and the thought carried home that more carefully-prepared witnesses are yours to be called up at all times and for the asking.

Agreeing that a common condition must be produced by a common cause, in order to understand its life anywhere, we need only confine ourselves to a study of the crowded district that is familiar to the witness you have called up to-day. As it is a crowded district of our metropolis, it belongs to all the country, and therefore is yours . . .

The nurses never overcome the fear of trampling on the children in the hall or on the street, a sound warning them when to tread carefully, or sometimes out of the darkness a tiny hand on the railing shocking suddenly with the sense of accident averted. It is not uncommon to go in daytime into the closet-room with candle in hand, in order to be able to see the patient at all. Nor is it uncommon to go at night and see ten or eleven people occupying two small rooms — people who have been working all day, freed for the night's rest, stretched on the floor, one next to the other, dividing the pillows, different sexes, not always the same family, for there are "boarders," who pay a small sum for shelter, among their own, the family glad of the help toward paying the rent. The price of rooms in the most wretched basement in the rear tenements is so high in comparison with the wage earned that it is for those who have employment based on something like regular income about one-fourth of the whole. But it must be remembered that few trades give employment all the year round. We hear more often than any other plaint that of the uncertainty of having a roof: the failure comes so often, and with it the "dispossess paper," that the sight of the household effects on the sidewalk following its presentment is too common to collect a crowd, where crowds collect quickly.

During the hot months of July and August is the time to observe a crowded district at its worst. The vermin and the heat drive the people to the streets, which are crowded with these unfortunates the greater part of the night. Mothers sit on the curbstone with nursing babies, and the cool of the door-stone is coveted for a pillow, or the refreshment of sleep on the roof or in the courts between the houses is sought, unless, indeed, the odors of the closets there are worse than the vermin or the heat within.

On the other hand, within these tenements are sometimes found the most scrupulously kept rooms; plants by the windows, happiness, and a real home; courtesy, devotion, and charity, such as one may seek for among the elect of the earth, and reverence; sufficient evidence of the original nobility of character, which can remain high despite all discouragements.

But the more frequent picture is that of the overcrowded rooms, denying the privacy and sacredness of home-life. Outside the house there is almost no park or playground for the children — nothing but the sidewalks and streets. Games for the boys are of necessity reduced to "leap-frog," "craps," or tossing pennies.

School-time comes, and the population increases so rapidly that, with the best intentions, it seems impossible to provide place, with a less keen sense of responsibility, the worst occurs. An unlettered, indifferent parent, exhorted and then informed that education is compulsory, finally does exert himself to claim the place for his children in the school, to learn that compulsory education acts and truant officers are superfluous matters, since there is no place in the school for his children. There is considerable discrepancy in the figures giving the number of children out of school at present. To avoid inaccuracy, I will only state that there are many thousands — 400 in one school alone of the region I am making special reference to to-day.

The law says that the child must be in school until fourteen, that he or she may not be employed under that age; and as nothing more than the parent's testimony is required to give the child to the shops, the temptation to perjury is apparent.

We now come to the sweat-shops, labor in which is the principal occupation of our neighbors. Where a "union" has been established and is strong, the work-day may be ten hours; where the trade is unorganized (and that is more likely to be among the unskilled, therefore the poor, therefore the least educated) the work-day is more often fourteen hours. Have you heard of the diseases most prevalent among people who work in contaminated air, and then go home to sleep under the same conditions? In the Nurses' Settlement consumption is spoken of as the "tailors' disease."

Have you watched the drive, drive, drive of men and women at the machines, over cigar or cigarette making? Have you peeped down into the cellars, and seen the rags sorted, the shirts made, the washing done, shoes cobbled, cheese and bread made? Have you watched the making of the collars, passementerie, clothing, cloaks and artificial flowers, the curling of feathers, the streaming of hats, the manufacture of neckties and boxes, the production of the whole long list of necessaries and luxuries for other people? Have you watched where the workers were laboring under the indifference or absenteeism of the employer? — working, working, working, until the pain in watching the ceaseless strain becomes unendurable, and you cry out against the inhumanity of it all? Cry out because you can see how impossible it is for these men and women to have the leisure or the strength to rear their children into stalwart men and women, into citizens with intelligent reasoning of how to govern themselves or to choose their governors.

I bring up again for the thousandth time in excuse for uncleanliness or a low standard of social or moral ethics, when such exist, no education, crowded, dark rooms for a home, no time or opportunities for proper cleanliness, no opportunities for healthful pleasures; grinding work and small pay; no work, and then the necessaries of life a gift. "Charity covers a multitude of sins," but does not wipe them out. Anxiety lest ends might not meet excludes even conversation in the home. All negatives are shifts to make ends meet; laws are evaded, breeding a contempt for law and order. Finally, there is the dumb discontent provoked into loud resentment; the district of class, creating leaders of their own who know what they have not, who can comprehend what they want. There can be no denial that the poor are poorer, than what is called "class feeling" has been intensified. This last election made many people see for the first time that there was what one side called revolt, that a "campaign of education" seemed necessary to save our institutions.

I am fully conscious of not bringing you a complete picture of even the small section of one city; there is too much to be said. Many dark pictures have been omitted. There has been no reference to the peddlers who have no trade, only the instinct of trade, many of whom, however are skilled workmen with no demand for their skill, obliged in dull seasons to do *anything*, and that means a basket, a box, or a push-cart, with some small outlay for stock; not that the occupation is desirable, but because that is all that is left, and work in the busy season has not paid enough to carry the family over.

Also should I like to dwell upon the affection and sobriety of our neighbors; the gratitude for courtesies, and the response to efforts for education among the children; the honest return of money loaned to them; the eagerness to show their patriotism, as instanced when the Russian brought his violin to show us how well he had learned "our" national air, and forth played "After the ball is over" — he had come here three years ago, when that seemed the song of America — and the pride in having attained citizenship, when they do, framing and hanging the official testimony on the wall, though the vaccination certificate has been thus honored also . . .

I might appeal to your self-interests to recognize the close relationships between the crowded districts of great cities and the more fortunate regions; might prove that the danger of infected and unsanitary tenements are your direct affairs; tell of the things made in rooms where infectious diseases were or had been; — evidences of the dying consumptive working at cigarettes; of the filthy basement where the sick girl lay, and where candy was being made; of the felt slippers sewed in the room where scarlet-fever and diphtheria were; or of the servant-girl coming home to visit in similar circumstances and returning to the baby.

There is a higher juster appeal that your own sins of responsibility will make to you. If the homes are poor, build others; not as charities, but as investments, satisfied with a four per cent return, in planning which have the comfort and education of the tenants in view. The testimony of people here and elsewhere who have had practical experience proves that such investments pay in every way, and that almost all have given a satisfactory return upon the investment of money. Time and education, both of which are slow, are required to alter many things; but you can begin it for others and yourselves. You can help the labor difficulty by comprehending what a fair condition of labor is. If you have no "consumers' league" to receive your pledge, pledge its principles to yourself. If there is a strike, try to discover both sides of the question, not only the one vulgarly holding your butter, but the other's grievance also; not rejoicing in the workingman's failure without understanding (if that is possible) what was behind the discontent. Be fair enough to help that workingman in his way, if you can see that his way is right. Listen to the cries that come from crowded districts. Their people are patient, and are not demanding overmuch . . .

SELENA SLOAN BUTLER

"Repulsive," Selena Sloan Butler said when describing Georgia's convict lease system — so backward and barbaric one had to wonder, "Are we living in a period of the 'dark ages?'"

Butler was a Georgia native, born seven years after slavery was abolished, and a graduate of Spelman Seminary in Atlanta.

No one who heard her speech at the annual conference of the National Association of Colored Women in 1897 would have been surprised by the brutality of convict leasing. Travelers in the South in those years would have seen the laborers, mostly Black men, toiling by the side of the road, shackled to chain gangs with irons on their ankles.

Convict leasing had emerged from the ruins of the Civil War as a way to supply much-needed labor to plantations and businesses when the enslaved were set free.

Arrests of "criminals" were often made by professional crime hunters who were paid by the head. Prisoners received unduly harsh sentences, sometimes ten or more years for minor offenses. They were leased out to privately-operated companies, which assigned them to roadways, railways, sawmills, brickyards, farmsteads, and other hard labor sites, with no pay. Prisoners lived in crowded, filthy convict camps where disease was rampant.

As Butler's speech made clear, it wasn't just men who were caught up in the system. Women were also assigned to chain gangs, and were often sexually abused.

It was shockingly inhumane, everyone agreed — except perhaps those who rationalized the system as an antidote for the spurious charge of "black idleness."

And convict leasing was so much cheaper than bricks-and-mortar prisons — private industry was flourishing off the cheap labor, and leasing fees were replenishing state coffers. How could politicians be persuaded to abolish a system that was doing so much to restore the economic fortunes of the downtrodden South?

Activists like Butler, Anna Julia Cooper, Mary Church Terrell, and Ida B. Wells were among the many reform-minded women who protested against a system that was, as Butler put it, "a reflection upon any civilized people."

Because Butler wasn't able to attend the meeting, her fellow activist Margaret Murray Washington, the wife of Booker T. Washington, read the paper for her.

By raising public attention, Butler and her fellow advocates helped to turn the tide against an abusive and corrupt system. But change was slow to come. In 1908, after a flood of newspaper accounts and high-profile trials, Georgia finally ended convict leasing.

"THE CHAIN-
GANG SYSTEM"

September 16, 1897
Second Convention of the National Association of Colored
Women, Howard Congregational Church, Nashville, Tennessee

[B]ecause Butler was not able to attend, this paper was read to the members by Margaret Murray Washington.]

Madam President Delegates and Friends: —

I bring to you at this time, not an address filled with rhetorical figures and fine diction, which would fill your souls with admiration and cause your minds to soar to loftier realms, and bask themselves in all that is grand and noble; but I bring to you facts, pure and simple, of a system of dealing with human souls in this age of Christian civilization; intelligence and culture, that causes one to pause and ask the question: "Are we living in the nineteenth century, that boasts of its great advancements along the line of Christianity; or are we living in a period of the "dark ages?" The Armenian massacre, the butchery of the struggling Cubans and the horrors and cruelty of the Siberian prisons, all sink into oblivion when one knows the foul condition of affairs as they exist in the "Convict Lease System" of the South, and especially Georgia.

I shall confine my talk to the "Convict Lease System" as practiced in Georgia.

For the benefit of those who do not understand the system of leasing convicts in Georgia, I quote the following explanation of the three classes of convicts in the State:

First. "The felony convicts, sentenced to the Penitentiary and confined under the State lease system, and regularly inspected by the State Penitentiary Department."

Second. "Misdemeanor or county convicts, actually employed on the public works, either by the county in which they were convicted or a county to which they were leased, but subject to no State inspection and under the control of no State official."

Third. "Misdemeanor or county convicts, leased by the county authorities to private individuals, in direct violation of the law and subject to no inspection."

The legislature leased the first-class convicts for a term of twenty years to convict camp companies. In these camps are employed more than 2,000 convicts.

The State has no control over the county or misdemeanor convicts at all. They are sentenced by the county in which they were convicted, to the chain-gang, and must be employed upon the public works of said county, or they are leased to another county to perform the same kind of work. This is lawful; but if the county officials have contracted to furnish private individuals or corporations, they accordingly convict as many persons as possible, so as to fill the contract. This is illegal, but has been practiced for many years in the "Empire State of the South." There are at least as many legal county chain-gangs as there are counties in the State, but there are twenty-four operated by private individuals, that have been inspected by the commissioner sent out by the Governor. There may be many more hidden in some lonely part of the counties. The convicts in these private chain-gang camps are worked upon farms, in turpentine distilleries, saw mills, brick-yards, etc. Many of the counties lease their convicts to other counties at the rate of $3.00 per month for well and strong men, and $1.50 for women and men with physical disabilities.

The recent report, which is not yet published, shows that the convicts worked by the counties are well cared for, and only in a few instances, have they suffered from the want of food, clothing and from brutal treatment by chain-gang "bosses." It is those convicts leased to private corporations who suffer miseries which their poor, miserable selves and God know. The chain-gang bosses, as a rule, are selected from the lowest element in the white race, and rather glory in their office and the freedom of dealing out misery and cruelty to helpless convicts for small offences, and often for no offence at all. Many of the chain-gang camps are situated in places remote from settlements and public roads, where no one can interfere with the inhuman treatment these poor, helpless creatures receive from beings who would be a disgrace to the brute kingdom. Many of the prisoners have scarcely enough clothing on their uncared for bodies to protect them from the gaze of others, or from winter's cold or summer's heat. Many of them have garments in which they were convicted months ago, and which to-day are dirty, greasy and worn almost to shreds. The majority of the prisoners in these private camps are poorly fed. Their diet consists chiefly of corn bread and fat meat, and what is worse, many of them work from ten to twelve hours a day, after which they return to their sleeping quarters, to find not even the necessities and comforts which a prisoner is entitled to — good, wholesome food, well cooked, and a good, healthy place in which to sleep. These men return, after a long and hard day's work, to find no supper prepared, no fire to dry their wet clothes or warm their cold bodies, as the case may be. Each is given his ration, and in turn must cook it over a fire that has been made in the yard of the stockade, four or five using the same skillet to bake their bread and fry their meat.

From the facts just stated, you can judge the sanitary condition of these chain-gang camps. In one camp sixty-one men were found sleeping in a room not more than nineteen feet square and seven feet from the floor ceiling. How they came out alive the next morning, after having spent the night in this room, with but one opening, a door, is a wonder which would puzzle a scientist to solve. Many of these convicts know not the comfort of sleeping upon even a cheap mattress or a heap of straw, but must wrap about their tired and neglected bodies a blanket much worn and filled with dirt and vermin, and lie down, not upon a wood floor, but the dirt floor of a tent, to lose themselves in sweet sleep that knows no color or standing — sleep that will, perhaps, take them back to home, mother, and innocent childhood.

The sanitary condition is repulsive and a reflection upon any civilized people.

Most of the deaths in private camps are caused by the negligence on the part of the "bosses" to secure medical attention when it is needed. Little or no provision is made for the care of the sick; some have been forced to work till they fell upon the ground, dead. The recent report shows the death rate to be twice as large in the private camps as in the county camps. Men have been sent to these private camps, hale and hearty, with strong muscles, and apparently, a long lease on life, but having staid there a short time, exposed to the unhygienic surroundings and the inhuman treatment, if death does not come to them immediately, they leave the camp when their terms have expired, physical wrecks, mere shadows, that scarcely remind one of what the man once was. In some camps the convicts are whipped with a leather strap; in others they are strangled with water.

The convicts are very shy of visitors, and are afraid to expose the treatment received at the camp, especially while they are prisoners. During the trial of some of the lessees of the State, conducted by his excellency, Gov. W.Y. Atkinson, I saw, as did every one in the room, the shyness with which the convicts would answer questions put to them by the State, that would expose the treatment they received. They knew that on their return to their camps they would be at the mercy of their "bosses."

Many Negro boys are sent to these camps for a trivial offense, made to do hard work, endure cruel beating and to associate with men hardened to crime. This illustration will give you some idea of the treatment which some of the boys are subjected to. In a certain county, a Negro boy was sentenced to the chain-gang. The grand jury sent for this boy, and on his way it was noticed that instead of occupying a seat in the buggy, he rode astride a pole that rested upon the seat and the dash-board of the buggy. An investigation showed that the boy had been so cruelly whipped that he could not sit down.

What grade of citizenship can any town or State expect to have when it "sends up" a boy for thirty days for stealing five cents worth of peanuts, to take his first lesson in a place whose influence is everything that tends to destroy soul and body? In Wilkes county, an aged colored man was whipped so unmercifully that he fell upon the ground in a helpless state and said: "Boss, is you going to kill me?" With an oath, the inhuman white "boss" said "yes." Then the old man begged to be killed, that he might die immediately. After cruelly beating the old man, the young white "boss" dragged him to a tree and chained him up so that he could not lie down. In this position he remained only a short while for death relieved him of his earthly torture. His murderer is still in jail.

These are but mild illustrations of the torture that has been practiced in many of the private camps for years, not only upon men, but women, who have committed some small offense. In some camps men and women are worked indiscriminately, the latter being dressed in men's clothes. No provision is made for the separation of the sexes in the sleeping quarters. A young girl was sent to chain-gang camp in Wilkes county, where she was made to put on men's clothes and dig ditches, just as the men did. For any small offense the white "boss" would beat her on her bare back before the male convicts — her pleadings would have no effect on the white "boss." The Governor pardoned this unfortunate girl that she might be relieved of her sufferings.

One of the most touching cases that has come before the public, is that of a young girl at Camp Hardmont, a camp for women. The guards became so infatuated with her, that peace did not always reign within the camp among the guards. One day an offspring came; both mother and child died. The matter was kept quiet for some time. Finally one of the sensational papers gave it to the public as it really was. These two cases will give you an idea of the life of a woman committed to the chain-gang camps. Women, though already steeped in sin, find these chain-gang camps and "bosses," repulsive to their polluted lives.

I have given you but a brief talk on the "Convict Lease System" as it really is. There is much more to be said, but too awful to relate to such a gathering as this. Only a few weeks ago I sat by a young woman who sat in her bed, dying from a loathsome disease, brought on by exposure and aggravated by neglect, while serving out a sentence in these chain-gang camps. Her condition became so alarming that friends secured a pardon for her. She was taken to her home in an alley, where, soon after she died. In these chain-gang camps the women have no moral restraint thrown about them, no one to sympathize with and persuade them to lead better lives. Col. [Phill] Byrd, who was recently appointed by the Governor to investigate the chain-gang camps, has made a report that shows a state of affairs to be existing in these private camps, that reflects upon a civilized and a Christian led people. This report has so aroused the press and the good and law abiding people of Georgia, that as the nineteenth century closes this "Convict Lease System," which is not only illegal, but demoralizing, will be blotted from the records of Georgia.

Too much praise and appreciation cannot be given to Gov. William Yates for he has done more to bring Georgia to a higher point of civilization than any other Governor she has had.

CAROLINE BARTLETT CRANE

On February 26, 1898, at ten o'clock at night, a fire broke out at a chemical company in Kalamazoo.

Firemen had just about subdued the flames when two tremendous explosions blew the roof off the building, which "burst like a cannon rocket," reported a local Michigan paper. "The fire boys and citizens were working side by side, close up to the building, and no one had given the first thought of danger."

Ten men were killed, twenty-six seriously injured. Some of the firemen were hurled thirty feet away and died instantly.

Like any community, the people of Kalamazoo struggled to fathom what had happened. One week later it fell upon Caroline Bartlett Crane, minister of the Unitarian People's Church, to provide guidance. Her sermon tackled one of the enduring mysteries of theology: Why do bad things happen to good people?

There were two possible answers, Crane told the worshippers. The first was an idea that had been circulating in Kalamazoo: that the explosion was God's will. One resident was even going around town talking about "the sins of the city," by which he meant dancing and card games.

The second answer, which Crane favored, was the one produced by the official inquest — that the disaster was an accident caused by human error.

The people of Kalamazoo, she said, had learned the hard way not to allow a chemical plant to be built downtown, or bystanders so close to a fire, or chloroform, ether and alcohol to mix with flames.

A believer in the social gospel, Crane subscribed to a practical, human-centered Christianity. Her answer was not that God didn't play a role in human affairs, but that individuals were called upon to make choices within the realm of natural law.

Crane had come to the ministry after working in journalism, which shows in the way she embraced the evidence, and in the career she adopted after leaving the ministry.

In 1903, she invited a city meat inspector to speak to her Kalamazoo women's club. But all the inspectors were busy, so she visited the abattoirs and slaughter sheds herself. What she saw was horrifying: rotting carcasses, rats, filth.

She gave the lecture herself and began lobbying to make meal inspections mandatory. Soon she was an urban sanitarian, traveling the country to investigate fresh water sources, sewers, garbage collection, disposal systems, milk and meat supplies, and lecture on public health issues. In Minnesota alone, she delivered her findings in 47 public talks. That was typical.

By the mid-1920s she was an expert in household technology, economy, and home design, known as "America's housekeeper."

"IS GOD RESPONSIBLE?"

March 6, 1898
The People's Church, Kalamazoo, Michigan

A week ago last night our city suffered a great calamity. The fire has been extinguished, the dead have been buried, the eulogies have been pronounced. The people, having given generously of sympathy and help to the afflicted, turn to their accustomed occupations. But the shock and sadness and the loss still remain upon us all. And new duties and responsibilities are found to rest upon our city; and old, old problems, yet forever new, rise out of this catastrophe to question us afresh. We understand that ten are dead, and others wounded; we understand how hearts must suffer for these. But why are they dead? And why has such sorrow fallen upon these households and such loss upon this town?

We have received two answers. One is the answer that the people read in the evidence given before the court of inquiry. The other is the answer given by certain ones who have sought to interpret this calamity in the terms of theology. The one answer is, that the explosion with its terrible fatality was the result of the operation of natural law. The other answer is, that it was willed and brought to pass by God . . .

But what is the basis for this confidence? It is the always observed fact that, given certain causes, certain effects are produced, not "sometimes," not "usually," not "with rare exceptions"; but always, so far as human experience and observation can testify: and that, moreover, no effect transpires without its exact cause. This is the common sense and the common faith of intelligent mankind. This belief in the uniformity and the invariability of nature's operations is the basis of all our operations in life. We learn what to do and what not to do by learning what nature does in response to our initiative. But if we could not trust her always, under the same conditions, to give the same response, security would shift to chance and order to chaos. And thus it was that, when no cause was apparent, we yet sought with confidence for a cause; and thus it is that, finding the cause, we believe ourselves to have found the means to avert such catastrophes in future.

But now let us attend to the other answer that has been given not, as in the first case, by a hastily summoned jury of citizens, none of whom claim to be experts, but by those who profess that the causes of this disaster lie within their own special province, and must be explained, so far as they are explicable, by reference to theology. Here we may naturally look for expert testimony.

The consensus of theological opinion as expressed in this town is, that God caused the explosion; that God intended it and brought it to pass for some good and sufficient reason; and that if that reason is beyond finite comprehension it is, nevertheless, ours to bow in unquestioning resignation to this awful dispensation of the divine will. Most of those who have given utterance to these convictions have disavowed understanding of the painful mystery, devoutly expressing the faith that it was God's act, and God may do what He will with His creatures; that the finite cannot hope to comprehend the Infinite, but we know that "He doeth all things well:' and we must adore His awful power and submit to His inscrutable purposes.

But one gentleman, at least, does not find God's providence wholly inscrutable. We are told by him that "god has spoken to Kalamazoo," and that this calamity has been visited upon us because of our sins, — the sins of the city, of the churches, of society. It would seem to be more particularly because people at parties sometimes dance and play cards, that God set fire to a chemical factory (the hand of Providence would have been more evident had it been the playing card factory) and blew it up with the breath of His wrath, and hurled innocent by-standers and brave men in the discharge of their duty into eternity. Had *they* played cards? Here was left no chance to repent. But through the catastrophe which overwhelmed them, we are warned to flee from the wrath that hovers especially over whist tables and waxed floors. By what special revelation this astounding fact was graciously made known to one of our local clergymen, is still a mystery which perhaps needs investigation.

But to return to the general consensus of theological opinion freely expressed, that God willed and executed this calamity, and that while we may not comprehend His purpose, we should bow in unquestioning submission and unwavering faith: This is a very old idea which rises yet once again to confuse thought and hobble reason and intimidate our natural instincts and make monstrous our conception of God and His providence. It is an idea which is practically outgrown and left behind by every human institution except the church. It is an idea which is outgrown by the vast majority of the more intelligent members of the church, though they are perhaps unconscious of the fact. Let us see if this is not so. Do you believe that any man of average intelligence, let him be a member of whatever church, takes his pastor's preaching so to heart that, being summoned to act upon that jury of the disaster, he would find himself disqualified for service by the conviction that the explosion was due to a special act of God, and, as such, was out of the category of things to be rationally investigated and guarded against in future? It is idle to say that God uses natural means to bring about His will;

for, if it were God's will to do this thing, imagine a court of inquiry instituted to find out how we can circumvent God next time? And yet what minister will say that it is not our duty to in future circumvent the conditions which caused the explosion? Where, then, is submission to the supposed will of God?

The idea in question is clearly an unfit survival from long past ages before science was born. Then, to attribute every unusual or mysterious event to the special intervention of God, was not unnatural. Men knew very little of natural law, and few indeed had dreamed of its universal sway. They did not think that the growing grass and the falling rain were due to special divine intervention, or fraught with special messages, because these things were common, but a prolonged drought or an earthquake or an eclipse of the sun or the breaking out of a strange disease or a stroke of lightning or of blindness or of apoplexy — these were out of the range of common experience, the laws governing them were not understood, and they were therefore accounted as special acts of God designed for purposes of punishment or of warning. The Bible has many instances of this primitive mode of thought. We find in the earliest examples not only the belief in calamities as special acts of God, but the belief, also, that these calamities are invariably visited upon men or nations in punishment of sin.

Take, for example, the story of the destruction of Sodom and Gomorrah. Jehovah has heard of the great wickedness of these cities, and purposes to destroy them; but first he thinks it wise to come down and see if all he has heard is really true. He stops on the way to visit Abraham and to dine with him. After dinner they walk and discourse together concerning the doomed cities, Jehovah having confided to Abraham his purpose to destroy them. But Abraham has a nephew with his family living in Sodom, and being especially anxious to avert the destruction of the city, he takes the liberty of reminding Jehovah that if there are any good people there, it would be wrong to destroy the city. To this Jehovah agrees, but, as you remember, the story does not allow the existence of any good people (except Lot and his family who are warned to come away), and so the cities are utterly destroyed.

Yes, there was a time in Hebrew history when it was stoutly held that all calamity was a visitation of God's wrath for sin. If the question were asked how it was that innocent persons sometimes suffered misfortunes, the simple answer was made that it was not true. All suffering was held to come as the result of individual or family or national sin against the commandments of Jehovah.

But a certain event in Hebrew history — the defeat by the Egyptians of King Josiah. the most righteous, most (God-fearing king, who devoted his life to the service of Jehovah; who had purified the Temple of all heathen practices; who had bound Jehovah's law upon the necks of all the people so that they served him as never before; Josiah. who undertook this battle with the mighty Egyptians expressly in honor and defense of Jehovah's insulted divinity and majesty, with unquestioning faith that Jehovah's mighty arm would uphold him and smite his enemies dead — Josiah, had been killed and his forces had been ignobly routed, and the people reduced shortly afterwards to dependence upon a heathen king who despised Jehovah and worshipped bulls.

What could be said to this? There are pathetic evidences in more than one book of the Bible, how deeply was the faith of the race wounded, what dark and terrible problems were opened up to the minds and souls of this afflicted people. The book of Job had its origin probably out of the mental state of the people at this critical and terrible period, or out of the yet more trying Captivity soon following. Job, a pre-eminently righteous man, is visited by every conceivable species of calamity. His friends come to comfort him, but all they can do is to urge him, at first gently, but later with bitter insistence, to confess the secret fault or crime for which alone God would so punish him. This, you see, was the orthodox view of the time, — that Job must have been a hypocrite through all these years of his good reputation, and that now, at last, God was visiting his deserved punishment upon him. But Job humble yet emphatically protests his innocence. His conscience is at rest. His suffering cannot be a punishment for sin. And then he sets his mind upon the problem. But he, or the writer of the book, tho' he is great enough to see that the old answer is false, yet fails of the true one — fails to find an answer which even satisfies himself. For a time he tries to be satisfied with the idea that, as God is the creator of all things and has omnipotent power over all — therefore it is just for Him to do what He will with His creatures, — in other words, that "might makes right." But He cannot rest there — perhaps perceives that might makes, rather obligation to *do* right — and so in the ending scene of the drama he, or the writer rather, practically gives the problem up, by causing Jehovah to restore to Job twice as many cattle and sheep and twice as much money as he had before, together with other children to the number of those he had lost. A noble book, a noble landmark upon the highway of human reasoning into the inner counsels of God. Yet it does give up the problem of the relation of physical evil to conduct; the old idea still held sway, and theology sternly repressed any new and unconventional solution.

We can easily trace this doctrine and its effects through the centuries up to our own time. Throughout the middle ages, and almost into our own day, epidemics of deadly disease were held to be special visitations of God. To arrest the plague, long processions went chanting Te Deums through the filthy streets. So long as it was believed that the plague was a visitation of God's wrath, what more natural than that the people should all unite in supplications to God for its cure? Everywhere, pestilences resulting from neglect of most obvious precautions were called "inscrutable providences." Less than one hundred years ago, when epidemic disease made fearful havoc in Austria, the means of cure chiefly employed was praying before the image of St. Sebastian.

Scotland, whose cities even into our present century were given over to incredible filth, suffered thirty terrible epidemics between the thirteenth and seventeenth centuries. These epidemics were regarded as visitations of divine wrath against human sin, and the work of the authorities was to announce the particular sin and to thunder against it. But, strange to say, they seemed never to have hit upon sanitary sin as the cause of the plagues. In 1700 came the great fire of Edinburgh which cleared and cleaned the city and purged it of disease germs that had accumulated undisturbed for centuries. The town council of Edinburgh, however, declared this fire to be "a fearful rebuke of God." . . .

But let us return once more to our examination of the theory that God wills all disasters similar to that from which this city has just suffered, and see what this theory logically involves. It involves the terrible "Maine" disaster. Whether that were what we call an accident, or whether it were the deed of some miscreant, the ancient theory applied to our disaster here would apply equally there, also. If God had not willed it to be, it could not be; and if He willed it, it makes no essential difference by what means He brought it to pass. Upon this theory, also, it is God who is primarily responsible for the slaughter of the Cubans. No doubt ministers conducting the funeral services of Cuban soldiers and "Maine" victims have spoken of God's inscrutable providences which have caused these deaths. And when that murdered negro Post-master [Frazier B.] Baker of North Carolina, was buried with his little child murdered in its mother's arms, did some one speak above the coffin, of this strange manifestation of a mysterious Providence which takes this way of teaching us some needed lesson — we know not what?

If we believe that God willed and brought to pass our calamity of a week ago, we must believe that He wills and brings to pass all calamities; and this destroys all motive to avoid and prevent disasters by natural means. We have seen how this belief has worked out its legitimate result when it was really believed. When it was actually believed that all sickness was a visitation of God, it was held impious to seek medical aid. Let the sick call the priest, and let the priest, if the case be serious, bring some holy relic a bone or a tooth of some saint — and lay upon the afflicted part, and let the priest, if the case be desperate, bring the Holy Bambino, the sacred image of the Christ Child himself; and let the priest, if the case prove hopeless, shift his cure from body to soul, and administer the last sacrament! To call a physician was considered as a confession of impiety, and how the doctor and his profession were regarded is indicated by the popular mediaeval proverb: "Where there are three physicians there are two atheists." Possibly some kinds of atheism might he considered superior to some kinds of theism. You have perhaps heard the story of the conversation between Dr. Robert Collyer, I think it was, and a zealous minister of another persuasion who was earnestly discoursing to him of God — describing His power, His majesty, His judgment, His mercy to His elect and His everlasting condemnation of heathen and unbelievers. Dr. Collyer listened, and, from time to time, nodded and said "Yes, — yes, — yes," until the preacher had finished. And then he said cheerfully: "Why, I find we agree almost exactly, brother, — with just this one difference, — your God is my Devil.

I would not be irreverent, but nothing seems to me in fact so irreverent as these monstrous ideas of God that are set forth by good and sincere men who do not perceive the monstrousness because they veil it with words about "holy will" and "inscrutable wisdom," and the like. These are *words,* but what man or woman touched by real life believes their content? If men and women believed them, most of the work of the world would be done upon one's knees, imploring God to do as little injury as possible. But we are given, not knees alone, but brains and hands to work with — yea, and hearts to throb with diviner thoughts of God"; and conscience and judgment to see wherein we and others have committed mistakes and sins that have brought calamities. For example: We, with other nations, have believed in war. We have created a great naval ship and sent her into a hostile harbor. The wrong is not all ours; it is a part of the world's barbarism that still persists. And, whether the destruction of that ship were due to accident or to design, it is the spirit that creates th.mc engines of destruction to human life which made that horror possible and actual.

Again: Here we had in this town a danger that we knew not of, and yet perhaps we should have known. We will know from now forever after. If there is a lesson, it is not inscrutable, it is plain enough. Do not permit the carrying on of a dangerous occupation in the midst of the city. Do not allow bystanders near in case of fire. Be cautious how you treat with elements which, like fire, will overwhelm you if you yield the mastery.

And yet the qualities by which they overwhelm are the same qualities by virtue of which they serve us. Mix chloroform, ether and alcohol with good judgment and we have a merciful anesthetic. Mix them with fire, and we have an explosion. Why lay claim to the first result ourselves, and attribute the last to God?

And, terrible as the result of a mistake may be, I venture to believe that, for nature's laws not to act because of our mistakes, would be yet more terrible. Humanity learns its lessons by its mistakes; but more: If this be indeed a *universe,* if it be governed by universal law, the suspension for one instant of one law might throw the universe out of gear, and reduce law to anarchy and order to chaos. Think of it thus: If, for example, an inflammable gas refused to ignite in the presence of fire, here would be an area within which natural elements had changed their nature with no natural cause; an area, in other words, within which the law of cause and effect ceased to be operative. But, wherever we set the limits of that area, there must be a place where it joins on to the general law and order of the universe. But it cannot join on any more than unlike units in arithmetic can be added to each other. Not apples plus grapes, and not law and no law. It cannot join on; the majestic circle of universal order is broken, and the loose ends of the law fly wild, whipping the world to chaos.

The safety of God's universe is in the realm of universal law. The safety of men is to know and to regard these laws. I suppose we might have been made a mere part of the vast machinery — automata like the stars in their orbits which can do no violence, make no mistakes. But I agree to the sentiment that "a freely-acting sinner is better than an automatic saint," and that all our character and all our goodness depend upon our freedom to do right or wrong as we will; and that all our wisdom comes from making choices, wise or unwise, and learning by the experience; and that all our greatness and our humanhood, and the promise of that "which doth not yet appear" comes from our learning God's will through the operation of his laws in the outward world and the inward soul, and our choosing of our own volition to obey that will and help make that will be done on earth as in heaven. Helping, with the conviction that God expects us to help ourselves and Him.

We read of the little girl who was much distressed to find some bird-traps in the meadow. "I knelt right down," she said, "and prayed that God would not let the birds get into the traps. And then, I prayed that God would not let the traps catch the birds. And then," she added, "I got up and kicked the traps all to pieces."

Let us pray, if we will, that we may be spared calamities of all kinds; but let us, whenever we see a trap that may waylay even a little bird with calamity, consider it our part, also, to destroy the danger. I am sure our recent sorrow has taught this city some consideration, that will never again he overlooked. And the fearful lesson will reach far beyond the disaster to a hundred other cities warned through us . . .

NANNIE HELEN BURROUGHS

As Black Americans emerged from the hardships of slavery and Reconstruction, many women wanted to open doors for their people through reform work. But in the powerful Black Baptist church, the path to leadership for women was firmly shut — that is, until Nannie Helen Burroughs came along and pried it open.

In September 1900, she stepped up to the podium at the National Baptist Convention in Richmond, Virginia, and with a brief but fiery speech, shook up the denomination and won a wider role for women.

"For a number of years there has been a righteous discontent, a burning zeal to go forward in His name among the Baptist women of our churches," she told the audience. But with so much talent and zeal for reform, why weren't women allowed to become church leaders?

Baptist women wanted to serve the Church, she said, but like unpolished gems, they were a lost opportunity. "Will you . . . help by not hindering these women when they come among you to speak?"

After her speech, a man in the audience called out, "Why don't she sit down? She's always talking. She's just an upstart." To which Burroughs responded: "I might be an upstart, but I am just starting up."

Indeed she was. Thanks to that speech, Burroughs persuaded church leadership to approve a women's auxiliary. And at age twenty-one, Burroughs began to make a name for herself as a powerful speaker. One writer called her "the eloquent evangel."

In 1909 Burroughs appealed to the Baptist Convention to set up a school for young women and girls. With her church's support, six acres were purchased in northeast Washington, DC, to become the campus of the National Training School for Women and Girls. With Burroughs at the helm, the school educated Black women from around the world with a rigorous curriculum designed to make them independent and self sufficient.

"Many opportunities are going from the women of the negro race because of their incompetency," she told the Women's Auxiliary. "It is necessary that in this age of the world they should know how to work."

Burroughs introduced courses that would prepare her students for jobs traditionally held by men, such as gardening, shoe repair, printing, barbering, tailoring, power machine operation, and — a subject especially dear to her heart — public speaking. The Baptist church was always at the center of her work, and she required her students to be practicing Christians.

She led the school for half a century, devoting her life to the education and elevation of Black women.

"HOW THE SISTERS ARE HINDERED FROM HELPING"

September 13, 1900
Twentieth Annual Session of the National Baptist Convention,
Fifth Street Baptist Church, Richmond, Virginia

We come not to usurp thrones nor to sow discord but to so organize and systematize the work that each church may help through a Woman's Missionary Society and not be made poorer thereby. It is for the utilization of talent and the stimulation to Christian activity in our Baptist churches that prompt us to service. We realize that to allow these gems to lie unpolished longer means a loss to the denomination.

For a number of years there has been a righteous discontent, a burning zeal to go forward in His name among the Baptist women of our churches and it will be the dynamic force in the religious campaign at the opening of the 20th century. It will be the spark that shall light the altar fire in the heathen lands. We realize, too, that the work is too great and laborers too few for us to stand by while like Trojans the brethren at the head of the work under the convention toil unceasingly.

We come now to the rescue. We unfurl our banner upon which is inscribed this motto, "The World for Christ, Woman, Arise, He calleth for Thee."

Will you as a pastor and friend of missions help by not hindering these women when they come among you to speak and to enlist the women of your church? It has ever been from the time of Miriam, that most remarkable woman, the sister of Moses, that most remarkable man, down to the courageous women that in very recent years have carried the Gospel into Thibet and Africa and proclaimed and taught the truth where no man has been allowed to enter. Surely, women somehow have had a very important part in the work of saving this redeemed earth.

Praying the Great Head of the Church to bless all the departments of our national work, we are yours for the highest development of Christian womanhood.

CARRIE NATION

After ten months of marriage, she took her infant and walked out on her husband, who was a drunk. That was the spark that ignited Carrie Nation's crusade against the liquor trade.

As a temperance speaker, she joined a cause that had gotten its start in early 1800s America. Despite the early objections of men who didn't want women on the speaking platform, women joined the movement in droves, drawn in because they were the ones who experienced first-hand the corrosive effects of excessive drinking on family life at a time when there were no laws outlawing domestic violence, marital rape, or child abuse. Even if a woman managed to secure a divorce, her husband could easily obtain sole guardianship of the children.

That fundamental imbalance led many women to view alcohol as the source of intractable social problems, and they filled the ranks of the Women's Christian Temperance Movement.

Under the stewardship of Frances Willard, the WCTU mostly attracted middle and upper-class White Protestant women, by the hundreds of thousands, which gave the organization tremendous political heft.

Soon, practically every town in America had its female temperance speakers. But none compared to Nation.

She staged her first assault in 1900 on a saloon in Medicine Lodge, Kansas, by singing hymns and temperance songs until she shut the place down. On she went, from one watering hole to another, bringing a hatchet to smash up the bar mirrors. She called her events "hachetations" and even sold tiny "Hatchet Granny" lapel pins.

She was attacked, jailed, and fined. Her colorful remarks were catnip to the press, put a spotlight on public corruption, and focused attention on the fact that women were powerless and had no legal recourse for reform.

In 1902, on a balcony overlooking Lake Michigan, Nation raised a glass of cold, pure water and cried out to the crowd, "I always drink as Adam drank before there was any sin."

A man in the audience called out, "Who brought sin into the world?"

Nation shot back: "You're a drunken old rat."

In 1904 she paid a visit to the Kansas Capitol in Topeka, where a senator threatened to throw her out. "You are sent here to represent the interests of the mothers and their children," she chided him, "and you insult a representative mother because you are representing the interests of the brewers and distillers."

Of course, she was right.

What often gets overlooked about Nation is her genius at gaining public attention for her cause. Light years ahead of commercial radio, television, and social media, she understood the power of performance — and used it well.

"EFFECT OF THE HATCHET"

August 20, 1902
Lake Michigan Park, Muskegon, Michigan

D ear friends, I will introduce myself to you as your loving home defender. This is Hell's conspiracy... the only difference between the parties is that one is in office and the other is out. Both are the enemies of your homes. Any one that will vote for the interest of the breweries votes to destroy your homes.

The effect of the hatchet has been to wake up the nation and make it think about this question. It is my purpose to animate men so that they will get their hatchets out and vote right. A great many people have denounced me for things I said about [President William] McKinley. Mr. McKinley was in favor of the brewer and if Mr. McKinley was the ideal of the people then the brewer is the people's ideal. We want presidents that will protect our homes.

If one starts out to protect herself she is incarcerated. They put me in jail because I used the hatchet. The governor of Kansas would pardon murderers and thieves, but he would not pardon a woman who would protect herself with a hatchet. Are you going to vote against the Prohibition Party, men? If you do you will vote against the best friends you have — the women.

There is oppression in this town — oppression of widows and children. There is oppression and crime and groaning and poverty and shame in this town, voted here by your men. You see how the Republicans are robbing your children and breaking the hearts of your women. They stand for the brewers.

I would gladly have given up my life. It seems strange that men would vote for this thing, that the American people are so indifferent to their homes. No law can establish a business that is no benefit to the community. The dry goods store and the grocery are a benefit to you. The saloons are not. You have got them here by licensing them here. You have voted for them, you men in the Democratic Party; you have voted for their conspiracy against your neighbors. You hypocrite, if you set in the Amen corner and vote for it you are the Devil's own scullion.

You Republicans vote not only to send these people's souls to hell, but you are going to hell yourself.

["Cut it out!" yelled a man in the audience.]

You can't cut it out. It's the cause of humanity.

I told you this afternoon I would tell you why I did what I did in Kansas. We had dives in Kansas that had never been closed. I went to the prosecuting attorney and I said, "You swore to close those dives up. You have got to do it."

The law says when intoxicating liquors are sold in a place it is a nuisance. The common law says that when a nuisance exists a citizen or citizens can abate it. Two years ago God said to me, "Go to Kiowa and break up the joints and I'll stand by you." So I rolled up bricks and rocks in newspapers and put them in a basket and drove down to Kiowa. When I got there I went into the first place and said, "I told you to close this place. Now get out of my way, for I'm going to break it up." . . .

[At the close of the lecture, a man in the audience called out, "Who brought sin into the world?"]

"You're a drunken old rat."

MARY HARRIS "MOTHER" JONES

What does it mean to agitate?

That's the question Mary Harris Jones — more famously known as "Mother Jones" — asked in a 1903 speech in Toledo, Ohio. "I'm for agitation," she told the crowd. "It's the greatest factor for progress."

According to *Merriam-Webster*, one of the main definitions of "agitation" is "to stir up public discussion." Mother Jones agitated with the most powerful weapon she had: her voice.

In 1903, she agitated against "wage slavery." She agitated on behalf of a fifty-five-hour work week. She agitated against harsh conditions and ineffectual child labor laws in the coal mines and silk mills. She agitated to call attention to the killing of six miners during a strike at the Stanaford camp in West Virginia.

That's where a US deputy marshal, a local sheriff, and a hired security official had assembled a posse that gunned down the miners — three of them Black men — in the early morning hours. As she wrote in her 1925 *Autobiography of Mother Jones,* when she arrived she saw the miners' shack "riddled with bullets. In five other shacks men lay dead. In one of them a baby boy and his mother sobbed."

Jones was an Irish-born schoolteacher and dressmaker who suffered unfathomable tragedies. In 1867 her husband, an iron moulder, and all four children died of yellow fever in Memphis. She stayed put and nursed other victims until the plague was stamped out.

A few years later, her home and dress shop were burnt to the ground in the Great Chicago fire of 1871. That's when she became an organizer for the Knights of Labor and the United Mine Workers.

"It's high time you got out and worked for humanity," she told a mass audience in Toledo's Memorial Hall in 1903. Four months later, she organized a "children's crusade," a march on foot all the way from Philadelphia to the summer home of President Theodore Roosevelt on Long Island in New York. The children carried banners that said, "We want to go to school and not the mines."

When they finally arrived in posh Oyster Bay, the President refused to see them.

Mother Jones kept agitating. She remained a union organizer for the United Mine Workers into the 1920s, and spoke out about union affairs, child welfare, and better working conditions until the end of her life. She was called "the most dangerous woman in America."

What does agitation mean to us today? There's no shortage of issues that cry out for public discussion and action. The world is overflowing with problems that demand our attention and our voices.

How will you use yours?

"AGITATION — THE GREATEST FACTOR FOR PROGRESS"

March 24, 1903
Memorial Hall, Toledo, Ohio

F
ellow workers, 'tis well for us to be here. Over a hundred years ago men gathered to discuss the vital questions and later fought together for a principle that won for us our civil liberty. Forty years ago men gathered to discuss a growing evil under the old flag and later fought side by side until chattel slavery was abolished. But, by the wiping out of this black stain upon our country another great crime — wage slavery — was fastened upon our people. I stand on this platform ashamed of the conditions existing in this country. I refused to go to England and lecture only a few days ago because I was ashamed, first of all, to make the conditions existing here known to the world and second, because my services were needed here. I have just come from a God-cursed country, known as West Virginia; from a state which has produced some of our best and brightest statesmen; a state where conditions are too awful for your imagination.

I shall tell you some things tonight that are awful to contemplate; but, perhaps, it is best that you to know of them. They may arouse you from your lethargy if there is any manhood, womanhood or love of country left in you. I have just come from a state which has an injunction on every other foot of ground. Some months ago the president of the United Mine Workers [John Mitchell] asked me to take a look into the condition of the men in the mines of West Virginia. I went. I would get a gathering of miners in the darkness of the night up on the mountain side. Here I would listen to their tale of woe; here I would try to encourage them. I did not dare to sleep in one of those miner's houses. If I did the poor man would be called to the office in the morning and would be discharged for sheltering old Mother Jones.

I did my best to drive into the downtrodden men a little spirit, but it was a task. They had been driven so long that they were afraid. I used to sit through the night by a stream of water. I could not go to the miners' hovels so in the morning I would call the ferryman and he would take me across the river to a hotel not owned by the mine operators.

The men in the anthracite district finally asked for more wages. They were refused. A strike was called. I stayed in West Virginia, held meetings and one day as I stood talking to some break-boys two injunctions were served upon me. I asked the deputy if he had more. We were arrested but we were freed in the morning. I objected to the food in the jail and to my arrest. When I was called up before the judge I called him a czar and he let me go. The other fellows were afraid and they went to jail. I violated injunction after injunction but I wasn't re-arrested. Why? The courts themselves force you to have no respect for that court.

A few days later that awful wholesale murdering in the quiet little mining camp of [Stanaford] took place. I know those people were law-abiding citizens. I had been there. And their shooting by United States deputy marshals was an atrocious and cold-blooded murder. After the crimes had been committed the marshals — the murderers — were banqueted by the operators in the swellest hotel in Pennsylvania. You. have no idea of the awfulness of that wholesale murder. Before daylight broke in the morning in that quiet little mining camp deputies and special officers went into the homes, shot the men down in their beds, and all because the miners wanted to try to induce 'black-legs' to leave the mines.

I'll tell you how the trouble started. The deputies were bringing these strike-breakers to the mines. The men wanted to talk with them and at last stepped on ground loaded down with an injunction. There were thirty-six or seven in the party of miners. They resisted arrest. They went home finally without being arrested. One of the officials of the miners' unions telegraphed to the men. "Don't resist. Go to jail. We will bail you out." A United States marshal . . . sent back word that the operators would not let them use the telephone to send the message to the little mining camp and that he could not get there before hours had passed. The miners' officials secured the names of the men and gave their representatives authority to bail them out of jail the next morning. But when the next morning arrived they were murdered in cold blood.

These federal judges, who continue granting injunctions, are appointed by men who have their political standing through the votes of you labor union fellows! You get down on your knees like a lot of Yahoos when you want something. At the same time you haven't sense enough to take peaceably what belongs to you through the ballot. You are chasing a will-o-the-wisp, you measly things, and the bullets which should be sent into your own measly, miserable, dirty carcasses, shoot down innocent men. Women are not responsible because they have no vote. You'd all better put on petticoats. If you like those bullets vote to put them into your own bodies. Don't you think it's about time you began to shoot ballots instead of voting for capitalistic bullets.

I hate your political parties, you Republicans and Democrats. I want you to deny if you can what I am going to say. You want an office and must necessarily get into the ring. You must do what that ring says and if you don't you won't be elected. There you are. Each time you do that you are voting for a capitalistic bullet and you get it. I want you to know that this man [Samuel Milton] Jones who is running for mayor of your beautiful city is no relative of mine; no, sir. He belongs to that school of reformers who say capital and labor must join hands. He may be all right. He prays a good deal. But, I wonder if you would shake hands with me if I robbed you. He builds parks to make his workmen contented. But a contented workman is no good. All progress stops in the contented man. I'm for agitation. It's the greatest factor for progress.

I see a lot of society women in this audience, attracted here out of a mere curiosity to see that old Mother Jones. I know you better than you do yourselves. I can walk down the aisle and pick every one of you out. You probably think I am crazy but I know you. And you society dudes — poor creatures. You wear high collars to support your jaw and keep your befuddled brains from oozing out of your mouths. While this commercial cannibalism is reaching into the cradle; pulling girls into the factory to be ruined; pulling children into the factory to be destroyed; you, who are doing all in the name of Christianity, you are at home nursing your poodle dogs. It's high time you got out and worked for humanity. Christianity will take care of itself. I started in a factory. I have traveled through miles and miles of factories and there is not an inch of ground under that flag that is not stained with the blood of children.

You may think, as people sometimes do, that my pictures are overdrawn. But if you would come with me I could show you that I have not the power to describe in words the awful conditions existing in some districts and especially in West Virginia. I have not told the half. And, until you labor fallows wake up those conditions will grow from bad to worse.

ISADORA DUNCAN

Isadora Duncan was all the rage in the arty, avant-garde circles of Berlin. She had been born in San Francisco, but it was in Europe where she found a reception for her innovative form of dance. In 1903, she was performing nightly for the city's cultural elite in loose flowing gowns so scandalously sheer you could see the contours of her body. Her ankles were bare, her feet in sandals.

"Immoral," fumed the head of the Berlin Artists' Society.

An editorial in the *Morgen Post* asked, "Can Miss Duncan Dance?"

She shot back with a letter to the editor, asking "Can the Dancing Maenad Dance?" It was a reference to an ancient Greek statue in the Berlin Museum that, she pointed out, had been dancing far longer than she had in "neither corset nor tights."

Duncan was invited to speak at the Berlin Press Club. Her talk, "The Dance of the Future," was an expression of her artistic vision, an argument for unrestrained movement that was simple, free and natural — a rebellion against the rigid costumes, hard slippers, and punishing formalities of classical ballet.

She published the speech as a pamphlet in German and English, and it has become a celebrated manifesto of modern movement and feminism. In an age when most choreographers and dance theorists were men, Duncan boldly declared the liberation of women from all restrictions: artistic, social, and political.

"She shall dance the freedom of woman," she said. "O, what a field is here awaiting her! Do you not feel that she is near, that she is coming, this dancer of the future?"

The speech was heavily influenced by her explorations of German philosophy, in particular Friedrich Nietzsche's idea of the primitive Dionysian force that fueled humanity's instinctive, chaotic emotions.

Duncan's own life was filled with turbulence and tragedy. Ten years after that talk, her two little children accidentally drowned with their nanny outside of Paris when their car rolled into the Seine. Her husband, a Russian poet, committed suicide.

In 1927, Duncan died in a bizarre accident in Nice when her long silk scarf got caught in the wheel of her open car, hurling her onto the roadway.

She's remembered as an artistic revolutionary who left a profound imprint on modern dance. It's also hard to think of another dancer who engaged with the public so often through the spoken word, delivering statements to the press, giving impromptu talks, and using language to try and capture the ineffable.

As she once said: "If I could tell you what it meant, there would be no point in dancing it."

"DANCE OF THE FUTURE"

March 5, 1903
Berlin Press Association, Architectenhaus, Berlin, Germany

To express what is the most moral, healthful and beautiful in art — this is the mission of the dancer, and to this I dedicate my life.

These flowers before me contain the dream of a dance; it could be named: "The light falling on white flowers". A dance that would be a subtle translation of the light and the whiteness. So pure, so strong, that people would say: It is a soul we see moving, a soul that has reached the light and found the whiteness. We are glad it should move so. Through its human medium we have a satisfying sense of the movement of light and glad things. Through this human medium, the movement of all nature runs also through us, is transmitted to us from the dancer. We feel the movement of light intermingled with the thought of whiteness. It is a prayer, this dance, each movement reaches in long ondulations [sp] to the heavens and becomes a part of the eternal rythm [sp] of the spheres.

To find those primary movements for the human body from which shall evolve the movements of the future dance in ever variating natural unending sequences, that is the duty of the new dancer of to day.

To give an example of this, we might take the pose of the Hermes of the Greeks. He is represented as flying on the wind. If the artist had pleased to post his foot in a vertical position he might have done so, as the god, flying on the wind, is not touching the earth; but realizing that no movement is true unless suggesting sequence of movements the sculptor placed the Hermes with the ball of his foot resting on the wind, giving the movement an eternal quality.

In the same way I might make examples of each pose and gesture in the thousands of figures we have left us on the Greek vases and bas reliefs; there is not one which in its movement does not presuppose another movement.

This is because the Greeks were the greatest students of the laws of nature, wherein all is the expression of unending ever increasing evolution, wherein are no ends and no stops.

Such movements will always have to depend on and correspond to the form that is moving. The movements of a beetle correspond to its form. So do those of the horse. Even so the movements of the human body must correspond to its form. They should even correspond to its individual form. The dance of no two persons should be alike.

People have thought that so long as one danced in rythm [sic], the form and design did not matter; but no . . . one must perfectly correspond to the other. The Greeks understood this very well. One of our illustrations shows a dancing Cupid. It is a child's dance. The movements of the plump little feet and arms are perfectly suited to its form. The sole of the foot rests flat on the ground, a position which might be ugly in a more developed person, but is natural in a child trying to keep its balance. One of the legs is half raised: if it were out-stretched it would irritate us, because the movement would be unnatural. The satyr in the next illustration shows a dance that is quite different from that of the Cupid. His movements are those of a ripe and muscular man. They are in perfect harmony with the structure of his body.

The Greeks in all their painting, sculpture, architecture, literature, dance and tragedy evolved their movements from the movement of nature, as we plainly see expressed in all representations of the Greek gods, who, being no other than the representatives of natural forces, are always designed in a pose expressing the concentration and evolution of these forces. This is why the art of the Greeks is not a national or characteristic art but has been and will be the art of all humanity for all time.

Therefore dancing naked upon the earth I naturally fall into Greek positions, for Greek positions are only earth positions.

The noblest in art is the nude. This truth is recognized by all, and followed by painters, sculptors and poets; only the dancer has forgotten it, who should most remember it as the instrument of her art is the human body itself.

Man's first conception of beauty is gained from the form and symmetry of the human body. The new school of the dance should be that movement which is in harmony with and will develop the highest form of the human body.

I intend to work for this dance of the future. I do not know whether I have the necessary qualities: I may have neither genius, not talent, nr temperament, but I know that I have a Will; and will and energy is sometimes greater than either, genius or talent or temperament.

Let me anticipate all that can be said against my qualifications for my work in the following little fable:

The Gods looked down through the glass roof of my studio and Athena said: "She is not wise, she is not wise, in fact, she is remarkably stupid".

And Demeter looked and said, — "She is a weakling small thing — not like my deep-breasted daughters who play in the fields of Eleusis; one can see each rib, she is not worthy to dance on my broad-wayed Earth". And Iris looked down and said: "See how heavily she moves — does she guess nothing of the swift and gracious movement of a winged being?" And Pan looked and said "What, does she think she knows ought of the movements of my satyrs, splendid twyhorned fellows who have within them all the fragrant life of the woods and waters." And then Terpsichore gave one scornful glance: "And — she calls that dancing! Why, her feet move more like the lazy steps of a deranged turtle".

And all the Gods laughed: but I looked bravely up through the glass roof and said:

"O, ye imortal [sic] Gods who dwell in high Olympus and live on Ambrosia and Honey-Cakes and pay no studio rent nor bakers bills thereof, do not judge me so scornfully. It is true O, Athena that I am not wise, and my head is a rattled institution; but I do occasionally read the word of those who have gazed into the infinite blue of thine eyes and I bow my empty gourd head very humbly before thine altars. And, O, Demeter of the Holy Garland," I continued, "it is true that the beautiful maidens of your broad-wayed earth would not admit me of their company: still I have thrown aside my sandals that my feet may touch your life-giving earth more reverently and I have had your sacred Hymn sung before the present day Barbarians and I have made them to listen and to find it good.

"And, O, Iris of the golden wings, it is true that mine is but a sluggish movement; — others of my profession have luted more violently against the laws of gravitation, from which laws, O, glorious one you are alone exempt. Yet the wind from your wings has swept through my poor earthly spirit and I have often brought prayers to your courage-inspiring image.

"And, O, Pan, you who were pitiful and gentle to simple Psyche in her wanderings, thing more kindly of my little attempts to dance in your woody places.

"And you most exquisite one, Terpsichore, send to me a little comfort and strength that I may proclaim your power on Earth during my life; and afterwards, in the shadowy Hades my wistful spirit shall dance dances better yet in thine honor —." Then came the voice of Zeus the thunderer:

"Continue your way and rely upon the eternal justice of the immortal Gods: if you work well they shall know if it and be pleased thereof."

In this sense then I intend to work and if I could find in my dance a few or even one single position that the sculptor could transfer into marble so that it might be preserved, my work would not have been in vain; this one form would be a gain; it would be a first step for the future. My intention is, in due time, to found a school, to build a theatre where a hundred little girls shall be trained in my art, which they in their turn will better. In this school I shall not teach the children to imitate my movements, but to make their own, I shall not force them to study certain definite movements, I shall help them to develop those movements which are natural to them. Whosoever sees the movements of an untaught little child cannot deny that its movements are beautiful. They are beautiful because they are natural to the child. Even so the movements of the human body may be beautiful in every stage of development so long as they are in harmony with that stage and degree of maturity which the body has attained. There will always be movements which are the perfect expression of that individual body and that individual soul: so we must not force it to make movements which are not natural to it but which belong to a school. An intelligent child must be astonished to find that in the ballet school it is taught movements contrary to all those movements which it would make of its own accord.

This may seem a question of little importance, a question of differing opinions on the ballet and the new dance. But it is a great question. It is not only a question of true art, it is a question of race, of the development of the female sex to beauty and health, of the return to the original strength and to natural movements of a woman's body. It is a question of the development of perfect mothers and the birth of healthy and beautiful children. The dancing school of the future is to develop and to show the ideal form of woman. It will be as it were a museum of the living beauty of the period.

Travellers coming into a country and seeing the dancers should find in them that country's ideal of the beauty of form and movement. But strangers who to-day come to any country and there see the dancers of the ballet school would get a strange notion indeed of the ideal of beauty in this country. More than that, dancing like any art of any time should reflect the highest point the spirit of mankind has reached in that special period. Does anybody think that the present day ballet school expresses this?

Why are its positions in such a contrast to the beautiful positions of the antique sculptures which we preserve in our museums and which are constantly represented to us as perfect models of ideal beauty? Or have our museums only been founded out of historical and archeological interest and not for the sake of the beauty of the objects which they contain?

The ideal of beauty of the human body cannot change with fashion but only with evolution. Remember the story of the beautiful sculpture of a Roman girl which was discovered under the reign of pope Innocent VIII and which by its beauty created such a sensation that the men thronged to see it and made pilgrimages to it as to a holy shrine, so that the pope, troubled by the movement which it originated, finally had it buried again.

And here I want to avoid a misunderstanding that might easily arise. From what I have said you might conclude that my intention is to return to the dances of the old Greeks or that I think that the dance of the future will be a revival of the antique dances or even of those of the primate tribes. No, the dance of the future will be a new movement, a consequence of the entire evolution which mankind has passed through. To return to the dances of the Greeks would be as impossible as it is unnecessary. We are not Greeks and cannot therefore dance Greek dances. But the dance of the future will have to become again a high religious art as it was with the Greeks. For art which is not religious is not art, is mere merchandise.

The dancer of the future will be one whose body and soul have grown so harmoniously together that the natural language of the soul will have become the movement of the body. The dancer will not belong to a nation but to all humanity. She will dance not in the form of nymph, nor fairy, nor coquette but in the form of woman in it greatest and purest expression. She will realize the mission of woman's body and the holiness of all its parts. She will dance the changing life of nature, showing how each part is transformed into the other. From all parts of her body shall shine radiant intelligence, bringing to the world the message of the thoughts and aspirations of thousands of women. She shall dance the freedom of woman. O, what a field is here awaiting her! Do you not feel that she is near, that she is coming, this dancer of the future? She will help womankind to a new knowledge of the possible strength and beauty of their bodies and the relation of their bodies to the earth nature and to the children of the future. She will dance the body emerging again from centuries of civilized forgetfulness, emerging not in the nudity of primitive man, but in a new nakedness, no longer at war with spirituality and intelligence, but joining itself forever with this intelligence in a glorious harmony.

This is the mission of the dancer of the future. O, do you not feel that she is near, do you not long for her coming as I do? Let us prepare the place for her. I would build for her a temple to await her. Perhaps she is yet unborn, perhaps she is now a little child, perhaps O, blissful — it may be my holy mission to guide her first steps, to watch the progress of her movements day by day until, far outgrowing my poor teaching, her movements will become godlike, mirrowing [sic] in themselves the waves, the winds, the movements of growing things, the flight of birds, the passing of clouds and finally the thought of man in his relation to the universe. O, she is coming, the dancer of the future: the free spirit, who will inhabit the body of new women; more glorious than any woman that has yet been; more beautiful than the Egyptian, than the Greek, the early Italian, than all woman in past centuries: The highest intelligence in the freest body!

MARY CHURCH TERRELL

In 1906, the population of Washington, DC was nearly one third Black, and the city was known as "the Colored Man's Paradise."

But that didn't mean real racial equality had actually been achieved. If anything, Jim Crow segregation laws had only hardened in previous years, as Mary Church Terrell made painfully clear in her 1906 speech to a women's club. To her, conditions for Blacks in the city were "intolerable."

In wrenching detail, she described the day-to-day insults, inconveniences, and hardships for Black people, who were barred from hotels, restaurants, theaters, even houses of worship.

"I may walk from the Capitol to the White House, ravenously hungry and abundantly supplied with money with which to purchase a meal, without finding a single restaurant in which I would be permitted to take a morsel of food," she told her audience. As for an equal shot at a job, "the door is shut in my face."

One of the country's first Black college-educated women, Terrell had lived in the nation's capital for fifteen years. She was a former high school teacher and member of the District of Columbia Board of Education. As a founder of the National Association of Colored Women, she focused her activism on ending discrimination and empowering Black women. She once famously noted, "We labor under the double handicap of race and sex."

She gave hundreds of speeches around the world, trying to force Whites out of their complacency and spur social change. In her autobiography, she described the racism of White America as "assault and battery committed on a human being's soul."

As she told it, she once gave a speech in Fort Worth, Texas, about "the race problem," and afterwards a woman called her "bitter." That word would come up again and again.

"Colored people so seldom tell certain truths about conditions which confront their race that, when they do," she said, "White people who are interested in them feel that they must be "bitter."" But she was only stating facts.

Segregation in Washington, DC, would not end until the early 1950s. One of the first hammer blows was a 1953 Supreme Court decision that desegregated restaurants. That case was *District of Columbia v. John R. Thompson Co., Inc.*, and involved a diner on 14th Street that refused to serve three Black patrons — one of them was Terrell, still fighting for her rights at age 87.

The following year, just three months before Terrell passed away, came the Supreme Court's landmark decision in *Brown v. Board of Education*, which began the process of dismantling racial segregation nationwide.

"WHAT IT MEANS TO BE COLORED IN THE CAPITAL OF THE UNITED STATES"

October 10, 1906
United Women's Club, Washington, DC

Washington DC has been called "The Colored Man's Paradise." Whether this sobriquet was given to the national capital in bitter irony by a member of the handicapped race, as he reviewed some of his own persecutions and rebuffs, or whether it was given immediately after the war by an ex-slaveholder who for the first time in his life saw colored people walking about like free men, minus the overseer and his whip, history saith not.

It is certain that it would be difficult to find a worse misnomer for Washington than "The Colored Man's Paradise" if so prosaic a consideration as veracity is to determine the appropriateness of a name.

For fifteen years I have resided in Washington, and while it was far from being a paradise for colored people when I first touched these shores it has been doing its level best ever since to make conditions for us intolerable. As a colored woman I might enter Washington any night, a stranger in a strange land, and walk miles without finding a place to lay my head. Unless I happened to know colored people who live here or ran across a chance acquaintance who could recommend a colored boarding-house to me, I should be obliged to spend the entire night wandering about. Indians, Chinamen, Filipinos, Japanese and representatives of any other dark race can find hotel accommodations, if they can pay for them. The colored man alone is thrust out of the hotels of the national capital like a leper.

As a colored woman I may walk from the Capitol to the White House, ravenously hungry and abundantly supplied with money with which to purchase a meal, without finding a single restaurant in which I would be permitted to take a morsel of food, if it was patronized by white people, unless I were willing to sit behind a screen.

As a colored woman I cannot visit the tomb of the Father of this country, which owes its very existence to the love of freedom in the human heart and which stands for equal opportunity to all, without being forced to sit in the Jim Crow section of an electric car which starts form the very heart of the city — midway between the Capital and the White House. If I refuse thus to be humiliated, I am cast into jail and forced to pay a fine for violating the Virginia laws. Every hour in the day Jim Crow cars filled with colored people, many of whom are intelligent and well to do, enter and leave the national capital.

As a colored woman I may enter more than one white church in Washington without receiving that welcome which as a human being I have the right to expect in the sanctuary of God. Sometimes the color blindness of the usher takes on that peculiar form which prevents a dark face from making any impression whatsoever upon his retina, so that it is impossible for him to see colored people at all. If he is not so afflicted, he will ungraciously show these dusky Christians who have had the temerity to thrust themselves into a temple where only the fair of face are expected to worship God to a seat in the rear, which is named in honor of a certain personage, well known in this country, and commonly called Jim Crow.

Unless I am willing to engage in a few menial occupations, in which the pay for my services would be very poor, there is no way for me to earn an honest living, if I am not a trained nurse or a dressmaker or can secure a position as teacher in the public schools, which is exceedingly difficult to do. It matters not what my intellectual attainments may be or how great is the need of the services of a competent person, if I try to enter many of the numerous vocations in which my white sisters are allowed to engage, the door is shut in my face.

From one Washington theater I am excluded altogether. In the remainder certain seats are set aside for colored people, and it is almost impossible to secure others. I once telephoned to the ticket seller just before a matinee and asked if a neat-appearing colored nurse would be allowed to sit in the parquet with her little white charge, and the answer rushed quickly and positively thru the receiver — NO. When I remonstrated a bit and told him that in some of the theaters colored nurses were allowed to sit with the white children for whom they cared, the ticket seller told me that in Washington it was very poor policy to employ colored nurses, for they were excused from many places where white girls would be allowed to take children for pleasure.

If I possess artistic talent, there is not a single art school of repute which will admit me. A few years ago a colored woman who possessed great talent submitted some drawings to the Corcoran Art School, of Washington, which were accepted by the committee of awards, who sent her a ticket entitling her to a course in this school. But when the committee discovered that the young woman was colored they declined to admit her, and told her that if they had suspected that her drawings had been made by a colored woman they would not have examined them at all. The efforts of Frederick Douglass and a lawyer of great repute who took a keen interest in the affair were unavailing. In order to cultivate her talent this young woman was forced to leave her comfortable home in Washington and incur the expense of going to New York. Having entered the Woman's Art School of Cooper Union, she graduated with honor, and then went to Paris to continue her studies, where she achieved signal success and was complimented by some of the greatest living artists in France.

With the exception of the Catholic University, there is not a single white college in the national capitol to which colored people are admitted. A few years ago the Columbian Law School admitted colored students, but in deference to the Southern white students the authorities have decided to exclude them altogether . . .

Altho white and colored teachers are under the same Board of Education and the system for the children of both races is said to be uniform, prejudice against the colored teachers in the public schools is manifested in a variety of ways. From 1870 to 1900 there was a colored superintendent at the head of the colored schools. During all that time the directors of the cooking, sewing, physical culture, manual training, music and art departments were colored people. Six years ago a change was inaugurated. The colored superintendent was legislated out of office and the directorships, without a single exception, were taken from colored teachers and given to the whites. There was no complaint about the work done by the colored directors, no more than is heard about every officer in every school. The directors of the art and physical culture departments were particularly fine. Now, no matter how competent or superior the colored teachers in our public schools may be, they know that they can never rise to the height of a directorship, can never hope to be more than an assistant and receive the meager salary therefore, unless the present regime is radically changed.

Not long ago one of the most distinguished kindergartners in the country came to deliver a course of lectures in Washington. The colored teachers were eager to attend, but they could not buy the coveted privilege for love or money. When they appealed to the director of kindergartens, they were told that the expert kindergartners had come to Washington under the auspices of private individuals, so that she could not possibly have them admitted. Realizing what a loss colored teachers had sustained in being deprived of the information and inspiration which these lectures afforded, one of the white teachers volunteered to repeat them as best she could for the benefit of her colored co-laborers for half the price she herself had paid, and the proportion was eagerly accepted by some.

Strenuous efforts are being made to run Jim Crow cars in the national capital. "Resolved, that a Jim Crow law should be adopted and enforced in the District of Columbia," was the subject of a discussion engaged in last January by the Columbian Debating Society of the George Washington University in our national capital, and the decision was rendered in favor of the affirmative. Representative

Heflin, of Alabama, who introduced a bill providing for Jim Crow street cars in the District of Columbia last winter, has just received a letter from the president of the East Brookland Citizens' Association "Endorsing the movement for separate street cars and sincerely hoping that you will be successful in getting this enacted into a law as soon as possible." Brookland is a suburb of Washington.

The colored laborer's path to a decent livelihood is by no means smooth. Into some of the trades unions here he is admitted, while from others he is excluded altogether. By the union men this is denied, altho I am personally acquainted with skilled workmen who tell me they are not admitted into the unions because they are colored. But even when they are allowed to join the unions they frequently derive little benefit, owing to certain tricks of the trade. When the word passes round that help is needed and colored laborers apply, they are often told by the union officials that they have secured all the men they needed, because the places are reserved for white men, until they have been provided with jobs, and colored men must remain idle, unless the supply of white men is too small.

I am personally acquainted with one of the most skillful laborers in the hardware business in Washington. For thirty years he has been working for the same firm. He told me he could not join the union, and that his employer had been almost forced to discharge him, because the union men threatened to boycott his store if he did not. If another man could have been found at the time to take his place he would have lost his job, he said. When no other human being can bring a refractory chimney or stove to its senses, this colored man is called upon as the court of last appeal. If he fails to subdue it, it is pronounced a hopeless case at once. And yet this expert workman receives much less for his services than do white men who cannot compare with him in skill.

And so I might go on citing instance after instance to show the variety of ways in which our people are sacrificed on the altar of prejudice in the Capital of the United States and how almost insurmountable are the obstacles which block his path to success. Early in life many a colored youth is so appalled by the helplessness and the hopelessness of his situation in this country that in a sort of stoical despair he resigns himself to his fate. "What is the good of our trying to acquire an education? We can't all be preachers, teachers, doctors and lawyers. Besides those professions there is almost nothing for colored people to do but engage in the most menial occupations, and we do not need an education for that." More than once such remarks, uttered by young men and women in our public schools who possess brilliant intellects, have wrung my heart.

It is impossible for any white person in the United States, no matter how sympathetic and broad, to realize what life would mean to him if his incentive to effort were suddenly snatched away. To the lack of incentive to effort, which is the awful shadow under which we live, may be traced the wreck and ruin of scores of colored youth. And surely nowhere in the world do oppression and persecution based solely on the color of the skin appear more hateful and hideous than in the capital of the United States, because the chasm between the principles upon which this Government was founded, in which it still professes to believe, and those which are daily practiced under the protection of the flag, yawns so wide and deep.

AURORA LUCERO-WHITE LEA

By 1910, the character of the Hispanic Southwest was changing. The majority of citizens in the New Mexico Territory still spoke Spanish as their main language, but population growth, the arrival of the railroads, and industrialization had brought profound change. Although they accepted the US political system and welcomed citizenship, they also feared their religious and cultural values were being undermined by "Americanization."

Even as a teenager Aurora Lucero was a proud Nuevomexicana, immersed in cultural issues and values — so it made sense that in 1910 she would speak at an oratory contest on the importance of the Spanish language.

Her passionate argument was in response to an immediate threat: a law that would require all government officeholders in New Mexico to be fluent in English. One powerful influence was her father, a Spanish language professor and editor of a newspaper, *La Voz del Pueblo*.

As his daughter came of age, the territory was abuzz with discussions about New Mexico's preparation for statehood and the framing of the new state constitution, which would be approved by the voters the next year.

At the national level, the changing face of America had become a political flashpoint. In the previous three decades, some fifteen million immigrants had poured into the United States, and President Theodore Roosevelt was responding to an anti-immigrant backlash. He argued that English should be the sole language for newspapers, government and schools.

In a 1918 speech in Des Moines, Iowa, Roosevelt said: "Let us say to the immigrant not that we hope he will learn English, but that he has got to learn it. Let the immigrant who does not learn it go back."

Then came his most uncharitable, inflammatory comment: "This is a nation, not a polyglot boarding house."

Even though in her own speech Lucero romanticized the culture of the Conquistadores and their high-blown Castilian literature, not the native Indigenous culture, she later became a renowned folklorist.

As superintendent of schools for San Miguel County, she traveled all over New Mexico, recording the folk tales, ballads, dances, children's games, and songs of the Hispanos and Pueblo Indians and becoming their fiercest champion.

Her masterpiece was *Literary Folklore of the Hispanic Southwest*, a 1953 compilation that helped preserve and revive that vital part of Southwestern history.

Twenty years later, New Mexico became the first state in the nation to pass a bilingual multicultural education law, providing school districts with funding for programs in both English and Spanish.

"PLEA FOR THE SPANISH LANGUAGE"

c. 1910
Interscholastic Oratorical Association, New Mexico
Normal University, Las Vegas, New Mexico

The territory of New Mexico has undergone many changes, politically and socially, it has solved many problems and now, upon the eve of statehood, a new problem is being discussed in every hamlet, village and city:

"Shall the Spanish language continue to be taught in our public schools?"

It seems beyond all doubt that New Mexico is soon to take her place as one of the states, in the grand sisterhood of commonwealths of this mighty union. That boon which for 60 long years she has sought in vain seems now within her reach, and to all appearances she has but to extend her hand in order to gain it: yet in her enthusiasm and eagerness to obtain it, she must not forget that she has problems to meet and solve such as no other state ever had.

In order to understand this problem thoroughly, let us state the peculiarities of our achievement. There is to the south of this rich and vast domain a population of more than 60,000,000 people, all descended from the Spanish Conquistadores. To the north, are found the homes of at least 90,000,000 of another people, nearly all of Anglo-Saxon blood, speaking an entirely different language. New Mexico is the meeting ground of these representatives of the Romanic and Germanic races, and no one can fail to see, even now, that their amalgamation is but a question of time. What the final outcome of such a union will be, of course no one can predict with absolute certainly, but if it be true that history repeats itself under analogous conditions, then we may venture the prediction that a new race will spring from such a union that will far surpass either of its factors in all those traits and characteristics that make man better fitted for high responsibilities. The past history of these two races is a record of glorious deeds and notable achievements. Both have in their natures elements of greatness, and the union of the calm, business like spirit of the Anglo-Saxon with the sanguine, chivalrous enthusiasm of the Castilian will be such a blending of all that is best in human nature that we fail to see how anything better for the wealth of humanity could possibly happen.

A difficulty presents itself at the very beginning; no matter how eager one may be that a new race should people these plains and hills, his hopes will be blasted if the essential means are ignored, means efficacious to the desired end. One of these is the cultivation of a thorough acquaintance, one with the other — the Anglo-Saxon with Castilian — the Anglo-American with the Spanish-American. How can this be done unless each understands the other's language?

In New Mexico, English and Spanish are the leading languages of the territory. The English language is the language in which the great bulk of the business of the country is transacted. The Spanish language, the language of the Spanish-Americans, the language of the Cortezes, the De Sotos and the Coronados, has been for more than three centuries the home language of the territory. Now, however, it has been proposed by the president and the congress of the United States to deprive the territory of this language; that is, they seem to wish to break into fragments at a single blow this strong and marvelous link in the chain of events, which has connected and held together the history of the old and new worlds; for this is exactly what the Spanish language has done, is doing, and will continue to do as long as it is not eliminated from the public schools and driven out of the territory.

In the act enabling New Mexico to become a state, passed by congress, it was provided that none except those who speak, read and write the English language with sufficient correctness shall be eligible to the legislature of the new state, or to any of the state public offices. It is claimed by some of those who passed this act that the Spanish-American will become a better citizen by depriving him of the use of his vernacular. In resorting to such a course, it would seem that the contrary effect might be produced in him by the unwarranted interference of congress with his natural rights, and instead of becoming a better, he might be made a worse citizen. Yet the Spanish-Americans of New Mexico have never been bad citizens. They have more than once proved their loyalty to the government and their love for the "Stars and Stripes," as their conduct in the Civil and the Spanish-American wars, and in many of the Indian wars, abundantly testifies.

It is impossible to understand why, in view of such a record, the people of New Mexico should be so unceremoniously deprived of a right which flows from the very essence of their manhood, for the right of language in man is a God-given right, and as such it is guaranteed and secured to him by the federal constitution when it declares that the natural rights of all men are inalienable. To single out New Mexico, then, for such unprecedented treatment, at the very moment that she is welcomed into sisterhood, is not only a gratuitous insult to the intelligence of her people, but it is also a proceeding as untenable in principle as it seems to be outrageous in its intent . . .

There is a host of Spanish writers who have beautified and ennobled Spanish literature to at least as high a degree as have the Chaucers, Drydens, Miltons, Byrons and Websters, uplifted the English language. We have our De Vegas, Calderon, Escriches, Castellars, Bellow and Arboledas, whose talents make them fully the compeers of the best Saxon bards and prose writers and whose pens have made Spanish literature the delight of scholars in every age and clime; while towering above them all stands the colossal genius, the author of "Don Quixote," whose superb merit is universally acknowledged and whose fame is rivaled but not surpassed by that of the great bard of Avon.

Yet this grand array of illustrious scholars, not to mention a vast number of others not less brilliant, will be lost to the youth of New Mexico when the Spanish language ceases to be taught in her schools.

Then consider the great commercial importance of this language. Besides being spoken in Spain and the Philippines, it is spoken in all countries south of the United States. These countries offer an unlimited field for the investment of American energy and enterprise. The advice of Horace Greeley to the young men of our country: "Go West" was heeded and the West became a blooming garden and a mighty empire: But the West is now filling up rapidly and those young men must soon turn south to these Spanish-American countries. If then we would cultivate their friendship and good will, get them to do business with us, admit us into their society, we should be able to greet them with a "Cómo está Usted?" as well as that they should be able to greet us with a "How do you do?"

Our public schools must have the Spanish language for the same reason that other modern languages are taught in them; they must have it as the inseparable companion of her sister, the English; they must have it if we wish that our youth shall be fully prepared to meet the duties which are awaiting them in all the Spanish-American countries — duties which they will in vain try to perform, without a thorough knowledge of the Spanish language.

The Spanish language is the language of our fathers, it is our own language, and must be now and hereafter the language of our children and our children's children. It is the language handed down to us by the discoverers of this New World. We are American citizens, it is true, and our conduct places our loyalty and patriotism above reproach.

We want to learn the language of our country, and we are doing so; but we do not need, on that account, to deny our origin or our race or our language or our traditions or our history or our ancestry, because we are not ashamed of them; and we will not do it, because we are proud of them.

The Spanish, next to the English, is the language most widely spread throughout the world; and though now the sun sets on the dominions of the actual successor of Charles V, it does not set, nor will it ever, on the dominion of the Spanish language. It is spoken in the far-off Philippines, and far along, from frozen mountain peaks to blooming valleys, it leaps with ever-increasing echo from

Mexico and Central America down to the Straits of Magellan. All the islands cradled in the bosom of the Atlantic rejoice in its grandeur and its majesty. Lastly it is spoken, written and sung in Spain — romantic Spain — the land of knighthood and the mother of heroes, the power that saved Europe from the fate of the Roman Empire, the hand that first unraveled the mystery of the sea, to give a New World to civilization, and to hoist the ensigns of Christianity on the Teocalis of the Incas and the Montezumas.

Such is the language against which it is proposed to close the doors of the public schools of this territory. A language with such a record, such a history, such traditions and backed, as in the Spanish by the moral influence of so many civilized countries, deserves a place not only in the public schools of New Mexico where it belongs by inheritance the right which three centuries of permanency therein give it, but in the best colleges of the United States in the proudest seats of learning in the world.

Therefore, in the name of all that is noble, grand and beautiful in the literature of the world; in the name of the broadening of the fields of our business interests, and in the expansion of trade relations with our immediate neighbors; in the name of the Anglo-Saxon youth of this territory who are everywhere endeavoring, with an earnestness fully worthy of the excellent cause to learn the Spanish; in the name of the rights which the people of New Mexico have as citizens of this great republic; in the name of its duty to them, as contracted most solemnly before the world at Guadalupe Hidalgo; in the name of honesty and justice, let us by all means see to it that the Spanish language is not driven from the public schools of New Mexico.

ROSE SCHNEIDERMAN

At five o'clock on a March afternoon in 1911, a fire broke out on the top floor of a factory in Manhattan.

The building was home to the Triangle Shirtwaist company, one of thirteen garment companies in New York that had resisted attempts at unionizing. A young Polish-born organizer, Rose Schneiderman, had helped lead an unsuccessful strike for better working conditions at that same factory a little more than a year earlier.

Conditions had not improved. As the fire raced across the ninth floor, bolts of cloth and paper patterns burst into flames. Trapped behind locked doors, dozens of workers clawed their way through the smoke and fire to windows, then leapt to their death on the pavement below. Girls as young as fourteen from Russia, Eastern Europe, and Southern Italy perished that day, a total of 146 dead.

One week later, at a mass meeting at the Metropolitan Opera House in Manhattan, Schneiderman was among the speakers who gave voice to the horror and outrage felt across the country.

"This is not the first time girls have been burned alive in the city," she said. ". . . every year thousands of us are maimed. The life of men and women is so cheap and property is so sacred . . . it matters little if 146 of us are burned to death."

Schneiderman later said she was so upset she could hardly speak above a whisper, but "the words poured out."

She had come to the US from Poland at age eight. Her family was so poor she left school after the sixth grade. By sixteen she was working as a lining stitcher in a cap factory, and she picked up English at Friday night talks at the Manhattan Liberal Club.

At age twenty-one, she began organizing workers for the New York Women's Trade Union League. She had a knack for explaining to the workers the meaning of trade unionism and how it could help them. Her first speech was at a 1903 strike in Bayonne, New Jersey. The employers had moved their factory from Manhattan to avoid the unions.

"When I was called on to speak, my knees turned to putty," she recalled. But she found the words and went on to become one of the labor movement's most fiery orators.

"Little Miss Schneiderman," as *The New York Times* called her — she was only four foot nine — spoke in auditoriums and church halls, in basements and at street meetings, and eventually on the radio. To critics she was "the Red Rose of Anarchy," a play on her flaming red hair.

At a labor speech in Cleveland in 1912, she said: "The worker must have bread, but she must have roses, too" — the right not just to subsistence but also beauty and meaning.

"TO THE VICTIMS OF THE TRIANGLE SHIRTWAIST FIRE"

April 2, 1911
Metropolitan Opera House, New York City, New York

I would be a traitor to these poor burned bodies if I came here to talk good fellowship. We have tried you good people of the public and we have found you wanting. The old Inquisition had its rack and its thumbscrews and its instruments of torture with iron teeth. We know what these things are today; the iron teeth are our necessities, the thumbscrews are the high powered and swift machinery close to which we must work, and the rack is here in the firetrap structures that will destroy us the minute they catch on fire.

This is not the first time girls have been burned alive in the city. Every week I must learn of the untimely death of one of my sister workers. Every year thousands of us are maimed. The life of men and women is so cheap and property is so sacred. There are so many of us for one job it matters little if 146 of us are burned to death.

We have tried you citizens; we are trying you now, and you have a couple of dollars for the sorrowing mothers, brothers and sisters by way of a charity gift. But every time the workers come out in the only way they know to protest against conditions which are unbearable the strong hand of the law is allowed to press down heavily upon us.

Public officials have only words of warning to us — warning that we must be intensely peaceable, and they have the workhouse just back of all their warnings. The strong hand of the law beats us back, when we rise, into the conditions that make life unbearable.

I can't talk fellowship to you who are gathered here. Too much blood has been spilled. I know from my experience it is up to the working people to save themselves. The only way they can save themselves is by a strong working-class movement.

CRYSTAL EASTMAN

In the early 20th century, the majority of women in the United States did not work in "the man's world" outside the home.

But when she examined the US census data for the year 1900, Crystal Eastman saw cause for celebration in the dramatic uptick in the number of women classified as "breadwinners, or as engaged in gainful occupations." As the data showed, very few occupations excluded or were closed to women.

"That census man, whoever he is, is a feminist. I wish we could find him and put up a statue to him," Eastman exuberantly told the crowd at New York City's Cooper Union in the winter of 1914. The rally was billed as "the first feminist mass meeting in the United States." Eastman joined twelve other speakers on the dais, including workers' rights advocate Frances Perkins, who would become the first woman to serve in a presidential cabinet, as US Secretary of Labor.

Eastman knew how to parse numbers. To her, the 1900 census was a gold-mine. "I believe in statistics just as firmly as I believe in revolutions," she said. A labor lawyer with a master's degree in sociology, she had worked as a safety researcher in Pittsburgh, collecting data and exposing the scanty protections and inadequate compensation for work-related accidents. She drafted worker safety legislation and developed the nation's first legal argument for workers' compensation.

She campaigned for equal working conditions and pay equity for women, arguing that these concrete matters had to be settled before women could experience true freedom.

She called her speech "What Feminism Means to Me," and what it meant was this: "Economic independence, without which the other kinds of freedom are hardly worth talking about. It will make freedom of choice in love and marriage possible for the first time."

That was just one of dozens of speeches Eastman made for women's rights and civil liberties. In 1917, she was a co-founder of the National Civil Liberties Bureau (later the ACLU), to fight government suppression of dissenters during World War I. With Alice Paul, she also drafted the Equal Rights Amendment, introduced to Congress in 1923.

Eastman believed women in the US were just getting started. She was already anticipating the work needed to achieve full equality. "The hardest part of the battle is yet to come," she said, "the battle with ourselves, with our inherited instincts, with our cultivated taste for leisure, with our wrong early training, with our present physical unfitness."

In the end women would win that battle too. American women would be ready, she said. "That is my feminist faith."

"WHAT FEMINISM MEANS TO ME"

February 17, 1914
Mass meeting, Cooper Union, New York City, New York

The most important contributor to feminist literature up to date is, in my opinion, an unknown man in the Census Bureau. Isn't that the last place in the world you would expect to find one? There is a certain table of statistics in a volume of the 1900 Census entitled Women at Work, which can transform me at one glance from the serene and confident feminist I usually am into a positively exultant fanatical believer. It is a table which classifies all the women engaged in gainful occupations in the United States in the year 1900. I am sorry these figures are not up to date, but the corresponding volume for the 1910 Census is not yet out. Perhaps we can make a few honest and conservative deductions for the year 1914. Anyhow, the figures for 1900 are exciting enough.

To begin with, gainful occupations in general are classified under 303 headings, and in all but nine of these 303 occupations some women were found employed. The nine in which no women were engaged turn out to be: soldiers, sailors, marines, firemen, street-car drivers, telegraph and telephone linemen, helpers to brassworkers, apprentices to roofers and slaters, helpers to steam boiler makers. That was in 1900, remember, fourteen years ago. There may be still no women soldiers, sailors, or marines. (It isn't lack of initiative on women's part that prevents that.) but I would be willing to guess there are by now a few women street-car drivers in the US, half a dozen linemen or so, and an appreciable number of "apprentices to roofers and slaters", to say nothing of "helpers to steam boiler makers".

But let us stick to the census. It goes on to say that while there were no women found in these nine occupations, there were found five women steamboat pilots, 45 railroad engineers and firemen, 31 railroad brakemen, ten baggagemen, 26 switchmen, seven conductors, 185 blacksmiths, 508 machinists, 31 charcoal, coke and lime burners, 11 well borers, 8 boiler-makers, six ship carpenters. These examples of women's initiative are selected by the census man as the most striking in his list. His own comment is profoundly interesting to me. "Such figures as these," he says, referring to those I have just given, "have little sociological significance beyond indicating that there are few kinds of work from which the female sex is absolutely debarred, either by nature, law, or custom." Isn't that great? Don't you love him for it? I tell you that census man, whoever he is, is a feminist. I wish we could find him and put up a statue to him.

Now let us turn from these figures to some from the same list which undoubtedly do have sociological significance. There were in 1900, in addition to all those women coke-burners, well-borers and ship carpenters, 770,000 women farmers and agricultural laborers, 8,000 government officials, 7,000 physicians, 8,000 hotel keepers, 33,000 merchants, 17,000 packers and shippers, 142,000 saleswomen, 85,000 stenographers, 21,000 telegraph and telephone operators. Add to that, 1,000,000 women engaged at that time in mechanical and manufacturing pursuits, i.e. in factory work, and 2,000,000 in domestic or personal service, and we begin to be able to appreciate the fact that there were nearly 5,000,000 women of sixteen years and over engaged in gainful occupations in 1900.

But I must not pause here. There are two questions which must be on the tip of the tongue of every statistics-lover: (1) What proportion of the total number of women over sixteen was this 5,000,000 women in gainful occupations? (2) Is the number of women in gainful occupations growing relatively to the population ? Let us dispose of the first question. The 5,000,000 women working in 1900 were twenty per cent. of the total number of women over sixteen. Second, is this tendency on the part of women to work for a living on the increase, on the decrease, or stationary? To answer this question we must go back to 1890. From 1890 to 1900 the number of women working for a living increased 35 per cent., while the population increased only twenty per cent. I think that establishes the fact that the tendency of women to enter gainful occupations is decidedly on the increase — the number of women earning their living grows at least three-fourths again as fast as the population grows. But let us examine that 35 per cent. increase a little. It is, from a feminist point of view, exceedingly significant that while the number of women engaged in domestic, and personal service increased only 26 per cent., women factory workers increased only 26 per cent., and women teachers only 33 per cent. (all of which have been for some time established occupations for women) — the number of women engaged in scientific and literary pursuits jumped 116 per cent., the number of women clergymen, journalists, architects and lawyers increased 221 per cent., stenographers and typewriters 305 per cent., saleswomen 156 per cent., packers and shippers 203 per cent., etc. In short, not only is the proportion of women in gainful occupations increasing, but that increase is taking place not so much in the old traditional occupations of teaching and domestic service, not so much in factory work where women's economic usefulness has long been established, but most emphatically in a great variety of commercial, agricultural and professional pursuits.

These facts, — that women are venturing into nearly every occupation there is, that their numbers are increasing by leaps and bounds, out of all proportion lo the increase in population, that while 15 per cent. of all women were at work in 1890, 20 per cent. were at work in 1900, and roughly 25 per cent. in 1910, — these facts are to me the most interesting, most hopeful, most stimulating facts in the world. They thrill me as no other statistics ever did.

In fact there is only one other way in which I can get a corresponding thrill. That, if you believe me, is by going to the circus. Doubting or troubled feminists should haunt the circus. There at last you can sit and observe your own sex with unqualified admiration. Watch the trapeze performers. There is no more beautiful sight in the world than those fearless creatures, men and women, with their lithe, perfectly trained bodies, swinging, balancing high in the air for our breathless delight. And, thank God, not one whit do the women fall short of the men in skill, endurance, suppleness or muscular co-ordination.

And the lady bare-back rider on the big white horse, is her performance any less brilliant than that of her gentleman partner on the black? No! and again, thank God.

And, as for the purely dare-devil feats of spectacular courage, aren't the performers a little more apt to be women? How many times have I sat and watched a women climb into a little red automobile on a platform way up at the top of the circus tent, wave a greeting to the audience below, and then start down the mad incline, take the death leap, turn two sommersaults and land three seconds later right side up and smiling!

And while the thousands clapped and thundered, I have sat still and gloried in her, and dreamed dreams of a future world in which women shall be free and strong of body, daring in spirit, lovers of games, excelling in feats of physical prowess.

To all weak-kneed sisters, to all who have listened to great doctors and scientists declaring the essential weakness of women, to all of us who have to confess that we cannot pick up a trunk and carry it upstairs as our brothers can, to all of us who admit to our own souls a sort of shrinking instinct to dodge behind a man when we hear a big dog jump out and bark in the night, — I recommend a seat at the circus. It's bound to cure your doubts, to re-establish your faith in the future. You come away regretful and determined, musing to yourself: —

"Yes, it's too late for me, I missed my chance; but my daughter can be as strong as her brother, — and my grand daughter, by all that I hold dear, she shall have the powerful, trained, active body of a young Diana. Why not? There's the circus to prove it."

I have brought in these facts from the humdrum working world, and these visions from the circus, because they suggest what feminism means to me. It means freedom for women, all kinds of freedom. But these two kinds, freedom in work and freedom in play, are the important ones to talk about, it seems to me. All the other kinds will follow in their train. Freedom in work, when once we have taken possession of it, will mean economic independence, without which the other kinds of freedom are hardly worth talking about. It will make freedom of choice in love and marriage possible for the first time. And nothing else will.

Freedom in play will mean free bodies, and a final escape from the very serious limitations put upon women's activities by their clothes.

Now a final word about this freedom of which we talk so eagerly; it was not easy to get and it is not easy to take, now that we almost have it. Most of the outside barriers are down, thanks to the pioneers. But the hardest part of the battle is yet to come; the battle with ourselves, with our inherited instincts, with our cultivated taste for leisure, with our wrong early training, with our present physical unfitness. In the end, though, we shall win this battle too. God meant the whole rich world of work and play and adventure for women as well as men. It is high time for us to enter into our heritage — that is my feminist faith.

MABEL PING-HUA LEE

Mabel Ping-Hua Lee was a Chinese patriot who dreamed of returning to her native country to help women enter the modern age. "The symbol of the new era," wrote the *Los Angeles Tribune*. "All Chinatown is proud of little Miss Mabel Lee."

As an immigrant to New York City, she had quickly taken up the ways of American women, including the fight for the vote. In 1912 she rode on horseback at the head of a suffrage parade on Fifth Avenue, leading a brigade of Chinese-American women. They were chosen because, with the revolutionary overthrow of the Qing dynasty in 1911, women in China had already won the right to vote. They proudly carried the flag of the new Chinese Republic and a sign that proclaimed, "Light from China."

"Perhaps because we were held back so strongly for so many years, there is now a great awakening," Lee told one newspaper reporter. "The accumulated need of centuries is bursting out."

Her speaking career began at age eighteen, when she took part in an oratory contest on "Chinese patriotism." In 1915, she spoke at a New York City "suffrage shop," a temporary storefront set up by the Women's Political Union.

As Lee made clear, Chinese women still had a long way to go to achieve equality. "I plead for a wider sphere of usefulness for the long-submerged women of China," she declared, then listed the dismal factors that had held women back: the lack of educational opportunities, the forced seclusion, the practice of foot binding, the inability to choose their own mate, the sexual double standard, and polygamy.

But the situation had changed for the better. Mass meetings for women were becoming commonplace. There was a daily newspaper for women. And, she noted with amazement, there had even been an all-female battalion in the Revolution. "China's submerged half has begun to emerge," she announced with pride.

Going forward, she said, the very future of China as an independent nation would depend on its ability to unshackle its women and develop them morally and intellectually.

Lee tried to keep ties with China, and she made three trips there between 1923 and 1937. She considered staying to open a school for girls, but the civil war between Nationalists and Communists made that difficult. After Japan's invasion in 1937, she stopped going altogether.

When her father died, she took over as director of the First Chinese Baptist Church in Chinatown and opened a Chinese community center. She spent the rest of her life serving the Chinese-American community in New York City, her adopted home.

"CHINA'S SUBMERGED HALF"

1915
Women's Political Union "suffrage shop," New York City, New York

I plead for a wider sphere of usefulness for the long submerged women of China. I ask for our girls the open door to the treasury of knowledge, the same opportunities for physical development as boys and the same rights of participation in all human activities of which they are individually capable.

By the beginning of the 20th century the conditions of the great masses of Chinese women may be thus briefly summarized. Politically, of course, they were nonentities. The scheme of education left them out of consideration because learning was deemed unnecessary for the discharge of their duties as wives and mothers. Those who obtained the rudiments of learning were so rare as to attract notice. The custom which dictated the seclusion of women forbade social intercourse with the other sex. The custom of foot-binding robbed them of freedom of movement and crippled them from their girlhood to the time when earthly sufferings end.

Except in rural communities where they worked like the men and alongside of them, the Chinese women's sphere was enclosed by the walls of their homes.

In China the female of the species never could be deadlier than the male because at all times she was under control. According to a famous writer, "At home, the girl follows her parents; after marriage she follows her husband; and at his death, she follows her son."

An old custom based on a false philosophy deprived her of the choice of her mate. An iniquitous law made it easier for the husband to divorce his wife than for her to divorce him. In no country is the double standard of morals so deeply entrenched as in China.

This is a sombre picture indeed — not pleasant to contemplate, but it is necessary to present it first in order to show the improvement made in recent years.

I have not mentioned the blighting effects of the institution of polygamy, for, with enlightenment and bodily freedom of women the custom of annexing extra wives will be "more honored in the breach than the observance." A drastic law forbidding the practice will go far towards its abolishment. But the solution of the question is largely in women's hands as this story will show:

An American missionary in China was taking tea with a mandarin's eight wives. The Chinese ladies examined her clothing, her hair, her teeth, and so on, but her feet especially amazed them.

"Why," cried one, "you can walk and run as well as a man." "Yes, to be sure", said the missionary.

"Can you ride a horse and swim, too?"

"Yes."

"Then you must be as strong as a man!"

"I am."

"And you wouldn't let a man beat you — not even if he was your husband — would you?"

"Indeed, I wouldn't," the missionary said.

The mandarin's wives looked at one another, nodding their heads. Then the oldest said, softly:

"Now I understand why an American never has more than one wife. He is afraid."

Any picture showing the condition of Chinese women throughout the by-gone past, though dark in the main, must be a moving picture to be strictly truthful. Glimpses of light run through every scene. Women of learning, women versed in statecraft, women of commanding intellect and heroines in every walk of life emerged from cramping surroundings and played their parts in the long drama of Chinese history . . .

After China opened five ports under the treaty with England in 1848, the education and uplift of Chinese women was taken up by missionaries. After they had devoted 55 years of patient and persevering labours to this noble cause, the work was undertaken by the Chinese themselves, who established the first school for girls in Foochow in 1897. Need we wonder that this new school was considered by our missionary friends as the greatest achievement of the age, and that Dr. Young J. Allen, one of the venerable workers invited to speak at the first commencement exercises, declared, as he stood before the assembled students and guests, that he felt inclined to say, "Lord, now lettest Thou Thy servant depart in peace?"

A new day has dawned [for the hitherto secluded and uneducated women of China] and no patriot or friend of China can fail to rejoice at the change. Hampered by crippling foot-bandages and the ever more rigid bonds of old social customs, our women have known no horizon beyond the four walls of their houses. They have received so little education, if any at all, that even in thought they have been practically limited to the area within these walls. That they, in spite of these limitations, have exercised such undeniable influence from time to time, is significant of the power which will be exercised by the Chinese women of the future, who with unbound feet and untrammeled minds, will face a new and dazzling era in the history of her sex.

Edicts have been issued against slavery and foot-binding, schools are being established for women and girls, and polygamy has been condemned as incompatible with modern civilization. These are evidences of the change of attitude toward women and her place in life. In the past she had no recognized place in society. To-day, not a few appear as equals in social and public gatherings and voice their sentiments.

The wives and daughters of leading Chinese officials attended with their husbands or fathers the inauguration ball given by President Yuan Shin Kai and there met the foreign diplomats and members of their families. Truly, the worm had burst its chrysalis; the women of China had taken their rightful place in society.

One of the most striking signs of the times is a daily newspaper for women edited by Mrs. Chang and published in Peking. This newspaper has been a power for good ever since it was started in 1906.

Mass meetings of Chinese women are now of such common occurrence as almost to have lost their novelty. A public meeting for women was called in Kiukiang some months before the opening of the National Industrial Exposition at Nanking for the purpose of urging the women to send thither specimens of their work "and so widen their interests and at the same time promote a worthy enterprise."

What better proof can you have of the change that has come over the country in the attitude of its leaders towards their women than the presence of these Chinese girls in the educational institutions of America?

As patriots and workers for China we cannot but be happy in our hearts to hear of the facts and know that Chinese women have proved themselves able to receive and wisely use their education. It is practically an established fact that every Chinese student is wishing God-speed and success to the nation-wide propaganda for the uplift and betterment of our women. But is this wish alone sufficient to bring its realization? To hope success and to achieve success are entirely different propositions.

Our statesmen for centuries back have felt the need for female education and must have wished for it. But what was the good of their mere wishing?

The missionaries came in their turn. They not only wished and prayed, but they labored. And it is largely due to their untiring efforts in the face of obstacles well-nigh insurmountable, that the present interest in women's education owes its existence.

Now it is our turn. What are we going to do in answer to the call of duty?

What good are laws and edicts if they are not enforced? Who of us does not know that at this very day foot-binding is still going on unhindered, that educational opportunities for girls are few and far behind those for boys, and that polygamy is an everyday practice even among some officials?

The Great Charter was wrung from King John 700 years ago — but the fight for freedom and human rights is still going on in England itself. How many years will it take for us to fully raise the submerged half of our country?

Friends and fellow-students: China's submerged half has begun to emerge, and when you recall that a battalion of Chinese young women was organized and drilled for service in the late revolution, and that a militant woman suffragist used violence towards a deputy of the Nanking Assembly for refusing to vote for woman suffrage, you will agree with me that a part of that half has emerged with a vengeance.

Still, all that is but a beginning. The great mass of the people has yet to be aroused to the necessity for action. The neglect and indifference to women's welfare in the past must be remedied — not only laws must be passed in the interest of the future mothers of the new Republic, but they must be religiously enforced. Prejudice must be removed and a healthy public sentiment created to support the progressive movement.

In furtherance of such a cause we students should take a leading part. To us girls especially, who are among the first to emerge, will fall the duties of pioneers and, if we do our share, ours will be the honor and the glory.

The welfare of China and possibly its very existence as an independent nation depends on rendering tardy justice to its womankind. For no nation can ever make real and lasting progress in civilization unless its women are following close to its men if not actually abreast with them.

In the fierce struggle for existence among the nations, that nation is badly handicapped which leaves undeveloped one half of its intellectual and moral resources.

If, according to President Lincoln, the Federal Union could not endure half free, half slave, how can China maintain her position among independent nations half free and taught, half shackled in body and in mind?

INEZ MILHOLLAND

In late summer 1916, the campaign for the woman's vote hit a wall. After decades of petitioning, lobbying, negotiating, strategizing, and many thousands of editorials, articles, and speeches, American women still had not secured the federal right to cast a ballot.

With President Woodrow Wilson coming up for re-election in November, suffragists decided to focus on the White House.

They unleashed a powerful weapon: a battalion of women speakers fanning out across the Western states, where suffrage had already been secured at the state level. The mission was to persuade the four million voting women of the West to support their non-voting sisters of the East by turning the president and Democrats out of office.

Inez Milholland was one of the most prominent of the speakers, known for her glamorous looks and fierce oratory. From 1911 to 1913, it was Milholland who rode astride a horse at the head of several suffrage parades, a living embodiment of the New Woman.

In early October 1916, she boarded a train for Cheyenne, Wyoming — the first stop in a whirlwind, 12,000-mile Western tour, on which she was scheduled to deliver more than fifty speeches. At each stop, she would speak for about two hours, linger for questions, then get back on the train.

Everywhere crowds were enthusiastic and press reports glowing. Milholland declared: "You women must assert yourselves if you are to help reshape the world."

But it was exhausting, and Milholland was in poor health. She wrote home to her husband about "doctoring" herself to get through the trip with iron, arsenic and strychnine. At one point she told reporters: "I cannot see how I keep going, but I just have to."

On October 23, 1916, at Blanchard Hall in Los Angeles. Milholland began to deliver a passionate speech to an audience of more than a thousand. "Women of the West, stand by us in our crisis," she cried out the crowd. "Give us your help, and we shall win. Fight on our side and liberty is for all of us!"

Midway through the speech, she delivered a defiant challenge: "Will you join us by voting against President Wilson and the Democratic candidates for Congress?"

With that, she collapsed. Ten weeks later she died of pernicious anemia, age thirty.

Her words lived on. "How long, Mr. President, must women wait?" became the slogan for picketers who stood silently for two and a half years in front of the White House, pressuring Wilson to change his mind. Eventually, in 1918, he did.

"APPEAL TO THE WOMEN VOTERS OF THE WEST"

October 22, 1916
National Woman's Party Assembly, Blanchard Hall,
Los Angeles, California

The unenfranchised women of the nation appeal to you for help in their fight for political freedom. We appeal to you to help us, for you alone have both the power and will.

The dominant political party — the Democratic party — has the power to liberate the women of the United States, but they have refused to exercise that power on our behalf, and on behalf of justice and of freedom. They have refused to put the party machinery back of the constitutional amendment. They have blocked the amendment at every turn. The Democratic leaders in the Senate forced it to defeat through a premature vote. In the House they have buried it in committee. Fourteen times the President has refused his help.

Therefore, women of the West, let no free woman — let no woman that respects herself and womankind, lend her strength to the Democratic party that turns away its face from justice to the woman of the nation.

Politically speaking, the women of America have been a weak and helpless class without the political pressure to push their demand.

Now, women of the free states, we are no longer helpless.

Now, for the first time in our history, women have power to force their demands, and the weapon with which to fight for woman's liberation. You, women of the West — who possess that power — will you use it on behalf of women? We have waited so long and so patiently and so hopelessly for help from other political sources. May we not depend upon the co-operation and good-will of women in politics? Shall we not feel that women will respond to the appeal of women, and shall we not see their hands stretched out to us in sympathy and help?

Women of the West, stand by us now. Visit your displeasure upon that political party that has ignored and held cheaply the interests of women.

Let no party, whatsoever its name, dare to slur the demands of women, as the Democratic party has done, and come to you for your endorsement at the polls. Make them feel your indignation. Let them know that women stand by women. Show them that no party may deal lightly with the needs of women and hope to enlist your support.

Women of the western states, it is only thus that we shall win.

It is only by unity, and a common purpose, and common action, and by placing the interests of women above all other political considerations, until all women are enfranchised, that we shall deserve to win.

Liberty must be fought for. And, women of the nation, this is the time to fight. This is the time to demonstrate our sisterhood, our spirit, our blithe courage, and our will.

It is women for women now, and shall be 'til the fight is won.

Sisters of the West, may we count on You? Think well before you answer. Other considerations press upon you. But surely this great question of women's liberty comes first.

How can our nation be free with half of its citizens politically enslaved?

How can the questions that come before a government for decision, be decided aright, while half of the people whom these decisions affect are mute?

Women of the West, stand by us in this crisis. Give us your help, and we shall win. Fight on our side and liberty is for all of us. For the first time in the world women are asked to unite with women in a common cause. Will you stand by?

Women of the West, if you can love and respect your sister women, if you hate unfairness and contempt, if you cherish self-respect, you must send the Democratic party, which has abused the interests of women, down to defeat in the suffrage states in November.

Make it plain that neglect of women's interests and demands will not be tolerated. Show a united front, and, whatever the result in November, there never again will be a political party that will dare to ignore our claims.

You know that politicians act when it is expedient to act; when to act means votes, and not to act means loss of votes.

President Wilson made this plain when he supported the eight-hour day measure for railway workers. If he cared about principle per se he would himself have urged an eight-hour day. But this was not worth while. What is worth while is to act for those who have organization, unity, and political strength behind them.

We have but to exhibit organization, unity, and political strength, and victory is ours. More, I say only when we have done so, shall we deserve victory.

The gods of government help those who help themselves.

Therefore, women and sisters, and one day fellow voters, let us help ourselves. Say to the rulers of this nation:

"You deal negligently with the interests of women at your peril. As you have sowed so shall ye reap. We, as women, refuse to uphold that party that has betrayed us. We refuse to uphold any party until all women are free. We are tired of being the political auxiliaries of men. It is the woman's fight only we are making. Together we shall stand, shoulder to shoulder for the greatest principle the world has ever known — the right of self-government."

Not until that right is won shall any other interest receive consideration. This demand of ours is more urgent than all others. It is impossible for any problem that confronts the nation today to be decided adequately or justly while half the people are excluded from its consideration. If democracy means anything it means the right to a voice in government.

Women are as deeply concerned as men in foreign policy. Whether we are to have a civil or militaristic future is of deepest moment to us. If things go wrong we pay the price — in lives, in money, in happiness.

We care about what sort of tariff we shall have. If the cost of living goes up, we, as housekeepers, are the ones to suffer.

We are deeply interested in the question of national service. We know, and must help to decide, whether our sons are to be trained to peace or war.

To decide these questions without us, questions that concern us as vitally as they concern men, is as absurd as would be an attempt to exclude the mother from influence in the home or care of her family. We say to the government:

You shall not embark on a policy of peace or war until we are consulted.

You shall not make appropriations for the building of ships and engines of war until we, who are taxed for such appropriations, give our consent.

You shall not determine what sort of national defense we shall have, whether civil or military, until we co-operate with you politically.

You shall not educate our children to citizenship or soldierdom without our wisdom and advice.

You shall no longer make laws that burden us with taxes and high prices, or that determine how our commodities shall be prepared and by whom, or that regulate our lives, our purchasing capacities, our homes, our transportation and education of children, until we are free to act with you.

This is our demand.

This is why we place suffrage before all other national issues. This is why we will no longer tolerate government without our consent. This is why we ask women to rise in revolt against that party that has ignored the pleas of women for self-government, and every party that ignores the claims of women until we win.

Women of the West, will you make this fight? Will you take this stand? Will you battle for your fellow women who are not yet free?

We have no one but you to depend on. Men have made it plain that they will fight for us only when it is worth their while, and you must make it worth their while.

It is only for a little while. Soon the fight will be over. Victory is in sight. It depends upon how we stand in this coming election — united or divided — whether we shall win and whether we shall deserve to win.

We have no money, no elaborate organization, no one interested in our success, except anxious-hearted women across the country who cannot come to the battle lines themselves.

Here and there in farm house and factory, by the fire-side, in the hospital, and school-room, wherever women are sorrowing and working and hoping, they are praying for our success.

Only the hopes of women have we; and our own spirit, and a mighty principle.

Women of these states, unite. We have only our chains to lose, a whole nation to gain. Will you join us by voting against President Wilson and the Democratic candidates for Congress?

JEANNETTE RANKIN

Jeannette Rankin grew up on a ranch outside Missoula, in a politically active family. After graduating from the University of Montana with a degree in biology, she spent six years campaigning across the country for the woman's vote.

A naturally gifted orator, she spoke fluidly without notes. One reporter described her as "convincing" and "straight from the shoulder."

In 1911, she testified before the Montana legislature in support of women's suffrage. Six years later, the people of Montana sent her to represent them in Washington, DC, making her the country's first female member of Congress — and one of America's most famous women.

At the top of her legislative agenda was not only suffrage but the political reforms that would improve the fortunes of women. Her "special duty," she told *The New York Times*, was to express "the point of view of women."

Despite her "nay" vote in the spring of 1917, the US declared war on Germany and entered the First World War. The Great War, as it was called, made a profound impact on American women's lives, expanding their skills, opportunities, and independence. Millions filled jobs left behind by men who had gone off to fight, or took new positions created by the war effort.

In January 1918, with an armistice agreement still ten months away, Rankin stood up in the House of Representatives and introduced legislation proposing an amendment to the Constitution "extending the right of suffrage to women." She argued that universal suffrage was the only path for a civilized, democratic nation.

She reminded her fellow legislators that it was unjust to rely on women's wartime contributions and personal sacrifices, then deny them the full rights of citizenship.

Democracy should begin at home, she said.

"Today there are men and women in every field of endeavor who are bending all their energies toward a realization of this dream of universal justice. How shall we answer their challenge, gentlemen; how shall we explain to them the meaning of democracy if the same Congress that voted for war to make the world safe for democracy refuses to give this small measure of democracy to the women of our country?"

That resolution narrowly passed in the House but died in the Senate. A year later Congress passed the same resolution by overwhelming margins, and in 1920, the 19th Amendment was added to the Constitution.

Rankin knew she was forging a path for others. "I may be the first woman member of Congress," she observed. "But I won't be the last."

"ON WOMEN'S RIGHTS AND WARTIME SERVICE"

January 10, 1918
US House of Representatives, Washington, DC

M r. Speaker, we are facing to-day a question of political evolution. International circumstances have forced this question to an issue. Our country is in a state of war. The Nation has had a terrible shock. The result has been a sudden change in our national consciousness. The things we have for years been taking for granted are suddenly assuming a new significance for us.

We as a Nation were born in a land of unparalleled resources, of vast acreage of fertile soil, of minerals, of coal, oil, gas, of timber, and water power. The combinations in which these resources were found, together with our great natural highways, gave us opportunities for development which no other nation could boast. And we had people, people in whose veins ran the blood of all nations, people imbued with the buoyancy of youth, fearless, and with the will and energy to make their dreams of freedom come true.

Without restraint we drew upon the stored treasure of the past. We spent recklessly, and we wasted our natural resources and our human energy with youthful abandon.

And then came the world war, and with its coming our carefree attitude was suddenly replaced by a new seriousness. To-day we are mobilizing all our resources for the ideals of democracy. We are taking stock of our available energy. And we are finding that with all our past wastefulness we still have limitless resources upon which we can count. We have men — men for the Army, for the Navy, for the air; men for the industries, the mines, the fields; men for the Government. And the national leaders are now reaching out and drawing men of talent, picking those with the best minds, with expert knowledge, and with broad perspective, to aid in war work.

But something is still lacking in the completeness of our national effort. With all our abundance of coal, with our great stretches of idle, fertile land, babies are dying from cold and hunger; soldiers have died for lack of a woolen shirt.

Might it not be that the men who have spent their lives thinking in terms of commercial profit find it hard to adjust themselves to thinking in terms of human needs? Might it not be that a great force that has always been thinking in terms of human needs, and that always will think in terms of human needs, has not been mobilized? Is it not possible that the women of the country have something of value to give the Nation at this time?

It would be strange indeed if the women of this country through all these years had not developed an intelligence, a feeling, a spiritual force peculiar to themselves, which they hold in readiness to give to the world. It would be strange if the influence of women through direct participation in the political struggles, through which all social and industrial development proceeds, would not lend a certain virility, a certain influx of new strength and understanding and sympathy and ability to the exhausting effort we are now making to meet the problem before us . . .

To-day as never before the Nation needs its women — needs the work of their hands and their hearts and their minds. Their energy must be utilized in the most effective service they can give. Are we now going to refuse these women the opportunity to serve in the face of their plea — in the face of the Nation's great need? Are you gentlemen representing the South, you who have struggled with your negro problem for half a century, going to retaliate after 50 years for the injustice you believe was done you so long ago? Have you not learned in your struggle for adjustment in the South to be broad and fair and open-minded in dealing with another franchise problem that concerns the whole Nation?

The women of the South have stood by you through every trial. They have backed you in every struggle, and they gave themselves and all they held most dear for the cause for which their men laid down their lives. Now they are asking to help you again in a big, broad, national way. Are you going to deny them the equipment with which to help you effectively simply because the enfranchisement of a child-race 50 years ago brought you a problem you were powerless to handle?

There are more white women of voting age in the South to-day than there are negro men and women together. Are you going to say to these thoughtful women: "After 50 years we have been unable to accomplish more than a tempo-rary adjustment of our problem; and now we refuse to let you disturb us, even to help us?" Dare you say that in the face of our tremendous national crisis — in the face of problems too great to rest upon the old doctrines of our youth, but demanding the action of a Nation united in spirit and using all its power?

These are heroic times, and they call for the strength and the courage and the dignity to think and act in national terms. We thought in national terms when we restricted activities by the prohibition amendment a few weeks ago. Why can we not think now in national terms and extend opportunities?

Our President emphasized the great nationalizing process our country is undergoing when he took over the railroads of the country to meet this crisis.

The food and fuel problems must soon be solved by nationalization. We are working and thinking to-day not as separate States but as a Nation. We must discuss public affairs not as Montanans or New Yorkers or Floridians but as Americans, taking always a national perspective and looking toward the welfare of the entire country.

We have made the protection of our child workers a national question. We declared war not State by State but by Federal action. We mobilized and equipped our Army not State by State but by Federal action. We mobilized and equipped our Army not State by State but through Congress. Shall our women, our home defense, be our only fighters in the struggle for democracy who shall be denied Federal action? It is time for our old political doctrines to give way to the new visions, the new aspects of national and international relations, which have come to us already since the war began.

For we have had new visions; we have been aroused to a new way of looking at things. Our President, with his wisdom and astuteness, has helped us to penetrate new problems, to analyze situations, to make fine distinctions. He startled us by urging us to distinguish between the German Government and the German people. We who have been steeped in democratic ideals since the days when our forefathers signed the Declaration of Independence find it difficult to think of government as something separate from the people.

Yet, as we learn to make this distinction for Germany, will not our minds revert to our own situation and be puzzled? How can people in other countries who are trying to grasp our plan of democracy avoid stumbling over our logic when we deny the first steps in democracy to our women? May they not see a distinction between the Government of the United States and the women of the United States?

Deep down in the hearts of the American people is a living faith in democracy. Sometimes it is not expressed in the most effective way. Sometimes it seems almost forgotten. But when the test comes we find it still there, groping and aspiring, and helping men and women to understand each other and their common need. It is our national religion, and it prompts in us the desire for that measure of justice which is based on equal opportunity, equal protection, equal freedom for all. In our hearts we know that this desire can be realized only when "those who submit to authority have a voice in their own government," whether that government be political, industrial, or social.

To-day there are men and women in every field of endeavor who are bending all their energies toward a realization of this dream of universal justice. They believe that we are waging a war for democracy. The farmer who knows the elements of democracy becomes something of an idealist when he contemplates the possibility of feeding the world during this crisis. The woman who knits all day to keep from thinking of the sacrifice she is making wonders what this democracy is which she is denied and for which she is asked to give. The miner is dreaming his dreams of industrial democracy as he goes about 2,000 feet underground, bringing forth from the rock precious metals to help in the prosecution of this war.

The girl who works in the Treasury no longer works until she is married. She knows now that she will work on and on and on. The war has taken from her opportunities for the joys that young girls look forward to. Cheerfully and willingly she makes her sacrifice. And she will pay to the very end in order that the future need not find women paying again for the same cause.

The boys at the front know something of the democracy for which they are fighting. These courageous lads who are paying with their lives testified to the sincerity of their fight when they sent home their ballots in the New York election, and voted two to one in favor of woman suffrage and democracy at home.

These are the people of the Nation. These are the fiber and sinew of war — the mother, the farmer, the miner, the industrial worker, the soldier. These are the people who are resting their faith in the Congress of the United States because they believe that Congress knows what democracy means. These people will not fight in vain.

Can we afford to allow these men and women to doubt for a single instant the sincerity of our protestations of democracy? How shall we answer their challenge, gentlemen; how shall we explain to them the meaning of democracy if the same Congress that voted for war to make the world safe for democracy refuses to give this small measure of democracy to the women of our country?

RUTH MUSKRAT

The speaker was a 26-year-old Cherokee student, a lover of literature who rejected the romanticized "noble savage" of James Fenimore Cooper and wanted to set the record straight.

In December 1923, Ruth Muskrat found herself on the steps of the White House, sharing her views with President Calvin Coolidge in a speech that appeared in newspapers around the world. "Mr. President," she said, "May not we, who are the Indian students of America, who must face the burden of that problem, say to you what it means to us?"

Muskrat had grown up on the Delaware Nation reservation in Oklahoma. She had traveled to China on a Y.W.C.A. tour to speak about the lives of Native Americans — when she came home, she went on a speaking tour to tell Native Americans students all about China.

She appeared at the White House as part of a delegation advising the government on Indigenous affairs.

Dressed in buckskin and beadwork, Muskrat presented the president with a book, *The Red Man in the United States*, which described the problems facing Native Americans. Then she delivered her speech, a plea for the Indigenous to have a voice and determine their own future.

"This, Mr. President, is the Indian problem which we who are Indians find ourselves facing," she said. "No one can find our solution for us but ourselves."

Her references to the "Great White Father" and "semi-barbaric" make us wince today, but they were an accepted part of the discourse of the day, a reflection of how many people thought and expressed themselves.

As for Coolidge, he was so pleased he invited Muskrat in to lunch with his wife. Coolidge had made a point of engaging with Native Americans throughout his presidency. He even claimed his own lineage included a "marked trace of Indian blood."

He believed Native Americans should assimilate into mainstream US culture, and he did what he could to speed that up. In 1924 he signed the Indian Citizenship Act, granting automatic citizenship to all Native Americans.

It was a step, not a solution. Many were still treated like second-class citizens, subject to poll taxes and literacy tests, and therefore denied the vote.

Muskrat became a lifelong activist for her people.

Years later she wrote a textbook, *Indians are People Too*, in which she noted: "When all Indians were made citizens of the United States in 1924 by act of Congress, it was a grudging citizenship. They were not then and are not now accorded the full privileges of democracy enjoyed by other citizens of the land."

"ADDRESS TO PRESIDENT CALVIN COOLIDGE"

December 13, 1923
The White House, Washington, DC

Mr. President: —

This volume of *The Red Man in the United States* is presented to the "Great White Father" in behalf of the many Indian students of America. It is a book which bears the best we have to offer — the story of our struggles and our tragedies, of our victories and our developments. The volume presents the results of an exhaustive investigation made under the auspices of what is now known as the Institute of Social and Religious Research. It gives for the first time a comprehensive account of the social, economic, and religious conditions among my people, as they are today. It is the only study of its kind that has ever been undertaken, and it will perhaps remain unique in this respect since we may reasonably hope that when the time would ordinarily be ripe for another such study, what is known as the "Indian Problem" will have ceased to exist.

Back on the Cheyenne Reservation in Oklahoma Indian women have worked with loving and painstaking care to make this gift worthy for the "Great White Father," weaving into this beaded cover the symbolic story of our race — the story of the old type of Indian, greeting with the hand of friendship the founders of this great nation, and the story of the new Indian, emerging from his semi-barbaric state, till his soil, and building for citizenship under the guidance of the school.

Mr. President, there have been so many discussions of the so-called Indian Problem. May not we, who are the Indian students of America, who must face the burden of that problem, say to you what it means to us? You know that in the old days there were mighty Indian leaders — men of vision, of courage, and of exalted ideals. History tells us first of Chief Powhatan who met a strange people on the shores of his country and welcomed them as brothers; Massasoit, who offered friendship and shared his kingdom. Then appeared another type of leader, the war chief, fighting to defend his home and his people. The members of my race will never forget the names of King Philip, of Chief Joseph, of Tecumseh. To us they will always be revered as great leaders who had the courage to fight, "campaigning for their honor, a martyr to the soil of their fathers." Cornstalk, the great orator, Red Jacket of the Senecas, and Sequoyah of the Cherokees were other noted leaders of our race who have meant much in the development of my people. It was not accidental that these ancient leaders were great. There was some hidden energy, some great driving inner ambition, some keen penetration of vision and high idealism that urged them on.

What made the older leaders great still lives in the hearts of the Indian youths of today. The same potential greatness lies deep in the souls of the Indian students of today who must become the leaders of this new era. The old life has gone. A new trail must be found, for the old is not good to travel farther. We are glad to have it so. But these younger leaders who must guide their people along new and untried paths have perhaps a harder task before them than the fight for freedom our older leaders made. Ours must be the problem of leading this vigorous and by no means dying race of people back to their rightful heritage of nobility and greatness. Ours must be the task of leading through these difficult stages of transition into economic independence, into a more adequate expression of their art, and into an awakened spiritual vigor. Ours is a vision as keen and as penetrating as any vision of old. We want to understand and to accept the civilization of the white man. We want to become citizens of the United States, and to have our share in the building of this great nation, that we love. But we want also to preserve the best that is in our own civilization. We want to make our own unique contribution to the civilizations of the world — to bring our own peculiar gifts to the altar of that great spiritual and artistic unity which such a nation as America must have. This, Mr. President, is the Indian problem which we who are Indians find ourselves facing. No one can find our solution for us but ourselves.

In order to find a solution we must have schools; we must have encouragement and help from our white brothers. Already there are schools, but the number is pitifully inadequate. And already the beginnings toward an intelligent and sympathetic understanding of our needs and our longing have been made through such efforts as this book represents. For these reasons to-day, as never before, the trail ahead for the Indian looks clear and bright with promise. But it is yet many long weary miles until the end.

It is out of gratitude for the opportunities of education and culture which has been afforded us by the interest of the white man, and out of our love for this nation to which we are eager to contribute our best, that this book is presented to our "Great White Father" in behalf of the Indian students of America.

MARGARET SANGER

In 1929, Margaret Sanger took part in a free speech event in Boston. Displays of banned books decorated the hall, and on the dais sat Sanger and other "undesirables" whose works were outlawed by Mayor James M. Curley.

Because she was forbidden to speak in any public forum in the city, Sanger's speech was read by "roastmaster" Arthur M. Schlesinger, a Harvard historian.

First, he mockingly gagged her, then read her words as she silently punctuated with her bobbing head.

Afterwards, Schlesinger called Sanger the "outstanding social warrior of the century" while reporters snapped photos.

Sanger came from a working-class family. After eighteen pregnancies and eleven children, her mother died at 48 of tuberculosis. Sanger always believed her mother's multiple pregnancies undermined her health. Her early nursing experience with poor, immigrant women convinced her of the need for family planning. When she learned that women did not know how to control the size of their families, she was determined to get them that information.

Beginning in 1912, she published a series of articles tackling sensitive subjects like sex, reproduction, and sexually transmitted infections. Her journal, *The Woman Rebel,* was considered "lewd, lascivious, filthy, and of an indecent character" under US law, which led to Sanger's indictment. The charges were eventually dropped, not long after the death of her five-year-old daughter from pneumonia. The US attorney said he did not want Sanger to become a martyr. But she was repeatedly arrested, and later did jail time for publishing instructions on how to use a diaphragm.

Sanger popularized the term "birth control," opened the country's first family planning clinic in Brooklyn in 1916, and founded several organizations that became Planned Parenthood. She gave hundreds of speeches and worked tirelessly to make birth control available for all women, regardless of race, ethnicity, or class. She never supported abortion or forced sterilization.

It's important to note Sanger's enthusiasm for the specious and dangerous theory of eugenics. Many progressive intellectuals of the day, including feminists and leading Black scholars and activists, also saw eugenics as an enlightened, progressive cause, a scientific advancement over Darwin's brutal natural selection.

The Nazi's detestable racial ideology and, above all, the gas chambers, reversed public opinion on eugenics. Not until the 1960s did the disability rights movement get underway and Americans finally began to appreciate and celebrate individuals with differences and disabilities.

Sanger died in 1966, just months after the birth control bill became legal in the US.

"GAGGED FOR
FREE SPEECH"

April 16, 1929
Ford Hall Forum on Free Speech, Boston, Massachusetts

To inflict silence upon a woman is indeed a drastic punishment. But there are certain advantages to be derived from it nevertheless. Some people are so busy talking that they do no thinking. Silence inflicts thoughts upon us. It makes us ponder over what we have lost — and what we have gained. Words are after all only the small change of thought.

If we have convictions, and cannot express them in words, then let us act them out, let us live them! Free speech is a fine thing, it should be fought for and defended.

If my voice is silenced by the hypocritical powers of reaction, in Boston, so much the worse for me, but so much the better for you for this act of suppression is to test the courage of your convictions, if you desire free speech.

It becomes your cue to speak, to act, to demonstrate the valor of your thought.

Sometimes I think we all talk too much. We read too much. We listen too much. But we act too little. We live too little. The authorities of Boston may gag me, they do not want you to hear the truth about Birth Control. But they cannot gag the truth. We do not need words. We do not need to talk, because the truth speaks for itself. Use your eyes, use your ears, use your intelligence and you can find out for yourself all that I could tell you. You all know that I have been gagged. I have been suppressed. I have been arrested numerous times. I have been hauled off to jail. Yet every time, more people have listened to me, more have protested, more have lifted their own voices. Here have responded with courage and bravery.

As a pioneer fighting for a cause I believe in free speech. As a propagandist I see immense advantages in being gagged. It silences me, but it makes millions of others talk and think [about] the cause in which I live.

HELEN KELLER

Though she lived until eighty-seven and was a lifelong speaker and activist, in the popular imagination Helen Keller has been immortalized as a child.

In the US Capitol stands a bronze statue of the little deaf and blind girl at the water pump, at the moment when her persevering teacher Annie Sullivan spelled w-a-t-e-r in the palm of her hand.

What's often unappreciated, though, is Keller's lifelong commitment to speaking out in public on behalf of the poor, oppressed, and exploited, for socialism, women's rights and workers' rights, and for people with disabilities.

She delivered her first speech in 1913 at an elementary school in Montclair, New Jersey, establishing a theme she would use over and over: the blindness of most people to the suffering of their fellow human beings: "We are all blind and deaf until our eyes are open to our fellowmen," she told the students. "If we had a penetrating vision we would not endure what we see in the world to-day."

On behalf of the American Foundation for the Blind, she traveled constantly from 1924 until 1968, across the United States and to thirty-five countries, advocating for those with vision loss, and providing a powerful role model for children with disabilities. Her greatest regret was that she had not received speech training earlier in her life, because she knew that her voice was not easy to understand.

One of her most celebrated and controversial speeches was her "Strike Against War," delivered in 1916 at Carnegie Hall, in which she warned against US involvement in World War I, which she believed would benefit capitalists at the expense of the working class.

Those who urged preparedness for the war "only want to give the people something to think about besides their own unhappy condition."

In 1930 she spoke before a committee of the US House of Representatives. Although she had addressed legislative bodies in state capitals before, this was her first appearance in Congress. She was there to support a federally-financed program to create Braille books for blind adults.

"Books are the eyes of the blind," she told the legislators. Then she asked them to close their eyes and, for just a few moments, place themselves in a sightless world. Try to imagine, she told them, making their way to the window, where "everything is a blank — the street, the sky, the sun itself!"

It would take another year of congressional wrangling before President Herbert Hoover signed the Pratt-Smoot Act authorizing the creation and circulation of free Braille books to individuals with vision loss — later known as the National Library Service for the Blind and Print Disabled.

"EYES OF THE BLIND"

March 27, 1930
Committee on the Library, US House of
Representatives, Washington, DC

Mr. Chairman, and friends, the bill which you have under consideration to-day, asks for an appropriation to supply Braille books to a class of persons who, through no fault of their own, are unable to read regular print. I hope the bill passes. Giving the blind worth-while books is a practical way of helping them to overcome their handicap. Indeed, it is far more than a practical measure; it partakes of the nature of a boon.

Books are the eyes of the blind. They reveal to us the glories of the light-filled world, they keep us in touch with what people are thinking and doing, they help us to forget our limitations. With our hands plunged into an interesting book, we feel independent and happy.

Have you ever tried to imagine what it would be like not to see? Close your eyes for a moment. This room, the faces you have been looking at — where are they? Go to the window keeping your eyes shut. Everything out there is a blank — the street, the sky, the sun itself! Try to find your way back to your seat. Can you picture who is sitting in that chair, day in and day out, always in the dark gazing back of you? What you would not give to be able to read again! Wouldn't you give anything in the world for something to make you forget your misfortune for one hour? This bill affords you an opportunity to bestow this consolation upon thousands of blind men and women in the United States.

When you closed your eyes just now you were assuming the sable livery of the blind, knowing all the time how quickly you could fling it aside. You felt no heavier burden than a grateful sigh that your blindness was a mummery. We who face the reality know we cannot escape the shadow while life lasts. I ask you to show your gratitude to God for your sight by voting for this bill.

I thank you.

LILLIAN GILBRETH

In the spring of 1933, America was reeling from the Great Depression, the nation's worst crisis since the Civil War. Thousands of banks were failing, US productivity had plummeted, and nearly a quarter of the labor force was unemployed.

That summer, Lillian Moller Gilbreth joined women from fifty-four countries at a conference in Chicago.

Among the first women in the US to earn a doctorate in engineering, Gilbreth was a pioneer in industrial and organizational psychology. She and her husband Frank Gilbreth had studied the work habits of manufacturing and clerical employees in a variety of industries to find ways to increase output and make the work easier. They founded a consulting and engineering firm in New Jersey that specialized in saving time, reducing worker fatigue, and speeding up production on the factory floor.

Their business boomed during the post-World War I industrial expansion, as they also raised twelve children in a busy household that served as a laboratory for their theories about education and efficiency. But the idyll wasn't to last.

As told at the end of the 1948 bestseller about their madcap family adventures, *Cheaper By the Dozen*, Frank Gilbreth collapsed and died in 1924 while speaking to his wife from a phone booth, just as he was about depart for Europe to deliver two professional speeches.

After the funeral, Lillian Gilbreth set sail herself and delivered those speeches in London and Prague. For the next four decades she carried on the business, serving clients, authoring papers, speaking at conferences and universities, and becoming the country's first female engineering professor, at Purdue.

The question she posed in the summer of 1933 — can the machine "pull us out" of the Depression? — was the logical extension of ideas she and her husband had explored for years about the importance of "the human factor" in industry.

Ever since the Industrial Revolution, she noted, the machine had been the focus of manufacturing, not the human being who ran the machine. The human was reduced to just a "hand to operate a machine."

As she told her audience, the machine could indeed help restore economic prosperity, but only with a "shift from materialism to humanitarianism."

Her views are just as relevant today as digital technologies and artificial intelligence transform the workplace and raise questions about privacy, bias, security, and inequality — concerns not just for the workers in the factories, but also for the millions of consumers who buy and use "machines" in their daily lives.

As Lillian Gilbreth would say, it's not the machine that matters most, but the human being.

"CAN THE MACHINE PULL US OUT?"

July 17, 1933
Round Table Meetings, International Council of Women,
Women's Congress, Palmer House, Chicago, Illinois

I t is putting an enormous task to the machine to ask, "Can it pull us out?" The answer is, "It can help pull us out, if we will design and use it properly."

It is interesting, in trying to look ahead to what the machine can do, to look back to the derivation of the word itself. It is used, in strikingly similar forms, in English, German, Danish, French, Spanish, etc. It traces back to the Latin and the Greek, with no change of meaning. "An engine, a contrivance, a device," and then, "an instrument of force," and "any instrument for the conversion of motion." And there is a notation that it is "perhaps akin to the Anglo-Saxon *macian* and the English *make*."

These things all being true, it is not strange that we have come to call the age from which we are passing, "The Machine Age." That phrase has many interpretations. Some use it to mean an age in which the machine has come to dominate men and an age in which the machine products have piled up, to the point where the distribution of them furnishes an unsolved problem. Others, mostly the engineering group, feel that the machine is only the tool of power, and that we should be thinking in terms of power and what it can be made to do for us. Still others think of it as an age when the coming of the machine has created an industrial revolution, both in thinking and in emphasis. All would perhaps agree that the machine has occupied the most important place in industry and business.

A review of the impressive and rapidly growing literature in this field — books, pamphlets, magazines, and newspaper articles — shows that the so-called "industrial revolution" was not really caused directly by the invention of certain devices, like the textile machinery, important as these were from the mechanical standpoint, but by the thinking. The "machine" became the center of interest. Its invention was the chief pre-occupation of the engineers. Its use was the chief concern of industrialists. The machine must be adequately housed and operated. Its efficiency, as a means of producing goods, was the great problem of the times, times that stretched through centuries, and that covered a geographical expansion that is still going on.

Not only men, but women and children, became machine owners or machine operators, or an aristocracy that, in the last analysis, was often supported largely by the work of the industrialist. The worker became a machine operator, until his function came to be described accurately by the current name for him, a "hand." That was, in many cases, all that was needed of him, a hand to operate a machine.

There is no need to describe here, the inadequate, often disgraceful housing; the long work day, in surroundings which were inefficient for proper machine operation and stunting for human beings; dirt, darkness, clutter, grease, in factories; and home conditions among the workers that words can never adequately picture. It seems an insult to the word "home" to use it for typical factory housing, not only in the eighteenth and nineteenth centuries, but in many places even today. The long histories of industrial housing, sweat-shop work, night work, child labor, protective legislation for women, the shorter work day and week, tell the story. What was back of all these?

Not the machine, but the conception of its use and importance. It became the end instead of the means. Its design was governed by the desire to make it effective in producing goods, i.e., as nearly as possible a perfect piece of mechanism, self-contained, able to operate with the minimum of human assistance. It must be durable. The work of its operator was determined by its shape. It should shine and be symmetrical and occupy the least space possible and be operated with the least wear and tear to it. No matter if the shine caused glare to the operator, and the symmetry meant that he had needless motions and effort and fatigue from the operating and expended his energy to spare the machine.

It was not that kindliness and a love of humanity died out of the world, or even of the thinking of the industrialists. It was simply that the *machine*, the transforming of power into things, became the chief interest of life. This of course happened because of the tremendous importance of things, possessions, which ties back into the history of the race and is primarily the concern of those who study this. If you loved and wanted things, the things that made these for you became of great value. Things were worth working for. They were the end of the work and the preoccupation of the leisure.

A passionate enough concern with things will influence one's philosophy and test one's ethics. Materialism is easily adopted, and a great desire for things may influence one's way of getting them. Not only production, but distribution are influenced. If I want things and have power to get them, I may produce to get all that I can, directly by making, and indirectly by exchange or distribution to those who can purchase and pay me in currency that will buy me other things that I want.

An overwhelming desire may influence one's viewpoint as to what belongs to one, and what does not. There seems no particular reason why materialism should lead to a great desire for things-for-oneself. If one were unselfish, it might be supposed to lead to wanting other people to have plenty of things. But as a matter of fact, the love of things often does lead people to want the things for themselves, and ultimately to be less concerned constantly that other people have all the things that they can use.

It would be interesting to know what the coming of the machine did to affect materialism, the love of things, and the desire to possess them even at the expense of other people. The engineers who designed the machines do not seem to have been materialists, or to have developed a passion for the things that the machines made. They were research men, mechanically-minded, with constructive imaginations. They were noted for plain living and high thinking. They rejoiced in the effectiveness of their plans, the looks and the performance of their engines and machines, the quantity and quality of the things that these made, and not in the possession either of the machines or of the things that they made. Engineers have never made much money, because they cared for other things more than for money or the things it could buy.

The industrialists who owned the machines did not know them intimately. Not as the man who designs and makes them does, not even as the man who runs and perhaps repairs them does. The machines, the men who operated them, and the places where both machines and operators and their families were housed, were means for making things. In many cases, both the records and the fiction based on study of them would seem to show that, by and large, industrialists thought little of their workers as individuals, or as separated from the work, unless because the industrialist or the worker, or both, happened to be at the time young and impressionable. In the mind of the employer, materials, machines, men, factory buildings, and housing of the workers, all seemed to be fused into one thing — a project for production. Naturally, women and children as well as men, living in the industrial housing, became actual or potential workers in the factory. The smaller the number of families employed, the smaller the number of houses necessary. The larger the number of workers in each family, the smaller the wages could be, theoretically, and if no thought was given to the welfare of the individual or of the family groups.

It seems doubtful if most industrialists ever actually saw the conditions under which the work was done, and the rest of the twenty-four hours lived, with seeing eyes. If your attention is primarily on the product of the factory, it is only when the product is faulty and you are trying to see why, that you note the conditions that affect the production. Light, heat, ventilation, humidity, crowding, clutter, oil, grease, dirt, etc. — looked at from the standpoint of the product, they may be important or unimportant. Much as we may wish that this attitude were a thing of the past, one cannot go through factories, even efficient ones, offices, or any series of work places today, without seeing that that attitude is still prevalent. Otherwise why the clutter, the piles of old newspapers, books or cloth added to chairs to make the seats higher, the dirty window panes, often even where there is supposed to be progressive management? . . .

If we have really had an industrial revolution in thinking which puts the emphasis on the human element (this human element including all individuals as responsible for social betterment), then we need have no fear of the machine. It can fulfill its greatest possibilities. It can eliminate drudgery and increase leisure time. It can furnish sufficient products for every man, woman and child in the world to have all he needs or wants. It can be adapted to extend the personality of its user and restricted so that its work can best meet human needs. Wrongly used, the machine can be a peril. Rightly used, it can help pull us out of our depression, and it can help keep us out of another. In a world of men and women physically adequate, mentally alert, emotionally serene, and socially adjusted, the machine can be used as a part of our great endowment of power — further the prosperity of mankind. But the shift from materialism to humanitarianism is imperative.

DOROTHY THOMPSON

In the years after the Great Depression, the United States had become isolationist, even xenophobic, with an undercurrent of anti-Semitism fueled by men like aviator Charles Lindbergh, industrialist Henry Ford, and radio priest Father Coughlin.

As Adolf Hitler and Benito Mussolini consolidated their power in Europe, journalist Dorothy Thompson was one of the first Americans to argue that fascism across the Atlantic threatened the survival of Western democracy.

The daughter of a Methodist minister, she was raised in upstate New York. She began working for the woman's vote and gave her first suffrage speech in a tiny town south of Buffalo. In 1920 she took off for Europe to pursue journalism, a profession for which she had absolutely no training. Within five years she became the first female head of an American overseas news bureau.

In the 1930s, she reported on Hitler's rise from beer hall rabble-rouser to chancellor. She even interviewed Hitler in Munich and famously underestimated him as "the very prototype of the Little Man." Three years later, the Gestapo kicked her out of the country.

Back in America, Thompson's insight into geopolitics and her keen moral sensibility made her one of the nation's most sought-after speakers. She hammered away at Hitler and the Nazis in her speeches and radio broadcasts, reaching millions. One writer described her as "full of fire and fury." Her experiences in Europe inspired her husband Sinclair Lewis' satirical 1935 novel, *It Can't Happen Here*, about a power-mad politician who whips up populist fears and takes over the United States.

In 1937, she testified before Congress on President Franklin Delano Roosevelt's plan to pack the Supreme Court with justices favorable to his New Deal legislation, a move she feared would undermine public trust in the nation's legal institutions.

She described to the legislators what she had seen in Germany — how the National Socialists had methodically taken over the German parliament, the courts, the labor unions, and the press. A fascist coup d'état was not just a dystopian conceit, she warned — it could actually happen in America.

In a broadcast the following year, she defended seventeen-year-old Herschel Grynszpan, a German Jew whose assassination of a Nazi diplomat became the pretext for the murderous rampage known as Kristallnacht.

She argued that Grynszpan's desperate act lay on the conscience of the United States, which, like so many other nations, had refused to admit Jews who were frantically trying to flee Europe.

"They say he will go to the guillotine without a trial by jury . . . who is on trial in this case?" Thompson asked. "I say we are all on trial."

"MODERN COUP D'ETAT"

March 31, 1937
US Senate Judicial Hearings, Washington, DC

I have responded to the request to come here to-day and testify on the question of the proposal to enlarge the Supreme Court, because I feel very deeply about the issues involved. I am speaking entirely as a private citizen. I have never been a member of any political party. As a journalist I supported almost all of the objectives of President Roosevelt during the last administration, though with certain reservations and criticisms mostly concerning method. I regret that I have not a more profound knowledge to lay before this committee.

I am not an expert on constitutional law, and my only justification for taking your time is that I have been for some years, as a foreign correspondent, an observer at the collapse of constitutional democracies. You might say I have been a researcher into the mortality of republics. The outstanding fact of our times is the decline and fall of constitutional democracy. A great need of our time is for more accurate analysis of the pathology of constitutional government, of why constitutional government perishes. A great deal of such analysis has been made, but the more thoughtful students have not made much impress on public opinion. And there are a great many people in the United States, for instance, who think that fascism is completely described as a plot of big business to seize government and run it in their own interests, through a dictator who is their stooge. Or they think that fascism has come about through some evil man, perhaps an evil genius of overwhelming ambition, bent on personal power, who suppressed free institutions by violence. Or they think that fascism is a peculiar institution of certain peoples, arising from special and limited conditions. For instance, that Germany became national socialist because of the Treaty of Versailles; or that Italy became fascist because she did not get what she expected to get out of the war. Or they think that constitutional democracies have fallen because they "failed to meet human needs" and pass adequate social legislation. I refer to that because that, apparently, is the President's view. That is what he said, at his first speech in support of his proposals for reforming the judiciary. He said:

In some countries a royalist form of government failed to meet human needs and fell. In other countries a parliamentary form of government failed to meet human needs and fell.

In still other countries, governments have managed to hold on, but civil strife has flared, or threats of upheaval exist.

That is what the President said, and apparently the moral of that is that unless Congress is made perfectly free to make any sort of legislation it may hit upon and then pass it on to a Supreme Court representative of the ideas of the majority, we shall see the end of democracy. Also, Mr. Harry Hopkins, in a radio address recently said, "The cure for the evils of democracy is more democracy." That is just another expression of the thought that democracies perish if they are curbed, or if they fail to respond immediately to all the economic and social demands of powerful groups of the community.

Gentlemen, I have come to a quite different conclusion about why democracies collapse, and give way to tyrannies of one sort or another. This blanket definition of fascism is not very descriptive of what is going on. Italian fascism, German national socialism, the military dictatorship of [Jozef] Pilsudski and of his successor in Poland, the monarchial dictatorship in Yugoslavia, the Catholic and semi-military dictatorship in Austria, the brain-trust dictatorship in Portugal, and the dictatorship of Comrade Stalin in Russia cannot be described as belonging to any one system of ideas. In hundreds of respects they are completely dissimilar. But each of them was the answer of a particular people, with particular mores and particular traditions to governments which were failing, not to meet human needs — if by that you mean failing to pass social laws — but failing in the first function of government: Failing to keep order and social cohesion and respect for principles. And each of these dictatorships has the same essential function. Its function is to impose social disciplines; to impose those social disciplines by the edict and coercion of a single man and regime of men, because the people themselves had ceased to accept the discipline of law.

I think the disciplines of law are particularly needed in democracies and are especially needed at any moment when a powerful majority is in temporary control of the current political situation almost to the exclusion of minority representation. We have such a situation in this country now. The men who designed the structure of this Republic realized this. They did not believe that the cure for the evils of democracy was more democracy. They believed that the prevention against a democracy running away with itself, the prevention against a powerful majority riding roughshod over the temporary minority and selling short the whole future of the country, the prevention against today's majority mortgaging tomorrow's majority, lay in a written constitution and an independent Supreme Court to interpret that constitution.

There is a reason why Supreme Court judges are appointed for life, and removable only by impeachment. That reason is obvious. It was certain that successive executives and successive Senates would seek to put upon the Supreme Court Bench men responsive to their own ideas. Everybody is human, but it was arranged that the Supreme Court, only by the merest chance, by a very remote mathematical chance, would ever coincide with the majority of the moment. It was so arranged that the Court should represent, not the momentary dominant majority, but the continuity and tradition in American life.

The difference between a regime of pure democracy, which moves from majority to majority, one often overthrowing the other and seeking to destroy all or much of what its predecessor has done — the difference between that kind of government, which I do not think has ever worked on this globe — and our own constitutional democracy is the difference between legislation which is haphazard, which is directed by powerful forces at large in society, and legislation which is somewhat checked by the will to continuity. It is true that the Supreme Court is conservative. I think it is conservative by its very nature. And that, gentlemen, is its function — to conserve. It represents, the opponents, say, the past. Yes; perhaps it does. It represents continuity; it demands that today's laws shall be checked against the whole body of law and the principles governing the state, and thus it insures that new laws shall be designed in some conformity with certain long-established customs and ways of life. And just because it represents continuity, because it exerts a constant reminder on the people that they have a past, a past to which they have a duty; just because it reminds them that when they act, however radically, however drastically, they must keep an eye on long-established patterns of law and behavior — just for that reason I think it safeguards the future. For certainly those political democracies, gentlemen, have been proved safest which have the longest and most unbroken traditions. You might say that just because we have a past, we can be most confident that we have a future . . .

I am sorry, gentlemen, to take your time by what may seem to be a lot of political philosophizing. But this question is essentially a political, and not a juridical, one, and I do not know how to discuss it except on the basis of a philosophy of politics. I know that the President's proposal is legally constitutional. But I am convinced that it is not politically constitutional.

It strikes the Supreme Court and the Constitution in the most radical and drastic fashion imaginable. Because it proposes to switch the Supreme Bench into line with the current political majority. That was frankly admitted by the President in his metaphor about the three-horse team. It proposes to create a court whose eyes are fixed, not upon the Constitution, and upon the whole body of existing law, but upon the White House and the ruling majority in Congress. It proposes to make the Supreme Court the instrument of that majority. The proposal suggests that its framers were in a confusion about the functions of society, the State, and the Government.

The Supreme Court is essentially an instrument of the State, not of government, which is a temporary majority running the State machinery. That is to say, it is a part of the entire legal apparatus. It is not there to guarantee that the will of the majority shall be expressed but to see that the will of the majority does not infringe the basic guaranteed rights of any individual citizen who wants to appeal against that will to a higher institution of reference. In fact, the very existence of the Supreme Court is an affirmation not only that every individual citizen has equality before the law, but that any individual citizen may, at some point, assert his equality with the whole political set-up. The conception that the individual may appeal to a court of reference which is above the majority; that he can stand there, all alone, and demand a right which perhaps 99 percent of the people do not want or cherish, is the most grandiose concept of political freedom. It was recognized as such by foreign critics and students of our system of government, such as Lord [Henry] Brougham, [James] Bryce, and [William] Gladstone. Incidentally, 40 years ago Bryce pointed out that the power of the President to expand the Supreme Court was the weakest point in the whole system. And it has reality only if the Court is independent of the Government, and that independence has been arranged for by a way of appointment and removal which gives every mathematical chance of success. If it becomes the instrument of the majority today, what possible guaranty have you that it will not become the instrument of another majority tomorrow? If, in our desire — a desire which I share with many members of this administration — to see a greater national consolidation, to extend the economic control of government over chaotic economic forces — an objective with which in the large sense I am in sympathy — if in order to do that, we pack the Court, what possible guaranty have we that tomorrow a government which believes that a national emergency demands the curbing of free speech, the dissolution of certain political parties, the control over the radio will not pack it again?

We have had times in our history when honest men tried to suppress all civil liberties — we have been told a lot about Supreme Court decisions that have balked social legislation and we are asked to turn back history and remember the *Dred Scott case*, which, they say, brought on the Civil War. But some of you gentlemen in this committee are from the South, and I wonder if you are lawyers. Do you remember the role that the Supreme Court played in the reconstruction era, in the days of the carpetbaggers, when men like Thaddeus Stevens — who were the radicals of their day — convinced that they were trying to fasten a hideous tyranny forever on the South? In those days the Supreme Court alone stood between the people of the South and a black terror organized by white northerners. In those days the South was in the minority; in those days the North, in its own mind, represented all the forces of national union and solidarity, progressiveness, and enlightenment. And like lots of enlightened, progressive, world-savers in history they were ready to resort to any means whatever to make the forces of what they called justice prevail . . .

I have spoken occasionally of the dangers of dictatorship and been roundly trounced for it by my friends who call themselves liberals. I no longer know what a liberal or a conservative is. They say that I go around seeing bogeys. Perhaps I go around seeing bogeys because I have seen, in the last 15 years, so many bogeys suddenly take on flesh. In Germany in 1928 you could hardly find a civilized man who thought that the Republic was in serious danger. I remember in 1928 there was an election, and the German Social-Democrats, who were somewhat "new dealers" in Germany, came into power by a big majority, and Hermann Müller became Chancellor. I remember sitting in his office and talking with him about what I thought was the feeling in the country, a feeling of hostility and of disappointment and of rage, because they thought things were going too far, and he laughed at me. "Why," he said, "the Republic was never safer in the world than it is at this moment." Well, it was as dead as a doornail five years later. I have never suggested that President Roosevelt is trying to establish a dictatorship. I would not be so foolish. But I have said that if any President wanted to establish a dictatorship and do so with all the appearance of legality, this is the way he would take. The modern coup d'état, by which so many democratic systems have fallen, does not destroy the legal apparatus of the State. The modern revolution is not made by violence. It keeps it, for the coup d'état wishes to appear legal. It only alters its spirit and its aim. Mr. Hitler took an oath to the Constitution of Weimar, and he has never offered another constitution. He has just obliterated it by a series of decrees backed by a supine parliament . . .

Now, I know that many people will say that these are very poor analogies, and they are right. The United States is not Germany and not Italy. This country has a long tradition of free government. And those critics are correct. One must not push analogies too far. Analogies as well as metaphors are always dangerous. But neither can one divorce events in this country from ideas and tendencies which are manifest throughout the world. The problems which we face are not unique. Everywhere constitutional democracies have had to face the question of how to make new integrations between economic and political power. We want power. That is the whole problem, the basic problem, of the New Deal. Everywhere constitutional democracies have had to meet increased demands from the masses for a greater share of the national wealth and for more security. Everywhere there is a demand for more efficient instruments of political power. And accompanying these demands is a growing tendency toward personal leadership and personal government, and for a very simple reason: Personal leadership and personal government are the quickest and easiest way to get the things that people want. It is always easier to change the men than to change the law.

People grow restive under the checks imposed by a regime of law. And yet all history proves that what Aristotle said is correct — that regimes tend to turn into their opposites, if the political principle which they represent is allowed to develop to the bitter end. If democracy becomes so pure and so immediate that the popular will is subjected to no standards, it rapidly moves into tyranny.

The whole world today has a new vision of freedom; economic freedom. That actually means a redistribution of wealth which will diminish the privileges of the few for the sake of the under-privileged many. From both a moral and an economic viewpoint that demand is justified and made inevitable, by our era of mass production. But that economic freedom — I do not think this can be said too often — will prove a complete mirage unless it is accomplished with the maintenance of political freedom. Political freedom is the condition of all freedom, as the people of Russia have learned, as the people of Italy have learned, and as the people of Germany have learned. They gave up political freedom to get something else which they thought at the moment was very much more important, and then they found out that there is not anything more important. And the first condition of political freedom is that we should stick to a regime of law, and not move off the path toward a regime of men.

It is precisely because we live in a revolutionary age that it is most necessary for us to guard with the greatest caution the traditional procedures of government . . .

ELEANOR ROOSEVELT

On a tour of the Midwest in the spring of 1940, First Lady Eleanor Roosevelt stopped in Chicago to speak to a civil liberties group.

With war raging in Europe, goon squads beating up labor organizers in the South, and anti-Semitic thugs inspired by Father Coughlin arrested for conspiring against the government, the national mood was tense. Isolationist sentiment was widespread, and trumped up fears of "Fifth Column" Nazi spies helped turn popular opinion against immigration — just when thousands of Jews were desperate to escape the Nazis.

The First Lady was a divisive figure. In the 1930s she supported government relief programs, befriended prominent Black leaders like Mary McLeod Bethune, and arranged for Marian Anderson to sing at the Lincoln Memorial after she was turned away from Constitution Hall by the Daughters of the American Revolution. She even held a picnic for Black girls on the White House lawn, outraging many Southerners.

Time and again she used her visibility to speak out for humanitarian causes that her husband couldn't support for political reasons.

Now speaking to a friendly crowd, she didn't hesitate to bring up the race issue. She acknowledged that, "if we are honest with ourselves," we must admit that democracy in America was imperfect.

Someone had recently asked her, "What do you think should be done about the social standing of the Negro race in this country?" Her answer was unequivocal. "Those are basic rights, belonging to every citizen in every minority group. We have got . . . to stand up and be counted."

She added that in her travels across the country, she had seen up close the vulnerability of people who lacked the means to defend their rights.

Poor people, non-citizens, minorities, and immigrants all deserved equal protection under the law, and "the minute we deny any of our basic rights to any citizen, we are preparing the way for the denial of those rights to someone else. Who is going to say it is not right today to do this or that? Who is going to say it is not right tomorrow? And where does it stop?"

In times of war, the curtailment of civil rights could be necessary, she agreed. But the United States was still at peace, "and therefore we have to guard the mainstays of democracy."

Roosevelt was right to remind the audience that American democracy was flawed. In December 1941, with the attack on Pearl Harbor, the US ended its isolation and joined the war.

Two months later, President Franklin D. Roosevelt issued Executive Order 9066, leading to the forced internment of 120,000 Japanese Americans — one of the most senseless civil rights violations in American history.

"CIVIL LIBERTIES —
THE INDIVIDUAL AND
THE COMMUNITY"

March 14, 1940
Civic Opera House, Chicago Civil Liberties
Committee, Chicago, Illinois

Ladies and gentlemen: I am glad you gave an award to the press tonight because that gave them the opportunity to tell us just what they could do. They are always telling us what we can do.

Now we have come here tonight because of civil liberties. I imagine a great many of you could give my talk far better than I because you have first-hand knowledge of the things you have had to do in Chicago, over the years, to preserve civil liberties. But I, perhaps, am more conscious of the importance of civil liberties in this particular moment of our history than anyone else, because, as I travel through the country and meet people and see the things that have happened to little people, I am more and more conscious of what it means to democracy to preserve our civil liberties. All through the years we have had to fight for civil liberty, and we know that there are times when the light grows rather dim. Every time that happens democracy is in danger. Now, largely because of the troubled state of the world as a whole, civil liberties have disappeared in many other countries. It is impossible, of course, to be at war and to maintain freedom of the press, freedom of speech, and freedom of assembly. They disappear automatically. And so, in some countries where ordinarily these rights were inviolate, today they have gone. And in some other countries, even before war came, not only had freedom of the press, freedom of assembly, and freedom of speech disappeared, but also freedom of religion. And so we know that here in this country we have a grave responsibility.

We are at peace. We have no reason for the fears that govern so many other peoples throughout the world, and therefore we have to guard the mainstays of democracy. Civil liberties emphasize the liberty of the individual. In many other forms of government the importance of the individual has disappeared. The individual lives for the state. Here, in our democracy, the government still exists for the individual. But that does not mean that we do not have to watch, or that we do not have to examine ourselves to be sure that we preserve, for all our people, the civil liberties which are the basis of our democracy. Now, we know, if we are honest with ourselves, that, in spite of all we have said, in spite of our Constitution, we do not have — many of us in this country — real civil liberties. For that reason, everywhere in this country, every person who believes in democracy has come to feel a real responsibility to work, to know his community, to know the people of his community, and to take the trouble — each one as an individual — to try to bring about for all our people a full observance of their civil liberties.

There are many times when, even though there is freedom of the press and freedom of speech, it is hard to get a hearing for certain noble causes. I often think that we, all of us, should think very much more carefully than we do about what we mean by freedom of speech, by freedom of the press, by freedom of assembly. I sometimes am much worried by the tendency that exists among certain groups in our country today to consider that these are rights are only for people who think as they do, that they are not rights for the people who disagree with them. I believe that you must apply to all groups the same rights, to all forms of thought, to all forms of expression, the same liberties. Otherwise, you practically deny the fact that you trust the people to choose for themselves, in a majority, what is wise and what is right. And when you do that, you deny the possibility of having a democracy. You have got to be willing to listen, to allow people to state any point of view they may have or to say anything they may believe, and then to trust that, when everyone has had his say, when there has been free discussion and really free, uninfluenced expression in the press, in the end the majority of the people will have the wisdom to decide what is right. We have got to have faith, even when the majority decides wrongly. We must still hold to the fundamental principles that we have laid down and wait for the day to come when the thing that we believe is right becomes the majority way of the people.

Of course, that means that we must have a real belief that people have intelligence enough to live in a democracy. And that is something which we are really testing out in this country today, because we are the only great democracy, and we are the only great democracy that is at peace and can go on living in what we consider a normal and free way of life. It is only here that people don't have to tremble when they say what they think. I don't know how many of you have read a book that I have been reading, but I think it is a most vivid picture of the kind of fear that has gradually come to all the people of Europe. It is *Stricken Field*, by Martha Gellhorn, a young woman who was a war correspondent. The story tells, in novel form, about the time that Czechoslovakia was taken over, to show what happened to little people. Some of those people were Communists.

The authorities had certain types of treatment for people in Czechoslovakia who were considered dangerous to the new regime, and the whole description of what they call "going underground" — living in hiding, afraid to speak to each other, afraid to recognize each other on the streets for fear they would be tortured to death — is a horrible one. Only great fear could bring people to treat other people like that, and I can only say that it seems to me that we should read as vivid a story as that now, just to make us realize how important it is that for no reason whatsoever should we allow ourselves to be dominated by fear so that we curtail civil liberties. Let us see that everybody who is really dangerous in our community has, at least, his or her day in court. Constituted authority has to work under the law. When the law becomes something below the surface, hidden from the people — something which is underground, so to speak, and over which the people no longer hold control — there can be no civil liberty.

Never before was it so important that every individual should carry his share of responsibility and see that we obey the laws, live up to the Constitution, and preserve every one of those precious liberties which leave us free as individuals. One of the things to which we have to be particularly alert today is the growth of religious prejudice and race prejudice. Those are two things which are a great menace, for we find that in countries where civil liberties have been lost both religious and race prejudice have been rampant. I think it would be well for us if we could define what we mean when we say that we believe in religious freedom. I once sat at a desk in a political campaign. I was running an office for the National Committee of Democratic Women. Over my desk came literature and material which I did not suppose anyone would print in the United States, and much of it had been brought out by members of various denominations and religious bodies against other people of other religions. It seems to me that the thing we must fix in our minds is that, from the beginning, this country was founded on the right of all people to worship God as they saw fit, and if they do not wish to worship, they were not forced to worship. That is a fundamental liberty. When religion begins to take part in politics, we violate a principle which we have set up, and that is the division between church and state. I think people should hold carefully to that principle.

As for having respect for the religion of other people, and leaving them to live their lives the way they wish, I believe we should teach every child to grow up with respect for all religions. Every child should know that his religion is his own, and that nobody else has the right to question it. Nor has he the right to question what others may believe in.

In addition to that, I think we should begin much earlier to teach all the children of our nation what a wonderful heritage of freedom they have — of freedom from prejudice — because they live in a nation which is made up of a great variety of other nations. They have before them and around them every day the proof that people can understand each other and can live together amicably, and that races can live on an equal basis even though they may be very different in background, very different in culture. We have an opportunity to teach our children how much we have gained from the coming to this land of all kinds of races, of how much this has served in the development of the land. Yet somehow I think we have failed in many ways to bring early enough to children how great is their obligation to the various strains that make up the people of the United States. Above all, there should never be race prejudice; there should never be a feeling that one strain is better than another. After all, we are all immigrants — all except Indians, who, we might say, are the only inhabitants of this country who have a real right to say that they own the country. I think that our being composed of so many foreign peoples is the very reason why we should preserve the basic principles of civil liberty. It should be easy for us to live up to our Constitution, but there are many groups among us who do not live up to what was written in that Constitution.

I am very much interested to find that in our younger generation there is a greater consciousness of what civil liberty really means. I think that is one of the hopeful things in the world today: that youth is really taking a tremendous interest in the preservation of civil liberties. It is a very hard period in the world for youth because they are faced with new problems. We don't know the answers to many of the problems that face us today, and neither do the young people. But the problems are very much more important to the young because they must start living. We have had our lives. The young people want to begin, but they can't find a way to get started. Perhaps that has made them more conscious of civil liberties. Perhaps that is why when you get a group of them together, you find them fighting against the prejudices which have grown up in our country, against the prejudices which have made it hard for the minority groups in our country.

The other night someone sent up a question to me: "What do you think should be done about the social standing of the Negro race in this country?" Well, now, of course I think that the social situation is one that has to be dealt with by individuals. The real question that we have to face in this country is: what are we doing about the rights of a big minority group of citizens in our democracy? That, we all have to face. Any citizen of this country is entitled to equality before the law; to equality of education; to equality at earning a living, as far as his abilities make that possible; to equality of participation in government, so that he may register his opinion in just the way that any other citizen can do. Now, those are basic rights, belonging to every citizen in every minority group. We have got, I think, to stand up and be counted when it comes to the question of whether any minority group is not to have those rights, because the minute we deny any of our basic rights to any citizen, we are preparing the way for the denial of those rights to someone else. Who is going to say it is not right today to do this or that? Who is going to say it is not right tomorrow? And where does it stop? We have to make up our minds as to what we really believe. We have to decide whether we believe in the Bill of Rights, in the Constitution of the United States, or whether we are going to modify it because of the fears that we may have at the moment.

I listened to the broadcast this afternoon with a great deal of interest. I had almost forgotten how hard the working man had to fight for his rights. I knew there was a time when hours were longer and wages lower, but I had forgotten just how long had been the fight for freedom — freedom to come together, to bargain collectively — freedom of association. Sometimes, until some particular thing comes to your notice, you think that those rights have been won for every working man. But then you come across a case, as I did the other day in the South, where someone has taken the law into his own hands and beaten up a labor organizer. I didn't think we did those things any more in this country. But it appears that we do — unless someone is always on the lookout, ready to take up the cudgel to defend those who can't defend themselves. That is the only way we are going to keep this country a law-abiding country, where law is looked upon with respect, and where it is not considered necessary for anybody to take the law into his own hands. The minute you allow that, you have acknowledged that you are no longer able to trust in your courts and in your law-enforcing machinery. Civil liberties are not very well off when anything like that happens.

So, I think, after listening to the broadcast today, I should like to remind you that behind all those who fight for the Constitution as it was written, for the rights of the weak and for the preservation of civil liberties, there was a long line of courageous people. And that is something to be proud of and something to hold on to. But its only value lies in the premise that we profit by it and continue the tradition in the future; that we do not let those people back of us down; that we have courage; that we do not succumb to fears of any kind; that we live up to the things we believe in; that we see that justice is done to the people under the Constitution, whether they belong to minority groups or not; that we realize that this country is a united country, in which all people have the same rights as citizens; and that we are grateful for that; and finally, that we trust the youth of the nation to herald the real principles of democracy-in-action in this country and to make this even more truly a democratic nation.

CLARE BOOTHE LUCE

In the spring of 1945, with nations in ruin and the end of the World War II in sight, representatives of fifty countries gathered in San Francisco to create an international organization to keep world peace.

As they hammered out plans for the United Nations, Republican Representative Clare Boothe Luce was visiting the newly-liberated Buchenwald concentration camp in Germany, where 54,000 men, women and children were murdered. Among the horrors she witnessed, one that affected her most was an hideously emaciated six-year-old boy. "No one wants to believe these things," she told reporters, "but it is important that people know they are true."

Luce had never been known to mince words, not in her politics, her journalism, or the acid-toned humor of her Broadway plays. High profile and glamorous, she was married to one of the world's most powerful men, magazine titan Henry Luce.

Both husband and wife were formidable critics of President Roosevelt. He was, they thought, naïve about the threat of Soviet Communism. At the 1944 Republican National Convention in Chicago, she delivered one of her toughest speeches, "G.I. Joe and G.I. Jim," slamming Roosevelt as a "dictatorial bumbledom.'

But Roosevelt had died in April of a brain hemorrhage, and suddenly Harry S. Truman was president, with a host of problems to solve. He told reporters he felt as if "the moon, the stars, and all the planets had fallen" on him, and asked them to pray for him.

In her national radio broadcast, Luce painted a grim picture. She predicted that after the Japanese defeat, Russia would emerge as the world's second most powerful nation. The threat was real, she said, that Soviet-style Communism would sweep over Asia and Europe.

She reminded her listeners that Russia was a totalitarian state, without a free press or free speech, its people caught in "a vast concentration camp, imprisoned by their own leaders." That was why she wanted Truman and other world leaders to resist appeasing the Soviets in post-war negotiations — or face World War III.

Just two months later, Truman and Great Britain's Winston Churchill would sit down with the Soviet Union's Joseph Stalin at Potsdam to define the post-war balance of power. As Luce predicted, the conflict between Western democracies and the Soviet Union would come into sharp focus.

Luce could not foresee the resilience of Western European democracies, but her clear-eyed take on the potential for authoritarianism to ensnare much of the world's population in the post-war landscape turned out to be prophetic. The Cold War was coming.

"AMERICA AND THE KREMLIN"

May 29, 1945
Broadcast over WJZ Radio and the Blue Network

The other day I saw a reporter-friend just returned from the San Francisco Conference. "Day and night," he said, "there was only one topic: Soviet Russia. Sometimes I wondered if Russia's strength or ideas really merit so much attention."

Of course he knew the answer: They do.

In this war, Russia's physical strength has been proven in many mighty battles. We know that America's factories have sent Russia 12,850 combat vehicles, including tanks, approximately 175,000 guns, and unknown quantities of ships. Altogether American industrial workers and taxpayers have sent $8,000,000,000 of lend-lease material to our Russian allies. Even so, Russia's own great industry, fine generalship, and rich manpower have played a decisive part in the defeat of Germany.

And now the German war machine is destroyed and German industrial strength all but obliterated. This leaves Russia immeasurably the strongest military and industrial power in Europe.

Russia has a fresh, untried and powerful army in Asia. Because it is to Soviet Russia's own national interests to get into the Pacific war, that army is certain to be used against the Japanese before the final kill. When the Japanese are at last beaten to the ground, their Army destroyed, and their factories pulverized, Russia will emerge as the strongest military and industrial power also in Asia.

There is no question that Russian physical strength — her iron muscles and machine brawn — make her the world's No. 2 power, the military and industrial Titan of Eurasia. And this certainly merits the attention it has received from the men who seek peace in our time at San Francisco.

As for Red Russia's ideas — well, at this hour every government in central Europe is either controlled directly or indirectly by Moscow-minded rulers. This has been and is being accomplished by a three-point policy: (1) By a policy of fraternization with the conquered peoples. (2) By the liquidation of all anti-Communists. This means that if people resist communism, whether they are Fascists, Monarchists,

Socialists, Democrats or Liberals, they are shot, imprisoned, or deported by the tens, and, if necessary, by the hundreds of thousands. (3) By a policy of putting guns, money, and food, which is to say, political power, into the hands of all discontented minority groups which will agree to adopt the Soviet programs, regardless of those groups' previous political convictions.

In Greece and in Italy the groundwork is laid for the Communist or so-called Partisan, Patriot, Free Democratic, or Liberation elements to take over as Anglo-American armies leave.

There are already strong clamorous Communist Parties in Belgium, Holland, France, and Spain. In the Near East there is much Communist fire.

The young despairing intellectuals of India are increasingly looking toward their near and mighty neighbor, the Soviet Union, for guidance in the technique of revolution. They get it, increasingly.

We all know that there is a powerful Chinese Communist Party, oriented toward Moscow, whose great opportunity will come when Red Russian armies move against Japan and offer to "liberate" Manchuria.

Mexico, Central America, and South America are all well provided with strong Communist groups. I need remind no one that we have our own Earl Browder.

In view of these facts, we must say that Red Russia's ideas merit all the attention they get from the fascinated statesmen of many nations at San Francisco.

Naturally we must ask ourselves: Is this rising world tide of Moscow-controlled communism a good or evil thing for the world? Upon the individual American's answer to this question will depend the fate of all the peoples of Europe and Asia in the very immediate years ahead, and the ultimate destiny of America 20 years from now.

But before we answer that question let us talk for a moment about words — the words, for example, "good" and evil.

Do these words have any meaning to you? Of course they do. They are the words men have used since the most ancient times — indeed, since speech itself was born. Now, these words, when applied to fundamental political policies and actions, have about the same meaning to all average Americans. But do they mean the same to us as they do to Communist leaders in Europe or Asia or South America or North America today? The appalling fact is that good and evil not only don't have the same meaning for them — they sometimes have no meaning at all.

Let me give you an example. Do we not all sane men agree that murder is evil? I think we do. When a Nazi SS man seizes a Jew, without due process of law, and throws him into a concentration camp, where he is tortured or starved to death, we say that deed is murder. No Nazi nonsense about racism or international Jewish plots or the security of the Reich can change that judgment in the eyes of man or God.

When a Communist OGPU agent strips a Russian of his small farm and few pigs, without due process of law, and then allows him to starve to death, or sends him to a slave camp in Siberia, that deed is murder, too. And no Communist twaddle about implementing the peoples' revolution, international capitalistic plots, or the security of the proletariat should change that judgment in the eyes of man, or can change it in the eyes of God.

The imposed death or imprisonment of any individual who has not been tried by a free jury of his peers under laws which have been framed by the will of the people are, we say again, evil things called murder, called slavery. They were evil when the Nazis practiced them. They are evil when the Communists practice them as they do today on a wholesale scale in all of Russia and in central Europe.

Let us get down to three fundamental political tenets, which all Americans hold to be right, good, and just.

We believe in a free press, free speech, and free worship. The Communists wherever you find them in America, Mexico, China, or Europe, believe that the press should be pre-censored and controlled; that men should refrain from criticizing their leaders under pain of death; and that any religion not subject to state control should be liquidated. In short, we and the Communists are exactly 180 degrees apart on our most fundamental political concepts. Moreover, the very words "right," "good," and "just" mean exactly what Stalin says they mean — but only on Monday morning. For on Tuesday morning he may change his mind. If so, the Russian people are required and every Communist leader in the world is required, under pain of death or exile, to change their minds accordingly before Wednesday. For truth to a Communist and Moscow leader is never an absolute. Truth is exactly what suits the Communist leaders' political policy or purposes, or even personal whims, at any given moment.

I expect at this point you will say that in principle you agree with everything I have said. But, you say, that's the way the Communists see things. They have the right, haven't they, to see things and do things the way they choose?

If the Moscow Communist leaders and their agents and puppets outside of Russia have the right to communize all of Europe — and then all of Asia — by liquidating all non-Communists; if they have the right to work within all other countries to overthrow their systems of government by force and murder; and if they have the right to plead that this international technique of terrorization and subversion is morally justified by the need of security for the Soviet Union or the welfare of the masses, then, my friends, should it not logically follow that every other nation had or has that same right?

Well, we never thought the Nazis had this right yesterday. Logically then, we must agree that the Communist dictators don't have it today, either. It is hard to have to display this troublesome moral consistency in our great hour of military victory in Europe, and when our gratitude is so very, very great to the heroic people of Russia, who helped us gain that victory. But a decent respect for the opinions of mankind requires that we examine the immoral nature of this communism that is sweeping Europe. And we know that millions upon millions of individual souls there and in Asia are yearning for freedom — the freedom to talk, to speak, to worship, to work at that which lies to their hands or appeals to their minds. Yes, the Russians, too, this valorous and imaginative people — even they are yearning for freedom. Have we any proof of that? We have . . .

I know what you are thinking now; I can hear your thoughts.

And what shall we Americans do about it? What can we do about it? Well, no American wants to go to war about this. But surely we have learned in the last decade that appeasement is the road to war. And if we want to stay out of war with communism we must not appease communism.

First, we can get our own thinking straight. We can, as individuals, write a balance sheet — a strictly moral balance sheet on communism as it has been revealed in Europe, versus parliamentary and constitutional forms of government. When we have made that balance sheet, we can decide where we each, as individuals, stand. I think morally we will find communism in the red — blood red. And then when we've got that balance sheet clear in our minds, we can as individuals help our Government to act abroad.

And what should our Government do abroad?

First and foremost, use our great diplomatic power and vast military prestige — now — to help all Asiatic and European statesmen and officeholders — Frenchmen, Poles, Italians, Greeks, Belgians, Dutch, Germans, Austrians, who are not either Fascists or Communists, to stay in power providing — and only providing — they are willing to form, and do form, true representative parliaments and congresses, and grant constitutions, which guarantee the people freedom of press, speech, religion, and assembly, and other essential legal rights natural to freemen. Such governments, however imperfect at the beginning, will tend increasingly to respond to the real will of the people.

It is a heartbreaking pity that the heroic but enslaved Russian people — the common men of Russia — are not free to aid us in an effort to enlarge the area of human freedom. But we must understand that the plain people of Russia live in a vast concentration camp, the prisoners of their own leaders. When we remember this, we will never act or speak as some people do, as though the great Russian people were our enemies. The Russian people are and must continue to be our friends, for the peace of the world depends on that friendship.

We are the two most powerful peoples on earth, and all our national good will and international diplomatic efforts must be directed toward cementing our friendship. No American wants war again in our generation. But surely in this last decade we have learned in blood and toil and tears and sweat that appeasement is the road to war. If we want to stay out of war with communism we must not appease communism. And we dare not appease communism. This cannot long remain two worlds, as it is today — the world of totalitarianism and the world of liberty. Indeed, as our conflict with Nazi totalitarianism proved, these two worlds are doomed to come into conflict. It must, and will be one world sooner or later.

Shall it be one world in which all mankind crawls and cringes in the darkness of slavery? Or shall it be one world in which all the great nations of mankind love and live in the light of freedom?

HELEN GAHAGAN DOUGLAS

Elected to represent California in the House of Representatives in 1944, Helen Gahagan Douglas benefitted from the celebrity of her previous careers as a Broadway and Hollywood actress and opera singer to build broad political support and popularity.

She spoke to enthusiastic crowds on issues like postwar price controls and the regulation of atomic energy. At a time when Jim Crow laws prevailed in much of the country, she forcefully advocated for civil rights, and she pushed to desegregate restaurants in the nation's capital. She was also the first White member of Congress to hire Black staffers in her Washington, DC, office.

In her most visible and courageous stand, during a dark chapter in American history, she confronted the House Un-American Activities Committee, which was holding Congressional hearings to investigate alleged Communist sympathizers.

In March 1946, Douglas stood up on the floor of the House and cut to the chase. "Mr. Speaker," she began, "I think we all know that Communism is no real threat to the democratic institutions of our country."

She continued with a ringing endorsement of free enterprise, freedom of speech and religion, and decency in public discourse:

"We do not believe in name-calling. We do not agree that everyone who disagrees with us should be hunted down like a criminal, denied his civil rights, and deprived of his ability to earn a living."

For all her calm and balanced reasoning, that speech became political fodder for the anti-communist crusaders. Douglas was relentlessly attacked as a pro-Soviet "fellow traveler."

When she later campaigned for the Senate, in 1950 — at a time when anti-Red fever was at an all-time high — her primary opponent picked up on the theme and called her "the pink lady." She was, he said colorfully, "pink right down to her underwear."

During the general election, Douglas faced off against Republican Rep. Richard M. Nixon, whose work on the high-profile Alger Hiss case had built up his bona fides as an anti-Communist. Nixon's campaign manager ordered 500,000 anti-Douglas flyers printed on pink paper.

It was a cutthroat race, with Nixon assassinating Douglas' character, implying that she was a Communist fellow traveler. She lost by a wide margin, bringing her political career to a close.

But Gahagan exacted her revenge by popularized a nickname for Nixon during that campaign that has stuck: "Tricky Dick."

And her speech has gone down in history as a bold and principle stand at a time of massive political and social acquiescence.

"MY DEMOCRATIC CREDO"

March 29, 1946
US House of Representatives, Washington, DC

Mr. Speaker, I think we all know that Communism is no real threat to the democratic institutions of our country.

But the irresponsible way the term "Communism" is used to falsely label the thing that a majority of us believe in can be very dangerous.

I do not think Communism in Russia need prevent international cooperation in building the peace, any more than it prevented international cooperation in winning the war.

I know that the road ahead is not without difficulty or without its vexing problems, but, if we could solve all the difficulties and the problems that arose during the war, surely we can solve them in peace.

We solved them in war because we had to. If we had not, we would all now be slaves of the Axis Nations.

We will solve them in peace if we fully realize the grim fact that if we do not, civilization has run its course.

We have reached a point where war can no longer be the final recourse. We have reached a point where we either grow up or blow up.

If it is blow up, the issues over which we struggle today are meaningless. I have asked to talk about Communism. But I am also going to talk about democracy — democracy, which I strive daily to live — democracy which is the only form of society in which I believe — the principles of which were fed to me with my first spoon of cereal — democracy which my forefathers helped establish on this great continent.

I shall talk about democracy, because we it is democracy that we believe in and live by — or should live by. We are interested in Communism as a system that challenges democracy. I am not afraid of that challenge.

I do not think we value democracy highly enough. The great mass of the American people will never exchange democracy for Communism as long as democracy fulfills its promise. The best way to keep Communism out of our country is to keep democracy in it — to keep constantly before our eyes and minds the achievements and the goals which we, a free people, have accomplished and intend to accomplish in the future under our own democratic system . . .

It is as a representative of the people, a democratic people, who believe in the principles and future of democracy — that I now speak about Communism.

There is no word in the world today more misused or misunderstood. I, for one, would not pretend to give a final definition of the word.

I have no special contribution to make on the subject. I am not a student of Communism. I have not been to Russia.

That, however, does not mean that I have not thought about Communism and tried to understand it and take an objective view toward it. One of the most important things today is for the American people to try to understand the Russian people and the Russian people to understand us.

I think we do a disservice to democracy when we dismiss Communism as the devil's handiwork. Of course, there is competition between democracy and Communism in the world today.

There is no doubt in my mind that the result will continue to be triumph of democracy in the world if we spend our energy and genius on demonstrating to the world what democracy can do.

One-sixth of the globe today, an area as large as the United States, India and China combined, is inhabited by people who are living under a form of state socialism known as Communism.

Primarily as a result of geographic isolation, these people since the Middle Ages have lived under the cruelest, most barbaric autocracy in world history. Under the czars, the nobility held huge estates. There was a relatively small trading class, and working class of artisans. In 1917, when the revolution began, there were only 10,000,000 industrial workers in the whole country. There were many more millions of peasants who worked the land with the most primitive tools and methods; mentally and physically debased, almost to the level of animals, and who until less than a hundred years ago were bought and sold like the animals on the land of the big estates on which they lived and worked.

When Lenin with the philosophy of Marx and Engels arrived in Petrograd in the midst of a revolt against the czars and the war, there was small wonder that the Russian people followed him who promised bread and freedom. In other words, Communism was born out of hunger, slavery, illiteracy, superstition, degradation.

But, Communism has no place in our society. We have something better. We have democracy. Communist methods are foreign to ours. Their policies are superimposed from the top and you take it from the top whether you like it or not.

Under our democratic system, programs are proposed from many sources in the community. A candidate running for office stands for a certain program, and the people elect him or reject him on the basis of that program. In other words, the people themselves select or reject what is good for them. We do not believe that one man or a group of men can save the people. We believe that the people save themselves.

The Soviet have never developed certain rights which to us are fundamental — the civil rights we cherish, the political rights we so boisterously and vigorously enjoy. They have sacrificed the competitive free-enterprise system we believe in.

Since the war, I think we must all admit that some good things have been accomplished under Communism for the Russian people.

But, Communism is the receiver which takes over when bankruptcy takes place.

It is our job not only to see that bankruptcy never takes place here, but that through democratic processes the welfare and security of the people which are what make a society solvent increase day by day.

The fear of Communism in this country is not rational. And the irrational fear of Communism is being deliberately used in many quarters to blind us to our real problems. The spreading of this fear is in fact propaganda for Communism.

I am nauseated and sick to death of the vicious and deliberate way the word Communist has been forged into a weapon and used against those who organize and raise their voices in defense of democratic ideals — of hearing the very program initiated by Franklin Roosevelt and which the majority of American people voted for in four successive national elections and to which President Truman has dedicated himself in his twenty-one point program called Communistic by those who seek to defeat the majority will of the American people.

Communism could successfully invade only a weakened democracy. A vigorous democracy — a democracy in which there are freedom from want, freedom from fear, freedom of religion and freedom of speech — would never succumb to Communism or any other ism.

Our fight is not against the windmill of Communism in America. Rather it is against those who would make a treadmill of democracy through special privilege, bigotry and intolerance.

Those who serve democracy and the future of democracy best are those who believe that full employment and fair employment practices can be achieved under our free enterprise system and who fight for full employment and fair employment practices through the democratic process.

It is up to us, the people, to show that we can have full employment and full production and freedom at the same time. That is a test democracy faces.

Nobody believes in free enterprise or its future more than I do. I have had all the benefits of this free enterprise system. I was bred in a family that handed down its business from father to son, a family that believed and believes today that individual initiative is the source of our economic vitality. I have every advantage and every opportunity that a child born into that kind of family would have.

It is because I know what education and opportunity and the respect of the community mean in the development of human beings that I fight for them for everyone.

I have never been in a breadline. I have never had to live on a ditch bank. I am not one of the millions who have never known a doctor's care.

I was not one of those 200,000 women a year who gave birth to their children without medical attention. I do not belong to a minority — at least I think the Irish are not considered a minority in America anymore.

But I have been in the slums of America. I have been to the ditch bank and have seen the people who came out of the cities because there was no place for them there. I have seen the people who were blown off, tractored off, or, because of lack of markets, were pushed off the land.

I have seen their miserable cars with all their worldly belongings strapped to them wending their weary way through State after State, millions in all, hunting for a job, hunting for somewhere beside the road to lay their heads.

I have seen shanty towns where the dust blinded and choked — where there was no water to relieve the thirst — no water to wash sick children, or when it rained rivers ran through the tents or the improvised shanties.

I have seen the children with sore eyes and swollen bellies. I have looked deep into the despairing eyes of fathers and mothers without jobs — or hope of jobs. I have seen minorities humiliated and denied full citizenship. And I tell you that we betray the basic principle upon which this Government of the people finds a way by which all the people can live out their lives in dignity and decency.

Yes; I believe in free enterprise. I believe in it so much that the whole object of my participation in government as a representative of the people is to make it free, free for everybody . . .

This, the most powerful nation on earth, stands today as irrefutable proof that there is no danger in a conglomeration of peoples and ideas freely expressed. In fact, out of the very conglomeration a rich harvest, which is the growth of America, has been reaped.

There is danger in the hysteria that always follows war. That danger is suspicion — suspicion that breeds in ignorance, thrives on bigotry, reaches epidemic proportions on hysteria.

Tom Paine said:

"Suspicion is the companion of mean souls and the bane of all good society."

This is true at home and abroad, as true in 1946 as it was in 1776. And former Secretary of State and War Henry L. Stimson wrote a few days ago:

The chief lesson I have learned in a long time is that the only way to make a man trust-worthy is to trust him; and the surest way to make him untrustworthy is to distrust him and show your distrust.

Mr. Stimson said this in reference to the atomic bomb and our international relations, but what is true of international relations is also true here at the home.

We, the Members of this body, will fail in our duty if we permit suspicion of another's purpose to divert us from our own purpose — that of making democracy function at full efficiency for our own people.

To be sure, there are Communists in America. There are a few people in America who believe the free enterprise system has run its course. As I have made clear, here today, I share no such belief. But to attack each new development in progress of American Democracy as Communism is to dig the grave of government of the people, by the people, for the people.

If we succeed in the practice of democracy, Communism will never take over, as some faint-hearted but loud-mouthed have proclaimed.

We cannot fail if we carry forward into the future the principles which have made America great.

Mr. Speaker, this body must always be loyal to the principles of its founders and the teaching of its fathers.

It must never yield to the tyranny of bigotry.

It must never succumb to the ranting's of the demagog.

It must always be the forum where justice is dispensed and intolerance is despised.

It must be the protector of free speech and the guardian of free worship.

It must never become an arena where class is arrayed against class — where race hatreds are bred and suspicions nourished.

We, the Members of this Congress — chosen by a free people to protect their rights and to bring reality to their hopes and faiths — are not bigots. We do not believe in name calling. We do not agree that everyone who disagrees with us should be hunted down like a criminal, denied his civil rights, and deprived of his ability to earn a living.

We, the Members of this House, do not believe that Capitol Hill is a hill on which to kindle a fiery cross but rather one on which to display the shining cross which since Calvary has been to all the world the symbol of the brotherhood of man.

KATHARINE HEPBURN

Katharine Hepburn's leftist leanings surprised no one. She'd been raised in a progressive household, with radical thinkers, writers and artists at the dinner table. She stumped for Franklin D. Roosevelt and lent her name to Russian war relief efforts.

What astonished people was the blistering force of her attack on the enemies of freedom in the spring of 1947.

"Silence the artist and you silence the most articulate voice people have," she thundered to a crowd of 28,000 at a rally supporting the 1948 Progressive Party presidential candidate Henry Wallace.

Hepburn was infuriated that Rep. J. Parnell Thomas, chairman of the House Committee on Un-American Activities, had begun investigating Communist activity in Hollywood.

She stepped up to the microphone at Gilmore Stadium in a sweeping red gown — "flaming red," according to the right-wing press.

Again and again, she attacked HUAC's assault on liberty, pointing to attempts to suppress speech in the theatre, literature, education, art, and the movies. "American became great," she said, in her famous, aristocratic lilt, "not because of the Salem witch hunts, but in spite of them."

Hepburn's younger brother Bob later said his sister's famous speech "was made for Mother." That would be a reference to Kit Hepburn, a passionate social reformer, suffragist, and birth control supporter who'd worked closely with Margaret Sanger.

Kit Hepburn testified before Congress and gave many speeches herself, often for leftist causes. Newspaper editorials attacked her. Bricks went flying through the windows of their Connecticut home.

As a child, Katharine Hepburn had joined her mother at suffrage demonstrations. In 1913, when British suffragette Emmeline Pankhurst visited Hartford and delivered her famous "Freedom or Death" speech, she stayed with the Hepburns. The six Hepburn children were raised to think for themselves, engage with the world, and above all, speak their minds.

But the price of that independence could be high, and Hepburn's speech threatened to derail her movie career. Conservative media outlets questioned her loyalty. FBI Director J. Edgar Hoover opened a file on her.

Hepburn later explained why she delivered that speech, which actor Edward G. Robinson was originally supposed to make.

"He's Jewish and very left of center, so he would certainly be suspect by that committee," she explained. "My ancestors were on the Mayflower. There's nothing that they can tack onto me. I've never been a member of any organization of any kind in my whole life. I'll make the speech."

"SILENCE THE ARTIST"

May 19, 1947
Progressive Party rally, Gilmore Stadium, Los Angeles, California

Each of us who has spoken to you tonight has represented a different field of endeavor in American life. I want to speak about the attack on culture — not because I work in the field of culture. I speak because I am an American, and as an American, I shall always resist any attempt at the abridgement of freedom.

That is why I am here tonight. In a sense, we are telling the same story. Mr. Kenny, Dr. Pauling, Dr. Hudson, Earl Robinson and myself. Telling it from a slightly different point of view, perhaps, but in the main, concerning ourselves with varied aspects of the same picture. This is important to remember, I think. The attacks upon the scientists, upon the member of a minority group, upon the artists, are one and the same attacks, camouflaged to confuse us, to create disunity and defeat. We the writers, the actors, the scientists, the educators, have been chosen as a primary target for attack by the Rankins, the Tenneys, and others of that ilk.

There is a good reason why we were given such a high priority on their lists. The artists, since the beginning of time, have always expressed the admirations and dreams of its people. Silence the artist and you silence the most articulate voice the people have. Destroy culture and you destroy one of the strongest sources of inspiration from which a people can draw strength to fight for a better life.

Needless to say, the attack is pushed on all fronts. While the writer and educator are being smeared, the mechanic is being relieved of his hard-won rights to organize and bargain. And the white collar worker is being forced to accept a lower standard of living through unchecked inflation and growing unemployment.

This is the plan of those who would disunite us and lead us on the road to war. Let us consider how the master plan proceeds insofar as it applies to the cultural field. I shall cite some examples, which to my mind constitute an indictment. You may draw your own conclusion.

First, radio. You all know of Norman Corwin. He was honored last year. Last year, he was honored with the "One World Award" established by the Wendell Willkie Foundation. There are those in our country who look upon One World as a subversive concept. A series of Norman Corwin scripts were requested by the Un-American Activities Committee in an obvious attempt to frighten a strong, liberal voice into silence.

Item two, radio, continued. William L. Shirer and Frank Kingdon. They were attacked by that same committee, and this is most important — their programs not renewed. Did they commit the sin of thinking and speaking along lines which were not approved by the thought control merchants?

Item three, radio continued. A Los Angeles commercial announcer was warned by a station that because he had made recordings for labor groups, his voice would become identified and he would lose his value to his sponsor, and of course his job. This, mind you, despite the fact that his name was not used on the recording.

Next, the field of the theatre. The script of a famous play was investigated by the Thomas-Rankin committee. The reason? The play dealt with problems of Negroes in the South. The name of the play, "Deep Are the Roots." Explore the real problems of the people and you are rewarded with an investigation

Item two, the theater, continued. In two American cities, Peoria, Illinois and Albany, New York, Paul Robeson, an American citizen, was refused the right to speak at a public meeting. A great artist, the most articulate voice of the Negro people, Mr. Robeson was an obvious threat for the men who ignore the meaning of the Bill of Rights. He spoke of peace and tried to use his art for social good. Consequently, he was deprived of freedom of speech.

Nor has the field of literature been overlooked. Many of you have probably read Howard Fast's book *Citizen Tom Paine*. Just a minute, be careful what you're clapping for. This book has been banned in the high schools of New York City and Detroit. It presents a dynamic concept of democracy, and, uh, to certain people, this apparently is highly undesirable.

The banning of *Citizen Tom Paine* is closely related to the field of education, and hereto, the same people are very busy. Let me remind you of State Senator Tenney's activities. In the past, he has attacked dozens of university professors and administrative officials, from Provost Dykstra of the University of California at Los Angeles to students who sympathize with motion picture strikers.

Senator Tenney has just introduced eleven bills in the State Senate, which, if passed, will set California education back fifty years. These men have learned well that the hand which rocks the cradle shakes the world. They are determined to have thought control from cradle to grave. And, a synonym for thought control is mass ignorance.

The examples, regrettably, are endless, but let me mention just one more. Two years ago, the State Department purchased seventy-nine representative paintings by American artists. These paintings were sent around the world as an exhibit of American art and culture. But the exhibition was suddenly halted, and the paintings returned to the United States to be auctioned.

An explanation? The State Department said, quote, "This is being done in the best interests of the State Department in view of the controversial issues involved," closed quote. And, the, uh, the cursed press described the paintings as, and I quote, "degenerate portraits authored by radical artists," closed quote. Perhaps you may remember that in Hitler's Germany all works of art displeasing to the authorities were labeled decadent and Bolshevist inspired.

I have made frequent references to the Un-American Activities Committee. Certainly if this Committee truly were concerned with un-American activities, it could well afford to clean its own house.

No more flagrant un-American action can be found than the vicious unwarranted attacks by the chairman of this Committee on a man whose sole crime lay in speaking for peace. I refer of course to Henry Wallace.

His presence here tonight rather than in the Hollywood Bowl is another shocking instance of the attempted suppression of free speech. Nor have I given anything like a complete picture. In democratic United States, in the year of 1947, supposedly responsibly responsible government officials call for the outlawing of minority political parties — and blithely ignore the freedom shattering implication of their hysterical request.

The President of the United States calls for a loyalty check, which can only be compared to the thought police of imperial Japan when that country followed the fascist path to destruction and war.

But the American people are not so gullible. They have proved in the past that they do not take kindly to the tactics of demigods and organized parties of reaction.

In the period immediately following the first World War, the Attorney General of the United States, one A. Mitchell Palmer, attempted to make political capital of terror and repression. His Justice Department moved down upon and arrested thousands of innocent persons whose only crime was an alien status or holding a divergent political view from those of Mr. Palmer.

However, Mitchell Palmer's presidential cult faded with the rising tide of protests from the appalled public, and the party which instituted the political raids was defeated in the next national election.

Today, J. Parnell Thomas of the Un-American Activities Committee is engaged in a personally conducted smearing campaign of the motion picture industry. He is aided and abetted in this effort by a group of Hollywood super-patriots who call themselves the Motion Picture Alliance for the Preservation of American Ideals.

For myself, I want no part of their ideals nor those of Mr. Thomas. Suffice it to say that on June 28, 1944, shortly after the formation of the Motion Picture Alliance, approximately one thousand member delegates of seventeen motion picture guilds and unions met to repudiate this organization and everything for which it stands.

The validity of this action can be judged by the recent activities of the Alliance. They have enthusiastically supported the Rankin-Thomas Committee and their Executive Secretary, Dr. John Lechner took the liberty of releasing a list of films which were called subversive. Among the so-called subversive pictures are, get this, "The Best Years of Our Lives," "Pride of the Marines," "The Strange Love of Martha Ivers," "Boomerang," and "Margie."

The members of the Alliance, the Thomases, Rankins, and Tenneys are concerned about "The Best Years of Our Lives." This is a touching concern, no doubt, but why do the Thomases, the Rankins, and Tenneys, and their bosses, express no concern over the fate of the American people who face growing unemployment and a terrible Depression.

Their loud cries can be heard from one end of the country to the other bewailing the danger of a book on democracy, or a play about Negroes, but they are strangely silent on the subject of housing.

Which of them has ever raised voice for full employment, an adequate health program, and security for the American people? Who among them has cried the evils of discrimination against minorities, or protested the feudal anti-labor legislation just passed by the Congress? And where do these men stand in the fight for peace?

To achieve peace and lasting prosperity, there must be unity among us and among all the nations of the world — the same unity that won the war.

American became great, not because of the Salem witch hunts, but in spite of them. We are still great because the American people have always accepted the challenge of new ideas — from the day that freedom was born in 1776 to this very moment.

The American people eagerly grasped at fresh concepts when they created this nation. The men and women who rode covered wagons across the plains followed the road of vigor and youth to new freedoms and a fuller life. The path of Middle Age thinking not only sets back the clock, it leads only to the grave.

And today, we won't turn the clock back, and we won't stand still. We'll move forward — progressively forward. That is what the American people have always done. We will fight not only to prevent the abridgement of freedom, but to broaden the freedoms that already exist.

We will fight not only for what we have and hold dear, but for what we hope to have — and deserve to have — and can have! And that is why we are here tonight.

JOSEPHINE BAKER

We think of her dancing in the cabarets, or strolling down the Parisian avenues with her pet cheetah. She radiated joy, exuberance, liberation. But behind the glittering stardom was a dark past.

Josephine Baker was born in St. Louis in 1906. Her father abandoned the family. Her mother, a washwoman, struggled to make ends meet. When food was scarce, Baker would scavenge in garbage cans. Sometimes she slept beneath cardboard shelters.

Dancing on street corners bought in a bit of extra money, and soon she was working in vaudeville halls. When her troupe was booked into a New York City club, she left town for good and began her climb to fame.

By nineteen she was performing in Paris. Dancing in sequins and feathers — or even less — Baker became a sensation. She was on the stage, in the movies, making records, and rich beyond her dreams. During the Second World War, she served as an ambulance driver and joined the French Resistance. Through it all, Europe remained her home.

Then in 1951, she was invited back to the America for a booking at a Miami nightclub. But she refused to perform there until the owners agreed to deseg-regate the audience — which they did.

By then she was a national hero, celebrated on a country-wide tour that culminated in a New York City parade, where she rode through the streets of Harlem in the back of a convertible. Tens of thousands of residents packed the streets and fire escapes just to catch a quick glimpse and cheer.

In February 1952, Baker went back to her home of St. Louis for a benefit per-formance. On stage at the Kiel Auditorium, to a crescendo of applause, she greeted the crowd, "Hello St Looie . . . I'm one of your children!"

She performed a few love songs, and showed off some "wiggles and grinds," as the local paper put it.

Then she talked about the hardness of her childhood. She recollected how, when she was eleven, race riots broke out in East St. Louis. In the spring and summer of 1917, mobs swept through the Black part of town with weapons and torches. All that was left of rows of homes were ash heaps, crumbling chimneys, and ruins.

Baker recalled standing on the bank of the Mississippi at night and watching the glow of burning buildings on the opposite shore. "We children stood huddled together in bewilderment," she told the audience, "not being able to understand the horrible madness of mob violence."

Her parting words to her hometown expressed her vision of an egalitarian, post-racial nation: "Let us stop saying white Americans and colored Americans, let us try once and for all saying Americans. Let human beings be equal on earth as in heaven."

"HOMECOMING DAY"

February 3, 1952
Kiel Auditorium, St. Louis, Missouri

My being here in St. Louis brings me back thirty five years. I never dreamed that I would return to St. Louis as an entertainer. A year ago when I decided to come to North America, I had it put in my contract that I would not appear in any city where my people could not come to see me, and at each time that there has been an approach to my coming to St. Louis I have always refused. Oh, I have had several fantastic offers in the first class theaters and night clubs, but when the question arrived about my people coming to see me, immediately there was a silence.

It was not until Mr. Woods and Attorney Grant came to Chicago to speak to me about the need of money for our schools that I decided to come. . . My people needed me, that was enough to make me decide.

Ladies and gentlemen believe me when I say that it makes me profoundly happy...it makes my heart swell with pride to see in this beautiful audience tonight, salt and pepper. . . I mean by that colored and white brothers mingling. This brings tears to my eyes and I. . . I want to get on my knees to thank God for letting me see this sight today. Friends and brothers, God is good. . . powerful. . . understanding. And now I have hope that St. Louis will not be the last city to join in with the other American cities that are so strongly fighting against discrimination for all Americans.

Strange, it seems just like yesterday that I ran away from home, not because I lived in poverty or that I was living in the slums for I have never been ashamed of my childhood surroundings. On the contrary, I have been very proud of my start, because it has made me remain human, and in that way understand my fellow brothers of misery. Friends, did not our Lord Jesus Christ live in poverty? Did he not? Then I believe it a great privilege to have suffered during my childhood.

I ran away from home. I ran away from St. Louis, and then I ran away from the United States of America, because of that terror of discrimination, that horrible beast which paralyzes one's very soul and body. Those in this audience that felt discrimination know what I am talking about and those who understand human beings understand what I am talking about too.

The hate directed against the colored people here in St. Louis has always given me a sad feeling because when I was a little girl I remember the horror of the East St. Louis race riot. I was very tiny but the horror of the whole thing impressed me so that here today at the age of forty five years I can still see myself standing on the west bank of the Mississippi looking over into East St. Louis and watching the glow of the burning of Negro homes lighting the sky. We children stood huddled together in bewilderment, not being able to understand the horrible madness of mob violence but here we were hiding behind the skirts of grown ups frightened to death with the screams of the Negro families running across this bridge with nothing but what they had on their backs as their worldly belongings. Friends, to me for years St. Louis represented a city of fear. . . humiliation. . .misery and terror. . . A city where in the eyes of the white man a Negro should know his place and had better stay in it.

So with this vision I ran and ran and ran. I wanted to find freedom of soul and spirit. I wanted to do things to help freedom come to my people. I was ready to fight, if necessary to obtain it. I wanted to feel that I was a human being and that we were all human beings. I got on my knees asking God, in whom I profoundly believe, to show me the light. . . to give me the power to help my people. . . to put me in a position where the sunshine that I bring would serve to enlighten the whites of the existence of colored people throughout the world in which there are over 600 million. I wanted to get far away from those who believed in cruelty, so then I went to France, a land of true freedom, democracy, equality and fraternity. There my soul was at ease but after a certain time I started to wonder why it was that in St. Louis which, was at one time, a French colony that the colored people of St. Louis have no equal rights. . . wherein Paris we are loved and respected as human beings and both cities where the population is preponderantly white. I tried to understand why this was. . .I asked various people. . . sometimes Americans of the white race. Oh, we had interesting conversations on that subject but never were they able to give a plausible reason.

This problem became an incurable disease and between my great triumphs throughout France and Europe I could not feel satisfied. The race situation kept gnawing at my heart, paralyzing my brain. . . I could not stop thinking of the suffering of my people here in America. I was continually unhappy, no one could understand why I should be because at that time I was considered the greatest success in Europe but that glow in the sky of burning houses, the screams, the terror, the tears of the unfortunate children that had lost their parents — this kept coming before me on the stage, in the streets, in my sleep.

I was haunted until I finally understood that I was marked by God to try to fight for the freedom of those that were being tortured. Here tonight I am thinking of our men over there in Korea fighting, dying so that the American flag can wave in pride throughout the world.

These men want to love America which has become their country. They also want to love the white race, but, want to be respected by them. They want their wives, their mothers, children and family to be happy and at ease here in America while they are giving their blood over there. My people have a country of their own to go to if they choose. . . Africa. . . but, this America belongs to them just as much as it does to any of the white race. . .in some ways even more so, because they gave the sweat of their brow and their blood in slavery so that many parts of America could become prosperous and recognized in the world. I must admit they are right, this land does belong to them as much as it belongs to anyone apart from the real Americans which are the Indians, and who poor souls are having a hard time because they have no right to their country.

I believe if the white and colored people could get together and be let alone, they would understand each other and consequently love each other. There is good and bad in every race, no man in any race is perfect. But it grieves me to know that St. Louis is among some of the cities of North America that practice discrimination. . . St. Louis, the city which a Negro, Mr. W. C. Handy helped to make famous throughout the world, and where a few months ago he came to do a charity benefit, only to be refused accommodations in a white hotel. Not that it is so important to be in a white hotel, but, Americans of all races should have the right to go where they please.

I remember when Lindbergh arrived in Paris, I was one of the first persons to know about his landing, because as the French people know that I was born in St. Louis, thinking I would be very proud to announce it to the public, they gave me the news first. I was then starring in the Folies Bergere. I was told to announce the great news to the public, which I did...the show stopped.

I forgot that Lindbergh was a white man and that he came from St. Louis and might not have liked Negroes. I only remembered that he was an American and that he had done something great for the progress of the world. This happened at the height of the American tourist season in Paris. There were fifty percent of Americans in the audience.

My heart almost burst with pride and joy, both the American and French people were delirious with happiness. This celebration went on all night. My joy had no bounds. I kept thinking, he is an American from St. Louis. Paris was going mad with joy.

Friends of mine invited me to one of the most fashionable restaurants in Paris at that time. The word had got around, both Lindbergh and America were on the tongues of every person...this was indeed a great victory for America. The room was packed with people and all around us champagne corks were popping. Everybody was drinking to the health of Lindbergh from St. Louis and America, when all of a sudden a clear and loud voice sounded. . . A white couple called the head waiter and told him not to serve me because in America this is not done. . . at home they said a nigger woman belongs in the kitchen.

This brought a great silence in the restaurant. I felt that if the floor could have opened and swallowed me this would be a blessing. The manager, on hearing the disturbance from the white couple came over to find out what was going on, and the white woman said: I have never sat beside a nigger in my life . . . I never will. In reply the manager reminded them that they were in France where human beings were equal and I was in my country, and if they wanted to leave he could give them their bill. He also let it be known to the other American guests present that it was a shame that the North Americans believed that their almighty dollar could rule the world.

Americans, the eyes of the world are upon you. How can you expect the world to believe in you and respect your preaching of democracy when you yourself treat your colored brothers as you do? The south will never, never be able to live down the shame of the murder of Mr. [Harry] and Mrs. [Harriette] Moore recently in Florida.

People are dying so that you will be able to live in peace. Try to understand and love each other before it is too late. Don't let the same thing happen to America through hate and misunderstanding that happened to Germany. . . Believe that it can happen ... It would be a shame for good thinking members of the white race to suffer for the bad. God dislikes evil and no happiness can be built on hate. Love one another as brothers. God said that you should make this country a good and powerful one, where our forefathers came with hope. Let us stop saying white Americans and colored Americans, let us try once and for all saying. . . Americans. Let human beings be equal on earth as in heaven. I thank you for coming tonight. . . May God bless you.

LILLIAN SMITH

The Montgomery bus boycott began on December 5, 1955, four days after Rosa Parks refused to sit at the back of the municipal bus. An estimated 40,000 Black bus riders boycotted the city transportation system in the nation's first large demonstration against racial segregation.

One long weary year later, the boycott was still going on, but an end was in sight. The US Supreme Court had upheld a lower court ruling, and a few legal technicalities were all that was holding back an official end to Alabama's segregation.

While they waited, the Reverend Martin Luther King, Jr. and the Montgomery Improvement Association called for a weeklong "institute," with mass meetings, seminars, speeches, oratory contests for young people, fasting, and a day of prayer. On the agenda was well-known Georgia novelist and activist Lillian Smith.

She was a lonely figure in the Deep South, whose soul-searching led her to conclude that racial segregation was a psychiatric disease that corrupted the human spirit — she called it "spiritual lynching." Her bestselling novel *Strange Fruit*, about an interracial love affair, had established her as one of the nation's most outspoken writers on racial injustice.

Since the 1930s Smith had been giving hundreds of speeches at churches, college campuses, and interfaith groups. "I know all the temptations not to speak out, all the fears," she had written in 1944.

But speak out she did.

On the third evening of the mass gathering in Montgomery, Baptist educator Nannie Helen Burroughs captivated her listeners by likening the bus boycott to the American Revolution. "Work as if all depended upon you," she concluded, "and pray as if all depended upon God."

Then came the announcement that Smith, the much-anticipated next speaker, would not appear after all due to illness — she was suffering from cancer. As reporter Inez Baskin of the *Montgomery Adviser* wrote, "A feeling of sympathy permeated the atmosphere." Smith's speech was read out loud by a friend instead.

She took Southern liberals to task for their "fuzzy" moderation on race. Most Southern Whites, even of good will, were doing nothing about ending segregation. "The right way was not a moderate way," she said.

She was making the same observation that King would make seven years later in his "Letter From the Birmingham Jail" — that the White moderate "who is more devoted to order than justice" was a greater stumbling block to Black freedom than the Ku Klux Klan.

A week and a half after that mass meeting, on December 20, 1956, the Montgomery bus boycott officially came to an end after 382 days.

"THE RIGHT WAY IS NOT A MODERATE WAY"

December 5, 1956

**Institute on Nonviolence and Social Change,
Montgomery Improvement Association, Montgomery, Alabama**

I want to take my stand by your side because I respect the creative means you have chosen to use to secure your legal rights as American citizens.

These means are nonviolent. This way is the way of good will and intelligence and truth, and love. You have refused to use the crude and dangerous weapon of hate. You have refused to lie. You have not succumbed to retaliation or to resentment. You have used no harshness of word or of act.

You have behaved under stress like mature men and women — not like a mob.

But you have not been "moderates" nor have you kept in the middle of the road. No. You have shown the world that there are two extremes and they cannot be put in the same moral category. There is the extreme of hate, yes; but there is also the extreme of love. There is the extreme of the lie, yes; but there is also the extreme we call the "search for truth." There is the habitual thief who is certainly an extremist; there is the habitually honest man who is an extremist, also. But would you put the thief and the honest man in the same moral category? Would you put the person whose life radiates love in the same moral category with the man whose life radiates hate? Are they equally harmful? Or equally good? Those who think so have abandoned the concept of morality and the concept of quality, and sanity in human affairs.

So: You have been extremists: good, creative, loving extremists and I want to tell you I admire and respect you for it.

Moderation is the slogan of our times. But moderation never made a man or a nation great. Moderation never discovered anything, never invented anything, never built a skyscraper, never invented an airplane, never wrote a poem, never painted a great picture, never wrote a great play, never discovered a country, never explored a new frontier, never built a civilization and never dreamed a great religion. These great thrusts of the human imagination and spirit came out of daring to meet ordeal in a new way. It would be difficult to imagine Jesus as a "moderate." Imagine Leonardo da Vinci being a moderate. Imagine Gandhi as a moderate. Imagine Shakespeare or Einstein as a moderate. Imagine Lindbergh being a moderate. He may be one now but he was not one when he flew the Atlantic. It was the act of a daring extremist if there ever was such; but it was a creative act; it was not the act of a destroyer, nor the act of a hating man, nor the act of a violent man.

You have done many good things, down here in Montgomery. But one of the best, one of the most valuable, has been the fact that you have dramatized for all America to see that in times of ordeal, in times of crisis, only the extremist can meet the challenge. The question in crisis or ordeal is not: Are you going to be an extremist? The question is: What kind of extremist are you going to be?

Here, in Montgomery, you have decided what kind of extremist you are. You have chosen the way of love and truth, the way of nonviolence and understanding, the way of patience with firmness, the way of dignity and calm persistence.

You have done this as others keep talking about moderation.

What do people mean when they use that fuzzy word, moderation? Why do the mass magazines keep talking about it? What is the meaning of this hypnotic word?

Let's take it step by step: Let's be as fair as we can. Many mean simply this: "We want to freeze things as they are. We want to be neutral. We don't want to move a step either way. Things suit us as they are: Why should we change them? Change is painful so let's don't change." There are others, a few men of good will but with only a moderate amount of brains who intend no harm at all when they lean back on this slogan. They mean in a vague way: "Let's be tactful; let's talk in a quiet voice; let's don't stir things up; let's do a little bit but let's sleep through it and then maybe some day we'll wake up and find that everything has settled itself without our having to do anything about it." And there are the few sincere, even intelligent people who want moderation simply because to them it is a synonym for doing nothing. They are too frightened to move, to think, to find a new way to meet the challenge. It is known by all of us that our minds don't work well if we become too frightened, although they work best of all when we are a little frightened.

People behave this way in other crises too; not simply this one of race relations. There are people who react in a similar way when they are told they have cancer. They decide to be moderate and do nothing. Why? Because they are scared. And because they are very frightened they convince themselves that if they do nothing, the cancer will go away.

The tragic fact is, neither cancer nor segregation will go away while you close your eyes. Both are dangerous diseases because they spread, they metastasize throughout our country — and indeed, throughout the whole earth. Because this is so: because you cannot wall these problems in, you don't have time to lose with cancer nor today, do we have time to lose since the Supreme Court has spoken on segregation. The critical moment is on us. Now is the time to deal with it.

Why is there a crisis now when for fifty years we have not felt segregation had reached a critical peak? Why has the Supreme Court's decision precipitated this crisis?

As I see it, this is why:

The Supreme Court is the highest legal voice in our land. It interprets the US Constitution for us. We are not free, in this country ruled by law, to interpret the law for ourselves as Herman Talmadge says he does and that "everybody can do." The Supreme Court has spoken: It has said, segregation in the public schools must go because it is unconstitutional. The Supreme Court has, therefore, said in effect that all legal segregation must go. Once saying this, the crisis was upon us.

Why? Because now, if we do not take segregation out of our schools, we are defying the Supreme Court, we are subverting the Constitution. If we do not get rid of segregation in buses and trains and planes, we are defying the highest law-interpreting body of our land. If we do not now get rid of all forms of public segregation, we are subverting our form of government.

But to say the Supreme Court's decision precipitated the crisis is only half a truth. It spoke its decision. The actual crisis came because we did not listen. The ordeal began when the governmental leaders of our southern states spoke out and said they would not obey the Supreme Court's decision.

It takes two to make a crisis. And these political leaders, these governors, these attorneys-general, these US Senators who defy the Supreme Court and force us to defy the Supreme Court have, in effect, started a revolution against the legal structure on which our free and democratic government is based.

This is how the ordeal started; this is the situation we are now faced with: a different situation from that of three years ago.

Three years ago we had segregation. And it was the same old unchristian, undemocratic way of life we have had for fifty years and have now; and people, colored and white, were harmed by it. But the situation is different. Different because segregation is now against the law of our nation. Different because to maintain it we have to defy our own government.

How we deal with this critical situation will determine our moral health as individuals, our cultural health, our health as a nation, and as a leader of democracy throughout the world.

You know how the destructive extremists are dealing with it in the South. But how are the rest of the white southerners dealing with it? May I trouble the waters, a little, by telling you?

A few — perhaps far more than you know — are dealing with it creatively and honestly and with courage. There are many white southerners opposed to segregation; there are many more who are not opposed to segregation but who believe it is more important to obey the law of the land than it is to have segregation. Some of these are speaking out: some in their pulpits and some in their editorial chair. Some are meeting in small groups and probing deeply into this trouble in order to try to understand it. Others are taking, here and there, a bold stand. Some are losing their jobs, of course. They are the creative, nonviolent "extremists" who are quietly, with wisdom and tact and goodwill trying to bring change about as quickly as possible. How about the rest of the white southerners? The moderates? Those who are neither good extremists nor bad extremists? How about them?

Most are doing nothing. That does not mean they are not worried. It means they are suffering from temporary moral and psychic paralysis. They are working harder to be moderates and neutrals than they are working to meet the crisis. They are driving straight down the middle of the road with their eyes shut and you know what happens in traffic when you do that. But they are trying to believe there is no traffic. They are telling themselves nobody is on the road but themselves. They are, you see, trying very hard not to be extremists, they are trying to be neither good nor evil.

And all the time these moderates are doing nothing or almost nothing, men like Herman Talmadge, men like Senator Eastland are shouting at the tops of their voice; certain newspaper editors are writing violently against the good extremists and begging everybody to please freeze and do nothing.

And the mobs gather; and the crosses are burned; and the houses are dynamited; and the brave ones who speak out lose their jobs and so it goes, on and on. The White Citizens Councils mushroom, the Klan wakes up and wraps itself in its pillow case and sheet; and Negroes and whites working for integration are boycotted and penalized and cheated.

But the big middle group turn away and try not to see, whispering, "I must be moderate; I must not get worried; I must not mind when innocent people are hurt and brave people lose their jobs and lives."

And how are the moderates getting along? How are they faring? What kind of price are they paying for their moderation, for this desire of theirs to prolong segregation?

May I suggest how high this price is?

In order to maintain the status quo, to maintain segregation as long as possible even though the Supreme Court has spoken, to drive in the middle of the road, the white people are having to give up their freedoms. What freedoms?

Let me name a few:

    a. The freedom to do right. There are white Christians in the South who know segregation is wrong. They want to do right. But they are not free to do right. Every day they do what they know in their hearts is contrary to their Christian beliefs.

b. The freedom to obey the law. The Supreme Court has spoken. But we in the South are not free to obey the law. We obey our dictators instead; these are sometimes our governors; other times these dictators are our business employers, our school superintendents, or our Boards of Trustees of the church.

c. The freedom to speak out, or to write, or teach what one believes is true. We have almost lost this basic freedom now in the South. The penalties are heavy for those who dare speak out anyway. Loss of jobs; boycott; ostracism; violence, sometimes.

d. And of course, having lost those three big freedoms, we have also lost our freedom from fear. In old Reconstruction days, white people were afraid of freed Negroes. Or so they said. Today, they are afraid of each other and themselves. They fear. And that is the saddest loss of all, in this great, free country of ours.

The risk is too big, people say. Young brave men say "the risk is too great. I'd like to do something but the risk is too big."

I say, "The time has now come when it is dangerous not to risk. We must take risks in order to save our integrity, our moral nature, our lives and our country. We must do what we do with love and dignity, with nonviolence and wisdom, but we must do something big and keep doing it."

I was talking to a group of white students in one of our southern universities. They had sort of sneaked me in. Yes, really. They were afraid for people to know Lillian Smith was on the campus. So everything was hush-hush. I teased them a little. And they laughed. But they felt ashamed, too. Some of these young men had come home from Korea a few years ago. They knew what danger is; and had gladly run risks. Now, they were not running any more risks.

Not only the loss of our freedoms but the loss of our old gallant courage, is part of the high price we are paying today for our do-nothing attitude toward segregation. And worst of all, is the loss of belief. One young man said, "I'd risk anything for something I believed. I just don't think I believe in anything much, anymore."

Then I told them about your creative project in Montgomery. They had heard a little, of course. But they listened, these young white men and girls. And they grew excited and interested, and thrilled.

Do you realize that in helping yourselves to secure your freedom you are helping young white southerners secure theirs, too? This is a big thing. This is how the creative act works: it always helps somebody else besides you. In dramatizing that the extreme way can be the good way, the creative way, and that in times of ordeal it is the only way, you are helping the white South find its way, too. You are giving young white southerners hope. You are persuading some of them that there is something worth believing in and risking for. You are stirring their imaginations and their hearts, not simply because you are brave and are running risks but because you know that the means we use are the important thing: that the means must be right; the means must be full of truth and dignity and love and wisdom.

Because you are doing this, I want to close my greeting to you by saying thank you. Thank you for what you are doing for yourselves and what you are doing also for the entire South. Thank you for dramatizing before the eyes of America that the question is not, "Are you an extremist?," but "What kind of extremist are you?" Thank you for showing us all that there is always a creative, good, nonviolent way to meet ordeal.

RACHEL CARSON

In the spring of 1962, marine biologist and nature writer Rachel Carson delivered the commencement address at Scripps College in Southern California on the topic of "man's attitude toward nature."

With the Cold War and the threat of nuclear conflict as the backdrop, her speech was an elegiac warning about the dangers of assuming that the world had been created solely for human "use and convenience."

The universe was older than we could fathom, she said, and its interdependent life forms — including humankind — deserve far greater respect and humility.

"Instead of always trying to impose our will on nature," she told the students, "we should sometimes be quiet and listen to what she has to tell us."

What the audience couldn't know was that in a couple weeks, *The New Yorker* would publish the first of Carson's three-part exposé of the misuse of pesticides by the chemicals industry. When published the following September as a book called *Silent Spring,* it would explode into national consciousness.

Since her days at the US Fish and Wildlife Service, Carson had been concerned about the dangers of pesticides, especially DDT. She suspected it was not the harmless miracle substance scientists proclaimed it to be, and that DDT should be certified for safety before humankind caused irreparable damage to the planet, and itself.

The chemicals industry fought back with ferocity, unleashing an arsenal of editorials, articles, and "scientific" studies to discredit her argument. As one critic said: "Her book is more poisonous than the pesticides she condemns."

Suddenly Carson was in high demand as a speaker. In a talk to the Women's National Press Club in December 1962, she cautioned the audience to be wary of the information they received about the controversy, because much of it was industry propaganda. "I recommend that you ask yourself — Who speaks? And why?"

Despite the flood of speaking invitations, Carson had to conserve her strength as she underwent treatment for breast cancer. She knew her time was limited. When she testified before Congress in June 1963 on "pesticides and other poisons," she was so weak she had to hold her head up between her hands.

Carson passed away in the following spring without knowing how prophetic her words actually were. At the Scripps commencement, she had clearly seen the future.

"Your generation must come to terms with the environment," she warned the graduates. "You go out into a world where mankind is challenged, as it has never been challenged before, to prove its maturity and its mastery not of nature, but of itself."

"OF MAN AND THE STREAM OF TIME"

June 12, 1962
Commencement address, Scripps College, Claremont, California

I wish to speak today of man's relation to nature and more specifically of man's attitude toward nature. A generation ago this would perhaps have been an academic subject of little interest to any but philosophers. Today it is a subject of immediate and sometimes terrifying relevance.

The word nature has many and varied connotations, but for the present theme I like this definition: "Nature is the part of the world that man did not make." You who have spent your undergraduate years here at Scripps have been exceptionally fortunate, living in the midst of beauty and comforts and conveniences that *are* creations of man yet always in the background having these majestic and beautiful mountains to remind you of an older and vaster world a world that man did <u>not</u> make.

Man has long talked somewhat arrogantly about the conquest of nature; now he has the power to achieve his boast. It is our misfortune it may well be our final tragedy that this power has not been tempered with wisdom, but has been marked by irresponsibility; that there is all too little awareness that man is *part* of nature, and that the price of conquest may well be the destruction of man himself.

I think we must first try to find the true perspective against which to look at man in his relation to the physical world and to the other life with which he shares the earth. To do this we must go far back in time, to the sources of that stream of life that flowed out of the obscurity that shrouds the early history of the earth.

As yet no one knows how or where the first life came into being. We do not even know with precision how old the earth is, but we know it was formed several billions of years ago. The first life seems to have arisen in the sea perhaps two billion years ago, at a time when conditions were somehow right for the formation of the mysterious stuff called protoplasm. The first simple organisms would have given little indication of the incredible number and diversity of creatures into which they were to evolve. But over the periods and the eras of geologic time the stream of life flowed on, growing always more and more complex. By the beginning of Cambrian time, more than half a billion years ago, all the major groups of backboneless animals had become established in the sea.

More time, measured not in centuries but in the majestic and incomprehensible eras of the geologic scale, was to pass before the first colonists came out upon the bare continents simple plants to begin the work of soil building that prepared the way for the earth's green mantle. And at last the first animals crept out on land, in that era called the Silurian. But this was only a few hundred million years ago, so we see that for perhaps four-fifths or more of earthly time the continents were without life. Then followed in swift succession the age of reptiles, of birds, of mammals.

Measured against the vast backdrop of geologic time, the whole era of man seems but a moment but how portentous a moment! It was only within the past million years or so that the race of men arose. Who could have foretold that this being, who walked upright and no longer lived in trees, who lurked in caves, hiding in fear from the great beasts who shared his world who could have guessed that he would one day have in his hands the power to change the very nature of the earth the power of life and death over so many of its creatures? Who could have foretold that the brain that was developing behind those heavy brow ridges would allow him to accomplish things no other creature had achieved but would not at the same time endow him with wisdom so to control his activities that he would not bring destruction upon himself?

I like the way E. B. White has summed it up in his usual inimitable style. "I am pessimistic about the human race," said Mr. White, "because it is too ingenious for its own good. Our approach to nature is to beat it into submission. We would stand a better chance of survival if we accommodated ourselves to this planet and viewed it appreciatively instead of skeptically and dictatorially."

Our attitude toward nature has changed with time, in ways that I can only suggest here. Primitive men, confronted with the awesome forces of nature, reacted in fear of what they did not understand. They peopled the dark and brooding forests with supernatural beings. Looking out on the sea that extended to an unknown horizon, they imagined a dreadful brink lying beneath fog and gathering darkness; they pictured vast abysses waiting to suck the traveler down into a bottomless gulf.

Only a few centuries have passed since those pre-Columbian days, yet today our whole earth has become only another shore from which we look out across the dark ocean of space, uncertain what we shall find when we sail out among the stars, but like the Norsemen and the Polynesians of old, lured by the very challenge of the unknown.

Between the time of those early voyages into unknown seas and the present we can trace an enormous and fateful change. It is good that fear and superstition have largely been replaced by knowledge, but we would be on safer ground today if the knowledge had been accompanied by humility instead of arrogance.

In the western world our thinking has for many centuries been dominated by the Jewish-Christian concept of man's relation to nature, in which man is regarded as the master of all the earth's inhabitants. Out of this there easily grew the thought that everything on earth animate or inanimate, animal, vegetable, or mineral and indeed the earth itself had been created expressly for man.

John Muir, who knew and loved the California mountains, has described this naive view of nature with biting wit: "A numerous class of men," he wrote, "are painfully astonished whenever they find anything, living or dead, in all God's universe, which they cannot eat or render in some way that they call *useful* to themselves . . . Whales, he went on, "are storehouses of oil for us, to help out the stars in lighting our dark ways until the discovery of the Pennsylvania oil wells. Among plants, hemp is a case of evident destination for ships' rigging, wrapping packages, and hanging the wicked."

So Muir, with his pen dipped in acid, many years ago pointed out the incredible absurdity of such views. But I am not certain that in spite of all our modern learning and sophistication, we have actually progressed far beyond the self-oriented philosophy of the Victorians. I fear that these ideas still lurk about, showing themselves boldly and openly at times, at others skulking about in the shadows of the subconscious.

I have met them frequently, as I have pointed out some exquisite creature of the tide pools to a chance companion. "What is it for?" he may ask, and he is obviously disappointed if I can't assure him that it can be eaten or at least made into some bauble to be sold in a shop.

But how is one to assign a value to the exquisite flower-like hydroids reflected in the still mirror of a tide pool? Who can place in one pan of some cosmic scales the trinkets of modern civilization and in the other the song of a thrush in the windless twilight?

Now I have dwelt at some length on the fallacious idea of a world arranged for man's use and convenience, but I have done so because I am convinced that these notions the legacy of an earlier day are at the root of some of our most critical problems. We still talk in terms of "conquest" whether it be of the insect world or of the mysterious world of space. We still have not become mature enough to see ourselves as a very tiny part of a vast and incredible universe, a universe that is distinguished above all else by a *mysterious and wonderful unity* that we flout at our peril.

Poets often have a perception that gives their words the validity of science. So the English poet Francis Thompson said nearly a century ago,

"Thou canst not stir a flower
Without troubling of a star."

But the poet's insight has not become part of general knowledge.

Man's attitude toward nature is today critically important, simply because of his new-found power to destroy it. For a good many years there has been an excellent organization known as The International Union for the Protection of Nature. I clearly remember that in the days before Hiroshima I used to wonder whether nature in the broadest context of the word actually needed protection from man. Surely the sea was inviolate and forever beyond man's power to change it. Surely the vast cycles by which water is drawn up into the clouds to return again to the earth could never be touched. And just as surely the vast tides of life the migrating birds would continue to ebb and flow over the continents, marking the passage of the seasons.

But I was wrong. Even these things, that seemed to belong to the eternal verities, are not only threatened but have already felt the destroying hand of man.

Today we use the sea as a dumping ground for radioactive wastes, which then enter into the vast and uncontrollable movements of ocean waters through the deep basins, to turn up no one knows where.....

The once beneficent rains are now an instrument to bring down from the atmosphere the deadly products of nuclear explosions. Water, perhaps our most precious natural resource, is used and misused at a reckless rate. Our streams are fouled with an incredible assortment of wastes domestic, chemical, radioactive, so that our planet, though dominated by seas that envelop three-fourths of its surface, is rapidly becoming a thirsty world.

We now wage war on other organisms, turning against them all the terrible armaments of modern chemistry, and we assume a right to push whole species over the brink of extinction. This is a far cry from the philosophy of that man of peace, Albert Schweitzer the philosophy of "reverence for life." Although all the world honors Dr. Schweitzer, I am afraid we do not follow him.

So nature does indeed need protection from man, but man, too, needs protection from his own acts, for he is part of the living world. His war against nature is inevitably a war against himself. His heedless and destructive acts enter into the vast cycles of the earth and in time return to him.

Through all this problem there runs a constant theme, and the theme is the flowing stream of time, unhurried, unmindful of man's restless and feverish pace. It is made up of geologic events, that have created mountains and worn them away, that have brought the seas out of their basins, to flood the continents and then retreat. But even more importantly it is made up of biological events, that represent that all important adjustment of living protoplasm to the conditions of the external world. What we are today represents an adjustment achieved over the millions and hundreds of millions of years. There have always been elements in the environment that were hostile to living things extremes of temperature, background radiation in rocks and atmosphere, toxic elements in the earth and sea. But over the long ages of time, life has reached an accommodation, a balance.

Now we are far on the way to upsetting this balance by creating an artificial environment consisting to an ever increasing extent of things that "man has made."

The radiation to which we must adjust if we are to survive is no longer simply the natural background radiation of rocks and sunlight, it is the result of our tampering with the atom. In the same way, wholly new chemicals are emerging from the laboratories an astounding, bewildering array of them. All of these things are being introduced into our environment at a rapid rate. There simply is no time for living protoplasm to adjust to them.

In 1955 a group of 70 scientists met at Princeton University to consider man's role in changing the face of the earth. They produced a volume of nearly 1200 pages devoted to changes that range from the first use of fire to urban sprawl. It is an astounding record. This is not to say, of course, that all the changes have been undesirable. But the distinguishing feature of man's activities is that they have almost always been undertaken from the narrow viewpoint of shortrange gain, without considering either their impact on the earth or their long-range effect upon ourselves.

They have been distinguished, also, by a curious unwillingness to be guided by the knowledge that is available in certain areas of science. I mean especially the knowledge of biologists, of ecologists, of geneticists, all of whom have special areas of competence that should allow them to predict the effect of our actions on living creatures, including, of course, man himself.

This is an age that has produced floods of how-to-do-it books, and it is also an age of how-to-do-it science. It is the age of technology, in which if we know *how* to do something, we do it without pausing to inquire whether we should. We know how to split the atom, and how to use its energy in peace and war, and so we proceed with preparations to do so, as if acting under some blind compulsion; even though the geneticists tell us that by our actions in this atomic age we are endangering not only ourselves but the integrity of the human germ plasm.

Instead of always trying to impose our will on nature we should sometimes be quiet and listen to what she has to *tell* us. If we did so I am sure we would gain a new perspective on our own feverish lives. We might even see the folly and the madness of a world in which half of mankind is busily preparing to destroy the other half and to reduce our whole planet to radioactive ashes in the doing.

We might gain what the English essayist [H.M.] Tomlinson called "a hint of a reality, hitherto fabulous, of a truth that be everlasting, yet is contrary to all our experience," for "our earth may be a far better place than we have yet discovered."

I wish I could stand before you and say that my own generation had brought strength and meaning to man's relation to nature, that we had looked upon the majesty and beauty and terror of the earth we inhabit and learned wisdom and humility. Alas, this cannot be said, for it is we who have brought into being a fateful and destructive power.

But the stream of time moves forward and mankind moves with it. Your generation must come to terms with the environment. You must face realities instead of taking refuge in ignorance and evasion of truth. Yours is a grave and a sobering responsibility, but it is also a shining opportunity. You go out into a world where mankind is challenged, as it has never been challenged before, to prove its maturity and its mastery not of nature, but of itself. Therein lies our hope and our destiny. "In today already walks tomorrow."

PAULI MURRAY

Three months after the historic March on Washington, Pauli Murray blasted its male organizers for discriminating against the women working alongside them to make America more egalitarian. Speaking to a women's group in November 1963, she complained that of the fifteen speakers at the Lincoln Memorial, only one was a woman.

Murray was a Yale Law School fellow who was widely respected for her pioneering work on race and gender. She'd been arrested for refusing to sit at the back of the bus in Petersburg, Virginia, fifteen years before Rosa Parks in Montgomery. She'd organized restaurant protests in Washington, DC, twenty years before the Greensboro lunch counter sit-ins.

Her law school paper at Howard University had influenced Thurgood Marshall's strategy in *Brown v. Board of Education.* Her book, *States' Laws on Race and Color,* was considered "the Bible of the Civil Rights movement."

She knew that the lack of women speakers at the Washington march was no accident. Planners originally wanted no women to speak, not even during the section dedicated to "Negro Women Fighters for Freedom." Anna Arnold Hedgeman, the lone woman on the planning committee, had complained.

Finally, organizers consented to give a spot to Myrlie Evers, widow of the recently assassinated Medgar Evers. But when she got stuck in traffic, activist Daisy Bates filled in.

Black American women, Bates told the crowd on the Washington Mall, would sit-in, kneel-in, and lie-in if necessary, "until every Negro in America can vote."

All the other addresses were by men — including Dr. King's iconic "I Have a Dream."

For Murray, it was "bitterly humiliating." As she noted, two days before the March, organizer A. Philip Randolph had agreed to speak at the National Press Club — despite protests by female reporters that the club restricted women to the balcony. When Randolph asked, "What's wrong with the balcony?" the women shot back, "What's wrong with the back of the bus?"

He failed to see, Murray noted, "that he was supporting the violation of the very principle for which he was fighting: that human rights are indivisible."

She also lashed out at James Meredith, the first Black student admitted to the University of Mississippi, for saying picket lines were too dangerous for women. "His views will not win the civil rights fight," Murray said.

In the quest for racial equality, Black women had been willing to overlook gender discrimination. But women had too often carried the greatest burdens in the Black family, Murray said. "Would the Negro struggle have come this far without the indomitable determination of its women?"

"THE NEGRO WOMAN IN THE QUEST FOR EQUALITY"

November 14, 1963
Leadership Conference, National Council of Negro
Women, Statler Hilton, Washington, DC

Negro women, historically, have carried the dual burden of Jim Crow and Jane Crow. They have not always carried it graciously but they have carried it effectively. They have shared with their men a partnership in a pioneer life on spiritual and psychological frontiers not inhabited by any other group in the United States. For Negroes have had to hack their way through the wilderness of racism produced by the accumulated growth of nearly four centuries of a barbarous international slave trade, two centuries of chattel slavery and a century of illusive citizenship in a desperate effort to make a place of dignity for themselves and their children.

In this bitter struggle, into which has been poured most of the resources and much of the genius of successive generations of American Negroes, these women have often carried disproportionate burdens in the Negro family as they strove to keep its integrity intact against the constant onslaught of indignities to which it was subjected. Not only have they stood shoulder to shoulder with Negro men in every phase of the battle, but they have also continued to stand when their men were destroyed by it. Who among us is not familiar with that heroic, if formidable, figure exhorting her children to overcome every disappointment, humiliation and obstacle. This woman's lullaby was very often "Be something!" "Be somebody!" My friend and colleague, Mrs. Dovey J. Roundtree, who tells this story of her own grandmother[,] was never quite sure in childhood what it was she was supposed to be, but there was never any escape from the mandate . . .

In the course of their climb, Negro women have had to fight against the stereotypes of "female dominance" on the one hand and loose morals on the other hand, both growing out of the roles forced upon them during the slavery experience and its aftermath. But out of their struggle for human dignity, they also developed a tradition of independence and self-reliance. This characteristic, said the late Dr. E. Franklin Frazier, sociologist, "has provided generally a pattern of equalitarian relationship between men and women in America." Like the Western pioneer settlements, the embattled Negro society needed the strength of all of its members in order to survive. The economic necessity for the Negro woman to earn a living to help support her family — if indeed she was not the sole support — fostered her independence and equalitarian position.

In the human rights battle, America has seen the image of the Negro evolving through many women: Harriet Tubman and Sojourner Truth a century ago; Ida B. Wells in the latter part of the 19th century; Mary Church Terrell and Mary McLeod Bethune in an earlier generation; Mrs. Rosa Parks, Autherine Lucy, Mrs. Gloria Richardson, Mrs. Daisy Bates, Mrs. Diana Nash Bevel, Mrs. Constance Baker Motley, Mrs. Medgar Evers, Dorothy Height, Mrs. Anna Hedgeman, and many others in the contemporary struggle. Not only have women whose names are well known given this great human effort its peculiar vitality but women in the many communities whose names will never be known have revealed the courage and strength of the Negro woman. These are the mothers who have stood in school yards with their children, many times alone. These are the images which have touched America's heart. Painful as these experiences have been, one cannot help asking: would the Negro struggle have come this far without the indomitable determination of its women?

In the larger society, Negro and white women share a common burden because of traditional discriminations based upon sex . . .

Despite the common interests of Negro and white women, however, the dichotomy of the segregated society has prevented them from cementing a natural alliance. Communication and cooperation between them have been hesitant, limited and formal. Negro women have tended to identify all discrimination against them as racial in origin and to accord high priority to the civil rights struggle. They have had little time or energy for consideration of women's rights. But as the civil struggle gathers momentum, they begin to recognize the similarities between paternalism and racial arrogance. They also begin to sense that the struggle into which they have poured their energies may not afford them rights they have assumed would be theirs when the civil rights cause has triumphed.

Recent disquieting events have made imperative an assessment of the role of the Negro woman in the quest for equality. The civil rights revolt, like many social upheavals, has released powerful pentup emotions, cross currents, rivalries and hostilities. In emerging from an essentially middle class movement and taking on a mass character, it has become a vehicle of power and prestige and contain[s] many of the elements of in-fighting that have characterized labor's emergence or the pre-independence African societies. There is much jockeying for position as ambitious men push and elbow their way to leadership roles.

Part of this upsurge reflects the Negro males normal desire to achieve a sense of personal worth and recognition of his manhood by a society which has so long denied it. One aspect is the wresting of the initiative of the civil rights movement from white liberals. Another is the backlash of a new male aggressiveness against Negro women.

What emerges most clearly from events of the past several months is the tendency to assign women to a secondary, ornamental or "honoree" role instead of the partnership role in the civil rights movement which they have earned by their courage, intelligence and dedication. It was bitterly humiliating for Negro women on August 28 to see themselves accorded little more than token recognition in the historic March on Washington. Not a single woman was invited to make one of the major speeches or to be part of the delegation of leaders who went to the White House. This omission was deliberate. Representations for recognition of women were made to the policy-making body sufficiently in advance of the August 28 arrangements to have permitted the necessary adjustments of the program. What the Negro women leaders were told is revealing: that no representation was given to them because they would not be able to agree on a delegate. How familiar was this excuse! It is a typical response from an entrenched power group.

Significantly, two days before the March, A. Philip Randolph, leader of the March, accepted an invitation to be guest speaker at a luncheon given by the National Press Club in Washington in the face of strong protest by organized newspaper women that the National Press Club excludes qualified newspaper women from membership and sends women reporters who cover its luncheons to the balcony. Mr. Randolph apparently saw no relationship between being sent to the balcony and being sent to the back of the bus. Perhaps if he had been able to understand what an affront it is to one's personal dignity to be sent to the balcony at a meeting concerned primarily with the issue of human dignity, he would set as a condition for his appearance a non-segregated gathering. He failed to see that he was supporting the violation of the very principle for which he was fighting: that human rights are indivisible.

In 1840, a somewhat similar issue arose in the anti-slavery movement. William Lloyd Garrison and Charles Remond, the latter a Negro, refused to be seated as delegates to the World Anti-Slavery Convention in London when they learned that the women members of the American delegation would be excluded and could sit only in the balcony. Mr. Garrison dramatized his protest by joining the women in the balcony. The seed of the Seneca Falls Convention of 1848, which marks the formal beginning of the woman's rights movement in the United States, was planted at that London convention. One wonders what similar decisions were made by the spiritual successors to Harriet Tubman and Sojourner Truth on August 28.

This was not an isolated incident. Women who have been active in local branches of NAACP have observed the efforts of men to push them out of positions of leadership. And from Atlanta came the recent announcement of Mrs. Ruby Hurley, veteran NAACP field worker, that she was organizing women's auxiliaries for NAACP because "Negro women and white women, too, have a responsibility to carry a greater share in the civil rights protest than they do." A woman's auxiliary implies an adjunct to a male organization. Can it be that the movement which Mary White Ovington, a woman, helped to organize has become so male-dominated that women no longer feel like first class members and can be roused to action only through an auxiliary organization in which they are at least treated as equals?

More recently, Mr. James Meredith, hero of the University of Mississippi crisis, reportedly told *The Washington Post*:

My makeup won't allow me to go along with using women and children in certain exposed roles in our fight. I love them too much. I think it is the man's role to face danger and protect his women and children.

Two comments are relevant here. All Negroes are *born* involved in the civil rights fight and exposed to its dangers. Ironically enough, the very presence of women and children in the demonstrations has doubtless minimized the violence and aroused the sympathies of the American public. The grudging respect of some local police for an aroused public opinion has been a key factor throughout the mass demonstrations. No more dramatic illustration of the many roles which women have played in this struggle can be found than the news photos of Mr. Meredith himself in many tense situations with his legal counsel, Mr. [sic] Constance Motley, at his side. The plain fact is that in today's wars and social revolutions there are *no* civilians. The tragic death of six children in Birmingham on September 15th made this painfully clear.

The second and more important fact is that in the civil right revolution it has been the individual commitment of men, women and children to the struggle for liberty and without regard to age or sex which has made the movement so spectacular and won the respect of the American people. It cannot be too strongly emphasized here that part of what has set the American Negro off from other Americans is their commonly held view that Negroes are not part of the significant American traditions and movements. It is pointed out that Negroes are the one group whose immigration to the New World was not voluntary. Negroes were not intended to be included in the Declaration of Independence, we are told. Although 200,000 Negroes fought in the Civil War and their emancipation was a result of the war, it was not their war it is said. All too often, upon reading American history one is left with the impression that Negroes are a group about which history has been made but who themselves have not taken the initiative in making significant history. Few people bother to read the historical materials which refute these general impressions.

But the whole world knows today that the American Negro is making history on the front pages of every newspaper and that he is keeping alive the tradition of liberty upon which the United States was founded. The civil rights revolution has been called the Second American Revolution. Let us not forget that this began as a revolution of school children in the 1950s when they won worldwide acclaim for their courage in desegregating the schools. A Negro child can have no finer heritage to sustain him and give him a feeling of "somebodiness" than the knowledge that he himself or she herself has been physically a part of the great sweep of history. What we are learning in this struggle is that self-respect must be earned. No one can win it for anyone else. It is an individual matter. Hence, while Mr. Meredith is well-intentioned, his view will not win the civil rights fight.

To return to our central theme, it is also pointedly significant that in the great mass of magazine and newsprint expended upon the civil rights crisis, national editors have selected Negro men almost exclusively to articulate the aspirations of the Negro community. There has been little or no public discussion of the problems, aspirations and role of Negro women. Moreover, the undertone of news stories of recent efforts to create career opportunities for Negroes in government and industry seems to be that what is being talked about is jobs for Negro men only. The fact that Negro women might be available and, as we shall see, are qualified and in need of employment, is ignored. While this is in keeping with the general tenor of a male-dominated s society, it has grave consequences for Negro women.

If what has been described represents trends instead of mere coincidences, then Negro women need to face some hard questions. Are they *losing* or *gaining* ground in the transition from a segregated to an integrated society?

At the very moment in history when there is an international movement to raise the status of women and a recognition that women generally are under-employed, are Negro women to be passed over in the social arrangements which are to create new job opportunities for Negroes? Moreover, when American women are seeking partnerships in our society, are Negro women to take a backward step and sacrifice their equalitarian tradition?

Negro women have tremendous power. How shall they use their power? How can they help Negro men and themselves to achieve mature relationship[s] in the wider community without impairing this tradition? Or is it in inherent in the struggle that Negro men can achieve maturity only at the price of destroying in Negro women the very characteristics which are stressed as part of American tradition and which have been indispensable to the Negro's steep climb out of slavery? And if these qualities are suppressed in the women, what will be the effect upon the personalities of future generations of Negro children? What are the alternatives to matriarchal dominance on the one hand and male supremacy on the other hand? . . .

How these issues are resolved may very well determine the outcome of the integration effort. One thing is crystal clear. The Negro woman can no longer postpone or subordinate the fight against discrimination because of sex to the civil rights struggle but must carry on both fights simultaneously. She must insist upon a partnership role in the integration movement. For, as Mr. Justice William O. Douglas, speaking for the United States Supreme Court, has declared, "The two sexes are not fungible; a community made up exclusively of one is different from a community composed of both; the subtle interplay of influence of one on the other is among the imponderables." Clearly, therefore, the full participation and leadership of Negro women is necessary to the success of the civil rights revolution.

Moreover, Negro women should seek to communicate and cooperate with white women wherever possible. Their common problems and interests as women provide a bridge to span initial self-consciousness. Many white women today are earnestly seeking to make common cause with Negro women and are holding out their hands. All too often they find themselves rebuffed. Integration, however, is a two-way effort and Negro women must be courageous enough to grasp the hand whenever it is held out.

The path ahead will not be easy; the challenges to meet new standards of achievement in the search for equality will be many and bewildering. For a time, even, the casualties of integration may be great. But as Negro women in the United States enter their second century of emancipation from chattel slavery, let them be proud of their heritage and resolute in their determination to pass the best of it along to their children. As Lorraine Hansberry, the gifted playwright, has said, "For above all, in behalf of an ailing world which sorely needs our defiance, may we, as Negroes or women, never accept the notion of — "our place."

FANNIE LOU HAMER

In 1962, Fannie Lou Hamer was a sharecropper in rural Mississippi when civil rights workers came to her town and encouraged the Black community to vote. In late August, Hamer and seventeen others rode a bus to the country courthouse in Indianola and tried to register. "That was the day I saw more policemens with guns than I'd ever seen in my life," she recalled.

Because she failed a literacy test, Hamer and her comrades were turned away. Undeterred, she returned to retake the literacy test, but failed again. She told the registrar: "You'll see me every thirty days till I pass."

In January 1963, Hamer took the test for the third time and passed, and was informed she was an officially registered voter. But when she tried to vote, she was told the county also required her to have two poll tax receipts.

It was harassment plain and simple, and it was illegal — the state of Mississippi was doing everything possible to keep Black Americans from exercising their constitutional right to vote.

By now Hamer had become a civil rights activist herself. She and her fellow activists were arrested, thrown into jail, and savagely beaten in Winona, Mississippi.

"Is this America?" she thundered in her speech in the summer of 1964 to the Credentials Committee of the Democratic National Convention in Atlantic City. "The land of the free and the home of the brave, where we have to sleep with our telephones off the hooks because our lives be threatened daily, because we want to live as decent human beings, in America?"

Her words were broadcast on major news networks, giving visibility to the Mississippi Freedom Democratic Party and its push for racial parity.

Already involved in the Student Nonviolent Coordinating Committee, Hamer stepped up and became a voting rights campaigner. She led workshops and classes. She gathered signatures for petitions and worked with the Southern Christian Leadership Conference.

And she traveled the country, speaking whenever she could, at marches, protests, freedom rallies, church meetings and on college campuses, and in her unsuccessful campaigns for the US and Mississippi state senate.

One of her most heartbreaking lines comes from a speech she delivered in 1964: "I'm sick and tired of being sick and tired."

Hamer remained one of the nation's most compelling civil rights voices, inspiring multitudes to vote, mentoring younger activists, and challenging the nation to live up to its ideals.

She died in 1977 at the age of 59, and is buried in Ruleville, Sunflower County, Mississippi. The fight for equal voting rights in America goes on.

"I QUESTION AMERICA"

August 22, 1964
Credentials Committee, Democratic National
Convention, Atlantic City, New Jersey

M r. Chairman, and the Credentials Committee, my name is Mrs. Fanny Lou Hamer, and I live at 626 East Lafayette Street, Ruleville, Mississippi, Sunflower County, the home of Senator James O. Eastland, and Senator Stennis.

It was the 31st of August in 1962 that 18 of us traveled 26 miles to the country courthouse in Indianola to try to register to try to become first-class citizens. We was met in Indianola by policemen, Highway Patrolmens and they only allowed two of us in to take the literacy test at the time.

After we had taken this test and started back to Ruleville, we was held up by the City Police and the State Highway Patrolmen and carried back to Indianola where the bus driver was charged that day with driving a bus the wrong color.

After we paid the fine among us, we continued on to Ruleville, and Reverend Jeff Sunny carried me four miles in the rural area to where I had worked as a timekeeper and sharecropper for 18 years. I was met there by my children, who told me that the plantation owner was angry because I had gone down to try to register. After they told me, my husband came, and said that the plantation owner was raising cain because I had tired to register, and before he quit talking the plantation owner came, and said, "Fanny Lou, do you know — did Pap tell you what I said?"

And I said, "Yes, sir. «

He said, "I mean that" He said, "If you don't go down and withdraw your registration, you will have to leave." [He] said, " Then if you go down and withdraw," he said, "you still might have to go because we are not ready for that in Mississippi."

And I addressed him and told him and said, "I didn't try to register for you. I tried to register for myself." I had to leave that same night.

On the 10th of September 1962, 16 bullets was fired into the home of Mr. and Mrs. Robert Tucker for me. That same night two girls were shot in Ruleville, Mississippi. Also Mr. Joe McDonald's house was shot in.

And June the 9th, 1963, I had attended a voter registration workshop; was returning back to Mississippi. Ten of us was traveling by the Continental Trailway bus. When we got to Winona, Mississippi, which is Montgomery County, four of the people got off to use the washroom, and two of the people — to use the restaurant — two of the people wanted to use the washroom.

The four people that had gone in to use the restaurant was ordered out. During this time I was on the bus. But when I looked through the window and saw they had rushed out I got off of the bus to see what had happened. And one of the ladies said, "It was a State Highway Patrolman and a Chief of Police ordered us out."

I got back on the bus and one of the persons had used the washroom got back on the bus, too. As soon as I was seated on the bus, I saw when they began to get the five people in a Highway Patrolman's car. I stepped off of the bus to see what was happening and somebody screamed from the car that the five workers was in, and said, "Get that one there." When I went to get in the car, when the man told me I was under arrest, he kicked me.

I was carried to the county jail and put in the booking room. They left some of the people in the booking room and began to place us in cells. I was placed in a cell with a young woman called Miss Euvester Simpson. After I was placed in the cell I began to hear sounds of licks and screams, I could hear the sounds of licks and horrible screams. And I could hear somebody say, "Can you say, 'yes, sir,' nigger? Can you say 'yes, sir'?" And they would say other horrible names.

She would say, "Yes, I can say 'yes, sir.'"

"So, well, say it."

She said, "I don't know you well enough."

They beat her, I don't know how long. And after a while she began to pray, and asked God to have mercy on those people.

And it wasn't too long before three white men came to my cell. One of these men was a State Highway Patrolman and he asked me where I was from. I told him Ruleville and he said, "We are going to check this."

They left my cell and it wasn't too long before they came back. He said, "You are from Ruleville all right," and he used a curse word. And he said, "We are going to make you wish you was dead."

I was carried out of that cell into another cell where they had two Negro prisoners. The State Highway Patrolmen ordered the first Negro to take the blackjack. The first Negro prisoner ordered me, by orders from the State Highway Patrolman, for me to lay down on a bunk bed on my face. I laid on my face and the first Negro began to beat. I was beat by the first Negro until he was exhausted. I was holding my hands behind me at that time on my left side, because I suffered from polio when I was six years old.

After the first Negro had beat until he was exhausted, the State Highway Patrolman ordered the second Negro to take the blackjack. The second Negro began to beat and I began to work my feet, and the State Highway Patrolman ordered the first Negro who had beat me to sit on my feet — to keep me from working my feet. I began to scream and one white man got up and began to beat me in my head and tell me to hush.

One white man — my dress had worked up high — he walked over and pulled my dress — I pulled my dress down and he pulled my dress back up.

I was in jail when Medgar Evers was murdered.

All of this is on account of we want to register, to become first-class citizens. And if the Freedom Democratic Party is not seated now, I question America. Is this America, the land of the free and the home of the brave, where we have to sleep with our telephones off the hooks because our lives be threatened daily, because we want to live as decent human beings, in America?

Thank you.

LORRAINE HANSBERRY

Her memories were rooted in what she called "the tempo of my people" — the sounds of a summer night on the South Side of Chicago, screen doors swinging shut on back porches, the murmuring voices of neighbors, the warmth and safety of her community.

Her father, Carl Augustus Hansberry, was a real estate broker who for years supported the NAACP's fight against Chicago's "restrictive covenants," housing rules that allowed White neighborhoods to keep Blacks out.

To challenge the laws, he moved the family to a White-restricted neighborhood. Angry confrontations erupted. Mobs surrounded their house, and her mother bought a gun.

Hansberry's father fought the case all the way to the US Supreme Court and won in 1940. *Hansberry v. Lee* was decided twenty-eight years before the passage of the Fair Housing Act.

But by then, her father had become disillusioned with America's promise of equality. He was planning to move the family to Mexico when he suddenly collapsed and died. His death certificate said cerebral hemorrhage, but Hansberry always believed the cause was racism.

She transformed her family's experience into an award-winning play, *A Raisin in the Sun*. In 1961, Columbia Pictures turned the story into an acclaimed motion picture. For the first time, White audiences could see the lives of everyday Black Americans dealing with racism and inequality, while Black audiences could see their own struggles come to life on the stage and screen.

Hansberry became more radical and vocal, a recognized voice for Black America. She spoke at protest rallies. She spoke at Carnegie Hall. She spoke at a conference on Black writers, asserting that "the question is not whether one will make a social statement in one's work — but only what the statement will say."

In June 1963, civil rights activist Medgar Evers was assassinated. In August, the March on Washington drew a quarter million people to the National Mall. Just a few weeks later, on a quiet Sunday morning, an explosion tore through the 16th Street Baptist Church in Birmingham, and four little girls were dead. The civil rights movement was facing its darkest hour.

The following spring, Hansberry spoke at a luncheon in Manhattan to young Black students, winners of a writing contest sponsored by *Reader's Digest* and the United Negro College Fund. In their striving faces she saw a reflection of her younger self, and a future that required their talented voices. "You are young, gifted and Negro," she told them. "The nation needs your gifts."

Nine months later, Hansberry died of pancreatic cancer, age 34. On her gravesite in Croton-on-Hudson, New York, visitors leave pens and pencils.

"THE NATION NEEDS YOUR GIFTS"

May 1, 1964
Fourth Annual Creative Writing Contest,
Co-sponsored by *Reader's Digest* and the United Negro College Fund,
Waldorf-Astoria, New York City, New York

L adies and gentlemen, Fellow Writers:
 I have had an opportunity to read three of the winning compositions in this United Negro College Fund contest — and it is clear I am addressing fellow writers indeed. Miss Purvis, Miss Yeldell, and Mr. Lewis —

Apart from anything else, I wanted to be able to come here and speak with you this afternoon, because you are young, gifted and Negro. In the month of May in the year 1964, I, for one, can think of no more dynamic combination that a person might be.

You are, after all, the product of a presently insurgent and historically vivacious and heroic culture, a culture of an indomitable will for freedom and aspiration to dignity.

For, even though it is not as well known as it should be, our people have sustained one of the most heroic resistances to tyranny in the history of man. Our African ancestors came to the New World fighting slavery by mutiny on the high seas and by suicide. The character of slavery itself was defined by the black man's repudiation of his enslavement, which he daily did battle with by sabotage, work stoppage, acts of violence against those who enslaved him and, of course, most telling of all, by running away by the thousands from slavery. And when the time came to help give the fatal blow to the slave system our ancestors, now by the tens of thousands, fell into the ranks of Abraham Lincoln's Union Army to serve in any way they could to destroy that hideous cancer against human dignity that was the Confederacy. They served as cooks, they served as spies, they served as work battalions, men and women, thousands and thousands of them — but above all they served as the most determined fighting soldiers to don the Union blue and storm the barricades of the rebel camps!

And after that war, the Civil War, the Negro people and the poor whites of the South sent their own sons, for the first time, into the halls of Congress to represent them and create the finest democratic hour the South and this Nation have ever known. During the period of the Reconstruction, for example, the free public school system was made available for the first time to the Southland — whereas before, only the children of the rich had been able to enjoy the right to education.

It was against this brief upsurge of democracy for black *and* white, that the Bourbon South unleashed the night rider — to take away the ballot from the Negro, and thereby from his poor white brother as well. It was against this brief upsurge of equality that slavocrat apologist historians arose across the land to vilify and defame the Reconstruction and create an image of it that persists to this day. And it was against the threat of the return, ever again, of such an hour of democracy and opportunity for all — that the system of brutality, murder and economic intimidation we know today became the instruments used to guarantee the disfranchisement of the black men and degradation of the white men of the South.

It is this system which prevails today. And it is this system that, once again, shall compel this Nation to find better education or be torn asunder. Once again.

But apart from all these things — apart from this little known and much distorted history of the Negro's three-century struggle against oppression in the New World — is the fact of his culture: a culture which, since the Seventeenth Century, has thrust forward poets and, since the Nineteenth, novelists and journalists.

Contrary to the notion of the quiescent intellectuality of the American black man is the fact that he first began publishing his newspapers in 1827 while the greatest of his number were yet in chains. He began writing classical verse before America was a nation. More important, the inflected speech and idiom of our people continue to influence an entire nation, as indeed do our ever-replenishing dance and music forms continue to dominate our national arts and entertainments.

And that is why I say that, though it be a thrilling and marvelous thing to be merely young and gifted in such times, it is doubly so — doubly dynamic —to be young, gifted *and black.*

Look at the work that awaits you! There is a story to be told and retold again until no man can plead his ignorance of the things I have just ripped through in such paltry outline.

I suppose what I am trying to do is to urge you in an opposite direction from the more fashionable attitudes and vogues of our times. There are many who would have you believe that there is something wrong with you as writers if you concern yourselves with anything that I have just put before you — who would try to persuade you that genuine sophistication lies in the realm of psychoanalytical novel and the absurdist play drawn not from the world as it is, but from only your most highly internalized and overdistilled notions of that world. I am too young and unwise *not* to offer advice this afternoon — and I caution you as developing writers away from those seductions.

Language symbols, spoken and written, have permitted Man to abstract his awareness of the world and transmit his feelings about it to his fellows. That may be the most extraordinary accomplishment in the universe, for all we know. And, even if it is not, it is certainly one of the most wondrous and marvelous things to have happened since our particular group of megatons (or whatever) either fused or split to make this particular world of ours.

And it is certainly too important a gift to waste in not using it, to the best of one's ability, in behalf of the human race.

Write if you will: but write about the world as it is and as you think it OUGHT to be and must be — if there is to be a world. Write about not only exotic disappointments — but ordinary ones. Write about the sit-ins; write about the lady who bored you on the airplane; write about how the stars seem viewed from earth. Write about love; write about hatred, pride, jealousy. In short, write about all the things that men have written about since the beginning of writing and talking, and write *to a point* — and don't pretend that you can't find what the point in what you have written is. Throw that thing away and start over with honesty..

Write! Work hard at it, CARE about it. Eschew the unstructured and the undisciplined and the pointless; no matter what anyone tells you — they are cheap evasions of art. And write about our people, tell their story. Leave the convoluted sex preoccupations to the convoluted; you have something glorious to draw on begging for attention. Use it.

One day several years ago Mrs. Rosa Parks refused to move to the back of the bus in Montgomery, Alabama and gave the whole nation something to talk about — and write about. Don't pass it up. Use it. Good luck to you. The Nation needs your gifts. Perfect them!

DOLORES HUERTA

For weeks the workers marched from town to town up the San Joaquin Valley, waving flags and crying "Viva la Causa." Their aim: to draw attention to migrant farmworkers and their right to form a union. After a journey of 340 long dusty miles, the marchers reached Sacramento on Easter Sunday. There, on the steps of the state Capitol, Dolores Huerta made a blistering speech.

"The workers are on the rise," she called out to the crowd of several hundred. "The workers know that they are no longer alone."

A former elementary school teacher in Stockton, Huerta committed herself to the cause when she saw her young students, the children of farmworkers, coming to class hungry and shoeless.

She founded the Agricultural Workers Association, set up voter registration drives, and lobbied local governments for better services. Her advocacy helped secure Aid For Dependent Families and disability insurance for farm workers in California.

At thirty-two, she joined César Chávez, executive director of the Stockton Community Service Organization. Together they founded the National Farm Workers Association, the first successful union of agricultural workers in the US.

It was a David and Goliath story, the vulnerable migrant workers who put food on America's tables against the wealthy ranchers who harvested billions in fruit and vegetable profits each year. The workers wielded their power through grassroots campaigning and boycotts. Huerta became one of their most visible champions, making speeches and giving statements to the press.

"Sí, se puede!" — "Yes we can!" — became the motto of the farmworkers, a cry for justice and human dignity.

In the winter of 1965, a bitter, prolonged strike became a social movement. It was capped with the three-week "peregrinación," or pilgrimage, from the farm town of Delano to Sacramento, picking up followers and media attention along the way.

The marchers hoped to confront Governor Edmund G. "Pat" Brown at the Capitol, but he was in Palm Springs, spending the Easter holiday with his family at the home of Frank Sinatra. Incensed by the governor's absence, Huerta threatened a statewide strike and demanded "unconditionally" that Brown call a special session of the legislature to consider the marchers' demands.

"This is a revolution! Viva la huelga!" she shouted. The crowd roared, and the cameras rolled.

Nine years later, Gov. Edmund Brown, Jr. signed the landmark California Agricultural Labor Relations Act, giving farmworkers the right to collective bargaining, the first law of its kind in the nation.

"SPEECH AT CAPITOL RALLY"

April 10, 1966
California State Capitol, Sacramento, California

T his is the first time in [the] history of the United States that farm workers have walked three hundred miles to their state capitol; and the governor of this state is not here to greet them.

But this is not surprising. This is in keeping with the general attitude that the governor and the people have had toward farm workers. I can assure you that had doctors, lawyers, auto workers or any other organized labor group marched three hundred miles, the governor would be here to meet them.

We hope that the governor will not follow the example of Harlan Hagen, who has reciprocated the continual loyalty of the Mexican-American voter and the work of the CSO [Community Service Organization] in registering voters among the Spanish-speaking people in Kern, Kings and Tulare counties, with an unprecedented attack against the National Farm Workers Association and the Delano grape strikers and the efforts of the farm workers to uplift their cause.

The governor's indifference to our pilgrimage, Congressman Hagen's vicious slurs on our union both demonstrate that we should not be taken for granted by any political party. As of this moment we wish to inform the Democratic party of this state that we will be counted as your supporters, only when we can count you among ours. The Democratic party does not have us in its hip pocket.

The leaders in this association do not want to meet with the governor in a closed-door session. We have met with the governor and his secretaries before in a closed-door session. We are no longer interested in listening to the excuses the governor has to give in defense of the growers, to his apologies for them not paying us decent wages or why the growers can not dignify the workers as individuals with the right to place the price on their own labor through collective bargaining.

The governor maintains that the growers are in a competitive situation. Well, the farm workers are also. We must also compete — with the standard of living to give our families their daily bread.

In 1959, the CSO and organized labor tried the first legislative efforts to give the farm workers minimal social legislation needed to ameliorate their terrible oppression. At that time the farm workers were not aware these attempts were being made and were therefore not there to testify and lobby in their own behalf, except for a delegation that César Chávez brought up from Oxnard.

In 1961 and 1963 through efforts of the CSO, National Far Workers Association and the herculean efforts of then Assemblyman — now Congressman — Phil Burton we were able to obtain welfare legislation that would ameliorate some of the terrible suffering of the farm workers in the off-season.

And the growers are still complaining and fighting for adequate administration of that law. Gus Hawkins also passed disability insurance for farm workers. That was eight years ago and we still have yet to see the needed legislation for a minimum wage enacted in this state.

But this is 1966.

Farm workers have not been driven down to a small closed-door session to see what the state can dole out to us in welfare legislation. The grape strikers of Delano after seven months of extreme hardship and deprivation have walked step by step through the San Joaquin Valley — the valley that has been their "Valley of Tears" for them and their families. Not to beg, but to insist on what they think is needed for them.

The difference between 1959 and 1966 is highlighted by the peregrination, it is revolution — the farm workers have been organized.

In 1959 a small group of people who had been influenced by a great man, Fred Ross, who organized the CSO, met to discuss and digest the previous efforts of organizing work. We analyzed these attempts and found certain principles that had been used time and again and we though undesirable for organizing farm workers and striking. We decided that a strong nucleus of workers had to be organized before striking, then they could progress into the actual struggle of economic sanctions.

César Chávez began, as the *Corrido del Campesino* states, going through the San Joaquin Valley as a pilgrim inspiring the workers to organize; giving them the confidence they needed through inspiration and hard work, educating them for months to realize that no one was going to win their battle for them, that their condition could be changed by only one group of people — themselves.

He refused contributions and he did not solicit money from any area. This was prior to the strike of course. César felt that outside money for organization of farm workers was no good, and it would not do the trick, and that the workers had to pay for their own organizations — and this was accomplished.

The National Farm Workers Association prior to the strike was supported entirely by its membership through the dues that they paid. Furthermore, the members of the National Farm Workers Association put forth the programs that they felt were needed immediately, such as a credit union, a service program, a group life insurance plan — the credit union so they could save their money and borrow when necessary, a group life insurance plan for their families that would take care of emergencies that arise from sudden deaths, and the service program for their complaints of nonunion wages, injury and disability cases, etc., and other daily problems in which they are exposed and undefended.

Each worker that was helped by the association's program became an organizer and the movement has grown in this manner with each worker bringing in other members to make the union stronger. The foundation was built by César Chávez through his dedicated efforts and the successive sacrifices of his wife, Helen Chávez, and their eight children, and their relatives who assisted them during this crucial organizing period when financial aid was not forthcoming.

April 10, 1966, marks the fourth year of the organizing efforts of the National Farm Workers Association. And today our farm workers have come to the capitol of Sacramento.

To the governor and the legislature of California we say: You cannot close your eyes and ears to our needs any longer, you cannot pretend that we do not exist, you cannot plead ignorance to our problem because we are here and we embody our needs for you.

And we are not alone. We are accompanied by many friends. The religious leaders of the state, spearheaded by the California Migrant Ministry, the student groups and civil rights groups that make up the movement that has been successful in securing civil rights for Negroes in this country, right-thinking citizens, and our staunchest ally, organized labor, are all in the revolution of farm labor.

This support has been highlighted by the people who have joined us here today. Furthermore, these groups are committing themselves to help us until total victory is achieved.

The developments of the past seven months are only a slight indication of what is to come. The workers are on the rise. There will be strikes all over the state and throughout the country, because Delano has shown what can be done, and the workers know that they are no longer alone.

The agricultural workers are not going to remain static. The towns that have been reached by this pilgrimage will never be the same. On behalf of the National Farmworkers Association, its officers and its members, on behalf of all of the farmworkers of this state, we unconditionally demand that the Governor of this state, Edmund Brown, call a special session of the legislature to enact a collective bargaining law for the farmworkers of the state of California.

We will be satisfied with nothing less. The governor cannot, and the legislature cannot, shrug off their responsibilities to the Congress of the United States. We are citizens and we are residents of the state of California, and we want the rules set up to protect us in this state — right here.

If the rules to settle our economic problems are not forthcoming, we will call a general strike to paralyze the state's agricultural economy. We will call in a general strike to let the legislators and the employers know that we mean business. We will take economic pressures, strikes, boycotts to force recognition and obtain collective bargaining rights.

The social and economic revolution of the farmworkers is well underway and it will not be stopped until we receive equality.

The farmworkers are moving. Nothing is going to stop them. The workers are crying for organization and we are going to organize them.

We may act in strange and unusual ways in our organizing, but we're willing to try new and unused methods to achieve justice for the farmworkers.

This is a revolution! Viva la huelga!

MARTHA J. SARA

When Alaska became the 49th state in 1959, still unresolved were land claims going back a century or more by the new state's 65,000 Native Americans. The situation festered for years.

Then, in 1968, something happened to create an urgent need for a settlement: the discovery of a vast oil field in far north Prudhoe Bay.

To carry the oil south to the ice-free port of Valdez, oil companies wanted to construct a pipeline 900 miles straight through the state, crossing a huge expanse of land, much of it claimed by Native Alaskans. Scattered in communities and villages, the Eskimos, Aleuts and Indians, descendants of the state's earliest inhabitants, lived off hunting, fishing, and gathering. They needed that land to survive.

They also had to deal with competing claims by state and federal officials, and the bare-faced bigotry of those who said the Natives were uneducated and unprepared for land stewardship.

At Congressional hearings in 1969, a college student, Martha Jane Sara, stood up to prove the naysayers wrong. Native Alaskans, she said, were ready to determine their own fate. She told the lawmakers she'd become a registered nurse at nineteen and director of a state institution by twenty, and she had helped launch a prenatal care facility in her city. To make a razor-thin deadline, she said, she'd become "an amateur painter, plumber, carpenter, electrician, diplomat, beggar, and petty larcenist."

She pointed out that Native Alaskans had shared all the responsibilities of American citizenship, courageously fighting and dying for their country in WWII, the Korean War, and the present conflict in Vietnam.

Moreover, she insisted the land rightly belonged to them. The proposals, she said, represented a significant compromise from what her people were owed. "We are not asking for all our land," she said, "just a portion of it . . . we will have to strive very hard because what we are asking for is less than what we believe is fair.

"Do not refuse us" was the refrain she used, again and again — urging the legislators to fulfill their legal and moral commitments.

She concluded with "quyana caqneq — "thank you" in Yup'ik.

In 1971, the Alaska Native Claims Settlement Act was signed into law by President Richard M. Nixon, granting aboriginals full title to 40 million acres of land and nearly $1 billion in cash.

Controversial, still disputed, the ANCSA transformed Native Alaskans into large owners of land and capital assets, giving them a substantial economic stake and say in the future of their state.

"DO NOT REFUSE US"

October 17, 1969
US Congressional Subcommittee on Native
American Affairs, Fairbanks, Alaska

M r. Chairman, members of the board, my name is Martha Sara. I'm an Eskimo. I was born and raised in Bethel. I'm a junior at the University of Alaska. My major is Sociology and I plan to go on and become a social worker.

On behalf of the Theata Club, which is an organization of native students on the University of Alaska campus, and on behalf of myself, I would like to say that I'm grateful for the right and am happy to take the responsibility to testify on behalf on the Native Land Claims.

Along with hundreds of other native young adults, I've taken the responsibility of becoming educated to better equip myself for our coming responsibilities in the management of our own affairs.

This is not an easy undertaking.

Although I am not the best example available, I will use myself. After high school I entered a school of nursing in Los Angeles. It was difficult for me because I had to overcome handicaps not faced by most American youths. I entered a different culture. Along with the dynamic process of learning what the school offered, I also had to adjust to new values and surroundings. I graduated and became a registered nurse at the age of nineteen. I was filled with a sense of accomplishment and I applied for employment at the Public Health Service Hospital in Bethel. Never before had they employed an Associates in Arts degree registered nurse — and so young. They had to get permission from Washington; permission was granted. I worked only one year when our community decided to open a Prenatal Home in Bethel through the assistance of the Office of Economic Opportunity. A director was needed with the qualifications of a registered nurse. I enthusiastically wrote a letter of application even before applications were printed. I knew the people and a lot of the future clients having worked most of the year in the Maternity Ward in our hospital.

To my delight I was hired. Complications arose, however, because someone pointed out that in order to be a Director of a Prenatal institution in the State of Alaska one had to be twenty-five years old, and I was not yet even twenty-one.

Letters were written on my behalf and permission was granted from Juneau for me to keep and fill the position. The funding was unsure because the deadline for occupancy was nearing and the building was unfit for expectant mothers as far as the State Sanitarian, State Fire Marshall, and Child Welfare Institution Directors were concerned. Complete renovation of the physical plant and procurement of necessary equipment was urgent. Needless to say, I became an amateur painter, plumber, carpenter, electrician, diplomat, beggar, and petty larcenist. Local men did the plumbing, carpentry, and electrical work in conjunction with the BIA. Local boys under the Neighborhood Youth Program did the painting. Used furniture was procured from the hospital through GSA. Supplies were ordered and opening day saw us admitting our first lady. We struggled and worked for what we wanted and got it. Of course we had the assistance and backing of the agencies, but the native peoples involved made it work. We were competent and proved it.

I am here representing a body of eager, willing young adults ready to learn, work, and show our capability in the management of our own affairs. I am just one of many who are willing to struggle for an education, who are willing to work hard, the way we worked on the Bethel Prenatal Home.

We are not asking for all our land — just a portion of it — and if you grant it to us, we will have to strive very hard because what we are asking for is less than what we believe is fair. But we are capable of striving very hard.

And how shall you refuse us? You who have centuries of learning, education, civilization, colonization, expansion, domination, exploitation behind you? How shall you refuse us?

Do not refuse us because we are young! In youth there is energy, drive, ambition, growth, and new ideas. Do not refuse us because we are young! For we shall mature!

Do not refuse us because we are undereducated! We are learning fast; and utilizing our newly gained knowledge, comparing and weighing the truths and benefits of this knowledge. We know that the 40,000,000 acres we are asking for will provide a minimum protection to hunting and fishing. We understand that we need the identification with, and the feeling for our own land. We also realize that we need this land as an economic base for our people. The land will be used as a commodity in our economic base. We can accomplish this with 40,000,000 acres. $500,000,000 is a lot of money. We understand what a vital role this can play in the economic base of our people. We realize that with proper and careful handling and investment of this money we can make it work for us. We do not plan to make improvements without first establishing a sound economic base which will provide for growth and return. After this is established, then we can begin our improvements. We will then be able to maintain and expand these improvements. We realize that we can not only benefit our people, but all of

Alaska. All this for $500,000,000. Do not refuse us because we are still learning! For we are fast learning!

Do not refuse us the chance to progress! We too have a dream for the progress of our land. We hold a superior position to develop our country because it is our country, and we love it. We will be more cautious in its utilization — and I deliberately use the word "utilization" instead of "exploitation." We will weigh each prospect carefully to assure ourselves that we are making the best decision for our generation and those generations to come. We are not here to grab; we are here to live with the growth of our native land. Do not refuse us the chance for progress. For we too share the dream of progress.

Do not refuse us because you are afraid we don't have competent leaders! I represent a generation of paradoxes. We are paradoxes in the fact that we are the closest links to the parties farthest separated in this issue. One of these groups is our beloved elders whom we left back home only a short time ago, who, along with others, still cling to the old ways and depend upon the land for subsistence. Another group is made up of our able leaders, Native and White, who are presently in positions of decision. We are close to the old ones and the people back home because, having recently left them, their problems, worries, and fears burn deep in our hearts. We know what makes them happy; we know what can fill them with contentment; we know what gives them hope. At the same time we are close to our leaders in the fact that we are striving and aspiring to their positions of decision. Native young people are rising up to meet the demands and expectations of a foreign and sometimes hostile society. The day of our leadership is not too far off. When that day of fulfillment comes, I would like to think that we can proudly take our places side by side with the present leaders to direct the affairs of our own people. In their wisdom they can quell our fears, channel our energy, help shape our innovative ideas, direct our aggression, and interpret our anxieties. Together we can provide able leadership! Do not refuse us for fear of poor leadership! For we are capable leaders.

Do not refuse us simply because you purchased the sovereign right of our land! Our fathers since time began have paid dearly for our homeland every generation. They struggled against the harshest environment known to man and survived to teach us to do the same. Each generation paved the way for the next. Do not refuse us because you purchased this right! For our forefathers paid for it long before your forefathers had the money!

Do not refuse us because we are a minority! For this is America! We have proved in many ways that, not only do we take advantage of Our rights and freedoms along with other Americans, but we are willing to, and have, fought equally for all its privileges. Our native soldiers fought and died for the United States in World War II, the Korean War, and in the present war in Viet Nam. As American citizens, we have equal rights and have taken on equal responsibility. So do not refuse us because we are a minority! For this is America!

In closing I would like to say that competence is something that has to be proven. And as young native adults we have demonstrated our abilities and are now proving it.

I would like to add that we are deeply grateful to you all for taking time out of your busy schedules to come and hear our testimonies. It is deeply appreciated. Thank you! Quyana caqneq!

SHIRLEY CHISHOLM

"I have no intention of just sitting quietly and observing," declared Shirley Chisholm in 1968, while campaigning to become the first Black woman elected to the US Congress, representing a newly-created district in Brooklyn. "I intend to speak out immediately in order to focus on the nation's problems."

That she did, wasting no time making her priorities clear. Her first speech on the House floor was a scathing attack on President Nixon's proposal to spend money on ballistic missile defense. A better use of funds, she argued, would be childcare and social services.

Two months later, Chisholm rose again on the House floor to plea for the Equal Rights Amendment. First introduced in Congress in 1923, it had been reintroduced each year but never passed.

Chisholm began with an all-too-common story: "When a young woman graduates from college and starts looking for a job, she is likely to have a frustrating and even demeaning experience ahead of her. If she walks into an office for an interview, the first question she will be asked is, "Do you type?"

So deep rooted and insidious was the prejudice against women, she said, that despite making up more than half the US population, they had "not even reached the level of tokenism yet."

Chisholm spent her life pursuing equality and justice. She started out running a day-care center in Brooklyn — from that experience sprang her lifelong fight for early childhood education and child welfare. She never veered from the conviction that helping women, children, and the disadvantaged was the best investment America could make.

Public speaking was central to her advocacy, and her signature speaking style could be traced back to the Depression when she and her sisters went to live with their grandmother in Barbados. Chisholm studied in a one-room schoolhouse, where she picked up a British education and a touch of the island accent.

When she drove through her district in Brooklyn in her sound truck, her distinctive voice could be heard calling out: "Ladies and Gentlemen . . . this is fighting Shirley Chisholm coming through."

She understood the twin barriers of race and gender but did not perceive them as equal. Speaking to a subcommittee on Education and Labor she commented: "During my entire political life, my sex has been a far greater handicap than my skin pigmentation."

When she ran unsuccessfully for president in 1972, her defiant campaign slogan was "unbought and unbossed." These words became the title of her autobiography, and they're also carved on her gravestone in Buffalo.

"INTRODUCING
THE E.R.A."

May 21, 1969
US House of Representatives, Washington, DC

Mr. Speaker, when a young woman graduates from college and starts looking for a job, she is likely to have a frustrating and even demeaning experience ahead of her. If she walks into an office for an interview, the first question she will be asked is, "Do you type?"

There is a calculated system of prejudice that lies unspoken behind that question. Why is it acceptable for women to be secretaries, librarians, and teachers, but totally unacceptable for them to be managers, administrators, doctors, lawyers, and Members of Congress?

The unspoken assumption is that women are different. They do not have executive ability, orderly minds, stability, leadership skills, and they are too emotional.

It has been observed before, that society for a long time discriminated against another minority, the blacks, on the same basis — that they were different and inferior. The happy little homemaker and the contented "old darkey" on the plantation were both produced by prejudice.

As a black person, I am no stranger to race prejudice. But the truth is that in the political world I have been far oftener discriminated against because I am a woman than because I am black.

Prejudice against blacks is becoming unacceptable although it will take years to eliminate it. But it is doomed because, slowly, white America is beginning to admit that it exists. Prejudice against women is still acceptable. There is very little understanding yet of the immorality involved in double pay scales and the classification of most of the better jobs as "for men only."

More than half of the population of the United States is female. But women occupy only two percent of the managerial positions. They have not even reached the level of tokenism yet. No women sit on the AFL-CIO council or Supreme Court. There have been only two women who have held Cabinet rank, and at present there are none. Only two women now hold ambassadorial rank in the diplomatic corps. In Congress, we are down to one Senator and ten Representatives.

Considering that there are about three and a half million more women in the United States than men, this situation is outrageous.

It is true that part of the problem has been that women have not been aggressive in demanding their rights. This was also true of the black population for many years. They submitted to oppression and even cooperated with it. Women have done the same thing. But now there is an awareness of this situation particularly among the younger segment of the population.

As in the field of equal rights for blacks, Spanish-Americans, the Indians, and other groups, laws will not change such deep-seated problems overnight. But they can be used to provide protection for those who are most abused, and to begin the process of evolutionary change by compelling the insensitive majority to reexamine its unconscious attitudes.

It is for this reason that I wish to introduce today a proposal that has been before every Congress for the last forty years and that sooner or later must become part of the basic law of the land — the equal rights amendment.

Let me note and try to refute two of the commonest arguments that are offered against this amendment. One is that women are already protected under the law and do not need legislation. Existing laws are not adequate to secure equal rights for women. Sufficient proof of this is the concentration of women in lower paying, menial, unrewarding jobs and their incredible scarcity in the upper level jobs. If women are already equal, why is it such an event whenever one happens to be elected to Congress?

It is obvious that discrimination exists. Women do not have the opportunities that men do. And women that do not conform to the system, who try to break with the accepted patterns, are stigmatized as "odd" and "unfeminine." The fact is that a woman who aspires to be chairman of the board, or a Member of the House, does so for exactly the same reasons as any man. Basically, these are that she thinks she can do the job and she wants to try.

A second argument often heard against the equal rights amendment is that it would eliminate legislation that many States and the Federal Government have enacted giving special protection to women and that it would throw the marriage and divorce laws into chaos.

As for the marriage laws, they are due for a sweeping reform, and an excellent beginning would be to wipe the existing ones off the books. Regarding special protection for working women, I cannot understand why it should be needed. Women need no protection that men do not need. What we need are laws to protect working people, to guarantee them fair pay, safe working conditions, protection against sickness and layoffs, and provision for dignified, comfortable retirement. Men and women need these things equally. That one sex needs protection more than the other is a male supremacist myth as ridiculous and unworthy of respect as the white supremacist myths that society is trying to cure itself of at this time.

PATSY MINK

Had she gotten a job offer after graduating from law school at the University of Chicago, Patsy Mink always said, she never would have entered politics.

"I was going to be Lady Portia and change the world," she said. "I couldn't find a job." The reason had nothing to do with her degree. "Law firms I applied to said: 'Get married and have babies.'"

So she went back to her native Hawaii. Mink was a third-generation Japanese American — her grandparents had immigrated to the islands to work on sugar plantations.

In 1956 she won a seat in the Hawaiian Territorial Legislature, and later the Territorial Senate. In 1959, when Hawaii became a state, she ran for office and became the first woman of color and the first Asian-American woman in Congress.

In the 1960s, there was no groundswell of interest in women's issues. No one was thinking or talking much about sex discrimination, or even using the words "sexism" or "sexist." But Representative Edith Green from Oregon was, and in the summer of 1970 she held Congressional hearings on the various ways women faced discrimination in higher education.

One who testified was education specialist Bernice Sandler, who also arranged for a parade of witnesses to talk about academic departments that refused to hire women, or refused to promote them or give them tenure, or the women who received thousands of dollars less salary than their male counterparts, or who worked full-time without benefits, office, or even salary, because their husbands also taught at the same university.

Mink, another witness, framed the problem not just as a hindrance for women, but as a loss for the entire nation, which "can no longer afford this system which demoralizes and demeans half the population and deprives them of the means to participate fully in our society as equal citizens."

When that legislation failed to pass, Green and Mink repurposed its core language and drafted a new statute, Title IX of the Education Amendments. President Nixon signed the bill into law in June 1972.

Before Title IX, many of the nation's best universities didn't accept women. Law and medical schools had gender quotas. All that suddenly changed.

But Title IX didn't just affect college admissions. It revolutionized the entire education landscape, ensuring that schools treat all students the same — offer the same courses, the same housing, the same athletic programs. Because of Title IX, millions of girls across America now play sports.

After Mink's death in 2002, Title IX was officially renamed the Patsy Takemoto Mink Equal Opportunity in Education Act.

"DISCRIMINATION AGAINST WOMEN"

June 24, 1970
Special Subcommittee on Education, Committee on Education
and Labor, US House of Representatives, Washington, DC

Madam Chairman and distinguished members of the Subcommittee, I am delighted to have this opportunity to express my strong support of Section 805 of H.R. 16098, which has the purpose of amending the Civil Rights Acts of 1964 and 1957, and the Fair Labor Standards Act so as to prohibit discrimination against women in education, and other objectives.

Discrimination against women in education is one of the most insidious forms of prejudice extant in our nation. Few people realize the extent to which our society is denied full use of our human resources because of this type of discrimination.

- Most large colleges and universities in the United States routinely impose quotas by sex on the admission of students. Fewer women are admitted than men, and those few women allowed to pursue higher education must have attained exceptional intellectual standing to win admission.
- Scholarships and other forms of financial assistance are also distributed on a discriminatory basis, making it more difficult for women to afford a higher education.
- Universities discriminate against women in hiring faculty, with the effect that women students are instructed mainly by males. This reinforces the system of prejudice on our campuses that systematically deprives women of equal education. And when employed, women faculty members are frequently paid less than their male counterparts even though equally competent and equally experienced.
- Women faculty members are promoted less frequently than men. Even administration reflects the same pattern: deans of women are frequently paid less than deans of men.

Our nation can no longer afford this system which demoralizes and demeans half the population and deprives them of the means to participate fully in our society as equal citizens. Lacking the contribution which women are capable of making to human betterment, our nation is the loser so long as this discrimination is allowed to continue.

The most unfortunate thing of all is that education is the very process we rely upon to make the changes and advances we need and yet we find that even education is not imparted on a fair and equitable basis . . .

In the field of higher education, I am particularly concerned with the fact that there has been no reversal of the recent pattern of discrimination against women. Indeed, figures reveal that the proportion of freshmen students entering our colleges and universities is greatly biased in favor of men. Thus, even in our newest generation of young people starting out on their higher education, which will lead to advanced positions in industry, government, private life, and education itself, women are deprived of the opportunity for an equal chance.

There are disturbing indications that women's role is even diminishing in faculty ranks, rather than increasing as it should to offset previous generations of discrimination. The Women's Equity Action League reported, "In the last century, women held more than one-third of the faculty positions in colleges and universities; today the proportion of women is less than one fourth."

Recently, the Women's Bureau of the Department of Labor issued a fact sheet on the earnings gap which showed sex discriminations in rank and salary in schools. The report said, "in institutions of higher education, women are much less likely than men to be associate or full professors." Citing a 1966 study by the National Education Association, the report stated that in 1965-66, "women professors had a median salary of only $11,649 as compared with $12,768 for men." It found "comparable differences" at the other professorial ranks.

Clearly, these differences do not occur by accident. They are the direct result of conscious discriminatory policies made possible by a loophole in the 1964 Civil Rights Act. I see no justification whatsoever for the existence of this inducement to discriminate.

Moves are underway outside of Congress to eliminate some of these discriminatory practices, notably in the Labor Department's new guidelines to bar sex discrimination on Federal government contract work. These guidelines apply to contractors and subcontractors covered by Executive Order 11246 and were described by Mrs. Elizabeth Duncan Koontz, Director of the Women's Bureau, as constituting "a giant step forward for those Americans whose talents have too often been wasted simply because they are women."

Among other things, the new guidelines, effective immediately, forbid employees to make any distinction based upon sex in employment opportunities, wages, hours, or other conditions of employment.

In addition, the President's Task Force on Women's Rights and Responsibilities recently recommended a series of legislative actions to eliminate discrimination against women in our society. The legislation presently before you would implement some of these important recommendations, including the addition of sex discrimination to the Federal aid prohibitions in Title VI of the 1964 Civil Rights Act, extending the jurisdiction of the Civil Rights Commission to include denial of civil rights because of sex, and amendments to the Fair Labor Standards Act to extend coverage of its equal pay provisions to executive, administrative, and professional employees.

In view of the significance of these major efforts to improve the status of women and remove legal incentives to discrimination against them, it is imperative that the Legislative Branch move with equal determination in this vital field.

Congress must act now to eliminate such glaring favoritism in our laws. It is no longer a matter of just equity, although that alone would dictate the necessity for the changes contemplated by H.R. 16098. Our country is now in a position where it can no longer afford to rely on the anti-deluvian [sic] notion that men should rule the world. We need women; their abilities and talents must be fully utilized.

Our nation's future is the most compelling reason for the adoption of these provisions of H.R. 16098. I congratulate the Subcommittee for its action in bringing forth this legislation, and give the bill my complete support.

BETTY FRIEDAN

Her term as president of the National Organization of Women was over, and Betty Friedan was stepping down. Acrimonious infighting had splintered the women's movement, and it was time for her to move on.

Friedan had help found NOW, then become its first president. Nationally she was among the most recognized women in the country, thanks to her 1966 bombshell bestseller, *The Feminine Mystique*. A scathing critique of the idea that women were defined by their homes and families, it drew middle-class White women into the fight for equality.

True, it was not an inclusive vision. Black, Hispanic, Asian American, and Native American women were absent from the book, as were working-class and poor women. But in the turbulent Sixties, new factions were only just beginning to coalesce and demand change.

After the NOW board meeting, at a press conference to announce the new leadership, Friedan took the microphone and, without forewarning her colleagues, called for a strike, a nationwide women's walkout on August 26, the fiftieth anniversary of women's suffrage. It would be, she said, a total shut-down of the American workplace, an act of resistance against women's oppression.

"I propose that the women who are doing menial chores in the offices cover their typewriters and close their notebooks," she said, "the telephone operators unplug their switchboards, the waitresses stop waiting, cleaning women stop cleaning, and everyone who is doing a job for which a man would be paid more — stop."

It was an idea that perfectly captured the moment and galvanized women across the country. Five months later, tens of thousands of them marched through the streets of America, the first major women's protest since the suffrage marches. In New York, Friedan led 50,000 women down Fifth Avenue carrying signs like "Don't Iron While the Strike is Hot," and "End Human Sacrifice — Don't Get Married."

At Bryant Park, she called out to the crowd: "This is not a bedroom war, this is a political movement!" Bella Abzug jabbed her finger in announcing the strike's three principal demands: free abortion, community-controlled 24-hour daycare centers, and equal educational and employment opportunity. Eleanor Holmes Norton stressed that preventing job discrimination would be impossible "unless the women have a place to leave their children."

Much of the media coverage was hostile. The New York *Daily News* called the feminists "strident, snobbish homewreckers." But that day has been remembered as the first major protest of the womanpower movement. As Friedan told a journalist, "After August 26, our revolution will be a fact, and America will never be the same."

"FAREWELL SPEECH
TO NOW"

March 20, 1970
**Fourth Annual Convention, National Organization
for Women, O'Hare Inn, Des Plaines, Illinois**

O
ur movement toward true equality for all women in America in fully equal partnership with men has reached a point of critical mass. All of us this past year have learned in our gut that sisterhood is powerful. The awesome power of women united is visible now and is being taken seriously, as all of us who define ourselves as people now take action in every city and state, and together make our voices heard.

It is our responsibility to history, to ourselves, to all who will come after us, to use this power now, in our own lives, in the mainstream of our society, now in some abstract future, when the apocalypse comes. There is an urgency in this moment. We face recession in this country, and repression, with the babies overproduced in the postwar era of the feminine mystique moving into the job market; with inflation eating up all our dollars; with men taking over even those professions that used to be female, as automation replaces blue-collar work. And in this era of recession, if we are going to compete for jobs with men, as we must to support ourselves and our families, there is bound to be more resistance than we have yet encountered. We are going to have to show that we meant it, and use our economic power to break through the barriers of sex discrimination once and for all, if women are not again to be the first fired, the last hired, as they have been in all other economic depressions.

As we visibly become the fastest-growing movement for drastic social change in the country, it would be naïve not to recognize that there are, and will be, many trying to destroy our strength, to divide and divert us. I have said from the beginning that the enemy is not man or men, though individual men among bosses, politicians, priests, union leaders, husbands, and educators must be concretely confronted as enemies. Men are fellow victims; ours is a two-sex revolution.

The rage women have so long taken out on themselves, on their own bodies, and covertly on their husbands and children, is exploding now. I understand the conditions that cause the rage, the impotence that makes women so understandably angry, but if we define that rage as sexual, if we say that love and sex and men and even children are the enemy, not only do we doom ourselves to live lives less rich and human, but we doom our movement to political sterility. For we will not be able to mobilize the power of that great majority of women who may have been oversold on love as the end of life, but nevertheless have a right to love; who may be overdefined as sex objects, but nevertheless cannot be asked to suppress their sexuality. Nor will we be able to use the political power of the men who are able to love women, and perhaps even more importantly, to identify with them as people. We will not be able to use their power to help us break through sex discrimination and to create the new social institutions that are needed to free women, not from childbearing or love or sex or even marriage, but from the intolerable agony and burden those become when women are chained to them.

I would warn you that those societies where women are most removed from the full action of the mainstream are those where sex is considered dirty and where violence breeds, If we confront the real conditions that oppress men now as well as women and translate our rage into action, then and only then will sex really be liberated to be an active joy and a receiving joy for women and for men, when we are both really free to be all we can be. This is not a war to be fought in the bedroom, but in the city, in the political arena.

I do not accept the argument that to use this power to liberate ourselves is to divert energies to stop repression and the war in Vietnam and the crisis in the cities. Our movement is so radical a force for change that as we make our voices heard, as we find our human strength in our own interests, we will inevitably create a new political force with allies and a common humanistic frontier, with new effectiveness against the enemies of war and repression that affect us all as human beings in America. Either that energy so long buried as impotent rage in women will become a powerful force for keeping our whole society human and free, or it will be manipulated in the interests of fascism and death.

I therefore propose that we accept the responsibility of mobilizing the chain reaction we have helped release, for instant revolution against sexual oppression in this year, 1970. I propose that on Wednesday, August 26, we call a twenty-four-hour general strike, a resistance both passive and active, of all women in America against the concrete conditions of their oppression. On that day, fifty years after the amendment that gave women the vote became part of the Constitution, I propose we use our power to declare an ultimatum on all who would keep us from using our rights as Americans. I propose that the women who are doing menial chores in the offices cover their typewriters and close their notebooks, the telephone operators unplug their switchboards, the waitresses stop waiting, cleaning women stop cleaning, and everyone who is doing a job for which a man would be paid more — stop — and every woman pegged forever as assistant, doing jobs for which men get the credit — stop. In every office, every laboratory, every school, all the women to whom we get word will spend the day discussing and analyzing the conditions which keep us from being all we might be. And if the condition that keeps us down is the lack of a child-care center, we will bring our babies to the office that day and sit them on our bosses' laps. We do not know how many will join our day of abstention from so-called women's work, but I expect it will be millions. We will then present concrete demands to those who so far have made all the decisions.

And when it begins to get dark, instead of cooking dinner or making love, we will assemble, and we will carry candles symbolic of the flame of that passionate journey down through history — relit anew in every city — to converge the visible power of women at City Hall — at the political arena where the larger options of our life are decided. If men want to join us, fine. If politicians, if political bosses, if mayors and governors wish to discuss our demands, fine, but we will define the terms of the dialogue. And by the time those twenty-four hours are ended, our revolution will be a fact.

GLORIA STEINEM

In 1970, what had been a trickle of articles and interviews about the women's movement became a flood. Every national magazine, it seemed, was running a feature article on "women's lib."

The year before, freelance writer Gloria Steinem had published an article in *New York Magazine*, "After Black Power, Women's Liberation," with its provocative opening line: "Once upon a time — say, ten or even five years ago — a Liberated Woman was somebody who had sex before marriage and a job afterward."

Suddenly everyone was asking: What do women want? And Steinem was busy either writing about the women's movement, or being written about. She appeared on the David Frost and Dick Cavett shows. *The New York Times* called her "the quintessential liberated brain beauty."

Steinem had already been busting myths with her journalism. Writing for Esquire in 1962, she tackled contraception and the ways in which women were forced to choose between marriage, family, and career. The next year, she went undercover at the New York Playboy Club and published an exposé on how the women were exploited.

In 1970, she testified before a Senate subcommittee on behalf of the Equal Rights Amendment. Sitting at the witness table, she told the lawmakers that "all our problems stem from the same sex-based myths" — that women were biologically inferior to men, and that they were already treated equal to men.

She repeated the theme a few weeks later as commencement speak at Vassar College. What does it mean to be living the revolution? "Having the scales fall from our eyes," she said.

Afterward, she admitted to some fear that the speech might have been too hot for mainstream America to handle. *The Washington Post* published her speech along with an editorial note that said: "Miss Steinem says it was prepared with great misgivings about its reception."

She needn't have worried. In the Sixties, radical change was happening all over America. After hundreds of civil rights boycotts and protests, federal laws now prohibited race-based discrimination. The birth control pill was legal. The Summer of Love, Woodstock, and the sexual revolution were upending social norms.

"Make love, not war" was a popular slogan — and an alternative vision to the country's increasingly unpopular war in Southeast Asia.

Steinem told the Vassar students that racism and sexism were part of the same oppression, and that women's liberation aimed to liberate men, too. "The challenge to all of us, and to you men and women who are graduating today, is to live a revolution, not to die for one."

"LIVING THE
REVOLUTION"

May 31, 1970
Vassar Graduation, Poughkeepsie, New York

President Simpson, members of the faculty, families and friends, first brave and courageous male graduates of Vassar — and Sisters.

You may be surprised that I am a commencement speaker. You can possibly be as surprised as I am. In my experience, commencement speakers are gray-haired, respected creatures, heavy with the experience of power in the world and with Establishment honors. Which means, of course, that they are almost always men.

But this is the year of Women's Liberation. Or at least, it the year the press has discovered a movement that has been strong for several years now, and reported it as a small, privileged, rather lunatic event instead of the major revolution in consciousness — in everyone's consciousness — male or female that I believe it truly is.

It may have been part of that revolution that caused the senior class to invite me here — and I am grateful. It is certainly a part of that revolution that I, a devout non-speaker, am managing to stand before you at all: I don't know whether you will be grateful or not. The important thing is that we are spending this time together, considering the larger implications of a movement that some call "feminist" but should more accurately be called humanist; a movement that is an integral part of rescuing this country from its old, expensive patterns of elitism, racism, and violence.

The first problem for all of us, men and women, is not to learn, but to un-learn. We are filled with the Popular Wisdom of several centuries just past, and we are terrified to give it up. Patriotism means obedience, age means wisdom, woman means submission, black means inferior — these are preconceptions imbedded so deeply in our thinking that we honestly may not know that they are there.

Unfortunately, authorities who write textbooks are sometimes subject to the same Popular Wisdom as the rest of us. They gather their proof around it, and end by becoming the theoreticians of the status quo. Using the most respectable of scholarly methods, for instance, English scientists proved definitively that the

English were descended from the angels, while the Irish were descended from the apes. It was beautifully done, complete with comparative skull-measurements, and it was a rationale for the English domination of the Irish for more than 100 years. I try to remember that when I'm reading Arthur Jensen's current and very impressive work on the limitations of black intelligence. Or when I'm reading Lionel Tiger on the inability of women to act in groups.

The apes-and-angels example is an extreme one, but so may some of our recent assumptions be. There are a few psychologists who believe that anti-Communism may eventually be looked upon as a mental disease.

It wasn't easy for the English to give up their mythic superiority. Indeed, there are quite a few Irish who doubt that they have done it yet. Clearing our minds and government policies of outdated myths is proving to be at least difficult. But it is also inevitable. Whether it's woman's secondary role in society or the paternalistic role of the United States in the world, the old assumptions just don't work anymore.

Rollo May has a theory that I find comforting. There are three periods in history, he says — one in which myths are built up, one in which they obtain, and one in which they are torn down. Clearly, we are living in a time of myths being torn down. We look at the more stable period just past, and we think that such basic and terrifying change has never happened before. But, relatively, it has. Clinging to the comfortable beliefs of the past serves no purpose, and only slows down the growth of new forms to suit a new reality.

Part of living this revolution is having the scales fall from our eyes. Everyday we see small obvious truths that we had missed before. Our histories, for instance, have generally been written for and about white men. Inhabited countries were "discovered" when the first white male set foot there, and most of us learned more about any one European country than we did about Africa and Asia combined.

I confess that, before some consciousness-changing of my own, I would have thought the Women History courses springing up around the country belonged in the same cultural ghetto as home economics. The truth is that we need Women's Studies almost as much as we need Black Studies, and for exactly the same reason: too many of us have been allowed from a "good" education believing that everything from political power to scientific discovery was the province of white males. I don't know about Vassar, but at Smith we learned almost nothing about women.

We believed, for instance, that the vote had been "given" to women in some whimsical, benevolent fashion. We never learned about the long desperation of women's struggle, or about the strength and wisdom of the women who led it. We heard about the men who risked their lives in the Abolitionist Movement, but seldom about the women; even though women, as in many movements of social reform, had played the major role. We knew a great deal more about the outdated, male-supremacist theories of Sigmund Freud than we did about societies in which women had equal responsibility, or even ruled.

"Anonymous," Virginia Woolf once said sadly, "was a woman."

I don't mean to equate our problems of identity with those that flowed from slavery. But, as Gunnar Myrdal pointed out in his classic study, *An American Dilemma*, "In drawing a parallel between the position of, and the feeling toward, women and Negroes, we are uncovering a fundamental basis of our culture." Blacks and women suffer from the same myths of childlike natures; smaller brains; inability to govern themselves, much less white men; limited job skills; identity as sex objects — and so on. Ever since slaves arrived on these shores and were given the legal status of wives — that is, chattel — our legal reforms have followed on each other's heels. (With women, I might add, still lagging considerably behind. Nixon's Commission on Women concluded that the Supreme Court was sanctioning discrimination against women — discrimination that it had long ago ruled unconstitutional in the case of blacks — but the Commission report remains mysteriously unreleased by the White House. An Equal Rights Amendment, now up again before the Senate, has been delayed by a male-chauvinist Congress for 47 years.) Neither blacks nor women have role-models in history: models of individuals who have been honored in authority outside the home.

I remember when I was interviewing Mrs. Nixon just before the 1968 election, I asked her what woman in history she most admired and would want to be like. She said, "Mrs. Eisenhower." When I asked her why, she thought for a moment, and said, "Because she meant so much to young people."

It was the last and most quizzical straw in a long, difficult interview, so I ventured a reply. I was in college during the Eisenhower years, I told her, and I didn't notice any special influence that Mrs. Eisenhower had on youth. Mrs. Nixon just looked at me warily, and said, "You didn't?" But afterwards, I decided I had been unfair. After all, neither one of us had that many people to choose from. As Margaret Mead has noted, the only women allowed to be dominant and respectable at the same time are widows. You have to do what society wants you to do, have a husband who dies, and then have power thrust upon you through no fault of your own. The whole thing seems very hard on the men.

Before we go on to other reasons why Women's Liberation is Man's Liberation, too — and why this incarnation of the women's movement is inseparable from the larger revolution — perhaps we should clear the air of a few more myths.

The myth that women are biologically inferior, for instance. In fact, an equally good case could be made for the reverse. Women live longer than men. That's always being cited as proof that we work them to death, but the truth is: women live longer than men even when groups being studied are monks and nuns. We survived Nazi concentration camps better, are protected against heart attacks by our female hormones, are less subject to many diseases, withstand surgery better, and are so much more durable at every stage of life that nature conceives 20 to 50 percent more males just to keep the balance going. The Auto Safety Committee of the American Medical Association has come to the conclusion that women are better drivers because they are less emotional than men. I never thought I would hear myself quoting the AMA, but that one was too good to resist.

Men's hunting activities are forever being pointed to as proof of Tribal Superiority. But while they were out hunting, women built houses, tilled the fields, developed animal husbandry, and perfected language. Men, isolated from each other out there in the bush, often developed into creatures that were fleet of foot, but not very bright.

I don't want to prove the superiority of one sex to another. That would only be repeating a male mistake. The truth is that we're just not sure how many of our differences are biological, and how many are societal. In spite of all the books written on the subject, there is almost no such thing as a culture-free test. What we do know is that the differences between the two sexes, like the differences between races, are much less great than the differences to be found within each group. Therefore, requirements of a job can only be sensibly suited to the job itself. It deprives the country of talent to bundle any group of workers together by condition of birth.

A second myth is that women are already being treated equally in this society. We ourselves have been guilty of perpetuating this myth, especially at upper economic levels where women have grown fond of being lavishly maintained as ornaments and children. The chains may be made of mink and wall-to-wall carpeting, but they are still chains.

The truth is that a woman with a college degree working full-time makes less than a black man with a high school degree working full-time. And black women make least of all. In many parts of the country, New York City, for instance, woman has no legally-guaranteed right to rent an apartment, buy a house, get accommodations in a hotel, or be served in a public restaurant. She can be refused simply because of her sex. In some states, women cannot own property, and get longer jail sentences for the same crime. Women on welfare must routinely answer humiliating personal questions; male welfare recipients do not. A woman is the last to be hired, the first to be fired. Equal pay for equal work is the exception. Equal chance for advancement, especially at upper levels or at any level with authority over men, is rare enough to be displayed in a museum.

As for our much-touted economic power, we make up only 5 percent of all the people in the country receiving $10,000 a year or more. And that includes all the famous rich widows. We are 51 percent of all stockholders, a dubious honor these days, but we hold only 18 percent of the stock — and that is generally controlled by men. The power women have as consumers is comparable to that power all of us currently have as voters: we can choose among items presented to us, but we have little chance to influence the presentation. Women's greatest power to date is her nuisance value. The civil rights, peace, and consumer movements are impressive examples of that.

In fact, the myth of economic matriarchy in this country is less testimony to our power than to the resentment of the little power we do have.

You may wonder why we have submitted to such humiliations all these years; why, indeed, women will sometimes deny that they are second-class citizens at all.

The answer lies in the psychology of second-classness. Like all such groups, we come to accept what society says about us. And that is the most terrible punishment of all. We believe that we can only make it in the world by "uncle Tom-ing," by a real or pretended subservience to white males.

Even when we come to understand that we, as individuals, are not second-class, we still accept society's assessment of our group — a phenomenon psychologists refer to as Internalized Aggression. From this stems the desire to be the only woman in an office, an academic department, or any other part of the man's world. From this also stems women who put down their sisters — and my own profession of journalism has some of them. By writing or speaking of their non-conformist sisters in a disapproving, conformist way, they are essentially saying, "See what a real woman I am," and expecting to be rewarded by ruling-class approval and favors. That is only beginning to change . . .

With women, the whole system reinforces this feeling of being a mere appendage. It's hard for a man to realize just how full of self-doubt we become as a result. Locked into suburban homes with the intellectual companionship of three-year-olds; locked into bad jobs, watching less-qualified men get promoted above us; trapped into poverty by a system that supposes our only identity is motherhood — no wonder we become pathetically grateful for small favors.

I don't want to give the impression, though, that we want to join society exactly as it is. I don't think most women want to pick up slimline briefcases and march off to meaningless, de-personalized jobs. Nor do we want to be drafted — and women certainly should be drafted: even the readers of *Seventeen Magazine* were recently polled as being overwhelmingly in favor of women in National Service — to serve in an unconstitutional, racist, body-count war like the one in Indochina.

We want to liberate men from those inhuman roles as well. We want to share the work and responsibility, and to have men share equal responsibility for the children.

Probably the ultimate myth is that children must have fulltime mothers, and that liberated women make bad ones. The truth is that most American children seem to be suffering from too much mother and too little father. Women now spend more time with their homes and families than in any past or present society we know about. To get back to the sanity of the agrarian or joint-family system, we need free universal daycare. With that aid, as in Scandinavian countries, and with laws that permit women equal work and equal pay, men will be relieved of their role as sole breadwinner and stranger to his own children.

No more alimony. Fewer boring wives, fewer child-like wives. No more so-called "Jewish mothers," who are simply normal ambitious human beings with all their ambitions confined to the house. No more wives who fall apart with the first wrinkle, because they've been taught their total identity depends on their outsides. No more responsibility for another adult human being who has never been told she is responsible for her own life, and who sooner or later comes up with some version of, "If I hadn't married you, I could have been a star." And let's say it one more time because it such a great organizing tool, no more alimony. Women Liberation really is Men's Liberation, too.

The family system that will emerge is a great subject of anxiety. Probably there will be a variety of choice. Colleague marriages, such as young people have now, with both partners going to law school or the Peace Corps together: that's one alternative. At least they share more than the kitchen and the bedroom. Communes, marriages that are valid for the child-rearing years only . . . there are many possibilities, but they can't be predicted. The growth of new forms must be organic.

The point is that Women's Liberation is not destroying the American family; it is trying to build a human, compassionate alternative out of its ruins. Engels said that the paternalistic, 19th century family system was the prototype of capitalism — with man, the capitalist; woman, the means of production; children the labor — and that the family would only change as the economic system did. Well, capitalism and the mythical American family seem to be in about the same shape.

Of course, there are factors other than economic ones. As Margaret Mead says: No wonder marriage worked so well in the 19th century; people only lived to be fifty years old. And there are factors other than social reform that will influence women's work success. "No wonder women do less well in business," says a woman-executive. "They don't have wives." But the family is the first political unit, and to change it is the most radical act of all.

Women have a special opportunity to live the revolution. By refusing to play their traditional role, they upset and displace the social structure around them. We may be subject to ridicule and suppression, just as men were when they refused to play their traditional role by going to war. But those refusals together are a hope for peace. Anthropologist Geoffrey Corer discovered that the few peaceful human tribes had a common characteristic: sex roles were not polarized, boys weren't taught that manhood depended on aggression (or short hair or military skills), and girls weren't taught that womanhood depended on submission (or working at home instead of the fields).

For those who still fear that Women Liberation involves some loss of manhood, let me quote from the Black Panther code. Certainly, if the fear with which they are being met is any standard, the Panthers are currently the most potent male symbol of all. In *Seize The Time,* Bobby Seals writes, "Where there's a Panther house, we try to live socialism. When there's cooking to be done, both brothers and sisters cook. Both wash the dishes. The sisters don't just serve and wait on the brothers. A lot of black nationalist organizations have the idea of regulating women to the role of serving their men, and they relate this to black manhood. But a real manhood is based on humanism, and it not based on any form of oppression."

One final myth: that women are more moral than men. We are not more moral, we are only uncorrupted by power. But until the leaders of our country put into action the philosophy that Bobby Seals has set down until the old generation of male chauvinists is out of office — women in positions of power can increase our chances of peace a great deal. I personally would rather have had Margaret Mead as president during the past six years of Vietnam than either Johnson or Nixon. At least, she wouldn't have had her masculinity to prove.

Much of the trouble this country is in has to do with the Masculine Mystique: the idea that manhood somehow depends on the subjugation of other people. It's a bipartisan problem.

The challenge to all of us, and to you men and women who are graduating today, is to live a revolution, not to die for one. There has been too much killing, and the weapons are now far too terrible. This revolution has to change consciousness, to upset the injustice of our current hierarchy by refusing to honor it, and to live a life that enforces a new social justice.

Because the truth is none of us can be liberated if other groups are not. Women's Liberation is a bridge between black and white women, but also between the construction workers and the suburbanites, between Nixon's Silent Majority and the young people they hate and fear. Indeed, there's much more injustice and rage among working-class women than among the much-publicized white radicals.

Women are sisters, they have many of the same problems, and they can communicate with each other. "You only get radicalized, as black activists always told us, on your own thing." Then we make the connection to other injustices in society. The Women's Movement is an important revolutionary bridge. And we are building it.

I know it's traditional on such an occasion to talk about "entering the world." But this is an untraditional generation: you have made the campus part of the world. I thank you for it.

I don't need to tell you what awaits you in this country. You know that much better than I. I will only say that my heart goes with you, and that I hope we will be working together. Divisions of age, race, class, and sex are old-fashioned and destructive.

One more thing, especially to the sisters, because I wish someone had said it to me; it would have saved me so much time.

You don't have to play one role in this revolutionary age above all others. If you're willing to pay the price for it, you can do anything you want to do. And the price is worth it.

MADELINE DAVIS

In 1972, *Roe v. Wade* was argued before the US Supreme Court, Title IX was signed into law, and for the first time, a gay woman stepped out of the closet and up to the microphone at a national political convention and announced, "I am a woman and a lesbian."

Madeline Davis spoke those words at 5:10 a.m. on July 12 to an increasingly left-leaning political party that would nominate George S. McGovern, the liberal senator from South Dakota, for president. Her speech at the Democratic National Convention in Miami marked a milestone for gay rights.

"I am someone's neighbor, someone's sister, someone's daughter," Davis declared. "A vote for this plank is a vote not only for me but it is a vote for all homosexual women and men across the country to peaceably live their own lives."

The gay rights anti-discrimination plank did not pass, possibly because after Davis spoke, another female delegate, from Ohio, rebutted it using a phony argument that linked homosexuality with prostitution and pedophilia. It was still possible to say those kinds of things in America during the summer of 1972 — but not for much longer.

America was grappling with matters of personal choice, lifestyle, and private habits. Homosexuality was still classified as a mental disorder in the Diagnostic and Statistical Manual of Mental Disorders, but it was removed the following year. Across the country, states were repealing old sodomy laws.

Davis had come out as lesbian in the early Sixties and was active in the LGBT community in western New York. A musician and librarian, she marched and spoke at the first gay rights march on the state capitol in Albany. Her advocacy for gay rights attracted the attention of the New York State Democratic Party, which named her a delegate to the convention.

"I made that speech," Davis told a journalist, "because I knew there were gay people out there at four o'clock in the morning, sitting in front of their television sets, waiting to see one of their own people stand up."

They would also have heard Jim Foster, a gay delegate from San Francisco who had been discharged from the US Army for being "homosexual, who spoke just before she did.

Committed to educating the public and opening minds, Davis later taught a course, "Lesbianism 101," at the State University of New York at Buffalo. It was the nation's first college class on lesbian history and culture. True to a librarian, Davis also founded an archive of L.G.B.T.Q. materials. Originally housed in her basement, it's now at SUNY Buffalo.

A video copy of her historic speech is included in the archive, along with its introduction by news announcer Walter Cronkite, the reassuring voice of middle American values.

"I AM SOMEONE'S NEIGHBOR"

July 12, 1972
Democratic National Convention, Miami Beach, Florida

I am a woman and a lesbian, a minority of minorities.

Thank you for the opportunity to speak to you. Twenty million Americans are grateful and proud of the Democratic Party.

We are the minority of minorities. We belong to every race and creed, both sexes, every economic and social level, every nationality and religion. We live in large cities and small towns. But we are the untouchables in American society. We have suffered from oppression — from being totally ignored or ridiculed to having our heads smashed and our blood spilled in the streets.

Now we are coming out of our closets and on to the convention floor — to tell you, the delegates, and to tell all gay people throughout America that we are here to put an end to our fears. Our fears that people will know us for who we are, that they will shun and revile us, fire us from our jobs, reject us from our families, evict us from our homes, beat us and jail us. For what? Because we have chosen to love each other.

I am asking that you vote YES for the inclusion of this minority report into the Democratic platform for two major reasons:

First, we must speak to the basic civil rights of all human beings. It is inherent in the American tradition that the private life and life styles of citizens should be allowed and insured, so long as they do not infringe upon the rights of others. A government that interferes with the private lives of its people is a government that is alien to the American tradition and the American dream.

You have before you a chance to reaffirm that tradition, that dream. As a matter of practicality you also have the opportunity to gain the vote of 20,000,000 Americans that would help in November to put a Democrat in the White House.

Secondly, I say to you: I am someone's neighbor, someone's sister, someone's daughter. A vote for this plank is a vote not only for me but it is a vote for all homosexual women and men across the country to peaceably live their own lives.

I wish to remind you that a vote for this plank may now or someday be a vote for your neighbor, your sister, your daughter or your son.

We ask for your vote and we ask because our people have suffered long and hard. That you reaffirm for every human being the right to love.

BARBARA JORDAN

Already a distinguished politician in her home state of Texas, it was not until she landed a primetime spot in the impeachment trial of President Nixon that Barbara Jordan, Democratic member of Congress, was thrust into the national spotlight.

On a July evening in 1974, after a twelve-hour debate, Jordan introduced the Articles of Impeachment to members of the House Judiciary Committee and a nationally-televised audience.

But before she turned to the question of the hour — whether Nixon committed impeachable crimes in the Watergate scandal — she intended to clarify her relationship to the principles upon which that assessment would be based.

"'We, the people. It's a very eloquent beginning," Jordan said, referring to the Constitution. "But when that document was completed on the seventeenth of September in 1787, I was not included in that 'We, the people.' I felt somehow for many years that George Washington and Alexander Hamilton just left me out by mistake."

In other words: the very document she was there to uphold had been drafted by slaveholders who excluded Black Americans like her from its protections. Was that document worthy of her respect?

Yes, she answered the question, it was. Through amendments and the legal process, that historic wrong had been righted. "My faith in the Constitution is whole. It is complete," she said, with that deep incantatory voice that some would later call "the voice of God."

It was an unexpected beginning, to be sure. But with that point, Jordan upheld the moral stature of the Constitution before moving on to the fraught task of making a legal case against a standing president of the United States. Had she not done so, Jordan might not have completely won over the nation's trust.

With lawyerly precision, she walked her fellow Americans through the evidence: what the President knew, how he attempted to subvert the Constitution, and how he betrayed the public trust. The next day, the committee members agreed that Nixon had violated his oath of office through the abuse of power and obstruction of justice. The following month, Nixon resigned.

It's hard to imagine anyone other than Jordan pulling that off with as much unshakable gravitas.

Just two months before, she spoke at Howard University on the "erosion of civil liberties" and issued a warning that still reverberates: "The events of the past few years and even the past few days," she said, "have convinced us that it is possible for this country to stand on the edge of repression and tyranny and never know it."

"OPENING STATEMENT ON THE ARTICLES OF IMPEACHMENT OF PRESIDENT RICHARD NIXON"

July 25, 1974
US House Judiciary Committee, Washington, DC

Thank you, Mr. Chairman.

Mr. Chairman, I join my colleague Mr. Rangel in thanking you for giving the junior members of this committee the glorious opportunity of sharing the pain of this inquiry. Mr. Chairman, you are a strong man, and it has not been easy but we have tried as best we can to give you as much assistance as possible.

Earlier today, we heard the beginning of the Preamble to the Constitution of the United States: "We, the people." It's a very eloquent beginning. But when that document was completed on the seventeenth of September in 1787, I was not included in that "We, the people." I felt somehow for many years that George Washington and Alexander Hamilton just left me out by mistake. But through the process of amendment, interpretation, and court decision, I have finally been included in "We, the people."

Today I am an inquisitor. An hyperbole would not be fictional and would not overstate the solemnness that I feel right now. My faith in the Constitution is whole; it is complete; it is total. And I am not going to sit here and be an idle spectator to the diminution, the subversion, the destruction, of the Constitution.

"Who can so properly be the inquisitors for the nation as the representatives of the nation themselves?" "The subjects of its jurisdiction are those offenses which proceed from the misconduct of public men." And that's what we're talking about. In other words, from the abuse or violation of some public trust.

It is wrong, I suggest, it is a misreading of the Constitution for any member here to assert that for a member to vote for an article of impeachment means that that member must be convinced that the President should be removed from office. The Constitution doesn't say that. The powers relating to impeachment are an essential check in the hands of the body of the Legislature against and upon the encroachments of the Executive. The division between the two branches of the Legislature, the House and the Senate, assigning to the one the right to accuse and to the other the right to judge, the Framers of this Constitution were very astute. They did not make the accusers and the judgers — and the judges the same person.

We know the nature of impeachment. We've been talking about it a while now. It is chiefly designed for the President and his high ministers to somehow be called into account. It is designed to "bridle" the Executive if he engages in excesses. "It is designed as a method of national inquest into the conduct of public men." The Framers confided in the Congress the power if need be, to remove the President in order to strike a delicate balance between a President swollen with power and grown tyrannical, and preservation of the independence of the Executive.

The nature of impeachment: a narrowly channeled exception to the separation-of-powers maxim. The Federal Convention of 1787 said that. It limited impeachment to high crimes and misdemeanors and discounted and opposed the term "maladministration." "It is to be used only for great misdemeanors," so it was said in the North Carolina ratification convention. And in the Virginia ratification convention: "We do not trust our liberty to a particular branch. We need one branch to check the other."

"No one need be afraid" — the North Carolina ratification convention — "No one need be afraid that officers who commit oppression will pass with immunity." "Prosecutions of impeachments will seldom fail to agitate the passions of the whole community," said Hamilton in the Federalist Papers, number 65. "We divide into parties more or less friendly or inimical to the accused." I do not mean political parties in that sense.

The drawing of political lines goes to the motivation behind impeachment; but impeachment must proceed within the confines of the constitutional term "high crime[s] and misdemeanors." Of the impeachment process, it was Woodrow Wilson who said that "Nothing short of the grossest offenses against the plain law of the land will suffice to give them speed and effectiveness. Indignation so great as to overgrow party interest may secure a conviction; but nothing else can."

Common sense would be revolted if we engaged upon this process for petty reasons. Congress has a lot to do: Appropriations, Tax Reform, Health Insurance, Campaign Finance Reform, Housing, Environmental Protection, Energy Sufficiency, Mass Transportation. Pettiness cannot be allowed to stand in the face of such overwhelming problems. So today we are not being petty. We are trying to be big, because the task we have before us is a big one.

This morning, in a discussion of the evidence, we were told that the evidence which purports to support the allegations of misuse of the CIA by the President is thin. We're told that that evidence is insufficient. What that recital of the evidence this morning did not include is what the President did know on June the 23rd, 1972.

The President did know that it was Republican money, that it was money from the Committee for the Re-Election of the President, which was found in the possession of one of the burglars arrested on June the 17th. What the President did know on the 23rd of June was the prior activities of E. Howard Hunt, which included his participation in the break-in of Daniel Ellsberg's psychiatrist, which included Howard Hunt's participation in the Dita Beard ITT affair, which included Howard Hunt's fabrication of cables designed to discredit the Kennedy Administration.

We were further cautioned today that perhaps these proceedings ought to be delayed because certainly there would be new evidence forthcoming from the President of the United States. There has not even been an obfuscated indication that this committee would receive any additional materials from the President. The committee subpoena is outstanding, and if the President wants to supply that material, the committee sits here. The fact is that on yesterday, the American people waited with great anxiety for eight hours, not knowing whether their President would obey an order of the Supreme Court of the United States.

At this point, I would like to juxtapose a few of the impeachment criteria with some of the actions the President has engaged in. Impeachment criteria: James Madison, from the Virginia ratification convention. "If the President be connected in any suspicious manner with any person and there be grounds to believe that he will shelter him, he may be impeached."

We have heard time and time again that the evidence reflects the payment to defendants money. The President had knowledge that these funds were being paid and these were funds collected for the 1972 presidential campaign. We know that the President met with Mr. Henry Petersen 27 times to discuss matters related to Watergate, and immediately thereafter met with the very persons who were implicated in the information Mr. Petersen was receiving. The words are: "If the President is connected in any suspicious manner with any person and there be grounds to believe that he will shelter that person, he may be impeached."

Justice Story: "Impeachment" is attended — "is intended for occasional and extraordinary cases where a superior power acting for the whole people is put into operation to protect their rights and rescue their liberties from violations." We know about the Huston plan. We know about the break-in of the psychiatrist's office. We know that there was absolute complete direction on September 3rd when the President indicated that a surreptitious entry had been made in Dr.

Fielding's office, after having met with Mr. Ehrlichman and Mr. Young. "Protect their rights." "Rescue their liberties from violation."

The Carolina ratification convention impeachment criteria: those are impeachable "who behave amiss or betray their public trust." Beginning shortly after the Watergate break-in and continuing to the present time, the President has engaged in a series of public statements and actions designed to thwart the lawful investigation by government prosecutors. Moreover, the President has made public announcements and assertions bearing on the Watergate case, which the evidence will show he knew to be false. These assertions, false assertions, impeachable, those who misbehave. Those who "behave amiss or betray the public trust."

James Madison again at the Constitutional Convention: "A President is impeachable if he attempts to subvert the Constitution." The Constitution charges the President with the task of taking care that the laws be faithfully executed, and yet the President has counseled his aides to commit perjury, willfully disregard the secrecy of grand jury proceedings, conceal surreptitious entry, attempt to compromise a federal judge, while publicly displaying his cooperation with the processes of criminal justice. "A President is impeachable if he attempts to subvert the Constitution."

If the impeachment provision in the Constitution of the United States will not reach the offenses charged here, then perhaps that 18th-century Constitution should be abandoned to a 20th-century paper shredder! Has the President committed offenses, and planned, and directed, and acquiesced in a course of conduct which the Constitution will not tolerate? That's the question. We know that. We know the question. We should now forthwith proceed to answer the question. It is reason, and not passion, which must guide our deliberations, guide our debate, and guide our decision.

I yield back the balance of my time, Mr. Chairman.

GRAYCE UYEHARA

Grayce Uyehara was a California college student majoring in music when she and her family were forced to leave their homes and move to the Rohwer Relocation Center, a swampy, wooded camp in southwest Arkansas.

In miserable barracks, surrounded by barbed wire and armed guards, they lived for the next four years. Her family's experience was typical of the nearly 120,000 people of Japanese descent who were sent to detention camps by the US government during World War II.

After the war, Uyehara found her voice as a volunteer, and later, as one of the leaders of the Japanese-American Citizens League. Her calm, fact-based speeches and testimony helped persuade the nation that a great moral wrong had been committed.

The rounding up of Japanese Americans began immediately after the attack on Pearl Harbor on December 7, 1941, which drew the country into World War II. The following day, the government began arresting West Coast residents of Japanese descent.

Two months later, on February 19, 1942, President Roosevelt signed the notorious Executive Order 9066, and the following month, tens of thousands more Japanese Americans were given 48 hours to gather their possessions.

Army trucks pulled up to their homes and took them to assembly centers, and from there to internment camps across the country. National security was cited as the rationale. The real reason was racism.

When the war ended, the internees were allowed to go back home to try and pick up the pieces. Many had lost their property, businesses and savings. As the years passed, few were willing to confront what had taken place — no one in the government, nor its victims. Many Japanese Americans were bitter, angry, and ashamed, and just wanted to move on.

But in 1980, at the urging of Uyehara and other former internees, including California Congressman Norman Mineta, Congress established a bipartisan commission to investigate the possibility of compensation. Uyehara was one of more than 750 witnesses at hearings across the country. Some survivors sat before the commission and wept.

Uyehara argued that the wartime imprisonment was not just a Japanese-American issue, but the nation's issue — one that threatened the rights of every American citizen. "No one knows who the next victims might be," she said.

The conclusions were published as *Personal Justice Denied*, a report that formed the basis for the Civil Liberties Act of 1988. In April 1988, when the Senate voted to pay each interned individual $20,000 and issue a formal apology, Uyehara declared: "Our name has finally been cleared. We are Americans."

"WARTIME INTERNMENT"

June 17, 1987
Subcommittee on Federal Services, Post Office, and Civil Service of the Committee on Governmental Affairs, US Senate, Washington, DC

I am Grayce Kaneda Uyehara of West Chester, Pennsylvania. I serve as the Executive Director of the Japanese American Citizens League-Legislative Education Committee (JACL-LEC) in Washington, DC, I spent time in the Stockton Assembly Center and the Rohwer Relocation Center in Arkansas . . .

In 1980, Congress established the Commission on Wartime Relocation and Internment of Civilians to review the facts and circumstances surrounding Executive Oder 9066, issued February 19, 1942, to assess the impact and effects of that Order, and to recommend appropriate remedies.

The December, 1982 report of the Commission, issued in February 1983, unanimously found that the exclusion and detention of approximately 120,000 Americans of Japanese ancestry and resident aliens were grave injustices. The action was not based on military necessity but rather because of race prejudice, war hysteria and lack of political leadership.

The injustice of the removal, incarceration and relocation of Japanese Americans is conceded by all responsible people and groups, including the US Department of Justice.

On April 20, Solicitor General Charles Fried of the Department of Justice told the United States Supreme Court in United States v. Hohri, 86-510, that the evacuation and incarceration of Americans of Japanese ancestry were "frankly racist." Fried argued that the decisions to exclude and incarcerate were not based upon a factual assessment of military data and intelligence reports, but on a political judgment at the "highest levels" that Japanese Americans as a group were inherently disloyal and untrustworthy. He characterized this pseudo-anthropological justification as "our shame" and openly acknowledged that the Japanese American internment was "our greatest departure" from the principles of freedom for which we were fighting in World War II.

Thousands of loyal Americans who wanted only to raise their families, enjoy the blessings of liberty and fight for their country were summarily imprisoned on the sole basis of national origin, race and ethnicity.

To regain our honor and rightful place in the American community, to take responsibility as citizens, and to ensure that the Constitution lives and works for all, we take as our mantle the people's right to petition our government for redress.

The Magna Carta of 1215 was an inspiration behind the world's most enduring document, the Constitution of the United States. The following words are apropos to redress, "No free man shall be taken, outlawed, banished, or in any way destroyed, nor will we proceed against or prosecute him, except by the lawful judgment of his peers and by the law of the land." "Due process of law" and "law of the land" by the end of the 14th century were interchangeable. This principle has been the essential reality of life in the United States since the adoption of the Constitution in 1787. Tragically, in 1942 Japanese Americans were, without due process, arbitrarily presumed to be disloyal . . .

It is recognized that no amount of money can adequately compensate the Japanese Americans for the wrongs done to them. Nevertheless, common law, the American people and the federal government itself have made it a bedrock of our legal and political system that, where governments have caused substantial injury through the deprivation of liberty or other fundamental rights, remedies should be available to the damaged or injured parties. Hence that fundamental proposition supports the rightness of monetary remedy.

Put another way, if not monetary compensation for the specifically aggrieved, what then would anyone propose as meaningful? Handwringing and expressions of regret, however sincere, will not do; and the victims, the American way, and the Constitution are shamed . . .

We believe this Senate will enact S. 1009. I will paraphrase George Bernard Shaw: "You see things; and you say, "Why right now?" But I dream things and have hopes and aspirations for Japanese Americans and all Americans that never were and I say, "Why not now?"

The reality of time weighs more heavily. There are less than 60,000 survivors of the 120,000 who left their homes with such short notice after being publicly branded as potentially disloyal to their own country.

It is time for honesty in our nation that Japanese Americans were removed from their homes on the basis of "potential disloyalty" to their own country. It is time to recognize that Japanese Americans are Americans, too. It is time to make real the promise of liberty and justice for all.

From the CWRIC report developed from the testimonies of 750 witnesses at the 20 hearings and the research completed from records, from numerous researched books on Japanese Americans and from the hearings held by the Senate and House subcommittee since the redress legislation was first introduced, we can conclude today there is acceptance in American [sic] that the incarceration of 120,000 Americans of Japanese ancestry and resident aliens was not justified and that appropriate remedies should be made by Congress in recognition for the damages for the loss of personal freedom.

I have attempted to answer many questions raised by Senators on this bill to redress the Japanese Americans, particularly on the individual payments. The passage of S.1009 with the payment of $20,000 to each survivor of Executive Order 9066 will not set a precedent for compensation, since the payment is to be made only to the direct victims of the order and subsequent Acts which came from the initial order. This method of payment is the only workable plan after 45 years, rather than to set up an adjudicatory claims procedure which will take more years. In the meantime, the surviving victims who suffered the most and who never recouped after their isolation from the mainstream of American life. These people spent from one to four years as prisoners in their own country; make no mistake that this dislocation and removal of the whole West Coast population of Japanese Americans can be described in any other manner.

This nation is celebrating the Bicentennial of the United States Constitution. Besides correcting the travesty committed against loyal citizens, the passage of S. 1009 will be timely and will show the rest of the world that America admits its mistakes and makes amends to those who were damaged by its decisions and actions. How also will other nations understand what we say about human rights and individual freedom?

William B. Reynolds, Assistant Attorney General, Civil Rights Division, in his speech to the Federalist Society in January, 1987 said:

> All of us in government — officials of the Executive branch, Congressmen, judges — have taken an oath to uphold the Constitution. In taking this oath, we do more than merely promise to avoid committing federal crimes. We promise to take our responsibilities under the Constitution seriously. This will sometimes mean making unpopular decisions, taking political heat, (and heat from the press too), and accepting accountability. Yet too often, decisions with profound consequences for our constitutional government are made with no reference or thought given to the constitutional implications; those more profound considerations are all but forgotten in the rush to respond (invariably politically) to immediate political exigencies.

It is through our conduct, the choices we make, the objectives we set, that we decide our nation's course and pass on this liberty to future generations.

Time inexorably marches on beyond. In behalf of the less than 60,000 survivors of E.O. 9066, the Japanese American Citizens League and Legislative Education Committee turn to Congress and ask the Senate to support the passage of S. 1009 during this 100th Congress in response to the petition for redress of our grievances.

The ancient Greek scholar asked, "When will justice come? When those who are not injured are as indignant as those who are." Our hope is that the Senators will agree that S. 1009 is responsible legislation and good for our nation.

I am available to respond to any concerns raised by the members of the Governmental Affairs Committee.

Thank you, Mr. Chairman and members of the subcommittee for this wonderful opportunity to testify today.

JUDY HEUMANN

Judy Heumann contracted polio when she was eighteen months old, one of the nearly 43,000 American children affected by the polio epidemic of 1949. Then came three months in an iron lung and three years in and out of the hospital.

When it was clear that she would have to use a wheelchair for the rest of her life, her doctor recommended putting her in an institution. In those days, that was the norm.

But her parents would never have put their daughter in an institution, as she explained in her memoir, *Being Heumann*. As German Jews, they had come to the United States as teenagers and lost their own parents to the Nazis, who believed people with disabilities imposed a genetic and financial burden on society.

At age five, Heumann's mother tried to register her for kindergarten in Brooklyn but was turned away because the principal considered the little girl in the wheelchair "a fire hazard." So every morning, while the other kids went to off to school, she had to stay home and study.

For young Judy, that was the dawning of awareness of the "faulty logic" that excluded her and 43 million other disabled individuals from mainstream American life.

As a student at Long Island University, she organized rallies and protests. She successfully sued the New York Board of Education, which had denied her a teaching license.

Victory followed victory as the nation gradually accepted that disability rights were civil rights, and human rights.

In 1977, Heumann led a twenty-six-day takeover of the San Francisco regional office of the US Department of Health, Education and Welfare. The protestors wanted an end to years of delay in implementing Section 504 of the Rehabilitation Act, which forbade any entity that discriminated based on disability from taking federal money.

On April 5, she stood before the crowd, a "Sign 504" sticker on her jacket, choking up with emotion.

"For too long," she said, "we have believed that if we played by the rules and did what we were told, we would be included in the American Dream. We have waited too long, made too many compromises, and been too patient. We will no longer be patient!"

In 1988, at a Congressional hearing on the Americans with Disabilities Act, Heumann told legislators about the pain and shame caused by discrimination. "This stigma scars for life," she said.

Two years later, the ADA became federal law, prohibiting discrimination against the disabled across American life.

"BECOMING DISABLED"

September 27, 1988
Joint House-Senate Hearing on Discrimination
on the Basis of Disability, Washington, DC

It is really a privilege to be here with all of you today. My name is Judy Heumann. I am the oldest of three children born to an immigrant family. Like most other Americans I was born without a disability. When I was one and a half years old, I contracted polio. Becoming disabled changed my family's life and mine forever.

My disability has made me a target for arbitrary and capricious prejudices from many person with whom I come into contact. Over the years experience has taught us that we must be constantly aware of people's attempts to discriminate against us. We must be prepared at every moment to fight this discrimination.

The average American is not, nor should they have to be, prepared to fight every day of their life for basic civil rights. All too many incidences of discrimination have gone by undefended because of lack of protection under the law.

In the past, disability has been a cause for shame. This forced acceptance of second-class citizenship has stripped us, as disabled people, of pride and dignity. This is not the way we as Americans should have to live their lives.

When I was five, my mother proudly pushed my wheelchair to our local public school where I was promptly refused admission because the principal ruled I was "a fire hazard." I was forced to go on home instruction, receiving one hour of education twice a week for three and a half years. Was this the America of my parents' dreams?

My entrance into mainstream society was blocked by discrimination and segregation. Segregation was not only on an institutional level, but also acted as an obstruction to social integration. As a teenager, I could not travel with my friends on the bus because it was not accessible. At my graduation from high school, the principal attempted to prevent me from accepting an award in a ceremony on-stage simply because I was in a wheelchair.

When I was nineteen, the house mother of my college dormitory refused me admission into the dorm because I was in a wheelchair and needed assistance. When I was twenty one years old I was denied an elementary school teaching credential because of "paralysis of both lower extremities sequelae of poliomyelitis."

At the time I didn't know what sequelae meant. I went to the dictionary and looked it up and found out that it was "because of." So it was obviously because of my disability that I was discriminated against.

At the age of twenty five I was told to leave a plane on my return trip to my job here in the US Senate because I was flying without an attendant. In 1981, an attempt was made to forcibly remove me and another disabled friend from an auction house because we were "disgusting to look at." In 1983 a manager of a movie theater attempted to keep my disabled friend and myself out of his theater because we could not transfer out of our wheelchairs.

These are only a few examples of discrimination I have faced in my forty-year life. I've successfully fought all of these attempted actions of discriminations through immediate aggressive confrontation or litigation. But this stigma scars for life. Many disabled persons experience discrimination of the same magnitude, but not everyone possesses the intestinal fortitude and has the support of family and friends required to face up to these daily societal barriers.

Sadly, these are not isolated examples true only in the past tense. This is an ongoing social phenomenon which haunts our lives at every minute.

I have been told throughout my life to be understanding of these people's actions, "They don't know any better." Neither I, nor any one of the forty-two million other people with disabilities, can wait for the two hundred million nondisabled Americans to become educated to the fact that disability does not negate our entitlement to the same constitutional right as they have.

Just as other civil rights legislation has made previously sanctioned discrimination illegal, so too will the passage of the Americans with Disabilities Act of 1988 outlaw protectivist, paternalistic, ignorant discrimination against all persons with disabilities.

We, as disabled persons, are here today to insure for the class of disabled Americans the ordinary daily life that nondisabled Americans too often take for granted. The right to ride a bus or a train, the right to any job for which we are qualified, the right to enter any theater, restaurant or public accommodation, the right to purchase a home or rent an apartment, the right to appropriate communication.

Whether you have HIV infection, cancer, heart disease, back problems, epilepsy, diabetes, polio, muscular dystrophy, cerebral palsy, multiple sclerosis, are deaf or blind, discrimination affects all of us the same. Simply put, we are here today to say that people in our society have been raised with prejudicial attitudes that have resulted in extreme discrimination against the 42 million persons with disabilities in the United States.

Discrimination is intolerable. The US Congress is to be commended for its introduction of the Americans with Disabilities Act. The passage of this monumental legislation will make it clear that our government will no longer allow the largest minority group in the United States to be denied equal opportunity.

You have all heard our testimony today. But you have also been aware of these stories for many years. As elected representatives, you must act without delay to end these reprehensible acts of discrimination. To do any less is immoral.

SANDRA DAY O'CONNOR

On October 29, 1991, Supreme Court Justice Sandra Day O'Connor — the only woman on the nation's highest court — delivered a lecture at New York University Law School to mark the 100th anniversary of the school's admittance of women, one of the nation's first major law schools to do so.

Raised on an Arizona ranch, O'Connor had graduated third in her class at Stanford Law School in 1952, but the closest she had come to a job offer in the field was as a legal secretary. Nevertheless, she went on to serve as a Republican state senator, state judge, and finally, in a milestone appointment by President Ronald Reagan in 1981, the country's first female Supreme Court justice.

She also became a frequent speaker, and she liked to talk about her early days at an all-girls school in El Paso and the lasting impact of her drama teacher's "insistence on proper and clear enunciation."

She named her NYU speech after Portia, the character in Shakespeare who disguised herself as a man so she could represent a client in trial — and won the case.

O'Connor chronicled the many obstacles women have faced through the years not just to practice law, but to participate fully in the workforce. She disapproved of the "New Feminism," which she believed drew on old stereotypes about the supposed differences between women's and men's logic, behavior, and adjudication in order to showcase women's alleged strengths. That would only serve to revive the "old myths" about innate gender differences, which she warned would reopen the door to a renewal of sex discrimination.

While O'Connor was speaking, a noisy group of pro-choice demonstrators marched and chanted outside, with signs that said, "Sandra Day, you can't hide! Undue burden is a lie!" — referring to her use of the "undue burden" standard in legal decisions, which would later be used to allow states to chip away at abortion rights.

Ultimately, both ends of the political spectrum have recognized O'Connor as a principled moderate who held the center on an increasingly divided and politicized court, and as someone whose rise to the top of the American judiciary marked a historic achievement for American women.

O'Connor never failed to push through gender barriers and call out sexism when she saw it.

At an oral argument before the Supreme Court that same month that she delivered her NYU speech, a lawyer offhandedly said to the justices, "I'd like to remind you gentlemen of an important legal point."

Justice O'Connor looked squarely at him and asked, "Would you like to remind me too?"

"PORTIA'S PROGRESS"

October 29, 1991
23rd James Madison Lecture on Constitutional Law, New
York University School of Law, New York City, New York

I am very happy to be celebrating with you the One Hundredth Anniversary of Women Graduates from New York University School of Law. New York University showed great foresight by admitting women law students before the turn of the century. It was one of the first major law schools to do so. Columbia Law School did not admit women until 1927; Harvard Law School did not admit women until 1950. In fact, New York University flouted the wishes of Columbia Law School committee member George Templeton Strong, who had written in his diary: "Application from three infatuated Young Women to the [Columbia] Law School. No woman shall degrade herself by practicing law in New York especially if I can save her."

New York women wouldn't be saved, however. The first woman to sit on the federal bench was a New Yorker, as was the first woman admitted to practice before the Supreme Court. A New York woman wrote the state's first workmen's compensation laws, and a New York woman wrote the "Little Wagner" act that permitted New York City employees to bargain collectively without violating antitrust laws. And, a New York woman worked on every major civil rights case that came before the United States Supreme Court in the 1950s and 1960s. You all can be very proud of this tradition. But being an early woman lawyer was not an easy accomplishment, even for New Yorkers.

Most of the women legal pioneers faced a profession and a society that espoused what has been called "The Cult of Domesticity," a view that women were by nature different from men. Women were said to be fitted for motherhood and homelife, compassionate, selfless, gentle, moral, and pure. Their minds were attuned to art and religion, not logic. Men, on the other hand, were fitted by nature for competition and intellectual discovery in the world, battle-hardened, shrewd, authoritative, and tough-minded.

Women were thought to be ill-qualified for adversarial litigation because it required sharp logic and eschews negotiation, as well as exposure to the unjust and immoral. In 1875, the Wisconsin Supreme Court told Lavinia Goodell that she could not be admitted to the state bar. The Chief Justice declared that the practice of law was unfit for the female character. To expose women to the brutal, repulsive, and obscene events of courtroom life, he said, would shock man's reverence for womanhood and relax the public's sense of decency.

In a similar case, Myra Bradwell of Chicago, who had studied law under her husband, applied to the Illinois Bar in 1869 and was refused admission because as a married woman her contracts were not binding, and contracts were the essence of an attorney-client relationship." The Court also proclaimed that "God designed the sexes to occupy different spheres of action, and that it belonged to men to make, apply, and execute the laws."

The United States Supreme Court, I blush to admit, agreed with the Illinois court. Justice Bradley, concurring in the Court's opinion, cited the natural differences between men and women as the reason Myra Bradwell could not be admitted. He wrote, "Man is, or should be, woman's protector and defender. The natural and proper timidity and delicacy which belongs to the female sex evidently unfits it for many of the occupations of civil life."

Even Clarence Darrow, one of the most famous champions of unpopular causes, had this to say to a group of women lawyers: "You can't be shining lights at the bar because you are too kind. You can never be corporation lawyers because you are not cold-blooded. You have not a high grade of intellect. I doubt you can ever make a living." Another male attorney of the period commented, "[A] woman can't keep a secret, and for that reason if no other, I doubt if anybody will ever consult a woman lawyer.

Luckily for us women lawyers today, our female predecessors had far more spunk, spirit, and wit than they were given credit for. Clara Shortridge Foltz, the first woman lawyer in California and the first woman deputy district attorney in America, displayed the characteristic mettle of these early women lawyers. When an opposing attorney once suggested in open court that she had better be at home raising children, Foltz retorted: "A woman had better be in almost any business than raising such men as you."

A New York woman lawyer pioneer, Belva Lockwood, was in 1879 the first woman admitted to practice before the United States Supreme Court. To receive that honor, however, she had to try three times to get a special bill passed in the Senate to change the admission requirements. Inexhaustible, she rode her three-wheeler all over Washington, lobbying senators and explaining to the press that she was going to "get up a fight all along the line." In 1884, the redoubtable Mrs. Lockwood even ran for President, reasoning that even though women could not vote, there was nothing to stop them from running for office. Even without women voters, she garnered 4,149 votes in that election.

In my own time and in my own life, I have witnessed the revolution in the legal profession that has resulted in women representing nearly thirty percent of attorneys in this country and forty percent of law school graduates. Projections based on data from the Census Bureau and Department of Labor indicate that forty years hence half the country's attorneys will be women. I myself, after graduating near the top of my class at Stanford Law School, was unable to obtain a position at any national law firm, except as a legal secretary. Yet I have since had the privilege of serving as a state senator, a state judge, and a Supreme Court Justice.

Women today are not only well-represented in law firms, but are gradually attaining other positions of legal power, representing 7.4 percent of federal judges, twenty-five percent of United States Attorneys, fourteen percent of state attorneys, eighteen percent of state legislators, seventeen percent of state and local executives, nine percent of county governing boards, fourteen percent of mayors and city council members, six percent of United States congresspersons, and of course, just over eleven percent of United States Supreme Court Justices. Until the percentages come closer to fifty percent, however, we cannot say we have succeeded. Still, the progress in my own time has been astounding.

That progress is due in large part to the explosion of the myth of the "True Woman" through the efforts of real women and the insights of real men. Released from these prejudices, women have proved they can do a "man's" job.

This change in perspective has been reflected, as most social change eventually is, in the Supreme Court's jurisprudence. I would like to sketch briefly how the Justices' comments about gender differences have changed in direct response to the change in the position of women in our society.

The ratification of the Bill of Rights in 1791 had little immediate effect on the legal status or fights of women. Its strictures were limited initially to the federal government; the states were free to continue as before in fashioning the political and legal rights of their citizens. State legislation affecting women was drawn primarily from the British common law, which gave women few property or contractual rights. Only in the case of unmarried women were the laws in this country somewhat more generous than in England, at least insofar as property ownership and management were concerned.

As you know, it was not until after the Civil War and the resultant adoption of the thirteenth, fourteenth, and fifteenth amendments to our Constitution that there were national guaranties for certain individual liberties which the states could not abridge. But even these additions to our Constitution did not easily translate into concepts that benefitted women as a group until the last half of the twentieth century. Until that time, despite the efforts of women such as Elizabeth Cady Stanton, Susan B. Anthony, and Sojourner Truth, society as a whole, including the Court, generally accepted the separate and unequal status of women.

The fourteenth amendment prohibits states from "denying to any person. . . the equal protection of the laws." There is little evidence to suggest that at the time of its adoption in 1868 this amendment was seen as a vehicle of women's equality under law. In fact, the fourteenth amendment for the first time introduced sex-specific language into the Constitution. Section 2 of the amendment, which deals with legislative representation and voting, says that if the right to vote is "denied to any of the male inhabitants" of a state aged twenty-one or over then the proportional representation in that state shall be reduced accordingly. Moreover, the Supreme Court determined in 1873 in the Slaughter-House Cases that the equal protection clause should be narrowly interpreted to apply only to state laws that discriminate against blacks.

The same Court on the very next day handed down the *Bradwell* decision, mentioned earlier, denying Myra Bradwell's claim that the state of Illinois had denied her the privileges and immunities of United States citizenship when it refused, because of her sex, to give her a license to practice law.

For the first half of the twentieth century the Court continued to defer legislative judgments regarding the differences between the sexes. In 1948, Valentine Goesaert and three other women challenged the constitutionality of a Michigan statute forbidding a woman from being a bartender unless she was "the wife or daughter of the male owner" of the bar. The Court, in an opinion by Justice Frankfurter, rejected the claim that the statute violated the equal protection clause, saying that "despite the vast changes in the social and legal position of women," the state unquestionably could forbid all women from working as bartenders. Even as late as 1961, the Court reaffirmed Florida's practice of restricting jury service to men, unless women registered separately. The Court said, "Despite the enlightened emancipation of women from the restrictions and protections of bygone years, and their entry into many parts of community life formerly considered to be reserved to men, woman is still regarded as the center of the home and family life. "The Supreme Court began to look more closely at legislation providing dissimilar treatment for similarly situated women and men in the early 1970s. The first case in which the Court found a state law discriminating against women to be unconstitutional was *Reed v. Reed*. In *Reed*, the Court struck down an Idaho law giving men an automatic preference in appointments as administrators of estates. *Reed* signaled a dramatic change in the Court's approach to the myth of the "True Woman."

In subsequent cases, the Court made clear that it would no longer swallow unquestioningly the story that women are different from men. In 1972, striking down a federal statute which made it easier for men to claim their wives as dependents than it was for women to claim their husbands as dependents, Justice Brennan wrote: "There can be no doubt that our nation has had a long and unfortunate history of sex discrimination. Traditionally, such discrimination was rationalized by an attitude of 'romantic paternalism' which, in practical effect, put women, not on a pedestal, but in a cage."

Two years later, the Court struck down a Utah statute providing that child support was required for girls only until their legal majority at eighteen, while child support for boys was required until they reached the age of twenty-one. The state had justified the difference by arguing that women matured faster, married earlier, and tended not to require continuing support through higher education, while men usually did require this additional support. The Court took a hard look at these justifications, concluding:

A child, male or female, is still a child. No longer is the female destined solely for the home and the rearing of the family, and only the male for the marketplace and the world of ideas . . . Women's activities and responsibilities are increasing and expanding. Coeducation is a fact, not a rarity. The presence of women in business, in the professions, in government and, indeed, in all walks of life where education is a desirable, if not always a necessary, antecedent is apparent and a proper subject of judicial notice.

In 1976, the Court made its more careful standard of review explicit, ruling that sex-based classifications would be upheld only if they served important governmental objectives and were substantially related to the achievement of those objectives.

Through the next two decades, the Court invalidated, on equal protection grounds, a broad range of statutes that discriminated against women. The laws struck down included a Social Security Act provision allowing widows but not widowers to collect survivors benefits; a state law permitting the sale of beer to women at age eighteen but not to men until age twenty-one; a state law requiring men but not women to pay alimony after divorce; a Social Security provision allowing benefits for families with dependent children only when the father was unemployed, not when the mother was unemployed, and a state statute granting only husbands the right to manage and dispose of jointly owned property without spousal consent.

The volume of cases in the Supreme Court dealing with sex discrimination declined somewhat in the 1980s. Several of the more recent cases brought before the Court have involved interpretations of statutes such as Title VII rather than of the equal protection clause. In *Hishon v. King & Spalding,* for example, the Court held that once a law firm makes partnership consideration a privilege of employment, the firm may not discriminate on the basis of sex in its selection of partners.

In all of these cases, the Court has looked with a somewhat jaundiced eye at the loose-fitting generalizations, myths, and archaic stereotypes that previously kept women at home. Instead, the Court has often asked employers to look to whether the particular person involved, male or female, is capable of doing the job, not whether women in general are more or less capable than men.

Just when the Court and Congress have adopted a less sanguine view of gender-based classifications, however, the new presence of women in the law has prompted many feminist commentators to ask whether women have made a difference to the profession, whether women have different styles, aptitudes, or liabilities. Ironically, the move to ask again the question whether women are different merely by virtue of being women recalls the old myths we have struggled to put behind us. Undaunted by the historical resonances, however, more and more writers have suggested that women practice law differently than men. One author has even concluded that my opinions differ in a peculiarly feminine way from those of my colleagues.

The gender differences currently cited are surprisingly similar to stereotypes from years past. Women attorneys are more likely to seek to mediate disputes than litigate them. Women attorneys are more likely to focus on resolving a client's problem than on vindicating a position. Women attorneys are more likely to sacrifice career advancement for family obligations. Women attorneys are more concerned with public service or fostering community than with individual achievement. Women judges are more likely to emphasize context and deemphasize general principles. Women judges are more compassionate. And so forth.

This "New Feminism" is interesting, but troubling, precisely because it so nearly echoes the Victorian myth of the "True Woman" that kept women out of law for so long. It is a little chilling to compare these suggestions to Clarence Darrow's assertion that women are too kind and warm-hearted to be shining lights at the bar.

One difference between men and women lawyers certainly remains, however. Women professionals still have primary responsibility for children and house-keeping, spending roughly twice as much time on these cares as do their professional husbands. As a result, women lawyers have special difficulties managing both a household and a career.

These concerns of how to blend law and family we share with women lawyers of over one hundred years ago, who, like us, debated whether a woman could have both a family and a profession. The prevailing view then, as Mrs. Marion Todd put it in an 1888 letter to the Women Lawyers' Equity Club, was that a husband was simply "too great a responsibility." Today, while many women juggle both profession and home admirably, it is nonetheless true that time spent at home is time that cannot be billed to clients or used to make contacts at social or professional organizations.

As a result, women still may face what has been called a "mommy track" or a "glass ceiling" in the legal profession — a delayed or blocked ascent to partnership or management status due to family responsibilities. Women who do not wish to be left behind sometimes are faced with a hard choice. Some give up family life in order to attain their career aspirations. Many talented young women lawyers decide that the demands of a career require delaying family responsibilities at the very time in their lives when bearing children is physically easiest. I myself chose to try to have and enjoy my family and to resume my career path somewhat later.

The choices that women must make in this respect are different from the choices that men must make. Men need not take time off from work to have a family — not even the bare minimum amount of time needed to deliver a child. It is in recognizing and responding to this fundamental difference that the Court has had its most difficult challenges. The dilemma is this: if society does not recognize the fact that only women can bear children, then "equal treatment" ends up being unequal. On the other hand, if society recognizes pregnancy as requiring special solicitude, it is a slippery slope back to the "protectionist" legislation that historically barred women from the workplace . . .

The question of when equality requires accommodating differences is one with which the Court will continue to struggle. I think in recent cases the Court has acknowledged, along with the "New Feminism," that sometimes to treat men and women exactly the same is to treat them differently, at least with respect to pregnancy. Women do have the gift of bearing children, a gift that needs to be accommodated in the working world. However, in allowing for this difference, we must always remember that we risk a return to the myth of the "True Woman" that blocked the career paths of many generations of women.

I would hope that your generation of attorneys will find new ways to balance family and professional responsibilities between men and women, recognizing gender differences in a way that promotes equality and frees both women and men from traditional role limitations. You must reopen the velvet curtain between work and home that was drawn closed in the Victorian era. Not only women, but men too, have missed out through the division of work and home. As more women enjoy the challenges of a legal career, more men have blessings to garner from taking extra time to nurture and teach their children.

If we are to continue to find ways to repair the existing difference between professional women and men with regard to family responsibilities, however, we must not allow the "New Feminism" complete sway.

For example, asking whether women attorneys speak with a "different voice" than men do is a question that is both dangerous and unanswerable. It again sets up the polarity between the feminine virtues of homemaking and the masculine virtues of breadwinning. It threatens, indeed, to establish new categories of "women's work" to which women are confined and from which men are excluded.

Instead, my sense is that as women continue to take on a full role in the professions, learning from those professional experiences, as from their experiences as homemakers, the virtues derived from both kinds of learning will meld. The "different voices" will teach each other. I myself have been thankful for the opportunity to experience a rich and fulfilling career as well as a close and supportive family life. I know the lessons I have learned in each have aided me in the other. As a result, I can revel both in the growth of my granddaughter and in the legal subtleties of the free exercise clause.

Do women judges decide cases differently by virtue of being women? I would echo the answer of my colleague, Justice Jeanne Coyne of the Supreme Court of Oklahoma, who responded that "a wise old man and a wise old woman reach the same conclusion." This should be our aspiration: that, whatever our gender or background, we all may become wise through our different struggles and different victories, wise through work *and* play, profession *and* family.

MARY FISHER

Mary Fisher's life was a postcard of a certain kind of success: White, upper-class, educated, the daughter of a wealthy Detroit financier and Republican power broker.

One summer day 1991, her ex-husband called to say he'd been feeling sick, had taken a blood test for HIV, and tested positive. She was tested too. At a pay phone at LaGuardia airport, she got the results, and was ambushed by a positive test and a terminal prognosis.

Since the early 1980s, the HIV and AIDS crisis had swept across the world. In 1991 alone, nearly 30,000 Americans died from AIDS-related illnesses. The virus had spread to people of all sexual orientations and genders, but the stigma of the "gay plague" and the sharing of needles for drug use remained.

To be diagnosed with AIDS was more than a death sentence — it also meant blame and rejection.

But Fisher was not an IV drug user or someone with multiple sexual partners. She had committed no crime. She was 44, with two toddlers, and so far asymptomatic.

At first she felt paralyzed, then determined to change the story. She wanted to bring home the reality of AIDS to ordinary people, and people in power. "I have come tonight to bring our silence to an end," she told the audience at the 1992 Republican National Convention in Houston and the millions watching on national TV.

The number of AIDS deaths was doubling every six months. At the Democratic National Convention that summer, speaker Elizabeth Glazer bitterly blamed Ronald Reagan for her daughter's death from AIDS.

Prominent conservatives pointed fingers at those suffering from the disease. President George H. W. Bush promised to outlaw discrimination, but kept suggesting that people should "change their behavior."

In January 1991, AIDS activists shut down Grand Central Terminal in a "Day of Desperation." They called for more money to fight AIDS instead of the Persian Gulf War. A banner over the terminal said, "One AIDS death every 8 minutes." Downtown, protestors left empty coffins outside the federal office building.

Mary Fisher urged unity. This disease, she said, "does not care whether you are Democrat or Republican. It does not ask whether you are Black or White, male or female, gay or straight, young or old."

We retreat to our stereotypes, she said, but "HIV asks only one thing of those it attacks: Are you human? And this is the right question: Are you human?"

Confronting her mortality, Fisher asked the essential questions: What do we owe one another? What does it mean to be part of humanity?

"A WHISPER OF 'AIDS'"

August 19, 1992
Republican National Convention, Astrodome, Houston, Texas

L ess than three months ago, at platform hearings in Salt Lake City, I asked the Republican Party to lift the shroud of silence which has been draped over the issue of HIV/AIDS. I have come tonight to bring our silence to an end.

I bear a message of challenge, not self-congratulation. I want your attention, not your applause. I would never have asked to be HIV-positive. But I believe that in all things there is a good purpose, and so I stand before you, and before the nation, gladly.

The reality of AIDS is brutally clear. Two hundred thousand Americans are dead or dying; a million more are infected. Worldwide, forty million, or sixty million, or a hundred million infections will be counted in the coming few years. But despite science and research, White House meetings and congressional hearings; despite good intentions and bold initiatives, campaign slogans and hopeful promises — despite it all, it's the epidemic which is winning tonight.

In the context of an election year, I ask you — here, in this great hall, or listening in the quiet of your home — to recognize that the AIDS virus is not a political creature. It does not care whether you are Democrat or Republican. It does not ask whether you are black or white, male or female, gay or straight, young or old.

Tonight, I represent an AIDS community whose members have been reluctantly drafted from every segment of American society. Though I am White, and a mother, I am one with a Black infant struggling with tubes in a Philadelphia hospital. Though I am female, and contracted this disease in marriage, and enjoy the warm support of my family, I am one with the lonely gay man sheltering a flickering candle from the cold wind of his family's rejection.

This is not a distant threat; it is a present danger. The rate of infection is increasing fastest among women and children. Largely unknown a decade ago, AIDS is the third leading killer of young-adult Americans today — but it won't be third for long. Because, unlike other diseases, this one travels. Adolescents don't give each other cancer or heart disease because they believe they are in love. But HIV is different. And we have helped it along — we have killed each other — with our ignorance, our prejudice, and our silence.

We may take refuge in our stereotypes, but we cannot hide there long. Because HIV asks only one thing of those it attacks: Are you human? And this is the right question: Are you human? Because people with HIV have not entered some alien state of being. They are human. They have not earned cruelty and they do not deserve meanness. They don't benefit from being isolated or treated as outcasts. Each of them is exactly what God made: a person. Not evil, deserving of our judgment; not victims, longing for our pity. People. Ready for support and worthy of compassion.

My call to you, my Party, is to take a public stand no less compassionate than that of the President and Mrs. Bush. They have embraced me and my family in memorable ways. In the place of judgment, they have shown affection. In difficult moments, they have raised our spirits. In the darkest hours, I have seen them reaching not only to me, but also to my parents, armed with that stunning grief and special grace that comes only to parents who have themselves leaned too long over the bedside of a dying child.

With the President's leadership, much good has been done; much of the good has gone unheralded; as the President has insisted, "Much remains to be done."

But we do the President's cause no good if we praise the American family but ignore a virus that destroys it. We must be consistent if we are to be believed. We cannot love justice and ignore prejudice, love our children and fear to teach them. Whatever our role, as parent or policy maker, we must act as eloquently as we speak — else we have no integrity.

My call to the nation is a plea for awareness. If you believe you are safe, you are in danger. Because I was not hemophiliac, I was not at risk. Because I was not gay, I was not at risk. Because I did not inject drugs, I was not at risk.

My father has devoted much of his lifetime to guarding against another holocaust. He is part of the generation who heard Pastor Niemoeller come out of the Nazi death camps to say, "They came after the Jews and I was not a Jew, so I did not protest. They came after the Trade Unionists, and I was not a Trade Unionist, so I did not protest. They came after the Roman Catholics, and I was not a Roman Catholic, so I did not protest. Then they came after me, and there was no one left to protest."

The lesson history teaches is this: If you believe you are safe, you are at risk. If you do not see this killer stalking your children, look again. There is no family or community, no race or religion, no place left in America that is safe. Until we genuinely embrace this message, we are a nation at risk.

Tonight, HIV marches resolutely toward AIDS in more than a million American homes, littering its pathway with the bodies of the young. Young men. Young women. Young parents. Young children. One of the families is mine. If it is true that HIV inevitably turns to AIDS, then my children will inevitably turn to orphans.

My family has been a rock of support. My eighty-four-year-old father, who has pursued the healing of the nations, will not accept the premise that he cannot heal his daughter. My mother has refused to be broken; she still calls at midnight to tell wonderful jokes that make me laugh. Sisters and friends, and my brother Phillip (whose birthday is today) — all have helped carry me over the hardest places. I am blessed, richly and deeply blessed, to have such a family.

But not all of you have been so blessed. You are HIV-positive but dare not say it. You have lost loved ones, but you dared not whisper the word AIDS. You weep silently; you grieve alone.

I have a message for you: It is not you who should feel shame, it is we. We who tolerate ignorance and practice prejudice, we who have taught you to fear. We must lift our shroud of silence, making it safe for you to reach out for compassion. It is our task to seek safety for our children, not in quiet denial but in effective action.

Some day our children will be grown. My son Max, now four, will take the measure of his mother; my son Zachary, now two, will sort through his memories. I may not be here to hear their judgments, but I know already what I hope they are.

I want my children to know that their mother was not a victim. She was a messenger. I do not want them to think, as I once did, that courage is the absence of fear; I want them to know that courage is the strength to act wisely when most we are afraid. I want them to have the courage to step forward when called by their nation, or their Party, and give leadership — no matter what the personal cost. I ask no more of you than I ask of myself, or of my children.

To the millions of you who are grieving, who are frightened, who have suffered the ravages of AIDS firsthand: Have courage and you will find comfort.

To the millions who are strong, I issue the plea: Set aside prejudice and politics to make room for compassion and sound policy.

To my children, I make this pledge: I will not give in, Zachary, because I draw my courage from you. Your silly giggle gives me hope. Your gentle prayers give me strength. And you, my child, give me reason to say to America, "You are at risk." And I will not rest, Max, until I have done all I can to make your world safe. I will seek a place where intimacy is not the prelude to suffering.

I will not hurry to leave you, my children. But when I go, I pray that you will not suffer shame on my account.

To all within sound of my voice, I appeal: Learn with me the lessons of history and of grace, so my children will not be afraid to say the word AIDS when I am gone. Then their children, and yours, may not need to whisper it at all.

God bless the children, and bless us all.

HILLARY CLINTON

The speaker had "a genuine case of nerves." First Lady Hillary Clinton had spent weeks drafting and redrafting her speech, aware that "one wrong word might lead to a diplomatic brouhaha."

On September 5, 1995, she stepped up to the microphone at the United Nations Fourth World Conference on Women in Beijing, with tens of thousands in the audience, including her 15-year-old daughter, and millions watching around the world.

"It's time to break the silence," Clinton declared. "It's time for us to say here, for the world to hear, that it is no longer acceptable to discuss women's rights as separate from human rights."

Speaking to representatives of 189 countries — including many where the absence of civil rights and violence against women were commonplace — she took a stand, calling out the abuses one by one:

"It is a violation of human rights when babies are denied food, or drowned, or suffocated, or their spines broken, simply because they are born girls," she said, or "when women and girls are sold into slavery or prostitution for human greed. It is a violation of human rights when women are doused with gasoline, set on fire, and burned to death because their marriage dowries are deemed too small, or when thousands of women are raped in their own communities and when thousands of women are subjected to rape as a tactic or prize of war."

After centuries in which gender equality had been brushed off and sidelined as a "women's issue," here was a representative of the United States forcing the world to listen, confronting the devastating reality for millions of women, and declaring that "human rights are women's rights and women's rights are human rights, once and for all."

Her speech, and the subsequent Platform for Action, defined a new era for women's rights.

Clinton later said she worked hard to keep her delivery calm and factual. "Women are often criticized if we show too much emotion in public," she said, with understatement.

After nearly a half century in the public eye and hundreds of speeches — from her 1969 graduation address at Wellesley right up to her 2016 concession speech after her historic presidential bid — Clinton knew better than most the potential pitfalls for women speakers.

And in that concession speech, she reserved special words of encouragement for "all the little girls" who were watching her graciously accept defeat. "Never doubt that you are valuable," she told them, "and powerful and deserving of every chance and opportunity in the world to pursue and achieve your own dreams."

"WOMEN'S RIGHTS ARE HUMAN RIGHTS"

September 5, 1995
Plenary Session, UN 4th World Conference on Women, Beijing, China

T hank you very much, Gertrude Mongella, for your dedicated work that has brought us to this point, distinguished delegates, and guests: I would like to thank the Secretary General for inviting me to be part of this important United Nations Fourth World Conference on Women. This is truly a celebration, a celebration of the contributions women make in every aspect of life — in the home, on the job, in the community, as mothers, wives, sisters, daughters, learners, workers, citizens, and leaders.

It is also a coming together, much the way women come together every day in every country. We come together in fields and factories, in village markets and supermarkets, in living rooms and board rooms. Whether it is while playing with our children in the park, or washing clothes in a river, or taking a break at the office water cooler, we come together and talk about our aspirations and concerns. And time and again, our talk turns to our children and our families.

However different we may appear, there is far more that unites us than divides us. We share a common future, and we are here to find common ground so that we may help bring new dignity and respect to women and girls all over the world, and in so doing bring new strength and stability to families as well.

By gathering in Beijing, we are focusing world attention on issues that matter most in our lives — the lives of women and their families: access to education, health care, jobs and credit, the chance to enjoy basic legal and human rights and to participate fully in the political life of our countries.

There are some who question the reason for this conference. Let them listen to the voices of women in their homes, neighborhoods, and workplaces. There are some who wonder whether the lives of women and girls matter to economic and political progress around the globe.

Let them look at the women gathered here and at Huairou — the homemakers and nurses, the teachers and lawyers, the policymakers and women who run their own businesses. It is conferences like this that compel governments and peoples everywhere to listen, look, and face the world's most pressing problems.

Wasn't it after the women's conference in Nairobi ten years ago that the world focused for the first time on the crisis of domestic violence?

Earlier today, I participated in a World Health Organization forum. In that forum, we talked about ways that government officials, NGOs, and individual citizens are working to address the health problems of women and girls. Tomorrow, I will attend a gathering of the United Nations Development Fund for Women. There, the discussion will focus on local — and highly successful — programs that give hard-working women access to credit so they can improve their own lives and the lives of their families.

What we are learning around the world is that if women are healthy and educated, their families will flourish. If women are free from violence, their families will flourish. If women have a chance to work and earn as full and equal partners in society, their families will flourish. And when families flourish, communities and nations do as well. That is why every woman, every man, every child, every family, and every nation on this planet does have a stake in the discussion that takes place here.

Over the past 25 years, I have worked persistently on issues relating to women, children, and families. Over the past two and a half years, I've had the opportunity to learn more about the challenges facing women in my own country and around the world.

I have met new mothers in Indonesia, who come together regularly in their village to discuss nutrition, family planning, and baby care. I have met working parents in Denmark who talk about the comfort they feel in knowing that their children can be cared for in safe, and nurturing after-school centers. I have met women in South Africa who helped lead the struggle to end apartheid and are now helping to build a new democracy. I have met with the leading women of my own hemisphere who are working every day to promote literacy and better health care for children in their countries. I have met women in India and Bangladesh who are taking out small loans to buy milk cows, or rickshaws, or thread in order to create a livelihood for themselves and their families. I have met the doctors and nurses in Belarus and Ukraine who are trying to keep children alive in the aftermath of Chernobyl.

The great challenge of this conference is to give voice to women everywhere whose experiences go unnoticed, whose words go unheard. Women comprise more than half the world's population, 70% of the world's poor, and two-thirds of those who are not taught to read and write. We are the primary caretakers for most of the world's children and elderly. Yet much of the work we do is not valued — not by economists, not by historians, not by popular culture, not by government leaders.

At this very moment, as we sit here, women around the world are giving birth, raising children, cooking meals, washing clothes, cleaning houses, planting crops, working on assembly lines, running companies, and running countries. Women also are dying from diseases that should have been prevented or treated. They are watching their children succumb to malnutrition caused by poverty and economic deprivation. They are being denied the right to go to school by their own fathers and brothers. They are being forced into prostitution, and they are being barred from the bank lending offices and banned from the ballot box.

Those of us who have the opportunity to be here have the responsibility to speak for those who could not. As an American, I want to speak for those women in my own country, women who are raising children on the minimum wage, women who can't afford health care or childcare, women whose lives are threatened by violence, including violence in their own homes.

I want to speak up for mothers who are fighting for good schools, safe neighborhoods, clean air, and clean airwaves; for older women, some of them widows, who find that, after raising their families, their skills and life experiences are not valued in the marketplace; for women who are working all night as nurses, hotel clerks, or fast food chefs so that they can be at home during the day with their children; and for women everywhere who simply don't have time to do everything they are called upon to do each and every day.

Speaking to you today, I speak for them, just as each of us speaks for women around the world who are denied the chance to go to school, or see a doctor, or own property, or have a say about the direction of their lives, simply because they are women. The truth is that most women around the world work both inside and outside the home, usually by necessity.

We need to understand there is no one formula for how women should lead our lives. That is why we must respect the choices that each woman makes for herself and her family. Every woman deserves the chance to realize her own God-given potential. But we must recognize that women will never gain full dignity until their human rights are respected and protected.

Our goals for this conference, to strengthen families and societies by empowering women to take greater control over their own destinies, cannot be fully achieved unless all governments — here and around the world — accept their responsibility to protect and promote internationally recognized human rights. The international community has long acknowledged and recently reaffirmed at Vienna that both women and men are entitled to a range of protections and personal freedoms, from the right of personal security to the right to determine freely the number and spacing of the children they bear. No one — No one should be forced to remain silent for fear of religious or political persecution, arrest, abuse, or torture.

Tragically, women are most often the ones whose human rights are violated. Even now, in the late 20th century, the rape of women continues to be used as an instrument of armed conflict. Women and children make up a large majority of the world's refugees. And when women are excluded from the political process, they become even more vulnerable to abuse. I believe that now, on the eve of a new millennium, it is time to break the silence. It is time for us to say here in Beijing, and for the world to hear, that it is no longer acceptable to discuss women's rights as separate from human rights.

These abuses have continued because, for too long, the history of women has been a history of silence. Even today, there are those who are trying to silence our words. But the voices of this conference and of the women at Huairou must be heard loudly and clearly.

- It is a violation of human rights when babies are denied food, or drowned, or suffocated, or their spines broken, simply because they are born girls.
- It is a violation of human rights when women and girls are sold into the slavery of prostitution for human greed — and the kinds of reasons that are used to justify this practice should no longer be tolerated.
- It is a violation of human rights when women are doused with gasoline, set on fire, and burned to death because their marriage dowries are deemed too small.
- It is a violation of human rights when individual women are raped in their own communities and when thousands of women are subjected to rape as a tactic or prize of war.
- It is a violation of human rights when a leading cause of death worldwide among women ages 14 to 44 is the violence they are subjected to in their own homes by their own relatives.
- It is a violation of human rights when young girls are brutalized by the painful and degrading practice of genital mutilation.
- It is a violation of human rights when women are denied the right to plan their own families, and that includes being forced to have abortions or being sterilized against their will.

If there is one message that echoes forth from this conference, let it be that human rights are women's rights and women's rights are human rights once and for all. Let us not forget that among those rights are the right to speak freely — and the right to be heard.

Women must enjoy the rights to participate fully in the social and political lives of their countries, if we want freedom and democracy to thrive and endure. It is indefensible that many women in nongovernmental organizations who wished to participate in this conference have not been able to attend, or have been prohibited from fully taking part.

Let me be clear. Freedom means the right of people to assemble, organize, and debate openly. It means respecting the views of those who may disagree with the views of their governments. It means not taking citizens away from their loved ones and jailing them, mistreating them, or denying them their freedom or dignity because of the peaceful expression of their ideas and opinions.

In my country, we recently celebrated the 75th anniversary of Women's Suffrage. It took 150 years after the signing of our Declaration of Independence for women to win the right to vote. It took 72 years of organized struggle, before that happened, on the part of many courageous women and men. It was one of America's most divisive philosophical wars. But it was a bloodless war. Suffrage was achieved without a shot being fired.

But we have also been reminded, in V-J Day observances last weekend, of the good that comes when men and women join together to combat the forces of tyranny and to build a better world. We have seen peace prevail in most places for a half century. We have avoided another world war. But we have not solved older, deeply-rooted problems that continue to diminish the potential of half the world's population.

Now it is the time to act on behalf of women everywhere. If we take bold steps to better the lives of women, we will be taking bold steps to better the lives of children and families too.

Families rely on mothers and wives for emotional support and care. Families rely on women for labor in the home. And increasingly, everywhere, families rely on women for income needed to raise healthy children and care for other relatives.

As long as discrimination and inequities remain so commonplace everywhere in the world, as long as girls and women are valued less, fed less, fed last, overworked, underpaid, not schooled, subjected to violence in and outside their homes — the potential of the human family to create a peaceful, prosperous world will not be realized.

Let this conference be our, and the world's, call to action. Let us heed that call so we can create a world in which every woman is treated with respect and dignity, every boy and girl is loved and cared for equally, and every family has the hope of a strong and stable future. That is the work before you. That is the work before all of us who have a vision of the world we want to see — for our children and our grandchildren.

The time is now. We must move beyond rhetoric. We must move beyond recognition of problems to working together, to have the comment efforts to build that common ground we hope to see. God's blessing on you, your work, and all who will benefit from it.

Godspeed and thank you very much.

TEMPLE GRANDIN

Temple Grandin barely spoke until she was four, and when she did, her voice was flat. She had little interest in social interaction and preferred her own inner world.

Her parents knew something was different about her, but they didn't know exactly what was wrong, and the doctors weren't much help. The catch-all diagnosis was "emotional problems." One doctor told them she was brain damaged.

School was tough. Kids called her "tape recorder," she recalled. "Teasing hurts."

The only relief came from specialized school activities like the model rocket club, electronics lab, and horseback riding. At eighteen, while she was visiting her aunt's ranch in Arizona, she noticed how the cattle calmed down when they were confined to a tight-fitting chute. Back to school, with the help of her science teacher, she invented her own "hug machine."

In adulthood she was formally diagnosed with autism. But what exactly did that mean? It was more guesswork than science.

What Grandin did know was that she had fallen in love with animals — her condition gave her a special connection to their world. "Autism made school and social life hard," she said, "but it made animals easy."

By the time she wrote her first book, *Emergence: Labeled Autistic,* in 1986, she was a successful designer of feedlot and livestock equipment and completing a Ph.D. in animal science. Her dissertation was on the effects of environmental enrichment on the development of pigs — material that became the basis of her book *Animals Make Us Human.*

She was among the first to explain to the public how an autistic person's mental processes worked. Grandin first spoke publicly about it in the mid 1980s, at a conference of the Autism Society of America. She described the experience of being hyper-sensitive to sound: "Like being tied to the rail and the train's coming."

Audience members flooded her with questions: "Why does my son do so much spinning?" "Why does he hold his hands to his ears?" "Why doesn't he look at me?"

One ASA leader recalled "there were tears in more than one set of eyes that day."

In 1993, Grandin came to wider attention when neurologist Oliver Sacks profiled her in a *New Yorker* article, "An Anthropologist on Mars." The title came from a phrase Grandin used to describe how she observes ordinary social interactions to navigate daily life.

Grandin has become a sought-after speaker about autism spectrum disorder, animal welfare, and neurodiversity. The child who couldn't speak now uses her voice to talk about "harnessing the power of every kind of mind," and to remind us of infinite variety of ways to exist and flourish in the world.

"ANIMALS IN TRANSLATION"

January 23, 2007

G. Brown Goode Smithsonian Education Lecture Series, The National Zoo and Conservation Biology Institute, Washington, DC

I might just start out and just say a few things about, about autism. It is a neurological disorder that the person is born with. It varies all the way from somebody who's non-verbal all the way up to a scientist like Einstein. It's a very, very broad ranging continuum. And then there's the milder type; it's called Asperger's, where the child has normal speech development, but there's kind of a loner, the kind of odd kid, and a lot of these people, you know, make brilliant scientists.

In fact there's a very interesting book out called *On Asperger's and Self-Esteem*, and it's about famous scientists and musicians that probably were on the autism-Asperger's spectrum. Then, about half the people on the spectrum are going to remain non-verbal.

Now, to understand animal thinking you have to get away from verbal language. The normal human mind tends to think in language, categorize things with language-based ways of categorization, which tend to override the visual thinking, the smell thinking, the touch thinking, the auditory thinking, that we're going to share with animals.

You know some people think you have to have language to have thought. Well, if that's the case, well, then I guess I just can't think, I just can't agree with those philosophers.

So what is thinking in pictures? It's literally having videotapes in my head. I think in photo realistic pictures, you know, like movies.

Now there's another kind of mind, and when you look at people on the autism-Asperger's spectrum, I've found that you can have the visual thinking mind, like me, that thinks in pictures, [but] is horrible at algebra because there's nothing there to visualize.

There's a pattern thinker that thinks in patterns and music rather than photorealistic pictures, tends to be bad in English.

And then, there's kind of a word specialist mind that just knows every single, you know, weather statistic and baseball statistic. Well both people and animals think in details, because when you have sensory-based thinking it's going to be extremely detailed. Animals notice little things that we tend to not notice.

Okay [referring to a slide], here's the entrance going into the veterinary shoot at a feed yard, and look at the windmill there. On windy days the wind's gonna be turning that windmill. Also look at how dark the entrance is, and most animals, the grazing animals and the carnivores and things like this, are dichromats. They don't have a red sensor, they see yellow and blue, but one of the things dichromatic vision does is it makes you much more sensitive to sharp contrasts of light and dark.

Okay [referring to a slide], here's a cow's eye view into a chute, [it] needs to have some solid sides, because look at the people you can see. Also the grazing animals have their eyes on the side of their head, so they can scan the horizon. Fear's the main motivation in grazing animals, you know, where carnivores have got their eyes in the front of the head so they've got good depth deception.

Now, on sunny days, you'll often have a lot more problems getting animals to walk over shadows and things, may not have a problem with this on cloudy days. There can be a lot of time-of-day effects. Look at the shadows you've got there, there's a little piece of yellow tape on a pike, you know, flapping. Get rid of those sort of things.

I went out to a zoological park about a year ago, and they couldn't figure out why on some days the antelopes would go in and out of the exhibit just fine, and on other days they didn't. Well, there was a sign that would sometimes be leaning up against the fence, and other times it was not leaning up against the fence. It was in the middle of the alley and it was bright yellow on the back side, and I basically said, either throw that sign away or put it up on the fence so it stays up on the fence. You know, they didn't notice the detail though — sometimes the sign was against the fence where it didn't cause a problem, and another time the sign was out in the middle of the lane where it did cause a problem. Let's just get rid of it.

It's a very, very simple thing, and to the animal they noticed that, because it was different on different days. Now if the sign just stayed there on the fence all the time, they would get used to it. You know, let's say you have a drain in the middle of a floor, okay, they get used to walking over that drain, that's fine. A new animal is gonna balk at that drain, an animal that's lived there for a long time just walks right over it. The sign just stays in the same place all the time, it just sort of becomes part of the furniture. But if it's moving around, then it's going to cause a problem . . .

And when I was a little kid, loud noises really hurt my ears. A lot of animals have very sensitive hearing. Some research done up in Canada by Joe Stuckey found that yelling and screaming at animals is really stressful, they differentiate between a gate slamming that has no intent towards them and people yelling and whistling. The animal knows the difference, and the heart rate goes up more to the yelling and screaming than it does to gate slamming, because the animal knows the gate sound probably wasn't directed at him. And animals have extremely, you know, high frequency hearing, and some of these loud noises, they hurt my ear, like a dentist drill. I get very concerned about some of the animals in different places being subjected to noise. Some of the ventilating systems are really noisy, what's that doing to them, to the animals, well we don't know. Animals that have a flighty genetics, that startle really easily, are more sensitive to, guess what, rapid movement and high-pitched intermittent noise. You know, animals, just like people, have different, sensitivities to things.

Watch your ear radar on your grazing animals, on all your grazing animals, all the hoof stock. The ears work independently. See [slide] how the horse and zebra have an ear on each other and the other ear is on me taking the picture. Now when they get scared or they get aggressive the ears go flat back. Well watch the ear radar, that can be an early warning.

Fear — it's the main emotion in autism. Until I took antidepressant medication, I was in a constant state of panic attacks all the time. It was absolutely, totally terrible, and the hoof stock are going to have much higher fear than a carnivore. and fear is the scientifically correct word. There's a tendency in the veterinary literature and the agriculture literature to avoid this little word, "fear." People tend to avoid it, and you go into the neuroscience literature and the biology literature, they use the fear word. And it is a scientifically correct word where I found, you know, I've had journal article reviewers say that I have to call it excitement or agitation. Well I think some people don't want to admit that some of the stuff they're doing maybe is really frightening and scaring the animal.

Fear circuits in the brain have been fully mapped and they have been mapped for twenty years. A lot of that research is already reviewed in *Animals in Translation* — the brain stuff on this is known, this is not some idle speculation. You get into the whole thing about whether or not animals have emotions. Well they've got the same neurotransmitters we've got. Psychiatric drugs like Prozac and Valium work on animals. If their emotions were from another planet, those drugs wouldn't work on them, but they do.

Q: Could you tell us a little bit about how you used your instincts that came to you through autism to help promote and change the animal welfare in the farm industry, please?

A: Well, when I first started out working on handling cattle, people in the Seventies were incredibly rough with beef cattle, and the beef cattle didn't want to go through the veterinary chute. And I was one of the first people to get down in the chute and see what they're seeing. I said, well this animal's scared of this chain hanging down, this shadow, the sun's in their eyes, or it's too dark, and,

and nobody looked at that before. And people thought I was absolutely out of my mind and crazy that I would get in the veterinary chute to see what cattle were seeing, because one of the things I've found, if you just take these things they're afraid of out of the chute, you know, like I've done a lot of work for the meat plants on auditing meat plants for animal welfare. And they've got to be able to move a hundred animals and only have no more than three mooing and bellowing, you know, due to prodding and stuff like that.

And in order for the plants to pass the audit, they had to find these things the animals were afraid of, like a reflection on a floor, and maybe move a light three feet, a ceiling light three feet to get rid of the reflection, add a light on part of the chute that was dark, tie up a chain that's flapping, put up some conveyor belting so the cattle didn't see people up ahead. And you might have four of these, I call them the distractions. You might have four of these things and you got to track down all four of them, and find them and get rid of them. Then the animals will move up the chute easily . . .

Q: With your background, have you done very much research with autistic children and their communicating with animals?

A: Okay. The therapeutic riding programs are often very, very helpful because you have three good things over there. You have the relationship with the horse, but then you also have rhythmic motion and it's a balancing activity. And therapists have found that when you do rhythmic activities, this was with the non-verbal kids, and you do a balancing activity and riding is both.

Oftentimes speech come in, and I've had parents say to me their kids started talking for the first time on the horse, cause you're getting such a good combination of rhythm and balance, and then it's really a fun activity, where doing something in a gym isn't anywhere near as much fun. And as far as sort of the relationship with the animal, some autistic kids are really good with the animal, they really click with the animal, and others don't.

You know, there's a tremendous amount of variability in autism, and I get asked, well should I get a service dog for my kid. Well you got a look at how's this child gonna react to the dog. It might be a good thing; it might be a bad thing. I would say, on the whole, that the therapeutic riding programs for the people that are non-verbal, on the whole, tend to be really beneficial.

Q: What are your thoughts on the future of children diagnosed with autism today?

A: Well, the thing about autism is it's such a broad spectrum, you're going all the way from somebody is going to be very handicapped and have to be living in a supervised living situation for the rest of their life, up to Einstein. Einstein today would be diagnosed autistic because he had no language until age three. Then you have the milder Asperger's where there's no obvious speech delay. Well I'm gonna guess that if you didn't have the Asperger traits you wouldn't have electricity in this building today. Tesla, who invented the power plant, would be labeled autistic today.

Many good engineers and computer people have Asperger traits. You wouldn't have these cellphones and all these little technical toys and airplanes and everything else, if you didn't have people that were more interested in things than in being social. It's like a little bit of the autism genetics, you get a brilliant scientist or musician or mathematician; you get too much of it, you get somebody that's handicapped . . .

You know, not everybody is going to be super social. You've got to learn basic social niceties. But that doesn't mean you're going to be super social, and a lot of the more Asperger type of kids, they're gonna get social interaction through shared interests. You know, chess club, computer club, art club, drama club, band — get involved in these things where there's a shared interest.

You know, I talked to this one lady, she said her idea of a really great candlelit, really romantic dinner, you know, the finest wine, the finest restaurant, it sets the stage for a three-hour discussion on computer data storage systems. Because that is just the most interesting thing that there is! In fact, Nancy Minshew, a really top autism researcher, did a brain scan on me to look at my visual thinking circuits, and in all brains you've got a big internet line that runs from the visual cortex up to the frontal cortex, a big trunk line. Mine was twice as big, and they found that same thing in, in some of the other, other people.

Also, they did another thing to see whether you were interested in things or interested in people, and they showed all these old weird videos from the 70s of people and cars and food and all kinds of things, and my brain got activated by the things.

And . . . the thing is if you didn't have people that were interested in things, we wouldn't have any computers, we wouldn't have any electricity, you know, think about it. Back in the caveman days, the really social people did not make the first stone sphere.

MICHELLE OBAMA

Delivering the commencement address at City College of New York in the spring of 2016, First Lady Michelle Obama praised the contributions of "hope-filled immigrants" drawn to America from all corners of the world.

"Maybe your family has been in this city for generations," she said, "or maybe, like my family, they came to this country centuries ago in chains. Maybe they just arrived here recently, determined to give you a better life."

She talked about her own journey from working-class Chicago and her parents' struggle to educate their children. And she spoke about the place she now called home, the historic house in the nation's capital where she lived with her husband and daughters, the White House.

"Graduates," she said, "it's the story that I witness every single day when I wake up in a house that was built by slaves, and I watch my daughters — two beautiful, black young women — head off to school, waving goodbye to their father. . . "

The following month she told that story again before a nationally broadcast audience, at the Democratic National Convention in Philadelphia. And she added a vivid detail — she watched her daughters playing on the White House lawn with their dogs.

What could be more American?

But this time, her story unleashed a torrent of criticism. Some said it wasn't true, the White House was not built by slaves. Others said her remarks were "unpatriotic" and showed her "disdain" for America.

In fact, it was true.

The labor force that worked on the construction site beginning in 1792 was made up of both free and enslaved Blacks, plus local White laborers and immigrants from Scotland and Ireland. As the White House Historical Association was quick to point out, the federal government did not actually own the enslaved people, but it did hire them from their masters.

Obama's story lifted the curtain on something we thought we already knew, and revealed it to have a sinister side. But we shouldn't have been surprised — the foundational role of slavery and its integration into every aspect of American life had been there all along. She forced us to look the truth in the eye.

Her anecdote hit many people hard because it seemed to undercut a cherished national monument. But the opposite was also true — it celebrated the progress this country has made as Black Americans have gone from enslaved laborers to residents whose children innocently play with their dogs on the lawn.

"Don't let anyone ever tell you that this country isn't great," Obama said that day, using public oratory to clarify our values, express pride, and celebrate how far we have all come.

"HOUSE BUILT BY SLAVES"

June 3, 2016
Commencement address, City College of New York,
New York City, New York

Wow! Let me just take it in. First of all, it is beyond a pleasure and an honor to be here to celebrate the City College of New York Class of 2016! You all, I mean, this has been the most fun I think I've had at a commencement ever.

Let me just say a few thank yous. Let me start, of course, by thanking President [Lisa] Coico for that wonderful introduction, for her leadership here at City College, for this honorary degree.

I also want to recognize Senator Schumer, Chancellor Milliken, Trustee Shorter, Edward Plotkin, as well as your amazing valedictorian, Antonios Mourdoukoutas — did I get it right? And your amazing salutatorian, Orubba Almansouri. I really don't want to follow those two. If anybody is wondering about the quality of education, just listening to those two speakers lets you know what's happening here. And I'm so proud of you both — and to your families, congratulations. Well done. Well done.

And of course, let us not forget Elizabeth Aklilu for her amazing performance of the National Anthem earlier today. She blew it out of the water.

But most of all, I want to acknowledge all of you — the brilliant, talented, ambitious, accomplished, and all-around outstanding members of the class of 2016! Woo! You give me chills. You all have worked so hard and come so far to reach this milestone, so I know this is a big day for all of you and your families, and for everyone at this school who supported you on this journey.

And in many ways, this is a big day for me too. See, this is my very last commencement address as First Lady of the United States. This is it. So I just want to take it all in. And I think this was the perfect place to be, because this is my last chance to share my love and admiration, and hopefully a little bit of wisdom with a graduating class.

And, graduates, I really want you all to know that there is a reason why, of all of the colleges and universities in this country, I chose this particular school in this particular city for this special moment. And I'm here because of all of you. I mean, we've talked about it — Antonios, I'm going to talk a little bit about diversity, thank you.

Just look around. Look at who you are. Look at where we're gathered today. As the President eloquently said, at this school, you represent more than 150 nationalities. You speak more than 100 different languages — whoa, just stop there. You represent just about every possible background — every color and culture, every faith and walk of life. And you've taken so many different paths to this moment.

Maybe your family has been in this city for generations, or maybe, like my family, they came to this country centuries ago in chains. Maybe they just arrived here recently, determined to give you a better life.

But, graduates, no matter where your journey started, you have all made it here today through the same combination of unyielding determination, sacrifice, and a whole lot of hard work — commuting hours each day to class, some of you. Yes, amen. Juggling multiple jobs to support your families and pay your tuition. Studying late into the night, early in the morning; on subways and buses, and in those few precious minutes during breaks at work.

And somehow, you still found time to give back to your communities — tutoring young people, reading to kids, volunteering at hospitals. Somehow, you still managed to do prestigious internships and research fellowships, and join all kinds of clubs and activities. And here at this nationally-ranked university, with a rigorous curriculum and renowned faculty, you rose to the challenge, distinguishing yourselves in your classes, winning countless honors and awards, and getting into top graduate schools across this country. Whoa.

So, graduates, with your glorious diversity, with your remarkable accomplishments and your deep commitment to your communities, you all embody the very purpose of this school's founding. And, more importantly, you embody the very hopes and dreams carved into the base of that iconic statue not so far from where we sit — on that island where so many of your predecessors at this school first set foot on our shores.

And that is why I wanted to be here today at City College. I wanted to be here to celebrate all of you, this school, this city. Because I know that there is no better way to celebrate this great country than being here with you.

See, all of you know, for centuries, this city has been the gateway to America for so many striving, hope-filled immigrants — folks who left behind everything they knew to seek out this land of opportunity that they dreamed of. And so many of those folks, for them, this school was the gateway to actually realizing that opportunity in their lives, founded on the fundamental truth that talent and ambition know no distinctions of race, nationality, wealth, or fame, and dedicated to the ideals that our Founding Fathers put forth more than two centuries ago: That we are all created equal, all entitled to "life, liberty and the pursuit of happiness." City College became a haven for brilliant, motivated students of every background, a place where they didn't have to hide their last names or their accents, or put on any kind of airs because the students at this school were selected based not on pedigree, but on merit, and merit alone.

So really, it is no accident that this institution has produced 10 Nobel Prize winners — along with countless captains of industry, cultural icons, leaders at the highest levels of government. Because talent and effort combined with our various backgrounds and life experiences has always been the lifeblood of our singular American genius.

Just take the example of the great American lyricist, Ira Gershwin, who attended City College a century ago. The son of a Russian-Jewish immigrant, his songs still light up Broadway today. Or consider the story of the former CEO of Intel, Andrew Grove, class of 1960. He was a Hungarian immigrant whose harrowing escape from Nazism and communism shaped both his talent for business and his commitment to philanthropy.

And just think about the students in this very graduating class — students like the economics and pre-law major from Albania, who also completed the requirements for a philosophy major and dreams of being a public intellectual. The educational theater student from right here in Harlem who's already an award-winning playwright and recently spoke at the White House. The biomedical science major who was born in Afghanistan and plans to be a doctor, a policy maker and an educator. And your salutatorian, whose Yemeni roots inspired her to study Yemini women's writing and to advocate for girls in her community, urging them to find their own voices, to tell their own stories. I could go on.

These are just four of the nearly 4,000 unique and amazing stories in this graduating class — stories that have converged here at City College, this dynamic, inclusive place where you all have had the chance to really get to know each other, to listen to each other's languages, to enjoy each other's food — lasagna, obviously — music, and holidays. Debating each other's ideas, pushing each other to question old assumptions and consider new perspectives.

And those interactions have been such a critical part of your education at this school. Those moments when your classmates showed you that your stubborn opinion wasn't all that well-informed — mmm hmm. Or when they opened your eyes to an injustice you never knew existed. Or when they helped you with a question that you couldn't have possibly answered on your own.

I think your valedictorian put it best — and this is a quote — he said, "The sole irreplaceable component of my CCNY experience came from learning alongside people with life experiences strikingly different from my own." He said, "I have learned that diversity in human experience gives rise to diversity in thought, which creates distinct ideas and methods of problem solving." That was an okay quote. Okay, you're bright. I couldn't have said it better myself.

That is the power of our differences to make us smarter and more creative.

And that is how all those infusions of new cultures and ideas, generation after generation, created the matchless alchemy of our melting pot and helped us build the strongest, most vibrant, most prosperous nation on the planet, right here.

But unfortunately, graduates, despite the lessons of our history and the truth of your experience here at City College, some folks out there today seem to have a very different perspective. They seem to view our diversity as a threat to be contained rather than as a resource to be tapped. They tell us to be afraid of those who are different, to be suspicious of those with whom we disagree. They act as if name-calling is an acceptable substitute for thoughtful debate, as if anger and intolerance should be our default state rather than the optimism and openness that have always been the engine of our progress.

But, graduates, I can tell you, as First Lady, I have had the privilege of traveling around the world and visiting dozens of different countries, and I have seen what happens when ideas like these take hold. I have seen how leaders who rule by intimidation — leaders who demonize and dehumanize entire groups of people — often do so because they have nothing else to offer. And I have seen how places that stifle the voices and dismiss the potential of their citizens are diminished; how they are less vital, less hopeful, less free.

Graduates, that is not who we are. That is not what this country stands for. No, here in America, we don't let our differences tear us apart. Not here. Because we know that our greatness comes when we appreciate each other's strengths, when we learn from each other, when we lean on each other. Because in this country, it's never been each person for themselves. No, we're all in this together. We always have been.

And here in America, we don't give in to our fears. We don't build up walls to keep people out because we know that our greatness has always depended on contributions from people who were born elsewhere but sought out this country and made it their home — from innovations like Google and eBay to inventions like the artificial heart, the telephone, even the blue jeans; to beloved patriotic songs like "God Bless America," like national landmarks like the Brooklyn Bridge and, yes, the White House — both of which were designed by architects who were immigrants.

Finally, graduates, our greatness has never, ever come from sitting back and feeling entitled to what we have. It's never come from folks who climb the ladder of success, or who happen to be born near the top and then pull that ladder up after themselves. No, our greatness has always come from people who expect nothing and take nothing for granted — folks who work hard for what they have then reach back and help others after them.

That is your story, graduates, and that is the story of your families. And it's the story of my family, too. As many of you know, I grew up in a working class family in Chicago. And while neither of my parents went past high school, let me tell you, they saved up every penny that my dad earned at his city job because they were determined to send me to college.

And even after my father was diagnosed with Multiple Sclerosis and he struggled to walk, relying on crutches just to get himself out of bed each morning, my father hardly ever missed a day of work. See, that blue-collar job helped to pay the small portion of my college tuition that wasn't covered by loans or grants or my work-study or my summer jobs. And my dad was so proud to pay that tuition bill on time each month, even taking out loans when he fell short. See, he never wanted me to miss a registration deadline because his check was late. That's my story.

And, graduates, you all have faced challenges far greater than anything I or my family have ever experienced, challenges that most college students could never even imagine. Some of you have been homeless. Some of you have risked the rejection of your families to pursue your education. Many of you have lain awake at night wondering how on Earth you were going to support your parents and your kids and still pay tuition. And many of you know what it's like to live not just month to month or day to day, but meal to meal.

But, graduates, let me tell you, you should never, ever be embarrassed by those struggles. You should never view your challenges as a disadvantage. Instead, it's important for you to understand that your experience facing and overcoming adversity is actually one of your biggest advantages. And I know that because I've seen it myself, not just as a student working my way through school, but years later when I became — before I came to the White House and I worked as a dean at a college.

In that role, I encountered students who had every advantage — their parents paid their full tuition, they lived in beautiful campus dorms. They had every material possession a college kid could want — cars, computers, spending money. But when some of them got their first bad grade, they just fell apart. They lost it, because they were ill-equipped to handle their first encounter with disappointment or falling short.

But, graduates, as you all know, life will put many obstacles in your path that are far worse than a bad grade. You'll have unreasonable bosses and difficult clients and patients. You'll experience illnesses and losses, crises and setbacks that will come out of nowhere and knock you off your feet. But unlike so many other young people, you have already developed the resilience and the maturity that you need to pick yourself up and dust yourself off and keep moving through the pain, keep moving forward. You have developed that muscle.

And with the education you've gotten at this fine school, and the experiences you've had in your lives, let me tell you, nothing — and I mean nothing — is going to stop you from fulfilling your dreams. And you deserve every last one of the successes that I know you will have.

But I also want to be very clear that with those successes comes a set of obligations — to share the lessons you've learned here at this school. The obligation to use the opportunities you've had to help others. That means raising your hand when you get a seat in that board meeting and asking the question, well, whose voices aren't being heard here? What ideas are we missing? It means adding your voice to our national conversation, speaking out for our most cherished values of liberty, opportunity, inclusion, and respect — the values that you've been living here at this school.

It means reaching back to help young people who've been left out and left behind, helping them prepare for college, helping them pay for college, making sure that great public universities like this one have the funding and support that they need. Because we all know that public universities have always been one of the greatest drivers of our prosperity, lifting countless people into the middle class, creating jobs and wealth all across this nation.

Public education is our greatest pathway to opportunity in America. So we need to invest in and strengthen our public universities today, and for generations to come. That is how you will do your part to live up to the oath that you all will take here today — the oath taken by generations of graduates before you to make your city and your world "greater, better, and more beautiful."

More than anything else, graduates, that is the American story. It's your story and the story of those who came before you at this school. It's the story of the son of Polish immigrants named Jonas Salk who toiled for years in a lab until he discovered a vaccine that saved countless lives. It's the story of the son of immigrant — Jamaican immigrants named Colin Powell who became a four star general, Secretary of State, and a role model for young people across the country.

And, graduates, it's the story that I witness every single day when I wake up in a house that was built by slaves, and I watch my daughters — two beautiful, black young women — head off to school — waving goodbye to their father, the President of the United States, the son of a man from Kenya who came here to American — to America for the same reasons as many of you: To get an education and improve his prospects in life.

So, graduates, while I think it's fair to say that our Founding Fathers never could have imagined this day, all of you are very much the fruits of their vision. Their legacy is very much your legacy and your inheritance. And don't let anybody tell you differently. You are the living, breathing proof that the American Dream endures in our time. It's you.

So I want you all to go out there. Be great. Build great lives for yourselves. Enjoy the liberties that you have in this great country. Pursue your own version of happiness. And please, please, always, always do your part to help others do the same.

I love you all. I am so proud of you. Thank you for allowing me to share this final commencement with you. I have so much faith in who you will be. Just keep working hard and keep the faith. I can't wait to see what you all achieve in the years ahead.

Thank you all. God bless. Good luck on the road ahead.

OPRAH WINFREY

In your mind's eye you can just see that little girl, sitting on the linoleum floor in her mother's house, watching Sidney Poitier accept an Oscar at the 1964 Academy Awards.

"His tie was white and of course his skin was black," she said, and she "had never seen a black man being celebrated like that."

That little girl became the woman we know as Oprah Winfrey. And until the Golden Globes in 2018, when she gave this speech, we had never seen a Black woman being celebrated, while speaking out, quite like that.

That is the power of storytelling, the kind that makes you feel you are inside the little girl's head — and it's key to what makes Oprah such an exceptionally gifted communicator.

When she received the Cecil B. DeMille Award at the 75th Annual Golden Globes, it was just three months after The *New York Times* exposé revealing numerous sexual abuse allegations against film producer Harvey Weinstein.

Within a week, Weinstein had been fired from Miramax and expelled from the Academy of Motion Picture Arts and Sciences. Suddenly legions of high-profile men in Hollywood, Silicon Valley, the media, politics, the music and restaurant industries — everywhere, it seemed — faced fresh allegations of sexual abuse. Multitudes of women were coming forward to share their own #metoo stories.

Oprah expressed appreciation for those women, because "speaking your truth is the most powerful tool we all have."

Then she told another story — the kind that literally makes the hair stand up on your arms — about Recy Taylor, a young wife and mother from a sharecropping family who, walking home from church in Abbeville, Alabama, in 1944, was kidnapped, gang-raped, and left by the side of the road.

Taylor also refused to remain silent. She told her story to law enforcement, and to a young NAACP investigator by the name of Rosa Parks, who came down from Montgomery to investigate. She took on Taylor's case and sought justice. Parks gathered national support and ignited a movement to support Taylor.

Despite their confessions, the six White men who assaulted her were never prosecuted, never brought to justice.

Taylor paid a high price for using her voice. She received death threats and her home was firebombed, but she remained in Abbeville with her family for two decades after the attack. She passed away just ten days before the Golden Globes ceremony at 97. But as Oprah said, her truth "goes marching on."

As does the truth of all the little girls watching the Golden Globes that night, future leaders who, Oprah predicted, will fight hard for a time "when nobody ever has to say 'me too' again."

"TIME'S UP"

January 7, 2018
Cecil B. DeMille Award, 75th Golden Globe Awards,
Beverly Hilton, Beverly Hills, California

In 1964, I was a little girl sitting on the linoleum floor of my mother's house in Milwaukee watching Anne Bancroft present the Oscar for best actor at the 36th Academy Awards. She opened the envelope and said five words that literally made history: "The winner is Sidney Poitier." Up to the stage came the most elegant man I had ever seen. I remember his tie was white, and of course his skin was black, and I had never seen a black man being celebrated like that. I tried many, many times to explain what a moment like that means to a little girl, a kid watching from the cheap seats as my mom came through the door bone tired from cleaning other people's houses. But all I can do is quote and say that the explanation's in Sidney's performance in "Lilies of the Field": "Amen, amen, amen, amen."

In 1982, Sidney received the Cecil B. DeMille award right here at the Golden Globes and it is not lost on me that at this moment, there are some little girls watching as I become the first black woman to be given this same award. It is an honor — it is an honor and it is a privilege to share the evening with all of them and also with the incredible men and women who have inspired me, who challenged me, who sustained me and made my journey to this stage possible. Dennis Swanson who took a chance on me for "A.M. Chicago." Quincy Jones who saw me on that show and said to Steven Spielberg, "Yes, she is Sophia in 'The Color Purple.'" Gayle who has been the definition of what a friend is, and Stedman who has been my rock — just a few to name.

I want to thank the Hollywood Foreign Press Association because we all know the press is under siege these days. We also know it's the insatiable dedication to uncovering the absolute truth that keeps us from turning a blind eye to corruption and to injustice. To — to tyrants and victims, and secrets and lies. I want to say that I value the press more than ever before as we try to navigate these complicated times, which brings me to this: what I know for sure is that speaking your truth is the most powerful tool we all have. And I'm especially proud and inspired by all the women who have felt strong enough and empowered enough to speak up and share their personal stories. Each of us in this room are celebrated because of the stories that we tell, and this year we became the story.

But it's not just a story affecting the entertainment industry. It's one that transcends any culture, geography, race, religion, politics, or workplace. So I want tonight to express gratitude to all the women who have endured years of abuse and assault because they, like my mother, had children to feed and bills to pay and dreams to pursue. They're the women whose names we'll never know. They are domestic workers and farm workers. They are working in factories and they work in restaurants and they're in academia, engineering, medicine, and science. They're part of the world of tech and politics and business. They're our athletes in the Olympics and they're our soldiers in the military.

And there's someone else, Recy Taylor, a name I know and I think you should know, too. In 1944, Recy Taylor was a young wife and mother walking home from a church service she'd attended in Abbeville, Alabama, when she was abducted by six armed white men, raped, and left blindfolded by the side of the road coming home from church. They threatened to kill her if she ever told anyone, but her story was reported to the NAACP where a young worker by the name of Rosa Parks became the lead investigator on her case and together they sought justice. But justice wasn't an option in the era of Jim Crow. The men who tried to destroy her were never prosecuted.

Recy Taylor died ten days ago, just shy of her 98th birthday. She lived as we all have lived, too many years in a culture broken by brutally powerful men. For too long, women have not been heard or believed if they dare speak the truth to the power of those men. But their time is up. Their time is up.

Their time is up. And I just hope — I just hope that Recy Taylor died knowing that her truth, like the truth of so many other women who were tormented in those years, and even now tormented, goes marching on. It was somewhere in Rosa Parks' heart almost 11 years later, when she made the decision to stay seated on that bus in Montgomery, and it's here with every woman who chooses to say, "Me too." And every man — every man who chooses to listen.

In my career, what I've always tried my best to do, whether on television or through film, is to say something about how men and women really behave. To say how we experience shame, how we love and how we rage, how we fail, how we retreat, persevere and how we overcome. I've interviewed and portrayed people who've withstood some of the ugliest things life can throw at you, but the one quality all of them seem to share is an ability to maintain hope for a brighter morning, even during our darkest nights. So I want all the girls watching here, now, to know that a new day is on the horizon! And when that new day finally dawns, it will be because of a lot of magnificent women, many of whom are right here in this room tonight, and some pretty phenomenal men, fighting hard to make sure that they become the leaders who take us to the time when nobody ever has to say "Me too" again.

BINA VENKATARAMAN

What does it mean to have the courage of your convictions?

It's a question with as many different answers as there are women featured in this volume. Some women used their voices to take a principled stand and speak on behalf of an unpopular cause. Others proposed ideas they knew would invite abuse and vituperation. Some risked their professional reputations. Some risked their lives.

They spoke anyway. In the words of journalist Bina Venkataram, they knew how to "summon courage."

The daughter of immigrants from India who came to the United States in the late 1960s, Venkataraman began her journalism career feeling intimidated and often unsure of herself. As she confessed in her commencement address to the 2021 graduating class at the University of Southern California, "courage still doesn't always come easily to me. But I've discovered that I can find it in myself when I know I am fighting a good fight."

The particular fight she's referring to pitted her against one of the country's most powerful men, Massachusetts Senator Edward M. Kennedy. Venkataraman wrote an article about the Senator's hypocrisy — on the one hand touting renewable energy, on the other hand blocking a proposed source of renewable energy, a wind farm off the shores of Cape Cod.

One hundred and thirty giant wind turbines were to be anchored in the waters of Nantucket Sound, clearly visible from the Kennedy compound at Hyannis Port, marring views and perhaps even depressing property values along the wealthy coast. Kennedy and his Capitol Hill colleagues were trying to slip a last-minute amendment to kill the wind farm into a Coast Guard budget bill.

Kennedy did his best to quash Venkataraman's story, but she held firm — a position, she told the graduates, that turned out to be a career milestone.

Venkataraman went on to become a White House advisor on climate change and editorial page editor at *The Boston Globe*.

Among her parting words of advice to students was to seek out excellence in other human beings, but avoid putting those individuals on a pedestal, because they'll inevitably get knocked off. Expecting otherwise is a fool's errand.

"The talented artist or athlete can be an abuser," she noted, "just like a brilliant scientist can be a eugenicist. And a bold, progressive senator" — such as Kennedy — "can be a barrier to progress."

That's a cautionary note for graduating seniors, and the rest of us. Elevating individuals and making them into heroes is inherently dangerous. Human beings consistently confound our expectations. Far better to take a holistic view and see people for who they are, wisdom and warts, all part of the tangled skein.

"SUMMON COURAGE"

May 17, 2021
Commencement address, University of Southern California,
Los Angeles Memorial Coliseum, Los Angeles, California

I f you look back at the past few years, you're likely aware that your talents, your knowledge, and your hard work got you here. And all of that will serve you well in the years to come. But in my experience thus far in my life and career, the most rewarding and meaningful moments have come not from flexing my talent or my knowledge. They have come from learning to summon courage.

More than a decade ago, I was a lowly novice reporter in the newsroom of *The Boston Globe*. And I felt intimidated by the talent and knowledge of those around me. I often believed in other people more than I believed in myself. But because of something I cared about at the time, I dared to take on a fierce and powerful Senator from the most storied and famous Massachusetts political family — the late Ted Kennedy. I wrote a story about an offshore wind farm that he thwarted with his power in the Senate, and the Senator wasn't happy. In fact, he was pretty upset. Even though it was a Saturday, he called what seemed like every editor at the newspaper — all the way up the food chain, to complain about the story. Each of them in turn called me to ask me whether I had backup for what I'd written in my story. I told each of them the same thing — I did. I had done my work, called the senator's office, and my story was accurate. All these calls were an intimidation tactic.

Eventually the senator's office called the highest-ranking editor at the paper on duty that day, a woman by the name of Ellen. She called me and told me Senator Kennedy was livid, which I knew. She asked me whether I might have gotten it wrong and if we should just correct the story. At this point, as I was being questioned for maybe the tenth time, I chose to say: "Did it occur to you that the Senator is the one who is wrong and not me?"

Ellen hung up on me. I was shocked. But even more shocked by the way I'd snapped at someone in authority — not something I was so accustomed to doing. And now it was clear that this editor hated me and that my future in journalism had disappeared. Still, I kept doing my job and covering that idea for a wind farm — and avoiding Ellen in the newsroom.

That small, super unsexy moment in my career — answering calls about Ted Kennedy from editors — turned out to be pivotal. It was a moment when I stood up for myself. But, the way I found the courage to stand up for myself was by standing up for something larger. My courage came from wanting people to know the truth. It also came from wanting to keep political interference from thwarting progress on offshore wind power, an alternative to the fossil fuels warming the planet. I found courage because I cared about the future.

Flash forward ten years or so, and it was this same editor, Ellen, who recommended me to the publisher of *The Boston Globe* for one of the top jobs at the news organization, a position on its masthead as editorial page editor, which I hold today. She had also, years before, secretly recommended me to the job that led me to work in the White House. This was a person I was convinced hated me. Recently, I asked her about it. She said she appreciated my bravery in challenging the country's most powerful senator — and my conviction when she challenged me. The very thing I thought made her hate me, made her respect me.

Courage still doesn't always come easily to me. But I've discovered that I can find it in myself when I know I am fighting a good fight. When I worked in the Obama White House, I had many opportunities to flex my knowledge and my talent — to speak in front of large audiences, to tout the president's progress on climate change, and to be in the public eye. But the most rewarding thing I did during my time in government was behind the scenes. I refused to give up in getting an intelligence agency to declassify a dataset that could save the lives of people in poor nations by helping them better map the areas most likely to flood during devastating storms. I was told countless times that it was impossible to release the data. But a couple of my colleagues and I banded together and we kept asking, and I'm pretty sure that we annoyed everyone so much that they eventually decided whatever risk they were worried about was worth having us off their backs. People think of courage as entering the arena, standing before a crowd as I am now, or even as standing up for a friend in a barfight. But sometimes courage is just quietly asking "why not?" a million times — until everyone gets sick of you.

That's the thing — sometimes courage in a world where people don't want to rock the boat will mean making your social group or your political party upset — or that people won't like you. But in exercising it, you get something more valuable, which is learning to like yourself.

Here's something else I've figured out: When you look for other people to inspire and fortify you in practicing courage — don't have heroes — at least not in the conventional sense. Be skeptical of putting people on pedestals. Rare talent or genius is not the same as being a hero. And, as I'm sure you know, a talented artist or athlete can be an abuser, just like a brilliant scientist can be a eugenicist. And a bold, progressive senator can be a barrier to progress.

You can admire these people for their accomplishments and real achievements, but know that when you exalt people, when you expect them to be perfect and act like superheroes, you will inevitably need to tear them down from their pedestals when they turn out to be merely human.

Look for heroes not on the silver screen or the pedestal or even at this podium — but at eye level and within reach: the people in your life who have been afraid but done the right thing anyway, who have shown you by example how to be bold.

Prize bravery over bravado. Prize all moments of bravery, even the small and unrecognized ones. You can be heroic whenever you choose, whoever you are, without being perfect or celebrated or superbly talented.

Finally, I want to challenge you to summon another kind of courage that is sorely needed in this moment of history, the kind of courage that will set you apart in your career and in your life.

It's the courage of imagination. What do I mean? The courage to envision that the world can be different and better than it is today. The courage to care enough about the lives of others and to believe you can make a difference. It's the kind of courage that teams of vaccine makers had when they believed that a COVID-19 vaccine could beat the odds and be created more quickly than a vaccine ever before in human history — one of the reasons we're able to be here together today. It's the kind of courage that Frederick Douglass, Maria Stewart, and other abolitionists of the 19th century showed when they helped Americans imagine a society without slavery. It's the courage that Khaleel Seivwright, a Toronto carpenter showed recently when he built shelters for the homeless that the city wasn't able to pull off — imagining a solution to a problem that others said couldn't be solved and buoyed by the Toronto residents who gave him money to do it. And it's the kind of courage that groups of young people have today when they see not just the catastrophe of climate change but when they imagine ways to solve it.

This kind of courage can be hard to sustain but you can be fortified by banding together with fellow travelers. And you can gain perspective by looking beyond immediate obstacles to a longer-range future. Progress can take time. Just a few days ago, the US government announced that the country's first large-scale offshore wind farm, something I wrote about so long ago — which can power 400,000 homes — is finally going to be built off the coast of Massachusetts.

It's so easy to be cynical about the world's problems, especially today. But cynicism comes from a fear of disappointment. If you don't expect anything to be better, you won't be let down. And while I know many loveable cynics — and I'm sure you do too, there are limits to what they can accomplish in the world. It takes courage to ask the question: is it possible to do what people say is impossible? And when people tell you it isn't, to keep asking that question: why not?

SOURCES

Anne Hutchinson
"Heresy Trial"

The History of the Province of Massachusetts Bay Colony, Appendix, Number 11. The Examination of Mrs. Ann Hutchinson at the Court at Newtown, pp. 482-520.

Margaret Brent
"Vote and Voyce"

Proceedings and Acts of the Assembly of Maryland, January 1637-1638, Volume 1, p. 215, Published by the Authority of the State, Under Direction of the Maryland Historical Society, ed. William Hand Browne, (Baltimore: Maryland Historical Society, 1883).

Nanye'hi
"A Peace Treaty"

Cherokee Treaty, 1781, Box 5, Reel 2, Nathanael Greene Papers, Manuscript Division, Library of Congress, Washington, DC.

Priscilla Mason
"Salutory Oration"

The Rise and Progress of the Young-Ladies' Academy of Philadelphia: Containing an Account of a Number of Public Examinations & Commencements; The Charter and Bye-Laws; Likewise, a Number of Orations delivered by the Young Ladies, and Several by the Trustees of Said Institution (Philadelphia: Stewart & Cochran, 1794), pp. 90-95.

Deborah Sampson Gannett
"Life as a Revolutionary War Soldier"

An Address, Delivered with Applause, at the Federal-Street Theatre, Boston: Four Consecutive Nights of the Different Plays, Beginning March 22, 1802, and After, at Other Principal Towns, a Number of Nights Successively at Each Place (H. Mann, for Mrs. Gannett, at the Minerva Office, 1802).

Emma Willard
"Improving Female Education"
An Address to the Public Particularly to the Members of the Legislature of New York Proposing a Plan for Improving Female Education. (Middlebury: J. W. Copeland, 1819), pp. 13-17.

Frances Wright
"New-Harmony Hall"
The New-Harmony Gazette (New-Harmony, Indiana), Volume III, No 37, July 9, 1828, pp. 289-291.

Maria Miller Stewart
"Farewell Address"
Productions of Mrs. Maria W. Stewart, Presented to the First Africa Baptist Church & Society, of the City of Boston, Published by Friends of Freedom and Virtue, (Boston: W. Lloyd Garrison & Knapp, 1837) pp. 77-82.

Angelina Grimké
"At Pennsylvania Hall"
History of Pennsylvania Hall, Which Was Destroyed by a Mob on the 17th of May, 1838, ed. Samuel Webb (Philadelphia: Merrihew & Gunn, 1838), pp. 123-126.

Lucretia Mott
"Discourse on Woman"
Discourse on Woman by Lucretia Mott, Delivered at The Assembly Buildings, December 17, 1849, Being a Full Phonographic Report, Revised by the Author (Philadelphia: T. B. Peterson, 1850), pp. 3-20.
Ohio Women's Convention, Held at Salem, April 19th and 20th, 1850, with an Address by J. Elizabeth Jones (Cleveland: Smead & Cowles Press, 1850), pp. 44-51.

Sojourner Truth
"Ain't I a Woman?"
"I Am A Woman's Rights"
The Anti-Slavery Bugle (Salem, Ohio), Vol. 6 — No. 41, June 21, 1851.
New York Independent, April 23, 1863.

Lucy Stone
"Disappointment is the Lot of Woman"
The History of Woman Suffrage, Vol I, eds. Elizabeth Cady Stanton, Susan B. Anthony, Matilda Joslyn Gage, (Rochester: Charles Mann, 1889), pp. 165-167.

Jane Johnson
"Rather Die Than Go Back"
The Underground Railroad: A Record of Facts, Authentic Narrative, Letters, &c., Narrating The Hardships, Hair-Breadth Escapes And Death Struggles of the Slaves in Their Efforts For Freedom, as Related By Themselves and Others, or Witnessed by the Author, by William Still (Philadelphia: Porter & Coates, 1872), pp. 94-95.

Julia Branch
"Woman's Rights in a New Aspect"
The New York Times, June 29, 1858, p. 1.

Sarah Parker Remond
"Why Slavery is Still Rampant in the Land"
The Anti-Slavery Advocate, 34(2), October 1, 1859, pp. 74-75.

Anna Dickinson
"Why Colored Men Should Enlist"
Addresses of the Hon. W. D. Kelley, Miss Anna E. Dickinson, and Mr. Frederick Douglass: At a Mass Meeting, Held at National Hall, Philadelphia, July 6, 1863, for the Promotion of Colored Enlistments. Library of Congress, African American Pamphlet Collection, pp. 3-4.

Clara Barton
"Testimony on Civil War Prison Conditions"
Report of the Joint Committee on Reconstruction, 39th Cong, 1st Sess., (Washington, DC: US Government Printing Office, 1866), pp. 102-108.

Frances Ellen Watkins Harper
"We Are All Bound Up Together"

Proceedings of the Eleventh National Women's Rights Convention, held at the Church of the Puritans, New York, May 10, 1866 (New York: Robert J. Johnston, 1886), pp. 45-48.

Frances Thompson
"Memphis Riots and Massacres"

US Congress, House of Representatives, *Memphis Riots and Massacres*, 39th Cong., 1st sess., 1865-66, House Report No. 101. (Washington, DC: US Government Printing Office, 1866), pp. 196-197.

Susan B. Anthony
"Is it a Crime for a US Citizen to Vote?"

An Account of the Proceedings of the Trial of Susan B. Anthony, on the Charge of Illegal Voting, at the Presidential Election in Nov., 1872, and on the Trial of Beverly W. Jones, Edwin T. Marsh, and William B. Hall, the Inspectors of Election by Whom Her Vote was Received (Rochester: Daily Democrat and Chronicle Book Print, 1874), pp. 151-178.

Maria Mitchell
"Need of Women in Science"

Papers Read at the Fourth Congress of Women, Held at St. George's Hall, Philadelphia, October 4, 5, 6, 1876 (Washington, DC: Todd Brothers, 1877), pp. 9-11.

Susette La Flesche
"Plight of the Ponca Indians"

Speeches given by Susette La Flesche, Thomas Henry Tibbles papers, Series 1, Box 1, Folder 5, National Museum of the American Indian, Smithsonian Institution.

Sarah Winnemucca
"Testimony on Indian Affairs"

Congressional Record, US House of Representatives, Committee on Indian Affairs, For the Relief of the Piute Indians, H.R. 6973,.48th Cong., 1st Sess., (24 January 1884); RG 233, Center for Legislative Archives, National Archives and Records Administration.

Elizabeth Cady Stanton
"Solitude of Self"

The Woman's Journal, Vol. XXIII, No. 4, January 23, 1892, pp. 1, 32.

Anna Julia Cooper
"Woman's Cause is One and Universal"

The World's Congress of Representative Women, A Historical Résumé for Popular Circulation of the World's Congress of Representative Women, Convened in Chicago on May 15, and Adjourned on May 22, 1893, Under the Auspices of the Woman's Branch of the World's Congress Auxiliary, ed. May Wright Sewall, Volume II (Chicago: Rand, McNally & Company, 1894), pp. 711-715.

Clara Shortridge Foltz
"Public Defender Rights of Persons Accused of Crime"

Chicago Legal News: A Journal of Legal Intelligence, ed. Myra Bradwell, Volume XXV., September, 1892 to September, 1893. (Chicago: Chicago Legal News Company, 1893), pp. 431-432.

The Albany Law Journal: A Weekly Record of the Law and the Lawyers, Vol. XLVIII, July-December 1893 (Albany: Albany Law Journal Company, 1893), pp. 248-250.

Ida B. Wells
"Lynch Law in All Its Phases"

Our Day: A Record and Review of Current Reform 11, January-June 1893, (Boston: Our Day Publishing Company, 1893) pp. 333-347.

Ka'iulani
"The Rights of My People"

Los Angeles Times, March 2, 1893, p. 1.

Lillian Wald
"Crowded Districts of Large Cities"

Proceedings of the First Convention of the National Council of Jewish Women, Held at New York, Nov. 15, 16, 17, 18 and 19, 1896 (Philadelphia: The Jewish Publication Society of America, 1897), pp. 258-268.

Selena Sloan Butler
"The Chain-Gang System"

The Chain-Gang System, Read before the National Association of Colored Women at
   Nashville, Tenn., 16 September 1897, by Selena S. Butler, (Tuskegee: Normal
   School Steam Press Print, 1897) p. 7.

Caroline Bartlett Crane
"Is God Responsible?"

"Is God Responsible? A Sermon," by Caroline Bartlett Crane, Minister of the People's Church,
   Kalamazoo Michigan, (Michigan: The Young Men's Union, 1898), pp. 5-27.

Nannie Helen Burroughs
"How the Sisters are Hindered from Helping"

Journal of the Twentieth Annual Session of the National Convention, Held in Richmond,
   Virginia, September 12-17, 1900 (Nashville, TN: The National Baptist Publishing
   Board, 1900), pp. 196-197.

Carrie Nation
"Effect of the Hatchet"

The Chronicle, (Muskegon, MI) August 21, 1902.

Isadora Duncan
"Dance of the Future"

Der Tanz Der Zukunft, Eine Vorlesung (Leipzig: Eugen Diederichs, 1903), pp. 11-26.

Mary Harris "Mother" Jones
"Agitation — The Greatest Factor for Progress"

The Toledo Bee, March 25, 1903.

Mary Church Terrell
"What it Means to be Colored in the Capital of the United States"

The Independent, (New York City) Vol. 62, No. 3034 (January 24, 1907), pp. 181-186.

Aurora Lucero-White Lea
"Plea for the Spanish Language"
New Mexico Normal University Bulletin 23, January 1911.
Albuquerque Journal, February 1, 1911, p. 6.

Rose Schneiderman
"To the Victims of the Triangle Shirtwaist Fire"
The Survey, April 8, 1911, pp. 84-85.

Crystal Eastman
"What Feminism Means to Me"
The Vassar Miscellany, Volume XLIV, Number 21, June 15, 1915, pp. 670-673.

Mabel Ping-Hua Lee
"China's Submerged Half"
First Chinese Baptist Church, New York City.

Inez Milholland
"Appeal to the Women Voters of the West"
The Suffragist, October 14, 1916, pp. 8-9.

Jeannette Rankin
"On Women's Rights and Wartime Service"
Congressional Record, 65th Cong., 2nd Sess., (Washington, DC: US Government Printing Office, 1818), pp. 771-772.

Ruth Muskrat
"Address to President Calvin Coolidge"
The Pasadena Evening Post, December 14, 1923, p. 6.

Margaret Sanger
"Gagged for Free Speech"
Sophia Smith Collection, Smith College, Margaret Sanger Microfilm, S71:157.

Helen Keller
"Eyes of the Blind"
Hearings Before the Committee on the Library, House of Representatives, 71st Cong., 2d Sess. on H.R. 9042, March 27, 1930 (Washington, DC: US Government Printing Office, 1930), pp. 21-22.

Lillian Gilbreth
"Can the Machine Pull Us Out?"
MSP 8, Gilbreth Library of Management Papers, Purdue University, Box 115, Folder 2.

Dorothy Thompson
"Modern Coup d'Etat"
Congressional Record, Hearings on S. 1392. 75th Congress, 1st session, (Washington, DC: US Government Printing Office, 1937), pp. 858-884.

Eleanor Roosevelt
"Civil Liberties — The Individual and the Community"
"The Chicago Civil Liberties Committee: Address by Mrs. Franklin D. Roosevelt," 1940, Eleanor Roosevelt Papers, Franklin D. Roosevelt Presidential Library, Hyde Park, New York.

Clare Boothe Luce
"America and the Kremlin"
Vital Speeches of the Day, Vol. XI, August 15, 1945, pp. 647-649.

Helen Gahagan Douglas
"My Democratic Credo"
Congressional Record, Proceedings and Debates of the 79th Cong., 2nd Sess. US House of Representatives (Washington, DC: US Government Printing Office, 1946), pp. 2856-2858.

Katharine Hepburn
"Silence the Artist"
Audio Lab, Wisconsin Historical Society, Madison WI.

Josephine Baker
"Homecoming Day"
University of Missouri-St. Louis Black History Project, Western Historical Manuscript Collection, State Historical Society of Missouri Research Center, St. Louis, Missouri.

Lillian Smith
"The Right Way is Not a Moderate Way"
Phylon (1940-1956), Vol. 17, Number 4 (4th Quarter, 1956, Clark Atlanta University), pp. 335-341.

Pauli Murray
"The Negro Woman in the Quest for Equality"
The Acorn, Volume 10, No. 1, June 1964, pp. 13-19.

Rachel Carson
"Of Man and the Stream of Time"
Scripps College Bulletin, June 12, 1962.

Fannie Lou Hamer
"I Question America"
Mississippi Freedom Democratic Party Documents, Mississippi Civil Rights Collection, Veterans of the Civil Rights Movement, L. Zenobia Coleman Library Archives, Tougaloo College, Jackson, Mississippi.

Lorraine Hansberry
"The Nation Needs Your Gifts"
Negro Digest, August 1964, Vol. 13. No. 10, pp. 26-29.

Dolores Huerta
"Speech at Capitol Rally"
Delano Record, April 28, 1966.

Martha J. Sara
"Do Not Refuse Us"

Alaska Native Land Claims, Part II, Hearings Before the Subcommittee on Indian Affairs of the Committee on Interior and Insular Affairs, US House of Representatives, 91st Cong., 1st Sess., (Washington, DC: US Government Printing Office, 1970), pp. 465-467.

Shirley Chisholm
"Introducing the E.R.A."

Congressional Record, May 21, 1969, Extensions of Remarks E4165-6, (Washington, DC: US Government Printing Office, 1969), pp. 13380-13381.

Betty Friedan
"Farewell Speech to NOW"

It Changed My Life: Writings on the Women's Movement, by Betty Friedan, (New York: Random House, 1978), pp. 180-183.

Gloria Steinem
"Living the Revolution"

Vassar Quarterly, Fall 1970, pp. 12-17.

Patsy Mink
"Discrimination Against Women"

Hearing before the House Committee on Education and Labor, Special Subcommittee on Education, House of Representatives, on Section 805, H.R. 16098, 91st Cong., 2nd Sess., (Washington, DC: US Government Printing Office, 1970), pp. 433-434.

Madeline Davis
"I am Someone's Neighbor"

Dr. Madeline Davis LGBTQ+ Archive of Western New York, Buffalo State, The State University of New York.

Barbara Jordan
"Opening Statement on the Articles of Impeachment"

Debate on Articles of Impeachment, Hearings of the Committee on the Judiciary, US House of Representatives, 93rd Cong., 2nd Sess. (Washington, DC: US Government Printing Office, 1974), pp. 110-113.

Grayce Uyehara
"Wartime Internment"

Hearing Before the Subcommittee on Federal Services, Post Office, and Civil Service of the Committee on Governmental Affairs United States Senate, 100th Cong., 1st Sess. S. 1009, to Accept the Findings and to Implement the Recommendations of the Commission on Wartime Relocation and Internment of Civilians, June 17, 1987, (Washington, DC: US Government Printing Office, 1987), pp. 97-118.

Judy Heumann
"Becoming Disabled"

Joint Hearing Before the Subcommittee on the Handicapped of the Committee on Labor and Human Resources, United States Senate, and the Subcommittee on Select Education of the Committee on Education and Labor, US House of Representatives, 100th Cong., 2nd Sess. on S. 2345, September 27, 1988 (Washington, DC: US Government Printing Office, 1989), pp. 74-76.

Sandra Day O'Connor
"Portia's Progress"

N.Y.U Law Review, 66 N.Y.U. L. Rev. (1991), pp. 1546-1558.

Mary Fisher
"A Whisper of 'AIDS'"

The Papers of Mary Fisher.

Hillary Clinton
"Women's Rights are Human Rights"

United Nations Development Programme (UNDP).

Temple Grandin
"Animals in Translation"
The Papers of Temple Grandin.

Michelle Obama
"House Built by Slaves"
Archives of The White House, Office of the First Lady, June 3, 2016.

Oprah Winfrey
"Time's Up"
The Washington Post, January 7, 2018.

Bina Venkataraman
"Summon Courage"
The Papers of Bina Venkataraman.

PERMISSIONS

Margaret Sanger
"Gagged for Free Speech"
Reprinted by permission of the Estate of Margaret Sanger.

Lillian Gilbreth
"Can the Machine Pull Us Out?"
Courtesy of Purdue University Libraries, Karnes Archives and Special Collections.

Eleanor Roosevelt
"Civil Liberties"
Reprinted by permission of The Eleanor Roosevelt Estate.

Katharine Hepburn
"Silence the Artist"
Published by permission of The Estate of Katharine Hepburn.

Josephine Baker
"Homecoming Day"
Josephine Baker TM is a trademark managed by Sagoo.

Lillian Smith
"The Right Way is Not a Moderate Way"
Reprinted by permission of The Lillian E. Smith Center, Piedmont University.

Rachel Carson
"Of Man and the Stream of Time"
Copyright © 2022 by Roger A. Christie.
Reprinted by permission of Frances Collin, Trustee.

Sandra Day O'Connor
"Portia's Progress"
Reprinted by permission of *The N.Y.U. Law Review.*

Mary Fisher
"A Whisper of 'AIDS'"
Published by permission of Mary Fisher.

Temple Grandin
"Animals in Translation"
Reprinted by permission of Temple Grandin.

Michelle Obama
"House Built by Slaves"
Reprinted by permission of The City College of New York.

Oprah Winfrey
"Time's Up"
Reprinted by permission of Harpo, Inc. All rights reserved.

Bina Venkataraman
"Summon Courage"
Reprinted by permission of Bina Venkataraman.

ACKNOWLEDGMENTS

Many individuals have generously supported my work on this book for years with their time, encouragement, and friendship, including Lorraine Gracey, Lindsey Willis, Delia Rios, Ruth Chlebowski, Sandra Gregor, Janine Buis, Jezra Kaye, Arlene McGuire, Dave Lieber, Courtney Ramsey, Laurie Shwiff, Christina Baulch, Patrick Burke, Deborah Reidy, Howard Tomb, Marilyn Rubin, Joe Kolman, Lenore Skenazy, Barie Carmichael, Sue Lawley (and Sisters in Script), Lucy Rose, Nichole Wagner, Girish Dadlani, Rosemarie Gatzek, Noah Scheer, Oriana Leckert, Melody Sharp, Clinton McDade, Cornelia Cotton, Miriam Edelman, Pamela Toler, Michael Sales, Gigi Yellen, Michael Precker, Gabriella Stern, Jeff Levy, Harley Dembert, Mathieu Roberts, Bayer Lee, Elliot Brodsky, Cynthia Rubin, Margi Booth, Stephen Garrett, Valerie Wright, Michael Sales, Martha Hollander, Mike Klein, Sara Noble, Rob Cottingham, Jonathan Talbott, Susie Krumholz, Karen Cahana, Virgil Scudder, Molly Sargent, Cardinal Marking, David Marion, David Schulder, and Debbie Arnold.

Special thanks to all 699 supporters of my Kickstarter, an encouraging (and patient) community whose belief in this project has kept me going.

I am deeply indebted to the scholars who personally guided me and generously shared their insights and expertise, including Christa Dhimo, Shirley Raines, Alyce McKenzie, Elaine F. Weiss, Melissa R. Klapper, Lynn Garafola, Barbara Breaden, Rachel B. Tiven, Alison M. Parker, Julie Haynes, Maegan Parker Brooks, Amy Aronson, Anne F. Mattina, María M. Carreira, and George C. Wright.

I am also grateful for the insights of those scholars, some alive and others who have passed on, who have explored this topic before me, and enlightened me through the years. That includes academics in the fields of social history, rhetorical studies, and women's studies, including Gerda Lerner, Sandra J. Sarkela, Susan Mallon Ross, Margaret A. Lowe, Nancy Cott, Barbara Babcock, Karlyn Kohrs Campbell, Doris G. Yoakam, Lillian O'Connor, Patricia Scileppi Kennedy, Dale Spender, Blanche Wiesen Cook, Kathleen Hall Jamieson, Carol Faulkner, Nancy Hewitt, Linda K. Kerber, Beverly Wilson Palmer, Christopher Densmore, Gloria Hartmann O'Shields, Beverly Manning, Judith Anderson, S. Michele Nix, Virginia Irving Armstrong, Elizabeth R. Varon, Paula Giddings, Mia Bay, William J. Mann, Evan Thomas, Amy Sohn, Lori D. Ginzberg, Ann D. Braude, Marilyn J. Westerkamp, Karen A. Foss, Sonja K. Foss, Nell Irvin Painter, Lisa Tetrault, Kristin B. Waters, Margaret Rose Gladney, Alix Kates Shulman, Lisa Hodgens, Sara M. Evans, Rosemarie Zagarri, Nancy Cott, Mary Ellen Snodgrass, Eleanor Flexner, Elizabeth Fox-Genovese, Carolyn Eastman, Susan Rumsey Strong, Mary Beard, Nina Banks, Jessica Enoch, Granville Ganter, Christina Devereaux Ramírez, P. Jane Hafen, J. Matthew Gallman, Mary Sarah Bilder, Mary C. Kelley, and Lindal Buchanan. Their knowledge has been a gift. The errors are all mine.

Those of us who were fortunate enough to be acolytes of the late Denise Graveline know she would have celebrated this book. She might even have written it herself, had she not passed away too soon.

Thank you to the hardworking and talented team at RealClear Publishing and Amplify Publishing Group — Naren Aryal, Lauren Magnussen, Caitlin Smith, Nina Spahn, and Sky Wilson. Their thoughtful care and attention have shepherded this book into being.

I hit the lucky trifecta with my talented friend, editor, and publisher, Carl Cannon. And I am infinitely grateful for the love and support of my mother, Devora Rubin.

Finally, I want to acknowledge the thousands of intrepid women speakers through the centuries, many whose names we don't even know. They inspire me.